Red Hat® Linux® Network Toolkit

Red Hat® Linux®
Network Toolkit

Paul G. Sery

M&T Books
An imprint of IDG Books Worldwide, Inc.

Foster City, CA ® Chicago, IL ® Indianapolis, IN ® New York, NY

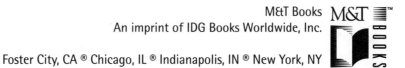

Red Hat® Linux® Network Toolkit

Published by
M&T Books
An imprint of IDG Books Worldwide, Inc.
919 E. Hillsdale Blvd., Suite 400
Foster City, CA 94404
www.idgbooks.com (IDG Books Worldwide Web site)

Library of Congress Catalog Card No.: 00-101651

ISBN: 0-7645-4656-2

Printed in the United States of America

10 9 8 7 6 5 4 3 2 1

1O/SR/QT/QQ/FC

Distributed in the United States by IDG Books Worldwide, Inc.

Distributed by CDG Books Canada Inc. for Canada; by Transworld Publishers Limited in the United Kingdom; by IDG Norge Books for Norway; by IDG Sweden Books for Sweden; by IDG Books Australia Publishing Corporation Pty. Ltd. for Australia and New Zealand; by TransQuest Publishers Pte Ltd. for Singapore, Malaysia, Thailand, Indonesia, and Hong Kong; by Gotop Information Inc. for Taiwan; by ICG Muse, Inc. for Japan; by Intersoft for South Africa; by Eyrolles for France; by International Thomson Publishing for Germany, Austria, and Switzerland; by Distribuidora Cuspide for Argentina; by LR International for Brazil; by Galileo Libros for Chile; by Ediciones ZETA S.C.R. Ltda. for Peru; by WS Computer Publishing Corporation, Inc., for the Philippines; by Contemporanea de Ediciones for Venezuela; by Express Computer Distributors for the Caribbean and West Indies; by Micronesia Media Distributor, Inc. for Micronesia; by Chips Computadoras S.A. de C.V. for Mexico; by Editorial Norma de Panama S.A. for Panama; by American Bookshops for Finland.

For general information on IDG Books Worldwide's books in the U.S., please call our Consumer Customer Service department at 800-762-2974. For reseller information, including discounts and premium sales, please call our Reseller Customer Service department at 800-434-3422.

For information on where to purchase IDG Books Worldwide's books outside the U.S., please contact our International Sales department at 317-596-5530 or fax 317-572-4002.

For consumer information on foreign language translations, please contact our Customer Service department at 800-434-3422, fax 317-572-4002, or e-mail rights@idgbooks.com.

For information on licensing foreign or domestic rights, please phone +1-650-653-7098.

For sales inquiries and special prices for bulk quantities, please contact our Order Services department at 800-434-3422 or write to the address above.

For information on using IDG Books Worldwide's books in the classroom or for ordering examination copies, please contact our Educational Sales department at 800-434-2086 or fax 317-572-4005.

For press review copies, author interviews, or other publicity information, please contact our Public Relations department at 650-653-7000 or fax 650-653-7500.

For authorization to photocopy items for corporate, personal, or educational use, please contact Copyright Clearance Center, 222 Rosewood Drive, Danvers, MA 01923, or fax 978-750-4470.

 is a registered trademark or trademark under exclusive license to IDG Books Worldwide, Inc. from International Data Group, Inc. in the United States and/or other countries.

 is a trademark of IDG Books Worldwide, Inc.

ABOUT IDG BOOKS WORLDWIDE

Welcome to the world of IDG Books Worldwide.

IDG Books Worldwide, Inc., is a subsidiary of International Data Group, the world's largest publisher of computer-related information and the leading global provider of information services on information technology. IDG was founded more than 30 years ago by Patrick J. McGovern and now employs more than 9,000 people worldwide. IDG publishes more than 290 computer publications in over 75 countries. More than 90 million people read one or more IDG publications each month.

Launched in 1990, IDG Books Worldwide is today the #1 publisher of best-selling computer books in the United States. We are proud to have received eight awards from the Computer Press Association in recognition of editorial excellence and three from Computer Currents' First Annual Readers' Choice Awards. Our best-selling *...For Dummies®* series has more than 50 million copies in print with translations in 31 languages. IDG Books Worldwide, through a joint venture with IDG's Hi-Tech Beijing, became the first U.S. publisher to publish a computer book in the People's Republic of China. In record time, IDG Books Worldwide has become the first choice for millions of readers around the world who want to learn how to better manage their businesses.

Our mission is simple: Every one of our books is designed to bring extra value and skill-building instructions to the reader. Our books are written by experts who understand and care about our readers. The knowledge base of our editorial staff comes from years of experience in publishing, education, and journalism — experience we use to produce books to carry us into the new millennium. In short, we care about books, so we attract the best people. We devote special attention to details such as audience, interior design, use of icons, and illustrations. And because we use an efficient process of authoring, editing, and desktop publishing our books electronically, we can spend more time ensuring superior content and less time on the technicalities of making books.

You can count on our commitment to deliver high-quality books at competitive prices on topics you want to read about. At IDG Books Worldwide, we continue in the IDG tradition of delivering quality for more than 30 years. You'll find no better book on a subject than one from IDG Books Worldwide.

John Kilcullen
Chairman and CEO
IDG Books Worldwide, Inc.

Eighth Annual Computer Press Awards ≥1992

Ninth Annual Computer Press Awards ≥1993

Tenth Annual Computer Press Awards ≥1994

Eleventh Annual Computer Press Awards ≥1995

IDG is the world's leading IT media, research and exposition company. Founded in 1964, IDG had 1997 revenues of $2.05 billion and has more than 9,000 employees worldwide. IDG offers the widest range of media options that reach IT buyers in 75 countries representing 95% of worldwide IT spending. IDG's diverse product and services portfolio spans six key areas including print publishing, online publishing, expositions and conferences, market research, education and training, and global marketing services. More than 90 million people read one or more of IDG's 290 magazines and newspapers, including IDG's leading global brands — Computerworld, PC World, Network World, Macworld and the Channel World family of publications. IDG Books Worldwide is one of the fastest-growing computer book publishers in the world, with more than 700 titles in 36 languages. The "...For Dummies®" series alone has more than 50 million copies in print. IDG offers online users the largest network of technology-specific Web sites around the world through IDG.net (http://www.idg.net), which comprises more than 225 targeted Web sites in 55 countries worldwide. International Data Corporation (IDC) is the world's largest provider of information technology data, analysis and consulting, with research centers in over 41 countries and more than 400 research analysts worldwide. IDG World Expo is a leading producer of more than 168 globally branded conferences and expositions in 35 countries including E3 (Electronic Entertainment Expo), Macworld Expo, ComNet, Windows World Expo, ICE (Internet Commerce Expo), Agenda, DEMO, and Spotlight. IDG's training subsidiary, ExecuTrain, is the world's largest computer training company, with more than 230 locations worldwide and 785 training courses. IDG Marketing Services helps industry-leading IT companies build international brand recognition by developing global integrated marketing programs via IDG's print, online and exposition products worldwide. Further information about the company can be found at www.idg.com. 1/26/00

Credits

ACQUISITIONS EDITOR
Laura Lewin

PROJECT EDITOR
Matthew E. Lusher

TECHNICAL EDITOR
Ken Hatfield

COPY EDITOR
S.B. Kleinman

PROJECT COORDINATORS
Linda Marousek
Joe Shines

PROOFREADING AND INDEXING
York Production Services

COVER DESIGN
Larry S. Wilson

GRAPHICS AND PRODUCTION
SPECIALISTS
Robert Bilhmayer
Jude Levinson
Michael Lewis
Ramses Ramirez
Dina F Quan
Victor Pérez-Varela

QUALITY CONTROL SPECIALIST
Laura Taflinger

BOOK DESIGNER
Jim Donohue

ILLUSTRATORS
Mary Jo Richards
Karl Brandt

About the Author

Paul Sery is a UNIX System Administrator for Productive Data Systems, Inc., in support of Sandia National Laboratories in Albuquerque, NM. He is a member of the Computer Service Unix, Special Projects (CSU SP), which specializes in managing and troubleshooting computer systems. Paul has a bachelors degree in Electrical Engineering from the University of New Mexico. He is the author of *LINUX Network Toolkit,* is the primary author of *Red Hat LINUX in Small Business* and the co-author of *Red Hat Linux for Dummies*, all from IDG Books Worldwide, Inc. When he is not beating his head against unruly computers, Paul and his wife Lidia enjoy riding their tandem through the Rio Grande valley. They also enjoy traveling throughout Mexico and especially Lidia's native Mexico City.

to my parents, Dr. Theodore and Doris Sery

Preface

Linux is, needless to say, a powerful tool. Networking and the Internet are also powerful tools. But they become extraordinarily powerful and useful when you know how to use them together.

Red Hat Linux Network Toolkit shows how to use Linux as the basis of your private network that is connected to the Internet. This book starts by describing how to install Red Hat Linux on a PC and then construct a simple, two-computer network. This basic network is then used to construct more complex networks later on. Simple examples are followed by more complex ones so that you can get started as quickly as possible before moving onto more advanced material. The elements (workstations and servers) of the example networks all have names and addresses that are used consistently throughout the book. By the time you complete this book, you should have your own fully functioning Linux network!

This book is intended to help you design, install and manage a Linux based network. The Linux computer or computers can be used to serve a combined network of Linux and Microsoft Windows computers (you can use Macintosh or UNIX workstations too but the instructions are not oriented to them). The Linux computers can also be used as workstations themselves. The book also shows how to safely connect computers or the network to the Internet.

Who Should Read This Book

This book shows how to create inexpensive, powerful networks of computers and manage them effectively. Those of you who are experienced with Linux computers should also be able to find useful information in this book. But my primary desire is to provide a basic tool especially for those folks who don't have access to many resources.

The instructions are oriented to the person with some Microsoft Windows experience. No Linux or UNIX experience is required, although it is helpful. This book is intended as a tutorial and not a reference. If you do not have any Linux or UNIX experience then I recommend you use one of the several good Linux reference books to augment my descriptions. (They are listed in chapter 3.)

If you are an experienced user of UNIX, you should be familiar with the general concepts and recognize the workings of Linux. You should be able to skip many sections where I give detailed instructions for installation or administration tasks. The Linux operating system is based on the Berkeley standard. Like all flavors of UNIX, it has evolved to a hybrid of System V and Berkeley.

How This Book Is Organized

This book is organized to help you construct your computer network quickly and efficiently. You may read it from cover to cover, or focus on those parts that interest you or meet your needs. I present information in this book in the same way as I try to learn a new system: read a brief description, try a simple example, read more of the details, try a more complex example, and so on. I offer relatively brief instructions on how to set up software that is described elsewhere – for example, Microsoft Windows and Linux itself. Many good books cover those topics, and I want to concentrate on the overall construction of a working network. The chapter themes are as follows:

◆ The introduction describes a bit of my own history as a computer and network administrator. It's included because my experience parallels a that of a lot of people who find themselves as the de facto administrator. It also introduces the Linux operating system and the client-server model, which is the basis for the networks described in this book.

◆ Chapter 1 describes how to install the Red Hat Linux operating system. It describes the step-by-step process in detail.

◆ Chapter 2 presents a simple example of a client-server network that you can quickly set up. This chapter describes the simplest client-server configuration, in which one computer acts as a file and print server to another computer. It uses the Linux computer as the server and a Windows computer as a network.

◆ Chapter 3 introduces the concept of troubleshooting. You solve an example problem by using the Microsoft Troubleshooter. I introduce the basic tools for troubleshooting Linux and Samba.

◆ Chapter 4 goes into some detail about how Linux and Samba work. This chapter describes the concept and the organization of Linux and Samba.

◆ Chapter 5 shows how to configure a Red Hat Linux computer. It introduces some administration commands. It also shows how to use the graphical configuration tools such as LinuxConf.

◆ Chapter 6 shows how to use and configure Samba. It uses several Samba examples to describe its use.

◆ Chapter 7 describes how to connect your local (private) network to the Internet. Several methods are described including the automatic diald system.

◆ Chapter 8 explains how to construct network services such as DNS, NFS, NIS and email. These services provide powerful capabilities to your network.

◆ Chapter 9 introduces the essential issues of systems administration: managing the computers, networks, people, and security.

◆ Chapter 10 introduces the Arkeia automated network backup system. Once your network grows into more than a couple of computers, backing it up becomes a major job. Arkeia allows you to backup one or more computers to a central server. (Note: Arkeia is included on the second CD-ROM.)

◆ Chapter 11 describes how to protect your network when it's connected to the Internet. Firewalls and IP-masquerading are introduced. Specific instructions are given for constructing IP filtering and masquerading firewalls (sample scripts are included on the companion CD-ROM).

◆ Chapter 12 discusses how to further secure your network. Tools and methods are described that will help you provide more security.

◆ The appendices describe the ubiquitous vi editor and a simple DHCP server. A DHCP server automatically and dynamically distributes IP addresses to workstations on a network.

◆ There are two virtual chapters included on the second CD-ROM. They are included to provide further background and help without increasing the size, and thus price, of the book. One gives a brief history of Linux and UNIX. The other describes how and where to find additional help.

Terms and Definitions

I should define some terms, to avoid confusion. The term *Linux* can mean two different things. First, it refers to the core operating system or kernel; the program – like DOS – that runs the computer. However, it also describes the entire system, including the Linux kernel, the file system and all the libraries, programs, and shell scripts and macros that start everything running when you power up the computer. Basically, the term *Linux* refers to everything off of the CD-ROM that you configure your computer with. Generally, I distinguish between the two by referring to the kernel as *Linux* and the distribution as either *the Linux distribution* or *RedHat*.

Samba is a system that allows your Microsoft Windows or DOS (Linux too!) programs to talk to your Linux server. Samba allows a Linux server to ``speak'' the SMB protocol that Microsoft Windows understands. Think of Samba as the glue that holds everything together. I describe the mechanics of Samba in more detail later in the book, but basically, Windows expects certain things to happen in certain ways and at certain times on the network in order to see things like files and printers on other computers. Until now, manufacturers such as Novell, Sun Microsystems, Intergraphics, and Microsoft have provided the software to do this – at a price. Now, with Linux and Samba you don't need them.

When I refer to the *DOS disk* I am referring to a FAT formatted disk. This is the traditional method. There are also newer methods such as VFAT for Windows95 and NTFS for Windows NT. I refer to the newer formats by name.

Conventions

I use several typographic conventions to identify particular types of information presented in this book:

◆ DOS commands that you are to execute are distinguished within normal text with bold, uppercase font (i.e., run **DIR**). Bold, italicized font is used for their parameters (i.e., run **FDISK** */MBR*).

◆ Linux commands that you are to execute are distinguished within normal text with bold, lowercase font (i.e., run **ifconfig**) and bold, italicized font for their parameters (i.e., run **ifconfig** *eth0*).

◆ Monospace text is used to distinguish Linux filenames, commands, command parameters and from normal text.

Icons

There are three types of Icons used in this book. They are used to introduce information about special subjects with the general flow of the book. They are:

Helpful hints for how to perform a task more efficiently, or special things to know about a particular topic of discussion.

These inform you about things that might cause you problems or harm.

General information displayed for your convenience.

Acknowledgments

The amount of help that I've received writing this book is extraordinary. The writing process goes by in a blur of coffee aided 18 hour days. Those days are only possible with the aid of many dedicated, tireless people. Their contributions are:

My wife, Lidia, whose support, advice and encouragement means everything to me.

Laura Lewin, Matt Lusher, and Stephanie Rodriguez put together this project and kept it going on a day-to-day basis. Matt also helped direct me through the production process, which, even after four times, is still a maze to me.

S.B. Kleinman edited every single sentence and helped me put them together in a coherent fashion – an amazing feat.

Ken Hatfield tested every single command and script and also made many technical suggestions. Every suggestion caused me to say "oh yeah, that's good."

All the other great people at IDGB.

Anne Hamilton got me my first gig – the original Linux Network Toolkit – in the "biz".

Milton Lau helped design most of the illustrations.

Pat Roache gave me my first job as a UNIX (and, yikes, VAX) administrator. He also let me experiment with Linux way back in 1994 to see if it would work for us.

Contents at a Glance

Contents

Part III   Expanding your Network Services

Introduction

I want to introduce you to the power of Linux. Linux is an operating system that was designed to work just like UNIX. It was written from scratch, however, and doesn't share any copyrights with UNIX. Therefore, it does not require any licensing fees and is can be distributed for no or little cost. Red Hat Linux is Linux plus a bunch of extras – this is called a Linux distribution. Red Hat, Inc. has added value to Linux in the form of extra tools and an installation system all bundled together.

Linux is an operating system that can act as a platform for most if not all of your computing needs. It can work as a file and print server for your Windows based computers. You can use it as your Internet gateway and firewall. Linux also works great as a platform for your personal workstation. You can get Linux off the Internet for free, get it with a book or purchase it preloaded on a CD-ROM for just a few dollars. It is a powerful system that is only limited by your imagination.

Computers Inherit the Earth – Sort Of

In the beginning of time – way back in the early 1980s – PCs computers were expensive oddities. Cumbersome and slow, they had little use beyond simple word processing and games. Sophisticated applications such as data bases quickly became available and But the PCs industry proliferated in the workplace, soon reached a critical mass and prices started dropping rapidly.

Today, the notion of PCs becoming ever more powerful while dropping in price is considered a law of the same level with Adam Smith's law of supply and demand. Adam Smith who? Moore's Law (the cofounder of Intel who predicted that the power of microprocessors would double every 18 months while the price would be cut in half during the same interval) rules my life. The fact that a Pentium costing $1,000 today outperforms a million-dollar mainframe of the recent past is almost a yawn.

After PCs had been around for a while someone figured how to interconnect them into networks of networks. The genius of interconnecting the world's networks – in the form of the Internet – has further changed the world. Now, PCs are used by all sorts of people in ever expanding and creative ways.

But while computer prices have plunged and internetworking has skyrocketed, the middle ground of plain-vanilla networks has remained, at best, moderately expensive. Compared to the cost of a standalone computer or Internet access, the cost of a simple network remains relatively high. The complexity of setting up and administering even a simple network typically pushes this cost well beyond the sum of the prices of the individual components.

Budget-minded businesses and individuals that need to have a small to moderate number of computers work together in a network have not prospered in the same way as individuals or large organizations have. The big shops can afford proprietary systems that offer economies of scale, and individuals just need a modem to get to the Internet. Those who are in-between need to struggle with the cost and complexity of Windows NT, Novell Netware or proprietary UNIX in order to have a small network.

Well, all that the balance of computing power has shifted with the invention of two amazing products. Linux is a UNIX-like clone developed by Linus Torvalds and a number of individuals. unwittingly looking to take over the world. Samba was designed by Andrew Tridgell and others and adds file and print sharing under Linux to Microsoft Windows–based computers. Together, Linux and Samba provide the framework for creating and managing powerful, robust networks. You no longer need to purchase Windows NT or Novell Netware for your computers to work together, because the folks who developed Linux and Samba have offered their work to anyone who wants to use it. Amazing. It is all free!

Although I provide in-depth coverage of these products, they are, in and of themselves, merely interesting devices. The other piece of the puzzle is the amorphous profession of systems administration. After you get your Linux-Samba network going, you have to manage it effectively. In addition to helping you set up your Linux-Samba network, I lay out a framework for mastering systems administration so that you can create and manage an inexpensive, professional system.

The Client-Server Model

As the first step to setting up and managing a network with Linux and Samba you need to understand the Client-Server model. This model forms the basis for the networks that I help you to build in this book. I think it wise to understand the basis for the networks that we will build. Figure 1 shows the Client-Server model, which defines the way that computers and computer software interact with each other. Simply put, a service is provided to a client. In practical terms, one or more server computers provide their resources to one or more client computers. In this way, resources and work are economized.

How does this happen? How does this model help you to economize your resources and work? In a small business, you may have several PCs. Each PC has its own resources such as disk drives, CD-ROMs, and maybe a few have printers. When you back up your disks, you might use floppies, a dedicated tape drive, or a portable Zip drive. To print, you use any of several printers. Figure 2 shows such a system. Well, this configuration suffers from a lot of nasty duplication of resources and purchase orders, to say nothing of confusion — for example, did I back up the right computer last night? With a simple client-server network, however, one printer, one tape drive, and one fairly large disk can reasonably serve quite a few PCs. Figure 3 shows this new client-server configuration. It helps to minimize waste of your money and time. Why make a backup of each machine when you can do one backup and go home early? Hey, that's the sign of a good systems administrator — okay, a great administrator, but it's worth a try.

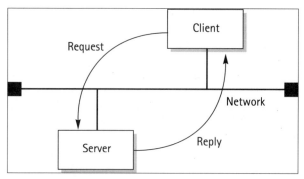

Figure 1: The client–server model

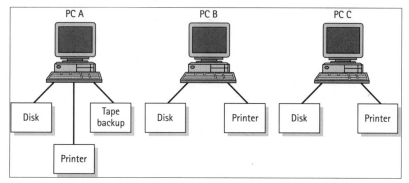

Figure 2: A diagram of an amorphous system

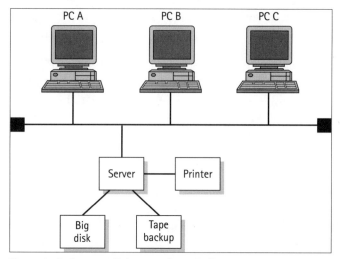

Figure 3: A diagram of the reconfigured client–server system

Keep in mind, however, that a client-server network does more than simply share computer hardware. It also helps to distribute your human resources. As more people work on a project, modifications of each other's work and files become disproportionately more difficult. Just two people working on the same spreadsheet can become intolerable as each modifies individual copies that differ only slightly from one another. Add an entire department and the work becomes very inefficient. On the other hand, if that spreadsheet exists in only one place and can be written to by only one user at a time, then work can continue. That is what the client-server does for you.

You may be thinking, "Well, I know all that, but the technology is expensive, and worst of all, is difficult to use; and I just want to run my business. I'll need a systems administrator and expensive consulting, too." My response is: Have you heard about LINUX and SAMBA? No? Well, read on. I might have a solution for you. *Solution* is a good word. With these powerful tools, you can easily set up and administer your own client-server network. In this book, I show you how to work with Linux and Samba to set up and run both simple and not-so-simple networks. I also offer guidance for handling the role of systems administrator – a role that Linux and Samba greatly simplify.

The History of a Dummy

A bit of retrospection is in order to show you the process that I hope you can avoid. My sordid history should scare you straight.

Ten years ago, I started a job as a scientific programmer. As the business grew from a couple of scientists and engineers – world-class ones, actually – I found myself increasingly in the role of managing the computers and their interaction. But we had very few capital equipment dollars and could not afford a Novell network or even a poor cousin. I hate to admit it, but we basically had a manually operated, RS-232 (serial) network. Later I used a switched network – of switch boxes to connect all our serial lines! Talk about advanced technology. Well, beat me over the head with a stick long enough and I'll get smart. What was my solution? We ended up with a terminal-based, multi-user version of WordPerfect for VMS on a MicroVAX II. For those of you who don't know what that means, just think of the phrase "slow and cumbersome." We did have a i386 SCO XENIX box running. I made several aborted attempts to get a terminal-based word processing system running on it. Needless to say it didn't work well enough either.

We finally entered the '70s around 1990.

I did have the luck of inheriting a black and white monochrome Sun SLC, which was slow even by 1990 standards. But it did run SunOS UNIX and it had an Ethernet port. I eventually hooked it to another workstation and was amazed when they were able to communicate.

The Sun eventually became the company file and print server, based on the Network File System (NFS). It was a vast improvement over our switched network, but was still shaky. Maintenance was difficult and expensive, and we were tied into a proprietary system. I kept it going on a shoestring while ever more demands were placed on it. It worked, but I never felt comfortable. I wished for a better way to run our system.

The more administration I did, the more I realized how much I didn't know. Taken individually, each task or system is not very complicated – but systems administration involves so many tasks and so many systems, and they all interact. I was trying to solve a big puzzle and I didn't know how many pieces it had. I started looking for a solution.

In part, I faced the chicken-and-the-egg dilemma. In other words, how do you maintain, upgrade, and manage such a system unless you know how to maintain, upgrade, and manage such a system? SunOS and Solaris weren't terribly difficult to manage if you know what you were doing. I knew some of the basics (performing backups, editing users, doing NFS exports), but I was concerned about what I did not know. I was always afraid that something bad would happen and some consultant would come in to clean up the mess and ask me how I could not know that the sky is blue. I wish that IDG Books had offered a *Systems Administration For Dummies* book back then. Very few classes or books dealt with the subject of systems (or network) administration – at least that I could find.

I gradually learned the trade in fits and spurts. In 1992, I took a very useful Networks course at the University of New Mexico (UNM). I had started the same course in 1985, only to drop it when we spent the first three weeks writing statistical equations for packet collisions or whatever. I was more than a little surprised and very happy when I came out of this course knowing that I had a good overview of networks and was finally in possession of some specific information.

In 1994, I ran across this interesting UNIX clone called Linux. I eventually realized that I had seen an advertisement for it distributed on a CD. That summer I purchased it. At first I pulled out my hair trying to get it installed. Then I found it really worked.

In 1995, I found this thing called Samba. At first glance, it looked like an NFS clone. I pulled it off the Net and was stunned when it compiled, installed, and worked right off the bat. I must not have believed my own eyes, because I promptly forgot about Samba and went on with my eternal NFS struggles.

In 1996 our Sun finally died. I had it in mind that when that occurred I would be able to substitute Linux and Samba for it. In just a handful of hours I got a Pentium PC running Linux-Samba to provide the same basic function as the Sun-NFS had provided. Within a couple of days I had our network working exactly as it had before. The dividend was that we eliminated the expensive, third-party software that had been required for our PCs to work with NFS.

Onward and Upward

My systems administration history is important, not because it is unusual, but because it is very typical. In businesses of any size that use computers and networks, people often inherit network and computer administration responsibilities even though they don't have much (or any) background in this field. If this is you, then this is your book. My hope is that by the time you finish this book, you'll have learned not only the essentials of installing, configuring and managing a Linux/Samba-based network, but that you'll have become an accomplished system administrator in the process.

Part I

The Simple Client–Server Network

Chapter 1

Installing Red Hat Linux

IN THIS CHAPTER

- ◆ Deciding how to partition or repartition your disk
- ◆ Deciding how to install Red Hat Linux
- ◆ Installing Red Hat Linux
- ◆ Configuring Red Hat Linux

THIS CHAPTER SHOWS YOU how to install and configure Red Hat Linux. Step-by-step instructions are given for accomplishing this task. The end result is a Linux computer that can be used as either a personal workstation or as a server – or both. The instructions given in Chapter 2 enable you to use your new Linux computer to construct a simple two-computer client-server network.

 This chapter gives you detailed instructions on two Linux installation methods. The first method allows you to modify your PC without eliminating your DOS or Windows operating system. However, please realize that these methods have associated risks. Specifically, you may accidentally erase your valuable data. All instructions have been tested on vanilla PCs, but that does not guarantee that you will not have problems with your particular setup. PCs, and especially laptops, vary a lot and you may have an unusual configuration that renders some of the instructions invalid. So please keep in mind that the devil is in the details and please, please back up anything that you do not want to lose!

This chapter shows how to install and configure Red Hat Linux. However, this chapter is more than simply an installation guide. This book shows you how to first construct a Linux computer, followed by a simple two-computer network, and from there increasingly more complex networks.

Looking Ahead

The Linux computer built in this chapter is used as a server for all subsequent example networks. This machine will take on several responsibilities as the book progresses:

- ◆ This Linux computer will be named chivas. Its network configuration is designed to work with all of the examples given throughout this book.

- ◆ chivas will function as the Samba file and printer server described in Chapters 2 and 6.

- ◆ It will optionally function as your Network File System (NFS), domain name server (DNS), Network Information Service (NIS), automounter, and e-mail server described in Chapter 8. These functions are optional because you may not want to run any of those services. You may also elect to place any or all of those services on a separate machine if you have the resources.

- ◆ It will optionally provide your network-based, automated backup services using the Arkeia system. This is optional again because you may not wish to run such a service, or you may wish to place it on another computer.

- ◆ Optionally, you can use it as your Internet gateway described in Chapter 7. Another machine – atlas – is introduced for that function, but depending on your circumstances, you may want to use chivas. (You can also configure chivas to look like atlas on the network. You can do this by assigning logical IP addresses to the Ethernet adapter. This process is described in Chapter 7.)

- ◆ Optionally, you can use it as your firewall described in Chapter 11. Again, atlas is introduced for that function, but depending on your circumstances, you may want to use chivas.

- ◆ A more secure firewall is described in Chapter 11 that uses chivas as a masquerading router. The firewall system requires atlas to reside on a network separate from the one that chivas resides on. chivas acts to route packets from the private network to the second network, which is called the DMZ.

The most important parameter described in the following installation is the Internet gateway address, also known as the default route. It is deliberately left blank because the protocol used to connect to the Internet, the Point-to-Point Protocol (PPP), dynamically creates the default route. You may specify it if you intend to use your own Internet connection and are experienced with such work. For instance, if you have a permanent Internet connection like Frame Relay, then you will want to specify the route explicitly. (However, keep in mind that you will have to modify the firewall and masquerading scripts provided on the CD-ROM.)

I highly recommend that you consider using either an old or brand-new hard disk for your initial Linux installation. Using a disk that you don't have to worry about backing up increases your freedom to experiment without the fear of significant damage to your valuable data. I have found usable 300MB disks for $30 and new multi-gigabyte disks can be found for around a $100. You can feel free to experiment on such disks. If you are serious about creating a real-world server, having an experimental disk allows you to try many different configurations.

You should also consider purchasing a separate disk even if you use the dual-boot system. If you have a separate disk, then you are protected from failures on the first one. It also simplifies the process of installing Linux because you don't have to worry about repartitioning the Windows disk.

Installing Linux is not much more difficult than installing Windows 95, 98 or NT. You do not need to make as many choices when installing those operating systems as with Red Hat Linux. That is because Red Hat is more flexible — and in my opinion more powerful — and you are given much more control over the beast. Freedom means more work, of course. Don't worry, the process is not very difficult and detailed instructions are given to guide you through.

Previewing the Installation Process

Linux may seem mysterious at first, simply because you are not familiar with it yet. Just keep in mind that it puts its pants on one leg at a time and the questions it asks are straightforward if you take them one by one.

Installing Red Hat Linux from a CD-ROM involves the following steps:

1. Deciding whether you will install Linux along with your existing operating system (typically Windows) or by itself.

2. Creating a boot disk (you can skip this process if you have a computer that boots from your CD-ROM).

3. Starting the Red Hat installation process.

4. Telling Red Hat what language you speak and keyboard you use.

5. Making choices about how to partition and format the disk.

6. Make some other installation choices.

7. Choosing the Red Hat software (called packages) to install.

8. Answering the system configuration questions that Red Hat asks you about your network, time zone, mouse type, and so on.

9. Configuring the X Window System, which is also known simply as X. X provides the platform for the graphical user interfaces (GUI) that Red Hat provides. The GUIs are GNOME and KDE and they provide the same functionality, and much the same look and feel as Windows Explorer.

Deciding How to Format your Disk

You have the following two choices for installing Red Hat Linux:

◆ Shrink an existing DOS file system with the FIPS program and then install the Linux file system – ext2 – on the freed-up space. This approach creates multiple partitions on a single disk and allows you to run either Windows or Linux when you start the PC.

◆ Format the entire disk for Linux, and run only Linux. You create a single partition using the entire disk and devote it to Linux. You cannot run any other operating system.

 This book does not give instructions for installing Linux alongside an NT computer using NTFS.

Table 1-1 summarizes your choices.

TABLE 1-1 DISK PARTITIONING OPTIONS FOR LINUX

Method	Advantages	Disadvantages
Single partition	Maximizes resources	Destroys existing data; requires dedicated disk
Multiple partitions	Retain data	Less space for Linux; potentially more difficult installation

No one method is best for all situations. This chapter, however, concentrates on using what is called a Linux "boot" floppy. This is a floppy disk that contains the basic Linux operating system, a number of modules to communicate with your hardware – disks, network adapters, and so on – and a minimal number of system and application programs. With it, you can start – boot – Linux and then mount the CD-ROM from which you can install a complete Linux system. This method works under more circumstances than the other methods, but requires a little more up-front work.

Of course, if you format an entire disk, you have use of the entire disk. This approach makes sense when you are ready to run your Linux box as a server or if you want to experiment on an unneeded disk. If you only want to experiment with Linux, use the multiple-partition method at first, as it is the least disruptive to your current setup.

Making Room for Linux

Before you can install Linux, you must make room for it. If you choose to use multiple partitions, you use a program called FIPS to shrink your current partition. If you decide to use a single partition, then you do not modify the disk partitions.

With the multiple-partition method, you start the installation process by completing the following steps:

1. Shrink the current partition with FIPS (this step makes room for both DOS/Windows and Linux on the same disk).

2. Create a boot floppy by copying a special file with the DOS program.

3. Boot the computer with the boot floppy.

4. Install and configure Linux via the Red Hat installation process that is included on the Red Hat Publisher's Edition CD-ROM. Adding the Linux partitions – in addition to the DOS partition – is part of the process.

With the single-partition (destructive) method, you begin the installation process by completing the following steps:

1. Create a boot floppy disk by copying a special file with the DOS program `rawrite.exe` if you are running Windows or DOS. Otherwise, use the `dd` program when running under Linux.

2. Boot the computer with the boot floppy. (If you have a newer computer, you should be able to boot directly off your CD-ROM.)

3. Install and configure Linux via the Red Hat installation process that comes on the boot. Partitioning the entire disk for Linux is part of the process.

Method 1: Installing Linux along with Windows (dual-boot)

You can repartition your disk without destroying the current operating system and data. This typically means that you'll install Red Hat Linux on the same disk as Windows. The First Nondestructive Interactive Partition Splitting Program (FIPS) is a DOS-based program, written by Arno Schaefer, that shrinks your DOS partition down by using any or all of the unused space on your disk. The freed space can then be used for one or more Linux partitions.

To prepare your disk, run ScanDisk and have it analyze your disk. You should also defragment the disk with Disk Defragmenter. You can run both programs from Windows 95:

1. Click the Windows 95 Start button.

2. Choose Programs → Accessories → System Tools.

3. You can select both utilities from the Systems Tools submenu. From the System Tools submenu, choose the ScanDisk utility.

4. In the ScanDisk-Ms-dos_6 dialog box, click the Thorough button, click the Automatically Fix Errors button, and then click the Start button. ScanDisk performs a check of your disk. (Be prepared for a long wait. ScanDisk must check every cluster on your disk as the last part of its check.) If ScanDisk encounters any problems, it asks you which action to take.

5. After ScanDisk has finished, repeat Steps 1 and 2, and from the System Tools submenu, choose the Disk Defragmenter.

6. When the Select Drive dialog box appears, select the appropriate drive and then click.

7. In the Disk Defragmenter dialog box that appears, click Start.

Note: You can also run these programs from DOS.

Read the documentation that comes with FIPS. You can find detailed instructions for using FIPS on the Red Hat CD in the first-level directory DOSUTILS. The CD-ROM contains more documentation in \DOSUTILS\FIPSDOCS. Several plain-text files can help you understand the process and the pitfalls of FIPS: README, FIPS, a FAQ, and other useful documents.

FIPS can't run in a multitasking environment, so complete the following steps to shut down Windows and boot in MS-DOS mode:

1. Click the Start button (lower, left-hand corner of your screen).

2. Click the Shut Down button.

3. Click the "Restart the computer in MS-DOS mode?" button.

4. Click Yes.

After your computer restarts in MS-DOS mode, you can run FIPS. There are two versions of FIPS. The version found on the Red Hat CD-ROM in the D:\DOSUTILS directory can be used on the older FAT file systems found on older versions of Windows 95. The version found in D:\DOSUTILS\FIPS20 works on FAT32 file system that Windows 98 uses. Note that this book assumes that the D:\ drive refers to the CD-ROM. If your system uses another letter to indicate the CD-ROM, then substitute that letter.
To run FIPS:

1. Change to the \DOSUTILS directory if you run a normal FAT file system (older versions of Windows 95), or the D\DOSUTILS\FIPS20 if you use FAT32 (newer versions of Windows 95, all Windows 98 and all NT) and start FIPS. Assuming the CD-ROM drive is drive D, you start FIPS from the prompt by entering the following command

   ```
   D:\DOSUTILS\FIPS
   ```

2. After you enter the command to start FIPS, you see the copyright and disclaimer screen. After you read it, press any key.

When FIPS prompts you to enter a character (for example, y, n, c, r), it does not require you to press Enter after the single character. When you press a valid key, FIPS accepts it and moves to the next step in its process.

3. If you are running under Windows or another multitasking system, FIPS displays the warning shown in Figure 1-1. Press N to exit FIPS and restart the computer under DOS. Otherwise, proceed at your own risk.

4. As shown in Figure 1-1, FIPS displays your present partition table. It displays the size of your disk and other information such as the number of cylinders. Press any key to continue.

5. FIPS calculates and displays a summary of your disk parameters. It asks you if you wish to save a copy of your root and boot sector to floppy. Load an unused, DOS-formatted and bootable floppy, and press Y.

6. FIPS then asks whether you have a floppy in drive A. Insert the floppy, press Y, and FIPS saves the information about your current boot sector setup on the floppy. Please make a backup!

```
This is free software, and you are welcome to redistribute it
under certain conditions; again see file COPYING for details.

Press any Key

WARNING: FIPS has detected that it is running under MS-Windows version 4.0
FIPS should not be used under a multitasking OS. If possible, boot from a DOS
disk and then run FIPS. Read FIPS.DOC for more information.

Do you want to proceed (y/n)? y

Partition table:

         |         |    Start         |      |    End         | Start |Number of|
Part.|bootable|Head Cyl. Sector|System|Head Cyl. Sector| Sector |Sectors  |  MB
-----+--------+----------------+------+----------------+--------+---------+------
1    |  yes   | 1    0     1|  06h| 15 1023     63|     63| 1032129| 503
2    |  no    | 0    0     0|  00h|  0    0      0|      0|       0|   0
3    |  no    | 0    0     0|  00h|  0    0      0|      0|       0|   0
4    |  no    | 0    0     0|  00h|  0    0      0|      0|       0|   0

Checking root sector ... OK

Press any Key
```

Figure 1-1: FIPS partition table

 TIP If you encounter problems later or simply want to return to your previous DOS setup, run the program RESTORRB.EXE (in D:\DOSUTILS) to restore the old boot sector to your disk. Then you can run FDISK to see that the old partition is reinstalled.

7. The next screen, shown in Figure 1-2, is a mini-partition table showing the current partition size in megabytes, the starting cylinder of the potential new partition, and the potential partition size. You alter the current and potential partitions with the left, right, up, and down keys. Each time you press the key, the partition changes in increments of several hundred KB. By pressing the cursor keys you increase/decrease the size of the new partition while decreasing/increasing the size of the old partition by the same amount.

```
Checking root sector ... OK

Do you want to continue or reedit the partition table (c/r)? c

New boot sector:

Bytes per sector: 512
Sectors per cluster: 16
Reserved sectors: 1
Number of FATs: 2
Number of rootdirectory entries: 512
Number of sectors (short): 0
Media descriptor byte: F8h
Sectors per FAT: 252
Sectors per track: 63
Drive heads: 16
Hidden sectors: 63
Number of sectors (long): 826497
Physical drive number: 80h
Signature: 29h

Checking boot sector ... OK

Ready to write new partition scheme to disk
Do you want to proceed (y/n)? _
```

Figure 1-2: The FIPS mini-partition table proceeded by the disk parameters.

8. Experiment with the possible configurations. You can install Red Hat Linux on as little as 50 MB for experimental purposes. A usable system requires as little as 100-150 MB, but if possible set up your system with at

least 200 MB – that is, enough space to install the basic file system, a fair number of utilities, and some data.

If you have a modern disk – 1.0 GB or larger – try starting with 500 MB. With that much space, you can comfortably load most everything you may want initially, including X Window. Obviously, the less space you have for Linux, the less you'll have to use for a file server. If you know for sure that you want to construct a file server that will store many megabytes or gigabytes of files, use the largest disk you can afford now. But if you are merely curious or want to use Linux as a home system, you can start with a relatively small space.

9. When you're ready to take the plunge, press Enter. FIPS displays the screen and prompts you to press c to continue or r to re-edit the partition. Make your choice, or exit completely by pressing Ctrl+C to go back to the DOS prompt.

10. FIPS recalculates the disk partition values and displays them, as shown in Figure 1-3. FIPS then asks if you are ready to write the new partition scheme to disk. Press y or n, and FIPS returns you to the DOS prompt.

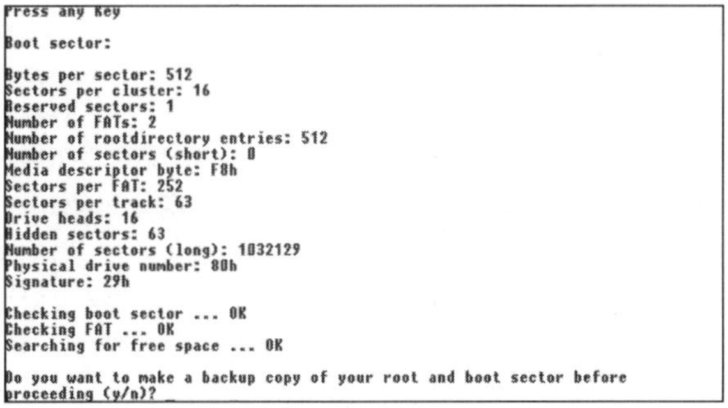

```
Press any key

Boot sector:

Bytes per sector: 512
Sectors per cluster: 16
Reserved sectors: 1
Number of FATs: 2
Number of rootdirectory entries: 512
Number of sectors (short): 0
Media descriptor byte: F8h
Sectors per FAT: 252
Sectors per track: 63
Drive heads: 16
Hidden sectors: 63
Number of sectors (long): 1032129
Physical drive number: 80h
Signature: 29h

Checking boot sector ... OK
Checking FAT ... OK
Searching for free space ... OK

Do you want to make a backup copy of your root and boot sector before
proceeding (y/n)? _
```

Figure 1-3: Are you ready to write the new partition to disk?

You can look at the new partition with FDISK.

If you reboot your computer at this point, the system may not recognize your CD-ROM with its current configuration. The system recognizes the partition you just created as drive D, which was probably the designation for your CD-ROM. In some cases, where you have two disk drives installed, the system may simply recognize the CD-ROM as drive E, which could cause problems.

You can delete that new partition with FDISK and eliminate the problem – doing so will not affect your Linux installation. However, FIPS labels the new partition as Red. The version of FDISK that I use with Windows 95 does not permit the use of lowercase letters when specifying the label during the delete process. Consequently, you have to live with the problem until you delete the new partition during the Linux installation process.

> Before you proceed, you should create a boot floppy, just as you have to do in the single-partition method. Just as you should make an emergency Windows 95 startup disk, you should have a boot floppy for emergencies. I provide instructions for creating a boot floppy a bit later in this chapter.

Method 2: Installing Linux by itself (destructive)

This is the method used in this book.

Using the entire hard disk for Linux is straightforward and conceptually simple. Whatever partition(s) you have are written over, destroying all the data on your disk. For this discussion, I assume that you have only one partition, which is typical of DOS and Windows installations.

MAKING A BOOT FLOPPY

It is generally necessary to create a boot floppy in order to start the Red Hat installation process. The floppy disk contains a basic Linux kernel and file system. (The file system provides a foundation from which the kernel can operate; it is essential to Linux's operation.) When you start your computer the boot floppy loads the basic Linux operating system and then starts the installation program.

> Newer computers have the ability to boot directly from the CD-ROM. If you have such a machine (you can tell by looking in the BIOS setup for the boot options), then it is not necessary to make a boot floppy. You can start the Red Hat installation process by booting off of the Red Hat installation CD-ROM. Change your BIOS setting to allow booting from the CD-ROM, save the setting, insert the CD-ROM and reboot your computer. You should see the start of the Red Hat installation process as described in the section "Installing Red Hat Linux" in this chapter. You can, of course, skip all of the instructions related to the boot floppy.

On the Red Hat CD-ROM, the directory D:\IMAGES contains a number of files that are images of a Linux kernel and file system. A program called RAWRITE — which you find in D:\DOSUTILS — transfers your kernel and basic file system image — containing the most essential system and application programs — byte-for-byte onto the floppy disk. When that disk is inserted into your floppy drive and you reboot your computer, Linux takes control and copies the file system into your system memory (ramdisk), and the Red Hat installation program starts. Then you can install a complete Linux system.

Here are the steps for creating a boot floppy:

1. Insert a floppy whose contents are disposable; all data will be irretrievably lost. Enter the following commands

```
D:\
CD \IMAGES
D:\DOSUTILS\RAWRITE
```

2. RAWRITE prompts you for the file you want to install and the location to install it. Enter BOOT.IMG – for a bootable image – and A for the floppy disk. RAWRITE puts the image onto the disk and returns to the DOS prompt.

TIP

If you intend to brave the rapids of installing Linux over a network, then you should make the boot floppy by using the bootnet.img or pcmcia.img file in place of boot.img. bootnet.img is intended for installing Linux on a computer that already has a working network connection. pcmcia.img is used on a computer — typically a laptop — that has a PCMCIA network adapter. Such installations are beyond the scope of this book.

3. Reboot the PC with the boot floppy inserted. The first prompt you see is boot. Simply press any key, unless you need to enter special parameters. You see the word linux displayed and then several lines of dots. This is the Linux kernel being loaded into memory. You see a screen full of information similar to the example.

```
Console: 16 point font, 400 scans
Console: colour VGA+ 80x25, 1 virtual console (max 63)
pcibios_init : BIOS32 Service Directory structure at
0x000f6f10
pcibios_init : BIOS32 Service Directory entry at 0xf6f20
pcibios_init : PCI BIOS revision 2.10 entry at 0xf6f41
Probing PCI hardware.
Calibrating delay loop.. ok - 35.94 BogoMIPSMemory:
63180k/65536k available(720k kernel code, 384k reserved,
1252k data)Swansea University Computer Society NET3.035 for
Linux 2.0
NET3: Unix domain sockets 0.13 for Linux NET3.035.Swansea
University Computer Society TCP/IP for NET3.034
IP Protocols: ICMP, UDP, TCP
VFS: Diskquotas version dquot_5.6.0 initialized
Checking 386/387 coupling... Ok, fpu using exception 16 error
reporting.Checking 'hlt' instruction... Ok.Linux version
```

```
2.0.30 (root@atlas.paunchy.net) (gcc version 2.7.2.1) #1 Thu
Aug 21 16:27:26 MDT 1997
Serial driver version 4.13 with no serial options enabled
tty00 at 0x03f8 (irq = 4) is a 16550A
tty01 at 0x02f8 (irq = 3) is a 16550A
Ramdisk driver initialized : 16 ramdisks of 4096K sizehda:
WDC AC21600H, 1549MB w/128kB Cache, LBA,
CHS=787/64/63
hdb: SANYO CRD-254P, ATAPI CDROM drive
ide0 at 0x1f0-0x1f7,0x3f6 on irq 14
Floppy drive(s): fd0 is 1.44M
Started kswapd v 1.4.2.2
FDC 0 is an 8272A
md driver 0.35 MAX_MD_DEV=4, MAX_REAL=8
scsi : 0 hosts.scsi : detected total.
eth0: 3c509 at 0x300 tag 1,BNC port, address  00 a0 24 2f 30
69, IRQ 10.
3c509.c:1.07 6/15/95 becker@cesdis.gsfc.nasa.gov
Partition check:
 hda: hda1
VFS: Mounted root (ext2 filesystem) readonly.
Adding Swap: 44348k swap-space (priority -1)
Swansea University Computer Society IPX 0.34 for NET3.035
IPX Portions Copyright (c) 1995 Caldera, Inc.
Appletalk 0.17 for Linux NET3.035
```

BOOTING FROM CD-ROM

You do not need to use a bootable floppy if you have a computer that can boot off of your CD-ROM. This capability became common around 1998. You need to look at your BIOS configuration in order to determine if your CD-ROM can boot your computer. Look at the boot sequence option to make that determination. It is beyond the scope of this book to describe how to do that. Please consult your computer system board, if you have one, for more information about the process. If you don't have documentation, then you can look at the boot options listed in your BIOS menu.

If you can and want to boot from CD-ROM, then configure your BIOS to do so. Restart your computer with the Red Hat Publisher's Edition CD-ROM inserted. Your computer will see the CD-ROM and start the installation process from it.

Installing Red Hat Linux

After you complete the dual-boot preparation, or decide to dedicate your entire disk to Linux, you can use the Red Hat installation program to install Linux. Insert the boot floppy disk into the floppy drive, or alternatively the Red Hat Publisher's

Edition CD-ROM into the CD-ROM drive and reboot the computer. The following instructions detail the Red Hat installation process.

Red Hat provides both a graphical user interface (GUI) and a text-based menu installation system. I've found that the text-based system works with a wider range of hardware than the GUI. I describe the text-based system here. Please use the GUI system if you wish – it is quite good. If you do use it, then you may wish to use these instructions as a general guideline because the GUI follows the same sequences as the text-based system.

For each step in the installation process, you see a different window. Most windows offer a sub-menu for selecting specific items, such as the type of CD-ROM drive. In other cases, however, you choose an option by selecting an onscreen button. You use the keys to select sub-menu options. You toggle the buttons on and off by pressing spacebar. You can also select a highlighted button by pressing Enter. The Tab key and the Shift+Tab key combination move the control from one place to another in the menu window. The F12 key moves the control to the next window, saving whatever selections you have already made (use with caution).

Within the sub-menus, use the keys to choose specific items, such as the network adapter model. Press Tab and Alt+Tab to move between a sub-menu and the command buttons such as Ok and Cancel.

 Unfortunately, the Red Hat installation system lacks an abort mechanism. After you start the installation, the system offers no way to exit gracefully. You must reboot.

Linux makes use of a facility called a virtual terminal. A virtual terminal allows you to make your single computer screen work like several separate terminals. By pressing Alt+CTRL+F1 through Alt+CTRL+F5, you can switch among the different screens, each independent of the others. Red Hat takes advantage of this feature by providing different information about your installation process in each terminal. The following table describes the function of each virtual terminal:

Key Combination	Displays
Alt+F1	Installation progress
Alt+F2	The shell prompt
Alt+F3	Installation log
Alt+F4	System log
Alt+F5	Program output

Starting the installation

Here are the steps for completing the Red Hat Linux installation process (each numbered item corresponds to an installation step):

1. Language Selection

   Linux is international. Select the language that you wish to use and press return.

2. Keyboard Selection

   Select your keyboard type. (You can modify your selection later by using the kbdconfig command.)

3. Installation Method

   You are asked to choose to install from your CD-ROM or hard drive. Select CD-ROM and press the Ok button.

TIP You can also install from a remote computer over a network by creating your boot floppy from the bootnet.img on the Red Hat Publisher's Edition CD-ROM. When you boot your computer you will be prompted for the type of method to use. It is beyond the scope of this book to describe how to perform that process. Please consult the documents on the CD-ROM in the docs directory.

4. Red Hat Linux

   This is the introduction and informational dialog box. Press any key to continue with the installation.

5. Installation Type

   Red Hat provides five different installation classes to choose from. I will use the Custom System in this book, but will briefly describe the other options first. They are

   - Install GNOME Workstation

   - Install KDE Workstation

   - Install Server System

   - Install Custom System

   - Upgrade Existing Installation

   The first three types write predefined partitions to your disk and also choose the software to be installed. The Install Custom System requires you to choose both the partitions and the software packages to install. The Upgrade Existing Installation doesn't change any of your existing partitions but merely installs new software. Please refer to the sidebar Using the Gnome/KDE workstation and server type installation for more information about those systems. This book describes the Install Custom System type of installation.

Select the Custom System.

Please keep in mind that if you use the Server or Workstation options, then your entire disk will be erased unless you choose the manual option.

Using the Gnome/KDE workstation and server type installations

If you choose either of the Gnome/KDE workstation or the server types, then you will be prompted to either allow Red Hat to create the partition(s) for you or do so manually. If you select the manual partition method, then you will use the Disk Druid system described in the section "Partitioning your Disk" to create your partitions. Please refer to steps 1 to 7 in that sectionfor more instructions.

If you choose to let Red Hat automatically set partitions, then your disk will be given a 64MB swap partition, a 16MB /boot partition and one large root (/) partition. The /boot partition contains the Linux kernel and supporting programs.

If you choose the Server with automatic partitions, Red Hat will attempt to write the five partitions shown in the following table to your disk.

Partition	Description
/	The root partition. The mount point of all partitions
/boot	Contains the Linux kernel and extras needed for booting
/usr	Libraries and other static files. Also extra applications
/var	Variable files such as logs and temporary files
/home	User home directories

The root (/) and var (/var) file systems are made equal in size to each other. The usr (/usr) and home (/home) partitions are allocated the same space too. The boot (/boot) partition is only allocated enough space — about 16MB — to store the Linux kernel and associated files needed to boot the computer. The root and var partitions are each given roughly 10% the disk space as the usr and home partitions.

Partitioning your disk

Your first major task will be to partition your disk. The following instructions describe going through this process using Red Hat's Disk Druid system.

1. Current Disk Partition (Disk Druid)

   Partition selection is a much more important consideration under Linux than with Windows. Windows is typically run on one or two partitions. Linux can also be run on a single partition but this can create problems down the line.

   There are different philosophies about how many partitions to use, and of what size. Those found in this book are based on the author's experience and best judgment.

   My suggested partitions for 1G and 4G disks are shown in Tables 1-2 and 1-3. You have much more breathing room if you use a bigger disk. The root partition size of 60MB is used in case you want to install all of the software contained on the Red Hat Publisher's Edition CD-ROM; it also leaves a little extra space for compiling multiple kernel versions (described in Chapter 4). Please use your best judgment for smaller or larger sized disks.

TABLE 1-2 SUGGESTED DISK PARTITIONS FOR A 1-GB DISK

Partition	Size	Function
/	60	Used as the root of all mounted file systems
/var	100	Used mostly for temporary files and logs
/usr	400	Used for static, or mostly static, files and libraries
/usr/local	200	Stores third-party and custom software storage
/home	100	User home directories
Swap	2 to 2.5 times RAM	Stores virtual memory to disk

TABLE 1-3 SUGGESTED DISK PARTITIONS FOR A 4-GB DISK

Partition	SizeB	Function
/	60	The root of all mounted file systems
/var	200	Used mostly for temporary files and logs

Partition	SizeB	Function
/usr	500	Used for static, or mostly static, files and libraries
/usr/local	1000	Third-party and custom software storage
/home	2000	User home directories
swap	2 to 2.5 times RAM	Stores virtual memory to disk

The Disk Druid system is used to partition your disk. If you are using a disk with existing partitions, then Disk Druid displays a screen that shows the partitions without any mount points; it will show the file system type, however. If you are using a new or reformatted disk like that shown in Figure 1-4, then you will not see any partitions. In this case it shows the entire disk as available to your new installation. Otherwise, you can delete each partition if you wish.

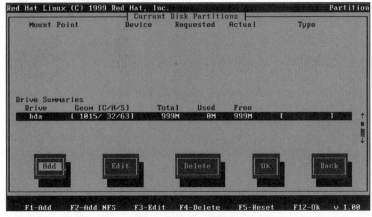

Figure 1-4: The Disk Druid Current Disk Partitions shows no partitions.

The column headers are pretty much self-explanatory.

- The Mount Point is the place where Linux will reference – mount – each file system.

- The Device is the logical piece of the disk – slice – that is used to store the file system partition.

- The Requested field shows how much space you have requested for the partition.

- The Actual field shows how much space is allocated for the partition.

- Type refers to the way in which the file system will be formatted. Linux uses the ext2 format by default. Windows uses FAT, FAT32 or NTFS for instance.

2. You can alternatively add and then edit partitions until you have a file system that meets your needs. First, use the Add button to create your root partition. Figure 1-5 shows the Edit New Partition dialog box.

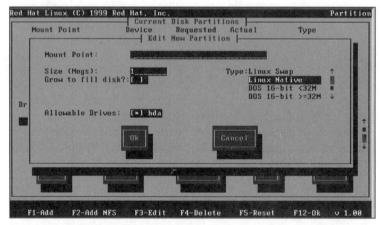

Figure 1-5: The Edit New Partition dialog box

3. In the Edit New Partition dialog box enter / as the mount point. Tab to the Size (Megs)box and enter 60 MB. Tab past the Grow to fill disk box. (Note, if you press the Space bar on the Grow to fill disk option, then Disk Druid will expand the partition to fill the remaining space on the disk. If you select this option on multiple partitions, then Disk Druid will attempt to evenly distribute the remaining disk space between the partitions.) Tab past the Type field because it defaults to the desired Linux Native. Tab down to the Ok button, as shown in Figure 1-6, and press the return key.

4. Repeat step 2 in order to create each new partition (/usr, /usr/local, /var, /home, swap and optionally /opt). Don't forget to create a swap partition (the swap partition does not have a mount point) You can use the Delete button to remove any or all partitions. You can also use the Edit button to modify the existing partitions. You should see a screen like shown in Figure 1-7.

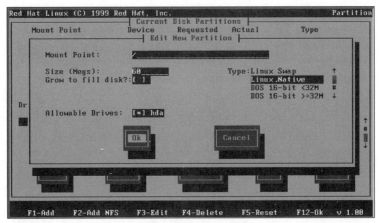

Figure 1-6: Enter the root partition information.

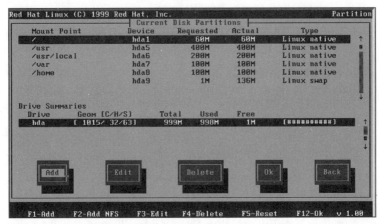

Figure 1-7: The Disk Druid Current Disk Partitions menu shows your new partitions.

TIP Linux is a demand-paged, virtual memory operating system. That means that it can "swap" out chunks of memory, called `pages`, to disk when its memory is filled up. The place on disk where it stores the information is the `swap` partition. A reasonable rule of thumb is to make the swap partition 2.5 times the size of the RAM in a computer.

5. After you've added all the partitions that you think you need you can go back and edit any or all of the partitions if necessary. Position the cursor on the desired partition and select the `Edit` option. Repeat step 2 to change any of the parameters.

6. Once you are satisfied with all your partitions press the `Ok` button. You are prompted to save the new partition table. Press `Ok` if you are satisfied with your choices. You can press `No` and return to the Disk Druid `Current Disk Partitions` window. You can also press the `Back` key and you'll go back one step.

    Once you have saved the new disk partitions, `Control` will return you to the Red Hat installation system.

7. Choose Partitions to Format

    You are asked to select which partitions to format. Formatting will erase all the information on a partition!

    ■ If you are installing on a new disk or do not care about the data stored on an old disk, then go ahead and select each partition to be formatted.

    ■ If you are re-installing Linux, and you have previously installed more than the single root (/) partition, then select only the `root` (plus the `/usr` and `/var` partitions, if you have them) partition to be formatted. However, if you are reinstalling and have any of the `/home`, `/usr/local`, `/opt` partitions, then don't format them and you will retain all of your existing data.

    ■ If you are using the multiple-partition method – to install Linux along with Windows, for instance – then make sure that you do not format the partition(s) with the other operating system(s). If you are already using Windows, for instance, then Disk Druid will automatically make the Windows partition `hda1` (assuming you are using the first IDE hard disk). Your Linux partitions will start at `hda5` and increment to `hda6`, `hda7`, etc. from there.

    You have the option of doing a more detailed format by selecting the `Check for bad blocks during format` option. That type of format will catch and exclude bad parts (blocks) of the disk drive and will also take a long time. If you are using an older disk, then it is best to select this option by pressing the spacebar.

Once again, use your best judgment and be careful proceeding.

Configuring LILO

1. LILO Configuration

   The LInux LOader (LILO) is the program that configures the boot sector on your hard drive to know about the operating system(s) on it.

   You need only enter information in this dialog box if you are using a SCSI disk drive(s). This book does not cover SCSI installations and it is left to you to decide what information, if necessary, to enter in this dialog box.

   Tab to the Ok button and press the return key.

2. LILO Configuration (continued)

   This step asks you where to install LILO on your hard disk. This book assumes a dedicated IDE hard disk and you will want to use the default /dev/hda. However, if you're using the multiple partitions method (typically referred to as a dual boot system), then you typically will still use /dev/hda. The exception is if you have Windows NT with NTFS on the first partition. In that case, select the partition where the /boot directory is located (typically /dev/hda1). You will typically need to use a boot floppy that has been configured to use the first Linux partition to start Linux (for instance, /dev/hda5).

   Tab to the Ok key and press the return key.

3. LILO Configuration (continued)

   If you are using a dedicated drive for Linux, then only one choice will be given here. However, if you are loading Linux onto a drive with another system on it – dual boot – then you can choose which one will be the default system here. Linux will be set up as the default by default.

   Tab to the Ok key and press the return key.

Configuring your network

The Network Configuration dialog box appears next. If you want your machine to be a stand-alone workstation, select No, press the enter key, and go on to the next section.

Otherwise, if your system is connected to a network, select Yes and press the enter key. The next two dialog boxes help you configure your system for a network.

> **TIP** As you fill in the dialog boxes, you may find that Linux guesses what information is needed and fills in some sections automatically. If Linux has guessed incorrectly, simply change the information.

Follow these steps to configure your system for a network

1. Hostname configuration

   You need to enter the name of your Linux computer. For instance, enter the name chivas at the prompt as shown in Figure 1-8, select the Ok button and press the return key.

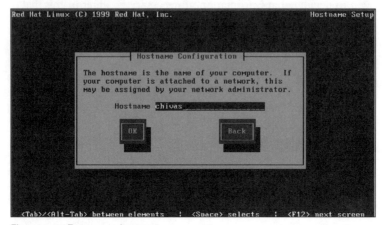

Figure 1-8: Enter your hostname.

2. Network Configuration

   Choose whether to enter your IP address manually or to have a BOOTP or a DHCP server hand you a dynamic IP. For this example, use the spacebar to toggle the bootp/dhcp selection off. That will activate the manual configuration, which includes the IP address, Netmask, Default gateway (IP) and Primary nameserver items.

> **TIP** The latter two options — BOOTP and DHCP — are not frequently used in home or small networks. This book uses and you should select the Static IP option.

Next, enter your values into the IP address, netmask, default gateway (IP), and primary nameserver entries as shown in Figure 1-9.

Figure 1-9: Enter your Network Configuration.

The IP address is the numeric address that every computer requires to use the TCP/IP protocol suite. The Netmask tells the host what kind of addressing scheme is used on the LAN. The Default Gateway refers to the computer – if any – that acts as the interface to the Internet. The Namesever entry is the IP address of the computer – if any – that translates the numeric IP address into the more familiar IP name and vice versa.

The following parameters are used to construct this Linux computer. These values are important because they fit into all the following examples throughout this book. If you are experienced setting up networks, or want this Linux computer to fit into an existing network, then go ahead an use your own values. However, if you don't have special needs, then please use these numbers. The values are also shown below.

- **IP address:** 192.168.1.250

- **Netmask:** 255.255.255.0

- **Default Gateway:** 192.168.1.254 (An Internet gateway will be configured in Chapter 7. It will be given the address 192.168.1.254)

- **Primary Nameserver:** 192.168.1.250 and/or your ISP's name server (A local nameserver will optionally be configured in Chapter 8.)

If you do not have an InterNic-registered – official – IP address, then you can, and should, use a public IP address. The most frequently used addresses are 192.168.1.X through 192.168.254.X, where X can be any number between 1 and 254. These addresses should use the 255.255.255.0 netmask.

If you are installing your new Linux box on an existing network that has a connection to the Internet or another network, then you should enter the IP address of that connection as the gateway. If your new Linux box is going to be the gateway, then enter its IP address there. Otherwise you can leave it blank and enter it later.

If you do not have access to an IP address, don't worry. The fine people who designed the internet protocols (notice the lower-case i) set aside some addresses for you to use as long as you do not use them outside your LAN. If you do not try to access the Internet – the WWW, e-mail, and so on – then the IP address spaces shown in Table 1-4 are legal. Chapter 8 discusses IP masquerading – that is, how to mask these addresses, or any IP, from the rest of the Internet – so don't worry about choosing this type of address now.

When you finish with this dialog box, select the Ok button and press Enter.

Internet addresses and the InterNic

The internet protocol is an impressive work (remember that the lower-case i refers to the protocols that make the Internet possible). It encompasses a huge number of disparate requirements and seamlessly glues the entire world together. Your TCP/IP local area network (LAN) contains nearly all the elements that allow it to scale up to network the entire world.

If you intend to advertise or use your network name out on the Internet, you must register it with the InterNic via an Internet service provider (ISP). See http://ds. internic.net and the Requests for Comment (RFC) rfc2050 for more information.

InterNic is getting stingier with IP addresses. All class C address spaces are distributed from Internet service providers (ISPs) who must prove to the InterNic that they are using more than 50 percent of their space. Therefore, you must now have at least 128 hosts to qualify for your own class C address space.

A new system under development will correct much of this problem. It is the Internet Protocol version 6, IPv6, and makes use of 128-bit-long IP addresses instead of the current 32-bit addresses. It is compatible with the current protocol but allows for considerably more growth. This is a lot of addresses and should be enough to assign an IP address to every home appliance and computer (and person) in the world.

TABLE 1-4 GENERAL-PURPOSE IP ADDRESSES

Network class	Start address	Last address	Subnet Mask
A	10.0.0.0	10.255.255.255	255.0.0.0
B	172.16.0.0	172.31.255.255	255.255.0.0
C	192.168.1.0	192.168.255.255	255.255.255.0

It is almost always best to use a class C address space. It can handle as many as 254 hosts, which should be enough. I prefer to assign my servers the highest addresses in the subnet, so I give it the address 192.168.1.250 (254 is used for the optional Internet gateway/firewall atlas described in Chapter 11). Clients, such as my Windows machines, get the low numbers starting at 192.168.1.1, Linux clients start at 100 and Linux servers occupy the addresses above 200. This convention makes it easy to remember which machines are the server(s) and which are the client(s).

3. Configure Network (continued)

Next, you need to enter the information on your domain name and extra name servers. This book uses the domain name of paunchy.net. You need to enter the IP address of your ISP's name servers (one or two).

The following bullets describe these parameters in more detail.

- **Domain name.** A domain name is, as you may guess, the name that your network is known as. It's like a nickname. For instance, paunchy.net is my registered domain name.

- **Host name.** This is the name of your computer with the domain name added. For instance, my domain name is paunchy.net, and this host name is chivas.paunchy.net.

- **Secondary and Tertiary nameservers (IPs).** These are the IP addresses of the second and third DNS servers that your computer will use. They are generally the addresses of your ISP nameservers.

When you finish filling in this dialog box, select the Ok button and press enter.

Continuing the configuration

1. Mouse Selection

   Select the mouse that you have. If you don't know, then use your best judgment and make a guess. Keep in mind that you can reconfigure the mouse by running the `mouseconfig` program after the installation is complete.

2. Time Zone Selection

   Select your time zone.

   Tab to the `Ok` key and press the return key.

3. Root Password

   Enter your root password. The root user has unlimited privileges and is the most powerful user on a Linux computer.

   When you enter the password, the system checks the second one against the first and forces you to reenter it if they do not match. It is essential to the security of your Linux box to use a proper password. Do not use a simple word or name or anything that can be easily guessed or associated with you. Instead, it is best to make up a simple phrase that is easy to remember but not found in any dictionary. Something like `car~lite` is appropriate. The idea is to be able to remember it and not have to write it down. The idea also is not to be able to find it in a dictionary where an automated program can find it. Please refer to Chapter 7 for more discussion.

   Tab to the `Ok` key and press the return key.

4. Add User

   You can add regular – non-root – users to your system in this dialog box. (If you don't want to any users, tab down to the `Ok` item and press the return key.) Choose a user ID, which is generally just a user name. For instance, I could enter `paul` or `psery` as my user name. You then can optionally enter the user's full name. Finally, you must enter your password twice as in the previous step. Repeat this process for each user that you wish to give access to your Linux computer.

   Tab to the `Ok` key and press the return key.

5. Authentication Configuration

   The Red Hat installation system uses shadow passwords with MD5 checksums by default. The traditional Linux/UNIX system stores your encrypted passwords in the `/etc/passwd` file by default. That file must be world-readable (any user can read – but not write – to that file) for a number of technical reasons. That makes it possible for a malicious or curious person to copy the encrypted passwords and then run a password-cracking program and possibly discover your passwords. Shadow passwords stores the encrypted passwords in another file — /etc/shadow — which is not world readable. This system makes your Linux computer safer. MD5 is an encryption method.

Chapter 8 describes how to set up an NIS server, so leave the Enable NIS option as is too.

Figure 1-10 shows the dialog box as it should be.

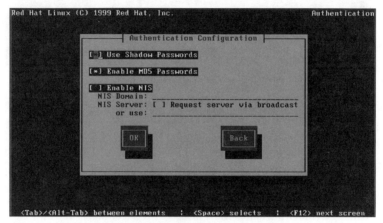

Figure 1-10: The Authentication Configuration dialog box

Tab to the Ok key and press Return.

Installing Red Hat software packages

1. Package Group Selection

This is the point where you get to choose which, if any, of the Red Hat software packages that come with the distribution to install. By default Red Hat installs not only the essential packages but also a selection of packages that it considers popular or useful. In many cases — and especially while you are suffering through the initial learning curve — it is reasonable to accept the default.

However, in Chapter 2 Samba is used to give Windows computers access files and printers on chivas. Go ahead and select Samba for installation by using the cursor keys to move down through the list. Use the spacebar to select the Samba package.

If you wish to further modify the software selection then you can make general or more detailed choices. The general choices fall into categories such as the SMB (Samba) Server component shown in Figure 1-11.

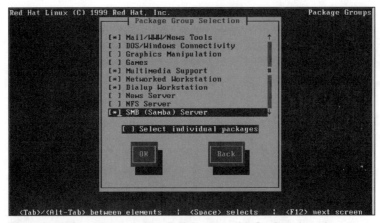

Figure 1–11: Components to install dialog box with Samba selected

You can also make more detailed selections if you choose the Select Individual packages. (Red Hat uses its own creation called the Red Hat Package manager (RPM) to store, install, remove and get information about all the software that it uses. RPM is has become a very popular system because it is an efficient, convenient and reliable software distribution method. It is discussed in more detail in Chapter 5.) When dealing with individual packages RPM is what the installation process is using.

This book uses the HOWTO and FAQ documents that are included on the companion CD-ROM. It is highly recommended that you install that documentation during this installation process. It only takes a few megabytes of disk space and is well worth its weight. Go towards the bottom of the installation dialog box and click on the Extra Documentation item to do so.

Once you finish selecting the software to install and press the Ok button, the software is copied onto your disk. A reasonably fast CD-ROM drive takes around 10 to 12 minutes. A simple progress display is shown. It is reasonably accurate in estimating the time to go.

2. You are shown a screen that indicates that overlapping packages are being resolved. This is a simple informational screen and does not require any response on your part.

Finishing up the configuration

1. Video Card Selection

   Red Hat provides a long list of video cards as shown in Figure 1-12. Use the arrow keys to move through the list. If you do not see your video card but you see a previous model by the same manufacturer, then select that. Press the Tab key to move to the 0k button and press Return. Once you select the video card, Red Hat will install the RPM video driver package from the CD-ROM.

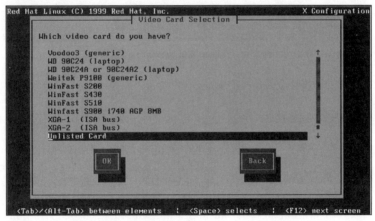

Figure 1-12: Choosing your video card

   If you do not see a video card that matches your equipment, then you have two choices. You can use (1) the Unlisted Card, which is the very last option in the menu or (2) Generic VGA option. If you choose the Unlisted Card, shown in Figure 1-13, then you go to another menu that lists generic video settings. In most cases, you'll select the SVGA option.

TIP   If you already have Windows installed, you can go to control panel→ display→settings→change display type to find out what video card you have.

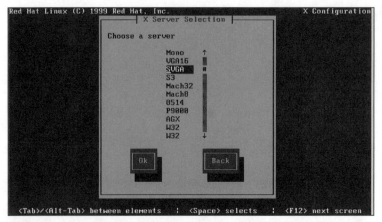

Figure 1-13: Selecting the SVGA in the X Server Selection dialog box

2. Bootdisk

   You can tell Red Hat to create a boot disk at the end of the installation process. You can use a boot disk to bypass the LILO system, start Linux directly and then mount your file systems. This is useful if LILO gets corrupted or misconfigured. Go ahead and select Ok and press the return key.

3. Installation to begin

   Press Ok and the Red Hat packages that you have chosen will be installed. This takes between 5 and 20 minutes in general depending on how fast your equipment is. Sit back and imagine the nirvana that will be yours!

4. Bootdisk

   If you elected to create a bootdisk in step 2, you will be prompted to insert a floppy disk. This disk will be completely overwritten so make sure that you use a blank or unwanted floppy.

   Insert the floppy disk, select Ok and press the return.

Configuring X

The final stage of the Red Hat installation process is to install the graphical X Window System, which is commonly referred to as X. This is optional but usually desirable. The most common reason not to run an interface is that you intend to run your Linux computer as a server. For instance, if you are using an older computer, then you will conserve resources by not running graphics. In this book, the graphics are installed.

Configuring X requires that you tell the Red Hat installation process what type of video adapter card and monitor that you have. Red Hat supplies numerous predefined settings, but if your equipment is not listed, then you can still use generic settings. The following instructions describe the process.

1. Monitor Setup

   Figure 1-14 shows the beginning of the list of monitors you can select from. Select a monitor that fits your own. If your monitor is not included in the list, then you can select Custom, Generic Monitor or Generic Multisync. In that case please see Chapter 7 for more instructions.

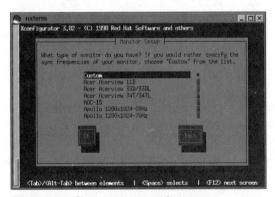

Figure 1-14: Choosing your monitor type

 Older monitors can't handle resolution rates and scan frequencies higher than those they were designed for. A monitor designed for a 640 x 480 resolution (and a low scan frequency) can't display 2,048 x 1,024 resolution (and a high scan frequency). More important, if you try to make the monitor display that high a frequency, it might burst into flames. (I didn't believe this either until I saw a monitor smoke.) Modern monitors, called Multisync, can automatically match themselves to a series of scan frequencies and resolutions. Some of these monitors are even smart enough to turn themselves off if the frequencies become too high, rather than burst into flames. It's best (particularly with older monitors) to find the documentation and match your vertical and horizontal frequencies properly. Lacking this, try a lower resolution (VGA or SVGA) first, just to get X Window System running.

3. Screen Configuration

To probe or not to probe? Probing tries to determine the configuration of your video card. If Red Hat is successful, then you don't have to make any guesses about your hardware. Give it a try but realize that some computers can hang up – that is, stop responding to your keyboard. If that happens you'll have to restart the installation process.

If you decide not to probe, then the next screen asks you to specify the amount of video memory that you have.

4. Video Memory

You use the dialog box to specify the amount of memory on your video card. (Note that this memory is different from the amount of main memory.) Most modern cards have 1, 2, 4, 8, or 16MB of video memory. Use your arrow keys to move down the list. When you select the memory amount, press the Tab key to select Ok, and then press Enter.

TIP If you do not know how much video memory your card has, try 1MB (the 1 meg option). Although this limits the resolution of your screen, you will probably be able to get X Window System going. Later, you can experiment with the Xconfigurator program described in Chapter 6 to figure out the best values for how much video memory you have, if the probe did not work properly.

5. Clockchip Configuration

Specify your video clockchip.

This specification is a vestige of older systems and older video boards. I recommend that you select No Clockchip Setting. When you have made your selection, use the Tab key to select the Ok button, and then press Enter.

Note that this dialog doesn't appear if the probe was successful.

6. Select Video Modes

You are asked to select the combination of screen resolution and the number of colors as shown in Figure 1-15. You need to make the choice because the memory in your video card must be used for both purposes. The fewer color bits you use, the fewer shades of color that your display will use. The higher resolutions pack more detail onto your screen.

Make a reasonable choice. If you are running Windows on your system already you can look at the `Control Panel->Display` dialog box to see how it is set up and then use that configuration as your starting point for Linux.

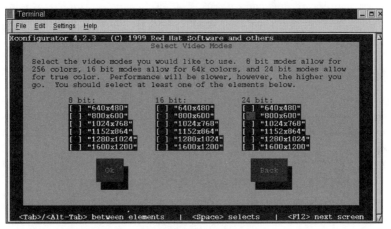

Figure 1–15: Selecting the resolutions and color depths

7. Starting X

Red Hat will now test your new X configuration. Select `Ok`.

8. Can you see this message?

If you configured X correctly, then you see this message. You have 10 seconds to either click the Yes button with your mouse or press the enter key.

9. Do you want to start X automatically at boot time?

You are given the option of starting X every time you boot or reboot your computer. This book uses that option and X Window System is the default environment used in all further discussions.

If you choose No, then your system will start up in character-cell or text mode. You can always manually start X with the `startx` command or modify the `/etc/inittab` file to automatically start X. The line `id3init-default` should be changed to `id5initdefault` in the `inittab` file to do that.

10. Configuration has been written.

This is an informational screen that tells you where the configuration file can be found. It also points you to the X `README.Config` file for more information.

If there is a problem with your X configuration, then you are regretfully informed of the situation. You have the option of quitting or going back and starting over. If you're game, go back and try, try again.

This autoprobe will not happen if the first autoprobe correctly found your video card, memory, and other settings.

If for some reason you can't get X Window System working at this point, you can always try finishing the configuration of X Window System later running the Xconfigurator program.

Done

That's it. You're done. Click Ok and you are prompted to remove the boot — or supplemental — floppy while the computer reboots. It should come back up running Linux and you are on your way!

Introducing the Red Hat Startup Process

When Red Hat Linux is booted numerous processes called daemons are started. The run level determines what daemons are started. Linux uses run levels to define the basic functions that the computer provides. Each level has certain daemons associated with it. For instance, the default run level as defined by the Red Hat installation process is 3. When booted to run level 3, the system works on a text-based terminal. Run level 5 and the X Window System is the default.

Within each run level the method for determining what daemons or processes are started is to place soft links in certain directories. A soft link is analogous to a pointer (UNIX) or a shortcut (Windows) but is really a file with the name of another file in it. The directories that contain the soft links are /etc/rc.d/rc0.d, /etc/rc.d/rc1.d, and ... /etc/rc.d/rc5.d. Each one, of course, corresponds to a run level. The run level is set in the /etc/inittab file.

The soft links point to programs or scripts that do the actual starting of the daemons. Therefore, when a file in the /etc/rc.d/rc5.d directory gets executed, the script that it points to in /etc/rc.d/init.d gets executed and any commands that it wants to run get run.

Troubleshooting

The art of troubleshooting is introduced in Chapter 2. However, there are some quick tips that should be covered here.

Fixing network problems

If the Red Hat installation process does not detect your Ethernet adapter (NIC), you will not see steps 2 and 3 in the section "Configuring your Network" in this chapter. In that case, please refer to the section "The Network Configurator" in Chapter 5. It describes using this system via the Control Panel. Enter the same information described in Configuring your Network. Alternatively, you can run LinuxConf and enter the information in the `Config` → `Networking` → `Client tasks` → `Basic host information` and ... `Client tasks` → `Name server specification` menus. If the installation system did not detect your NIC, then it's a good bet that you'll have to specify the NIC kernel module during configuration. For instance, if you have a 3Com `3c509` card (like I used to have), then enter that name in the Kernel module box.

Summary

This chapter covered the basics of installing Red Hat Linux. Installation is not an easy process, but can be made simpler if you learn some essential topics and make some basic preparations. When problems occur you can very often solve them by following basic troubleshooting techniques and knowing where the more common problem spots are.

Topics covered in this chapter:

- ◆ The overall process of installing Red Hat Linux. A simple list of the steps is given. That information helps provide a simple road map so you can look ahead and hopefully gain an understanding of the process.

- ◆ The process of installing Linux by itself or along with Windows. The Red Hat installation process can be a pretty straightforward one, but you may occasionally run into difficulties. If you prepare your system and follow the process precisely, then it can be a good experience.

- ◆ Detailed, step-by-step instructions to guide you through the Red Hat installation process. This book uses a coherent set of example computers and networks. You are given specific information to use during the installation process so that the computer you build will fit into the upcoming examples.

Chapter 2

Setting Up a Simple Network

IN THIS CHAPTER

◆ Wiring your network

◆ Configuring your Windows computer

◆ Configuring Samba

◆ Getting Windows computer to work with Samba

THIS CHAPTER SHOWS you how to construct a simple client-server network based on Linux, Samba, and Windows 95/98. The network consists of only two computers — one server and one client — yet it is a fully functional network. Figure 2-1 shows the topology (diagram) of the system. Think of this configuration as your basic building block. The more complex examples introduced later in the book build on this system.

The instructions in this chapter assume that you are an experienced computer user. That is, you are expected to be familiar with such basic concepts as directory structures and the difference between an operating system and an application. It helps if you have installed and configured your own computer at least once; the more times the better. The relatively simple (when everything goes as planned) process of setting up Microsoft Windows helps to prepare you for the unfamiliar task of installing Linux.

The process of answering installation questions and making decisions about the particulars of any operating system and application is basically the same no matter what system you use. I concentrate on providing detailed instructions in this chapter so that even without adequate experience you should be able to get this simple example running (however, you should expect to suffer some frustration as you tackle new concepts and the fickleness that accompanies computers in general). After you set up the simple client-server network you will have the basic building block necessary to evolve your network into a more complex, "real-world" system. Linux (and by default UNIX) concepts and facilities are introduced along the way.

Introducing the Simple Network

In this simple network, the server is running the Linux operating system. The Samba file and printer sharing system runs as an application on top of Linux. The client runs Windows 95, 98 or NT. Figure 2-1 shows the diagram of the network. The installation or Red Hat Linux is described in this chapter. The construction of a simple network – including Samba – is described. Subsequent chapters describe constructing more complex networks.

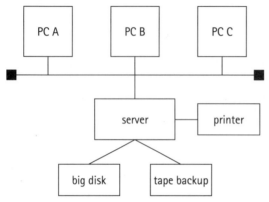

Figure 2-1: A simple client-server network

Installing the Network Wiring

For this simple network to work, you must connect it. Two primary types of cables exist: Twisted pair and Thinnet. Twisted pair is telephone wire. Several different grades of cable exist, the best being Category 5. Thinnet is coaxial cable like that used for cable TV, although it has 50-ohm impedance versus 75 ohm.

 The process of wiring your business or home for a network can be danger-ous. It is best to hire a licensed electrician or other professional. But if you de-cide to do it, please follow all related building codes and common sense.

Twisted pair is also referred to as 10baseT – 10 Mbps means 10 megabits-per-second, and T refers to twisted pair. (You can also run a faster version of Ethernet that runs at 100 Mbps and requires category 5 cable. It is referred to as 100baseT or 100baseTX). 10baseT requires an active hub or concentrator to work. (If you only have two machines, then you can connect them directly by using a cable with the trans-mit/receive wires crossed over. This is hardly worth the effort, however, because hubs can be purchased for as little as US $40.) It offers the advantage that individual hosts can be connected and disconnected independent of each other. The wiring can be conveniently connected to phone jacks. The disadvantage is that it costs extra to purchase and maintain the hub, which also adds another layer of complexity.

Thinnet is also referred to as 10base2. Its main advantage is that it's a passive system and requires no active circuitry to work; it simply connects to each Ethernet transceiver on the bus. Its main disadvantage is that it's a wave guide or transmission line and must be properly terminated to work. That means that each end of the cable must have a 50-ohm terminator attached to it and a proper BNC tee connector must be used at each Ethernet adapter. If it is not terminated or the cable is broken — either by disconnecting it or breaking it — the entire network will not work. (Note that as with 10baseT, the network speed of thinnet is 10Mbps.)

I use Thinnet on my network at home and have used it professionally. In many ways, it is cumbersome but its passive (does not need electronic hubs) and inexpensive nature makes it ideal for learning about your client-server network. This is the system used in this book.

Using coaxial cables (that is, cable TV-type wiring) can present special problems. It is possible to conduct dangerous currents across these types of cables if your building's grounding is not connected to a central ground. This situation occurs when one power circuit is grounded at one location and another circuit is grounded elsewhere. Please take note, that if you span the two locations with a Thinnet (10base2) coaxial cable, you have a conductor that bypasses the building grounds. If the Thinnet touches an open electrical circuit, or a short-circuit occurs in one of the connected computers, or the building's grounds are at different potentials, disaster can befall your computer equipment and you! Be careful and forewarned.

Configuring Windows for Network Operations

This network uses the TCP/IP protocol. TCP/IP is the protocol that holds the Internet together. TCP/IP is really a number of individual protocols that when used together allow two computers, or twenty, or the entire world's computers to connect and work together. It is truly amazing that it scales so well. For now, however, your concern is just to get two computers to work together. TCP/IP is described in more detail in Chapter 3.

For the purposes of this chapter, I assume you have a PC already running Windows 95 or 98. If you don't have Windows installed, don't worry — its installation is a relatively simple process. Follow Microsoft's instructions and in most circumstances you will be okay. If not, many good books can help you to set up Windows.

The Windows 95/98 network instructions are for configuring the network from scratch. If you do not have a network interface card installed or have not configured your network settings yet – other than a modem connection – you need to use the following instructions exactly. If you already have your network working, look through the instructions for those steps that you need to complete. For instance, if you have Netware or NetBEUI working, you need to install TCP/IP but not the network adapter.

Here are the steps you must complete to configure Windows 95/98 for network operations:

1. You might need to have your Windows 95 or 98 CD accessible for this process, so go ahead and mount it in your CD-ROM drive.

2. Click on the Start → Settings → Control Panel button. The Control Panel window opens.

3. In the Control Panel window double-click the Network icon. Windows opens the Network dialog box, shown in Figure 2-2.

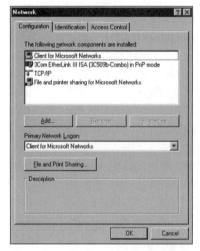

Figure 2-2: The Network dialog box

You will need to configure the following Windows functions

a. **Client.** You will want to use the Client for Microsoft Networks that allows your computer to work as a network client with a network server(s). This mechanism is necessary to work with Samba and every other network function.

b. **Adapter.** I happen to use a 3Com Etherlink III ISA Ethernet Card adapter (which is also known as a network interface card or NIC) on my computer.

c. **Protocol.** TCP/IP is the protocol you will want your PC to use in order to communicate with your LAN and the Internet. You can ignore other networking protocols such as IPX or NetBEUI if you already have them installed.

4. Click the Add button to open the Select Network Component Type dialog box shown in Figure 2-3.

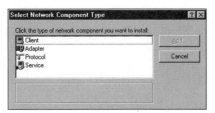

Figure 2-3: The Select Network Component Type dialog box

5. If you do not already have the Client for Microsoft Networks installed, select the Client option and then click the Add button, which becomes active after you select Client. The resulting Select Network Client dialog box, shown in Figure 2-4, gives you several choices. Select the Microsoft option in the Manufacturers section and the Client for Microsoft Networks under Network Clients. Click OK.

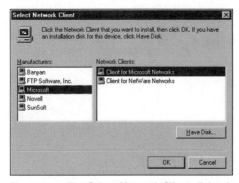

Figure 2-4: The Select Network Client dialog box

6. If you do not already have a network adapter installed, click the Add button again. The Select Network Component Type dialog opens again. Select Adapter and then click on the Add button. The Select Network Adapters dialog box opens.

7. The Select Network Adapters window gives you two subwindows for selecting the manufacturer and then the model of your adapter. As you can see in Figure 2-2, I select the 3Com Etherlink III ISA (3C509b-Combo) in PnP mode EthernetCard as the adapter. Find and select the appropriate adapter for your system and then click OK.

8. You are returned to the Network dialog box as you saw in Figure 2-2. Four components should be listed.

9. Next, add the TCP/IP protocol if it is not already installed. Click the Add button again. In the Select Network Component Type dialog box, select the Protocol component and finally click Add. In the dialog box that's displayed, select Microsoft in the Manufacturer subwindow and TCP/IP in the Network Protocols subwindow, as shown in Figure 2-5. Click OK.

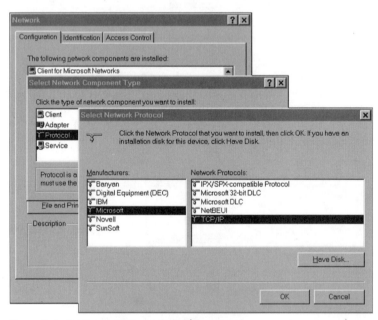

Figure 2-5: Adding the Microsoft TCP/IP protocol

10. Back at the Network dialog box again, you should see the screen similar to that shown in Figure 2-6. You can ignore protocols such as IPX and NetBEUI if you have them. They will not interfere with your TCP/IP configuration. If you do not use them, then you can remove each one by selecting and clicking on the Remove button. I remove such protocols in order to keep things simple for myself.

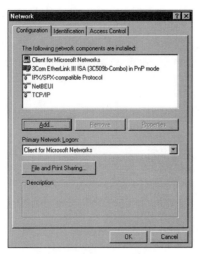

Figure 2-6: The Network dialog box displaying various components

11. Now you need to configure the Client for Microsoft Networks Properties.
Select Client for Microsoft Networks and then click the Properties button
and you see the dialog box shown in Figure 2-7. The Log on to Windows
NT domain button should be set and the Windows NT domainshould be
MYGROUP. The Logon and restore network connections button should
be set. Click 0k, and you return to the Network dialog box.

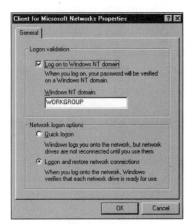

Figure 2-7: The Client for Microsoft Networks Properties dialog box

12. Next you need to configure the TCP/IP properties. Select the TCP/IP
protocol and then click the Properties button.

The TCP/IP Properties dialog box appears. Each of the six property types is important, but to get your simple client-server network running, you just need to set your IP Address option. Click the IP Address tab. Set the *Specify an IP address* radio button, and enter an address and a subnet address. I enter the values as shown in Figure 2-8 (192.168.1.1 and 255.255.255.0). Click OK and you return to the Network dialog box.

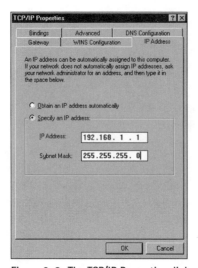

Figure 2-8: The TCP/IP Properties dialog box

The dialog box shown in Figure 2-8 lists my IP address and Subnet Mask. Recall from the discussion of IP addresses that the TCP/IP protocol allows for unregistered addresses as long as they don't appear out on the Internet. You are not currently connected, so this address is a good choice. As you can see, I am using the class C address space. My Linux server is 192.168.1.254 and I have chosen 192.168.1.1 for my Windows client. This is a class C address, so the standard Subnet mask is 255.255.255.0, which masks out the first three octets (255) for local communications.

13. Back at the Network dialog box again, click the Identification tab (at the very top, in the middle of the window) and you see the dialog box shown in Figure 2-9. Enter the name that you want to identify your PC as on the network. Initially, you want to set your Workgroup name to WORKGROUP, because that is Samba's default.

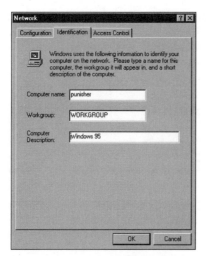

Figure 2-9: The Identification tab in the Network dialog box

14. In the Network dialog box, click the Access Control tab. The User-level access control button should be activated and the Obtain list of users and groups from should be set to WORKGROUP, as shown in Figure 2-10. Click OK.

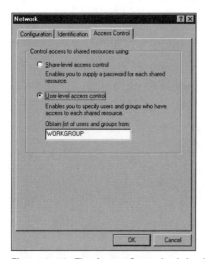

Figure 2-10: The Access Control tab in the Network dialog box

15. Windows displays the System Settings Change window. You must reboot your computer for the new Samba-ready configuration to work. After you reboot, you need to do a minimal configuration of Samba — create a lock file — on the Linux box to be able to access its files and printers.

16. Reboot your computer by clicking the Start button and then the Shutdown menu item. A Shutdown dialog box appears. Click the Restart button and then click OK. It may take awhile to finish so be patient.

Fixing an unresponsive network with the Windows 95/98 Registry

Sometimes after reconfiguring, an existing Windows 95/98 network configuration does not communicate on the network properly. Even after you reinstall the network adapter, client, and protocol from scratch, the problem is not resolved. The problem, as far as I can tell, is that Windows loses track of what is installed. It shows the proper items installed in the Network window but gets confused somewhere along the line.

Windows uses a system called the Registry to keep track of all hardware and software and configuration parameters. I use REGEDIT.EXE, which Microsoft supplies, to edit the Registry by double-clicking the keys shown. Remove the key `HKEY_LOCAL_MACHINE\ System\CurrentControlSet\ServicesVxD\MSTCP` (I've also had to remove the `HKEY_LOCAL_MACHINES\System\CurrentControlSet\Services\Class\Net Trans\0000` key at times) by clicking it and using the Edit menu to delete it. Reenter all the components in the Network window as described in the following steps. This process removes the erroneous information that Windows has stored about its network settings. After you redo the network setup and reboot the PC, everything should work.

To redo the network setup:

1. Open the Network dialog box by double-clicking the Network icon in the Control Panel window.

2. Click the Configuration tab at the top of the Network dialog box and then click the Add button.

3. In the resulting Select Network Component Type dialog box, select the Service option and then click Add.

   In the Select Network Service dialog box that's displayed, select Microsoft in the Manufacturer sub-window and then select the File and printer sharing for Microsoft Networks option in the Network Services sub-window.

5. Click OK to exit back to the Network window and then click OK once more.

6. Windows asks whether you want to reboot the PC. You must reboot to make the change take effect.

Configuring Samba

Red Hat Linux comes with Samba. Recall that Samba was one of the optional components that I suggested you install in Chapter 1. The heart of Samba consists of the configuration file smb.conf installed in /etc by default, and the smbd and nmbd daemons. (A *daemon* is a process that runs in the background in order to service requests on a continual basis. Please refer to the discussion of daemons in Chapter 3 for an explanation of what they do).

When Samba exports a directory for use by a computer or computers on the network, it is called a *Share*.

You can update Samba by getting patches or entire distributions off the Internet. The mother of all Samba Web Sites is at the following address:

http://www.samba.org

This site also lists numerous mirrors (computers that make frequent copies of the central site's files) that you should try to make use of to lessen the burden on Canberra's server.

Installing Samba

If you did not install Samba during Chapter 1, then you can do so now. Red Hat provides a mechanism for installing software called the Red Hat Package Manager (RPM). It is discussed in more detail in Chapter 5.

Log in as root and insert the Red Hat Publisher's Edition CD-ROM into the CD-ROM drive. Enter the following two commands to install Samba.

```
mount /mnt/cdrom
rpm -ivh /mnt/cdrom/RedHat/RPMS/samba*
```

This will install Samba on your system and also start the *smbd* and *nmbd* daemons.

Checking that Samba is running

The Samba daemons, *smbd* and *nmbd,* should already be running. Samba has also installed a simple configuration file, */etc/smb.conf.* It should be exporting one share, called *public,* to every computer on your network.

The heart of Samba consists of two programs — *smbd* and *nmbd* — that listen for SMB requests from clients and respond with SMB services. *smbd* handles file and print requests, and nmbd handles browsing. In the recent past, they could also be run on an as-needed basis whereby a program that runs all the time, *inetd*, launched them when they were called for. However, now *smbd* is only run as a daemon while nmbd can still be launched by inetd but will then work as a daemon. I guess it is still reasonable to run it from *inetd* in case the daemons stop, in which case it will be restarted the next time a request comes.

The configuration file that is in place will export your home directory on the chivas by default. The process of modifying the smb.conf configuration file is given in Chapter 6.

TIP

You can restart the daemons manually. However, you must do this as root, the all-powerful user. At the login prompt, simply enter the word **root** and its password. Then enter the following commands:

```
/etc/rc.d/init.d/smb restart
```

Verify the two Samba daemons are running by entering the following command:

```
ps -x |grep mbd
```

This command returns the following information on the Samba daemon processes:

```
[root@chivas /]# !ps
ps -x |grep mbd
  749  ?    S    0:00 smbd -D
  758  ?    S    0:00 nmbd -D
  763  p0   R    0:00 grep mbd
```

Note that the grep process displays itself as well as the two Samba processes. That is because the string "mbd," which is used to filter out the text that you want to view, also catches itself.

Configuring Samba for encrypted passwords

Windows 98, NT and newer versions of 95 use encrypted passwords. The default configuration of Samba is to use "user"-level authentication. This means that every Samba share that you attempt to access will require that your Windows box send a username/password pair. If those passwords are encrypted, then you have to configure Samba to use encryption too.

Samba encryption can be configured as follows:

1. Login as root.

2. Edit the /etc/smb.conf file. If you are unfamiliar editing Linux text files, then please consult Appendix AIntroducing vi. Vi is a text editor that is found on nearly every Linux and UNIX computer.

3. Locate the following two lines

   ```
   ;   encrypt passwords = yes
   ; smb passwd file = /etc/smbpasswd
   ```

4. The semicolon (;) at the beginning of the lines means that Samba treats them as comments. Remove the semicolon and the parameters will become active. They should look as follows

   ```
   encrypt passwords = yes
   smb passwd file = /etc/smbpasswd
   ```

5. Create the /etc/smbpasswd password file by entering the following command

   ```
   cat /etc/passwd | mksmbpasswd.sh > /etc/smbpasswd
   ```

6. Create a password for root by running the `smbpasswd` command. You will be prompted twice for the password. Enter the same password that you did while installing Red Hat Linux in Chapter 1. In order for Windows to access the root user share on the Linux server both passwords will have to match.

TIP

Note that we are creating a password for the root user because that is the only user that was created automatically during the Red Hat Linux installation process. Chapter 6 describes how to create Linux user accounts. Until then, the root user will be used for these initial demonstrations.

Testing Samba

If you have a LAN running and have already connected your Windows 95 and Linux-Samba box on it, you can go directly to the Network Neighborhood and start browsing. If this method doesn't work, enter the following command to see the resources that Samba exports:

```
smbstatus
```

If you have already browsed the server, the public share is displayed. Otherwise, you see just the header with the version number. However, this utility is very useful because it shows what services (printers and files) clients are accessing.

Red Hat supplies a Samba configuration file that comes with the RPM package. It is located at */etc/smb.conf.* The smbd daemon reads this file when it starts. This default configuration allows you to mount the home directory of the Linux user that matches the name of your Windows 95 computer as found in the Network configuration described in the section "Configuring Windows 95 for Network Operations." This capability is important because if your Windows 95 TCP/IP computer name matches a user name, you will automatically be able to browse and use the Samba service without having to modify the *smb.conf* file.

If you want to customize *smb.conf,* check out the appendix "Introducing vi," and then follow these instructions:

1. Save the *smb.conf* to *smb.conf.bak* by entering the following command

   ```
   cp /etc/smb.conf /etc/smb.conf.bak
   ```

2. Inspect the manual page, referred to as a man page, by entering the following command

   ```
   /bin/man smb.conf
   ```

   Pay close attention to the examples.

3. Open *smb.conf* with vi

   ```
   /bin/vi /etc/smb.conf
   ```

   I leave it to you to experiment on your own because I cover *smb.conf* in greater detail later in Chapter 6.

4. Samba must re-read the *smb.conf.* Run the Samba startup and stop scripts by entering the following commands

   ```
   /etc/rc.d/init.d/smb stop
   /etc/rc.d/init.d/smb start
   ```

It Works!

Hang on. You are in the home stretch now! See if you can browse your Linux server from Windows.

The Red Hat Samba configuration specifies *user* security. To access a Samba resource, a Linux user name must match a Samba share name. I have not had you configure any regular Linux users that you could match up with yet. However, you have configured the user *root*. Therefore, you need to log off of your Windows 95 system and then log back on as the user *Root*. After you logon to your Windows 95 box as *Root*, you will appear to the Linux box as *Root*, too:

1. Log out of your Windows box by clicking the Start button at the lower-left corner of the Desktop. Choose *Close all programs and log on as another user* and then select *Yes.* Your system closes all open programs and prompts you for your user name and password.

2. Login to your Windows box. The first dialog box asks you to log in as a Windows user. It defaults to the last user name that was logged on. Press the Shift+Tab to go to the user name box and enter the name **root**. Tab down to the password and enter the same one that you used in the Red Hat Linux configuration for *root.*

3. Assuming that you have never logged on as *root* before, Windows will prompt you for the password that you just entered twice. This step confirms that you got it right. Re-enter the password in both boxes. The system then creates the user id *Root*, which you can use in the future.

4. The question in the next dialog box looks ominous but isn't. The system thinks that it must find a domain server, but that is unnecessary in most situations and certainly for this example. Simply click the OK button.

When your computer has restarted, use the following steps to view your new Linux-Samba server.

1. Double-click the Network Neighborhood icon (generally in the upper left-hand corner of your screen) to open the Network Neighborhood window shown in Figure 2-11.

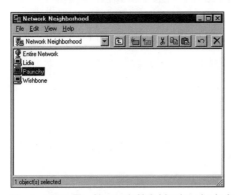

Figure 2-11: The Network Neighborhood window

6. Double-click the icon for your Linux-Samba server. In my case, it is the *Chivas* icon. The password that I entered for Windows 95 matches the one for Root on the Samba server, and I am given access to the home directory of Root as shown in Figure 2-12!

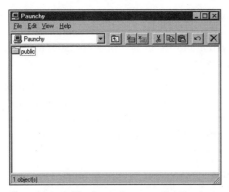

Figure 2-12: The Root share on the Samba server chivas

7. Finally, if you double-click on the Root icon you will see the contents of that directory. Since it has just recently been created, the only files are "dot" configuration files. (They are files whose names have a period as the first character. The default of the *ls* command is to hide files like that – you need to specify the -a option to see them. Since they are not displayed by default, the convention is to use them as configuration files.) Figure 2-13 shows the contents of the *Root* directory.

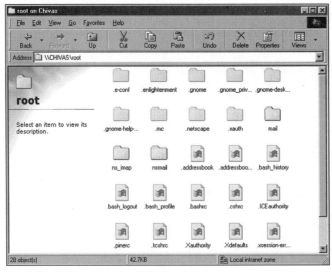

Figure 2-13: The contents of the Root share

If your Samba server does not appear in your Network Neighborhood, you can sometimes find it with Microsoft Explorer. The following steps describe that method:

1. Click the Windows 95 Start button. It is generally located in the bottom left-hand corner of your screen.

2. Open the Find menu.

3. Open the Computer menu.

4. Enter the name of your Samba server or its IP address (in our example, 192.168.1.254) in the FindComputer dialog box. Click the Find Now button. If the Windows 95 Explorer finds your server, it displays an icon representing the server. You can double-click the icon and access the server's resources just as if you had accessed it through the Network Neighborhood. Network browsing requires the server to broadcast the fact of its existence. When you use the FindComputer process, the client tries to locate the server. Sometimes this works more readily than browsing.

Summary

This chapter covers the following topics:

◆ Re-configuring Windows 95/98 for Samba. I provide detailed instructions to help the novice as well as experienced user through the entire process.

◆ Wiring your computers together. In these examples I use Thinnet coaxial cables because of their low cost and simplicity. However, you can readily use 10baseT if you want.

◆ Browsing the Samba resources from the Network Neighborhood. This capability gives you a way of seeing what is available and then connecting to it.

◆ Using the Microsoft Explorer as another method for finding and attaching to Samba shares.

Chapter 3

Troubleshooting

IN THIS CHAPTER

- ◆ Understanding the philosophy of troubleshooting
- ◆ Solving an example problem by using the Microsoft Troubleshooter
- ◆ Examining the Microsoft Troubleshooter fault tree
- ◆ Diagnosing the client-server network using Paul's Troubleshooter

FIXING PROBLEMS WITH COMPUTERS and networks is the one constant job of systems administration. The primary job of a systems administrator is to minimize problems by designing and managing the network properly and anticipating problems. That is why you install a tape backup drive on a server, and use it regularly to back up your data. Because you can't predict everything, however, you must learn how to deal with problems as they occur.

Troubleshooting is more an art than a science. The more intimately you know your system, the easier it is to deal with problems. Some people can see a problem and its solution better than others can. Unfortunately, you can't teach talent. However, the art of systems administration also includes some fairly simple science. You must deal with any problem that arises in a systematic fashion. You need to identify the problem and then systematically eliminate each possible cause, working from the simple to the complex, until you solve the problem.

Chapters 1 and 2 guide you through the process of installing Red Hat Linux and then creating a simple client-server network. However, that simple network has tens of thousands of lines of code. The network has many subsystems – disks, memory, interface cards, wires and so on – as well as all those interacting protocols (for example, *udp*, *tcp*, *icmp*, *ip*). Things need to work together in precisely the right way, and just one bad part can prevent that simple system from working. If something goes wrong and the network doesn't work, how do you fix it? The best way is to identify exactly what is causing the problem and eliminate each possible cause, one by one. This chapter describes some basic methods for solving problems this way.

Troubleshooting with the Fault Tree

The better you know your system, the greater the likelihood that you can fix it. You learn by struggling to get the simple things to work and then you struggle with the more complex problems. I have set up dozens of networks in my career, but not suprisingly I encountered some problems that I had never seen before while I was writing the example in Chapter 1. By solving those problems, I gained additional insights about my own system, and I can solve problems just a little bit better than before. You never stop learning.

The formal model that I use for understanding troubleshooting is the *fault tree*. In a fault tree, the trunk represents the problem, and each root represents a potential cause of the problem. This conceptual model simplifies the process of finding the solution. What if the client in Chapter 1 can't communicate with the server? If you are new to networks, this may seem like an impossible problem. However, the answer soon becomes apparent if you break it down into distinct parts.

How do you break down the problem? First, look at Figure 3-1, which shows a tree of the possible answers to the problem. The first root on the left involves problems with the physical connection: Do you have a network adapter? Is the Thinnet connected properly? Do you have a break in the cable? The second root deals with the network interface with Windows: Have you installed the network interface to the adapter or Microsoft Client for Networks or the TCP/IP protocol? The third root follows the thread of the network interface on the Linux box.

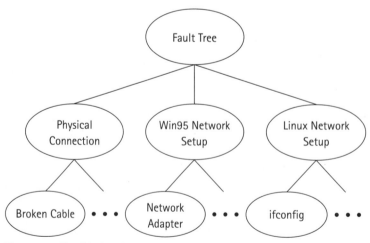

Figure 3-1: Troubleshooting by using the fault tree

Each sub-root deals with the specifics of the more general problem. For example, if the problem relates to the physical connection, you can trace the problem to one of several causes: no adapter, a misconfigured adapter, a break in the wire, a faulty connector, or no connector at all. Or if the problem involves the network configuration, you know that it can be only one of several things. By using the fault tree, you can break down any problem into simpler ones and eventually locate the root cause.

Your goal in troubleshooting problems with your network is first to identify the problem and then pick a plan of attack.

Solving a Sample Problem

Microsoft provides a helpful interactive fault-tree analyzer called the Network Troubleshooter. You access this informative tool via the Help system:

1. Click the Windows Start button and then choose Help from the resulting menu. As shown in Figure 3-2, Windows displays the Help TopicsWindows Help window.

Figure 3-2: The Help Topics window

2. Click the Contents tab and then double-click the Troubleshooter icon. (As you can see, Windows has a number of different troubleshooters that can come in handy.)

3. Windows opens the Network Troubleshooter window, shown in Figure 3-3.

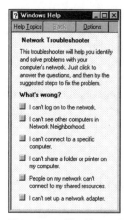

Figure 3-3: The Network Troubleshooter

For this example, I assume that you have configured Windows and mistakenly failed to install the network client. For instance, perhaps you have not configured a *Client for Microsoft Networks.* Thus, you can't get the Network Neighborhood window, because Windows has no way to access the network.

4. In the Network Troubleshooter, click the button labeled I can't see other computers in Network Neighborhood. The Network Troubleshooter responds by opening the window shown in Figure 3-4.

Figure 3-4: The Network Troubleshooter asks questions
to help you track down the cause of the problem.

5. Click the button next to the explanation that comes closest to describing your problem: I can't see any computers on the network. (In some cases, you have to make the best of the options that are available to you, even if they don't fit perfectly.)

   The Troubleshooter opens another window, shown in Figure 3-5, to ask if you see the Entire Network icon in Network Neighborhood.

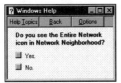

Figure 3-5: The Network Troubleshooter further
narrows down the problem.

6. Again, use your best judgment and answer *No.*

   Figure 3-6 shows the Troubleshooter's reply. This window gives you the
   probable explanation – you do not have the network software installed –
   and offers three paths that you can take.

Figure 3-6: The Network Troubleshooter
identifies the problem.

7. Click the button for the option labeled *View instructions on installing the
   network software,* and the Troubleshooter opens another help window,
   shown in Figure 3-7. This window details a four-step process for correct-
   ing the problem. It also gives a two-part explanation as to why your system isn't working. It also gives a shortcut to the Network window.

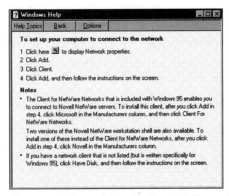

Figure 3-7: Network Troubleshooter tells you how to solve the problem.

8. Click the shortcut button, and the Network Troubleshooter opens the *Network* dialog box shown in Figure 3-8. The Troubleshooter was correct; you have no Microsoft Client or other Client installed. If this were a real problem, you would fix it by clicking the *Add* button and then proceed to install the Microsoft *Client for Microsoft Networks* as described in Chapter 1.

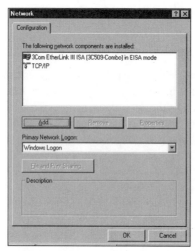

Figure 3-8: The Network Troubleshooter takes you straight to the dialog box you use for solving the problem.

That was a good example of troubleshooting. You often encounter relatively simple oversights such as leaving out an essential software component. The path to the answer was complicated by the real-world problem of having to answer the incomplete questions that the Troubleshooter asks. Nothing's perfect but every tool helps.

My colleague, Ken Hatfield, puts it this way: "One of the side benefits from lots of troubleshooting comes from what I call *The value of blind alleys*. Most often in troubleshooting, you go down blind alleys, or in your tree example, the wrong branches of the solution tree. In doing this however, you learn something. In the future, when you encounter a different problem down the road, that previous blind alley may be the road to the solution." Well said.

Microsoft's Network Troubleshooter

In this section, the Network Troubleshooter is described in more detail. As you may have guessed, I like it both as a basic problem-solving tool and as a teaching aid. Further examination is helpful to your education in the art and science of systems administration.

The first menu in the Network Troubleshooter offers a synopsis of all the primary problems that you can encounter with Windows networking. Figure 3-9 shows the menu again.

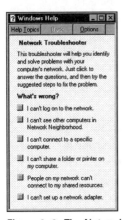

Figure 3-9: The Network Troubleshooter, again.

The first menu helps you identify what your general problem is. To work toward a solution, the Troubleshooter queries you further in order to traverse a fault tree and solve the problem.

If the Troubleshooter fails, consider the following possible causes for the problems with your network:

◆ A duplicate computer name exists on the network.

◆ You forgot your network password.

◆ A problem unknown by the Troubleshooter occurred – it could have nothing to do with the network.

The Troubleshooter contains lots of information. Much of it is repetitive, of course, but if you follow the logical structure, you can see how it thinks. The logic is general and can be adapted for solving almost any technical problem.

The Troubleshooter can't solve every problem. But even in those cases, it still serves its purpose. Sometimes, it is useful to know what you don't know. In those cases, the Troubleshooter narrows down the areas that you must search and frees up your resources to look elsewhere.

TIP

The original Windows network configuration seems to have a bug. (I have been informed that the version released in late 1996 may fix this problem.) While I was preparing the first two chapters in this book, I went through the process of configuring my network many times. Sometimes, I inexplicably could not access either the Samba services or the general network; other times, neither could be accessed. I performed all the setup exactly the same and had all my ducks in order. I was perplexed and discouraged.

I finally started looking through the Windows registry, which keeps all the configuration information on every aspect of the machine. Theoretically, the Network manager that you have been using should set everything in the registry up to date. I used REGEDIT.EXE to fix the problem. I started by removing the register *key*, shown in Figure 3-10, that stores some of the information about Windows the TCP/IP setup: `HKEY_LOCAL_ MA-CHINES\System\CurrentControlSet\ServicesVxD\MSTCP` or `HKEY_LOCAL_MACHINES\System\CurrentControlSet\Services \Class\NetTrans\0000` (or possibly 0001, or 0002, etc.) Then, I reentered all the components in the network window as I describe in Chapter 1. After I rebooted the PC, everything worked. Apparently, Windows can get confused after two or more network reconfigurations.

Figure 3-10: Using regedit to erase the TCP/IP parameters

Tools of the Trade

When you need to solve a problem, you must use the tools you have at your disposal — tools such as the Network Troubleshooter. An auto mechanic who figures out that you have a bad spark plug is of no use without a socket wrench and an extra plug. In the following sections, I discuss some of the other tools you can use to solve problems with your network.

Diagnosing the Linux box: My troubleshooter

Your Linux box is the foundation of your network. It must be set up correctly for anything to run. If you carefully follow the installation instructions that I provide in Chapter 1, your network should be up and running like a champ. If it isn't running, or if you have some unusual setup (or Murphy is in a bad mood), you can check for several different causes. The following sections describe several steps you can take. Think of the guidelines I offer in these sections as Paul's Troubleshooter.

If the network on your Linux computer is not working, use the following sections as a simple fault tree that you can follow to troubleshoot your network. I divide this troubleshooter into two major areas: Linux networking and Samba. The troubleshooter is not comprehensive, but it does cover some of the typical problems that I have encountered.

CHECKING LINUX NETWORKING

You can take several steps to check your network for problems. The following sections identify common problem areas to check. Over time, you'll find that these areas account for most of the problems you see.

IS THE POWER TURNED ON?   First, verify that you have turned on the power. Sounds simple, but hey, sometimes the simplest things go wrong. This is the problem I am best able to solve.

HAS YOUR NETWORK CABLE BEEN COMPROMISED?   Thinnet is topologically a bus structure. In other words, each computer on a Thinnet cable is connected electrically to all the other computers in the network. Each computer sees all the network traffic on that cable. If any part of that bus is compromised, all traffic ceases. For example, if you disconnect the terminator at either end of the cable, all communication ends. The best way to troubleshoot that type of problem is to start at one end and work your way down the line. Try to get just two computers connected, then three, and eventually you'll find the fault.

Determining whether your network cable has been compromised requires addressing the following issues:

◆ Make sure the "BNC" — Bayonet Nut Connector — connectors are securely attached if you are using Thinnet.

◆ Look at the interface between the coaxial cable and the BNC connector to make sure they are in good physical contact. Sometimes, the cable can pull out a little bit so the little pin in the center of the cable does not make contact with the other end of the BNC connector.

◆ Look at the cable itself and make sure it hasn't been cut or crushed.

◆ If you have an ohmmeter, test the continuity of both the center conductor and the outer shield conductor. Make sure the cable is not attached to anything.

◆ Make sure that the center conductor is not touching (short-circuited to) the shield (the thin, braided metal wires immediately under the outer insulation).

◆ Make sure that each end of the cable has a 50ohm terminator attached to it. A Thinnet must be terminated or else it will not work, just as it will not work if the cable is broken. The reason for this is that the radio frequency (RF) signal reflects from the un-terminated end and interferes with the in-coming signals.

If you have a cable that you know is good, try substituting it. The idea is to eliminate as many segments that you are unsure about as possible. If you have just two computers in close proximity and you suspect a problem with the cable you are using, all you can do is try another cable. If the computers are far apart and rely on several segments or a long cable, try moving them close together and using one short segment. If you have three or more computers, try getting just two of them working together. Then try adding another one. Proceed until you find the faulty segment.

IS YOUR NETWORK ADAPTER CONFIGURED CORRECTLY?

When I list commands or programs to execute in the following paragraphs, I show the absolute pathname. Red Hat sets up the path for most of these commands in the Root environment in much the same way that DOS uses the PATH= environmental variable. By giving the entire path, however, I assure that my examples will work no matter how you set up your environment, and I also give you a peek into the Linux file system.

Rather than give generic parameters, I use my own values (such as my IP address) in the commands that I describe in the following paragraphs. I also italicize the parameters. Use your own values where appropriate.

Sometimes a startup script is misconfigured and the startup screen goes by but you don't see an error message. Login as *Root* and from the shell prompt enter the command:

```
ifconfig
```

You see a listing of two different interfaces, as shown in Listing 3-1, or three interfaces if you have PPP configured. (I cover using PPP to establish network connections to the Internet in Chapter 8.) The program *ifconfig* tells the Linux kernel that you have a network adapter, and gives it an IP address and network mask. This is the first step in connecting your Linux box to your network.

Listing 3-1: Network interfaces listed

```
[root@chivas /]# ifconfig
lo        Link encap:Local Loopback
          inet addr:127.0.0.1  Bcast:127.255.255.255  Mask:255.0.0.0
          UP BROADCAST LOOPBACK RUNNING  MTU:3584  Metric:1
          RX packets:115 errors:0 dropped:0 overruns:0
          TX packets:115 errors:0 dropped:0 overruns:0

eth0      Link encap:10Mbps Ethernet  HWaddr 00:A0:24:2F:30:69
          inet addr:192.168.1.254  Bcast:192.168.1.255
Mask:255.255.255.0
          UP BROADCAST RUNNING MULTICAST  MTU:1500  Metric:1
          RX packets:16010 errors:18 dropped:18 overruns:23
          TX packets:7075 errors:0 dropped:0 overruns:0
          Interrupt:10 Base address:0x300
```

If you do not see the line containing lo, which is the loopback interface, or eth0, which is your network adapter, then your physical network connections have not been set up correctly. The loopback interface is not a physical device; it is used for the network software's internal workings. It must be present for the network adapter to be configured.

If the loopback interface is not present, enter the following command:

```
ifconfig lo 127.0.0.1
```

If the network adapter — generally an Ethernet card — is not present, enter the following command:

```
ifconfig eth0 192.168.1.254
```

Because this is a class C network address, *ifconfig* automatically defaults to the 255.255.255.0 netmask.

If you have an unusual netmask — which you shouldn't — enter the following command:

```
ifconfig eth0 192.168.1.254 netmask 255.255.255.252
```

Enter **ifconfig** and you should see your network adapter displayed correctly. If it is not, examine the manual page on *ifconfig*. You display this manual page by entering the following command and then pressing Enter:

```
man ifconfig
```

You can page through the document by pressing Return to go line by line, the spacebar to go forward a page at a time, Ctrl+b to page backward, or q to quit. It shows a great deal of information on how ifconfig works.

If you are still having problems, look at the Linux startup information by running the following command:

```
dmesg
```

You will see the information that was displayed during the boot process. Look for your Ethernet NIC, which should appear after the "Adding Swap" line as shown below.

```
Freeing unused kernel memory: 60k freed
Adding Swap: 13651k swap-space (priority -1)
Eth0:   3c509 at 0x310 tag1, BNC port, address ... aa,IRQ 11.
3c509.c:1.16 (2.2) 2/3/98 becker@cesdis.gsfc.nasa.gov
```

If you do not see your Ethernet adapter, then you might have a hardware problem. Check your adapter. Reseat it (take it out and put it back in) and see if it works. If not, then you probably need a new NIC.

If you do see the NIC, then look inside the Linux kernel and see which devices it has. Enter the command to change to a special directory called /proc where process information is located:

```
cat /proc/devices
```

You should see a line with your network adapter listed. If you don't, then Linux does not know that it exists. If the NIC is Plug 'n Play (PnP) compatible, then that is often the problem. Linux frequently has problems working with PnP NICs. It is best to turn PnP off. Run the following program to see if you have a PnP NIC.

```
pnpprobe
```

If you see that your Ethernet NIC is PnP, then you can use the *isapnp* program to reconfigure it. It is a difficult program to use and I prefer to use the configuration program that comes with the NIC. In my case I run 3c5x9cfg.exe, which runs under DOS for my 3Com 3c509 NIC. Use your NIC's configuration program and turn off PnP.

Try to run your Ethernet NIC again. If it still does not run then you need to find out more information about it. You might have an interrupt or address conflict. Look at the list of interrupts and then the *IO* addresses of all the devices that the kernel knows about by entering the following commands:

```
cat /proc/interrupts
cat /proc/ioports
```

The IO address is the actual location in memory where the device – such as the network adapter – is accessed by the microprocessor (that is, your Pentium or 486 chip). The interrupt is a way that the microprocessor is stopped – or interrupted – from whatever it is doing in order to process information that has arrived at the device that is sending the interrupt. Thus, when I stop to save this text, my Windows computer sends this new information to my Linux server. The Ethernet adapter sends packets containing this text and the Ethernet adapter on the Linux side collects a bunch of packets and then sends an interrupt to the processor. Linux picks up on what is happening and directs the information to Samba, which takes care of saving the data in the correct file. But I discuss the details of that process more thoroughly in Chapters 6 and 7.

Listing 3-2 shows both the interrupts and the IO addresses.

Listing 3-2: Linux interrupts listed

```
[root@chivas /proc]# cat /proc/interrupts
  0:    378425   timer
  1:      1120   keyboard
  2:         0   cascade
 10:     16077   3c509
 13:         1   math error
 14:     63652 + ide0

[root@chivas /proc]# cat /proc/ioports
0000-001f : dma1
0020-003f : pic1
0040-005f : timer
0060-006f : keyboard
0080-009f : dma page reg
00a0-00bf : pic2
00c0-00df : dma2
00f0-00ff : npu
01f0-01f7 : ide0
0300-030f : 3c509
```

```
03c0-03df : vga+
03f0-03f5 : floppy
03f6-03f6 : ide0
03f7-03f7 : floppy DIR
```

Look for your network adapter. In my case, it is the 3c509. No conflicts exist, or I would not be writing this page because my server would be dead in the water. If a conflict exists, you have to reconfigure the adapter. Run your Ethernet NIC configuration program and set the adapter's parameters in its EEPROM. Older adapters may have jumpers or little switches called DIP switches to set. If you think you have to do this, remember to write down all the other devices' interrupts and IO addresses so you don't end up conflicting with something else.

You also may be using a kernel that does not have networking installed. (This is unlikely in the newer versions of Red Hat because the daemon *kerneld* will automatically load networking – and other – modules on demand. However, it is still informative to go ahead and look at these files in order to gain an understanding of how Linux works.) Display the networking devices by entering the following command:

```
cat /proc/net/dev
```

Listing 3-3 shows that the kernel is configured for loopbackand an Ethernet NIC (eth0). The loopback (lo) interface is used only for internal networking. The Ethernet interface is what you want to see. If you don't see it, you may have an unsupported network adapter or a defective or misconfigured one. Red Hat installs, by default, the daemon kerneld that automatically loads modules as they are needed. You can look back at the results of your boot process by using the *dmesg* command. Look for a message that says `delaying eth0 configuration`. That most likely means that Linux was not able to load the network adapter module or the adapter is not working.

Listing 3-3: Linux kernel network configuration

```
[root@chivas net]# cat /proc/net/dev
Inter-|   Receive                  |  Transmit
 face |packets errs drop fifo frame|packets errs drop fifo colls carrier
   lo:    116     0    0    0    0     116     0    0    0     0    0
 eth0:  16292    19   19   23   19    7245     0    0    0    54    0
```

The next step is to make sure that your network routing configured correctly. Look at your routing table by entering the following command:

```
netstat -r -n
```

You should see a listing like the one shown in Listing 3-4. The *destination* is the location – IP address – that you want to send packets to; for instance, the address

192.168.1.0 refers to my local network. The *gateway* is the address (computer or router) where the packets need to be sent so they can find their way to their destination. In the case where the destination is the local network, then the 0.0.0.0 means "no gateway." The *genmask* is used to separate the parts of the IP address that are used for the network address from the host number (more on that in Chapter 10). The flags are used to indicate things like *U* for up and *G* for gateway. The metric is used as a measure of how far a packet has to travel to its destination (a number greater than 32 is considered to be infinite). The next two flags — *Ref* and *Use* — are not important for this discussion. Finally the *Iface* is self-explanatory.

Listing 3-4: Routing table displayed

```
Kernel IP routing table
Destination      Gateway   Genmask          Flags   MSS  Window   irtt Iface
192.168.1.0      0.0.0.0   255.255.255.0    U       1500      0      0 eth0
127.0.0.0        0.0.0.0   255.0.0.0        U       3584      0      0 lo
```

You must have a route to the loopback interface (also referred to as *lo*), which is the 127.0.0.0 address.

If you are missing either or both parameters, you must set them. To set the loopback device — which must be set for the network adapter to work — enter the following command:

```
route add -net 127.0.0.0
```

To set the route for the network adapter and your local network, enter the following command:

```
route add -net 192.168.1.0
```

This route is assigned automatically to your network adapter. However, if you wish to assign it explicitly, enter the command as follows:

```
route add -net 192.168.1.0 dev eth0
```

Run **netstat** *-r -n* to see your routing table. You should see entries for the loopback and the Ethernet, as shown in Listing 3-4.

If you do not see a route to your network interface, try repeating the preceding steps. You may have to delete a route. To delete a route, enter the following command:

```
route del 192.168.1.0
```

If the network adapter is configured correctly and the routing is correct, check the network. The best way to do this is to ping the loopback interface first and then the other computer. Enter the following command, let it run for a few seconds (one ping occurs per second), and stop it by pressing Ctrl+C:

ping *127.0.0.1*

You should see a response like the one shown in Listing 3-5.

Listing 3-5: Ping the loopback interface

```
[root@chivas /]# ping 127.0.0.1
PING 127.0.0.1 (127.0.0.1): 56 data bytes
64 bytes from 127.0.0.1: icmp_seq=0 ttl=64 time=2.0 ms
64 bytes from 127.0.0.1: icmp_seq=1 ttl=64 time=1.2 ms
64 bytes from 127.0.0.1: icmp_seq=2 ttl=64 time=1.1 ms
64 bytes from 127.0.0.1: icmp_seq=3 ttl=64 time=1.1 ms

--- 127.0.0.1 ping statistics ---
4 packets transmitted, 4 packets received, 0% packet loss
round-trip min/avg/max = 1.1/1.8/4.6 ms
```

Each line shows the number of bytes returned from the loopback interface, the sequence, and the round-trip time. The last lines are the summary, which shows if any packets did not make the trip. This is a working system, but if you don't see any returned packet, something is wrong with your setup and you should review the steps outlined in the preceding paragraphs.

Next, try to *ping* the Windows computer. Enter the following command, let it run for 10–15 seconds, and stop it by pressing Ctrl+C:

ping *192.168.1.2*

You should see a response like the one shown in Listing 3-6:

Listing 3-6: Ping the Windows PC

```
[root@chivas /]# ping 192.168.1.1
PING 192.168.1.2 (192.168.1.2): 56 data bytes
64 bytes from 192.168.1.1: icmp_seq=0 ttl=32 time=3.1 ms
64 bytes from 192.168.1.1: icmp_seq=1 ttl=32 time=2.3 ms
64 bytes from 192.168.1.1: icmp_seq=2 ttl=32 time=2.5 ms
64 bytes from 192.168.1.1: icmp_seq=3 ttl=32 time=2.4 ms

--- 192.168.1.2 ping statistics ---
4 packets transmitted, 4 packets received, 0% packet loss
round-trip min/avg/max = 2.3/2.5/3.1 ms
```

If you get a continuous stream of returned packets and the packet loss is zero or very near zero, your network is working. If not, the problem may be in the Linux computer or the Windows machine. Review the troubleshooting steps I describe in this chapter. Note that the ICMP is taking about 1 full millisecond (ms) longer to travel to my Windows box than to the loopback device. That is because the loopback is completely internal to the Linux box.

TIP If you can't locate the problem and you are using a PPP connection to an Internet Service Provider (ISP), establish a PPP connection and try to ping the computer where you have your account. It is considered a security breach to continuously ping someone else's computer — and at least bad manners — so don't leave it running. Also, the ISP's firewall may not allow the Internet Control Message Protocol (ICMP) packets that ping uses. ICMP packets are the simplest type of packet defined in the Internet Protocol. They are used for doing simple things like a ping.

CHECKING SAMBA'S SERVICES

If your basic networking is working but you can't access the Samba resources, the next likely culprit is Samba. The Samba suite of programs includes several tools that can help you troubleshoot problems. The following tests address a much wider range of problems than should occur if you have not modified the *smb.conf* file that Red Hat installed for you.

The Samba configuration file, *smb.conf*, is quite complex. It contains dozens of variables and they can interact in hundreds, if not thousands, of ways. Although I've kept the examples simple so far in this book, to get a useful client-server system going, you have to experiment. To facilitate that experimentation, and to help you troubleshoot problems, Samba provides a useful suite of test programs.

Start by making sure the daemons are running. From the command line, enter the following command:

```
ps x | grep mbd
```

As shown in Listing 3-7, you should see a line for smbd and one for nmbd. (Note that the grep command filters out all the output from ps except for those lines that contain the string mbd. Listing 3-7: Looking for the smbd and nmbd daemons)

```
[root@chivas /]# ps -x |grep mbd
  227  ?   S    0:00 smbd -D
  236  ?   S    0:00 nmbd -D
  360  ?   S    0:06 smbd -D
  742  p0  S    0:00 grep mbd
```

If the daemons are not running, start them by entering the following commands from root's command line:

```
/etc/rc.d/init.d/smb restart
```

Repeat the **ps** command, as shown in the previous paragraphs, to make sure they ran. If they didn't, enter the following command to make sure the files exist and are executable:

```
ls -l /sbin/smbd /sbin/nmbd
```

The second, third, and fourth characters in the resulting output should be "r," "w," and "x," respectively, and the owner should be "*root.*" If not, enter the following commands:

```
chmod 750 /usr/sbin/smbd /usr/sbin/nmbd
chown root /usr/sbin/smbd /usr/sbin/nmbd
```

Try running the daemons again. If they still don't work, they are probably corrupted and you have to reinstall them. See Chapter 7 for instructions on re-installing a Red Hat Package and try reinstalling the Samba package again.

If those processes are running, test the configuration by entering the following command:

```
testparm | more
```

TIP   The vertical bar (|) is called a *pipe* in the UNIX world. It is a mechanism to connect the output of one command or application to the input of another. The command **more** takes the voluminous output of testparm and allows only one page of text to be displayed at a time.

Several pages of Samba information are displayed. Listing 3-7 shows the first and last pages of the lengthy listing. The output reports any errors that occur, but sometimes you have to look closely to see through all the information that **testparm** displays.

Listing 3-7: First and last pages of output from testparm

```
Load smb config files from /etc/smb.conf
doing parameter printing = bsd
doing parameter printcap name = /etc/printcap
doing parameter load printers = yes
```

```
doing parameter log file = /var/log/samba-log.%m
doing parameter max log size = 50
doing parameter short preserve case = yes
doing parameter preserve case = yes
doing parameter lock directory = /var/lock/samba
doing parameter locking = yes
doing parameter strict locking = yes
doing parameter share modes = yes
doing parameter security = user
doing parameter socket options = TCP_NODELAY
Processing section "[homes]"
doing parameter comment = Home Directories
doing parameter browseable = yes
doing parameter read only = no
doing parameter preserve case = yes
doing parameter short preserve case = yes
doing parameter create mode = 0750
doing parameter allow hosts = maggie
Processing section "[printers]"
doing parameter comment = All Printers
doing parameter path = /var/spool/samba
doing parameter browseable = no
doing parameter printable = yes
doing parameter public = no
doing parameter writable = no
doing parameter create mode = 0700


   . . .


Service parameters [lp]:
    comment:
    path: /var/spool/samba
    create mask: 0700
    print ok: Yes
    printer: lp

Service parameters [lp0]:
    comment:
    path: /var/spool/samba
    create mask: 0700
    print ok: Yes
    printer: lp0
```

```
Service parameters [IPC$]:
    comment: IPC Service (Samba 1.9.16p11)
    path: /tmp
    status: No
    guest ok: Yes
```

Checking the smbd setup

The next test involves running a program that looks to see what shares Samba is exporting. As you may have guessed, my Linux server is named chivas. I use that name in my examples. Enter the following command:

```
smbclient -L chivas
```

This command returns the basic information about what services chivas is serving. This test is useful for detecting errors in your password setup or mistakes of that nature.

Listing 3-9 presents an outline of what you should look for depending on the output of **smbclient.**

Listing 3-9: If-then logic for smbclient

```
If you see the message "Bad Password" then
    Check your smb.conf for incorrect:
        Hosts allow, Hosts deny, or Valid users
    Then run testparam again and look specifically for these problems.

If you see the message "connection  refused" then
    The smbd daemon is probably not running. Check it again.

If you see the message "session request failed" then
    If it says "your server software is being unfriendly" then
        You may have an invalid entry (or entries) in smb.conf,
            or, smbd is not running,
            or another service may be running on port 139.
    You can check the first two as described previously;
    you can check the last one by running the following command:        netstat
-a
and looking for anything using port 139.
```

Checking the nmbd setup

You can check the status of the nmbd process by entering the following command:

```
nmblookup -B chivas
```

where *chivas* is my Windows client. You should get that PC's IP address back. If you do not, check the PC setup.

To do a general search of every PC on your network, enter the following command:

```
nmblookup -d 2 "*"
```

You should see a response from every client on the network, as shown below.

```
Added interface ip=192.168.1.250 bcast=192.168.1.255 nmask=255.255.255.0
Sending queries to 192.168.1.255
Got a positive name query response from 192.168.1.250 ( 192.168.1.250 )
Got a positive name query response from 192.168.1.101 ( 192.168.1.101 )
192.168.1.250 *<00>
192.168.1.101 *<00>
```

You can check your passwords more precisely by entering the following command:

```
smbclient '\\chivas\root' -U root
```

(I use the username *root* here because that is the only user that has to be installed during the Red Hat Installation process in Chapter 1. Adding users is discussed in the section "Adding Linux Users" in Chapter 6. The root service is used because it is the only service that I can guarantee to be available at this point.)

Enter the password for *root*. If you get the **smb: \>** prompt then your setup is correct. At the prompt, enter **?** to see the available commands. You should be able use the **dir, get,** and **put** commands.

Two of the common errors are "invalid network name" and "bad password." The first error probably means that the service for *tmp* is incorrectly set up in smb.conf. The latter error can have several meanings:

◆ You have shadow passwords without smbd support for them.

◆ You are using encrypted passwords without smbd support for them.

♦ Your smb.conf has misconfigured values for any of the following parameters:

- Valid users

- Password level

- Path

 TIP The Samba log files contain a lot of troubleshooting information. Check out the `/var/log/samba` directory for files that describe what is happening with both smbd and nmbd.

Checking Samba from your Windows Client

You conduct the last tests from your Windows PC. Execute the following command from a DOS window:

```
C:\net use g: \\chivas\root
```

Depending on the Windows user name that you are using and the configuration of your Linux-Samba server, you may or may not be prompted for a password. If your Windows user name matches a valid user name on the Linux server, you should be able to see the drive *g:* in your *My Computer* dialog box. If it doesn't appear, you'll be prompted for a password. If your Windows user name and the password match one on the Linux box, you will see drive *g:* show up in *My Computer*. Otherwise, return to Chapter 1 and follow the instructions for creating the user Root on your Windows box.

The final test is to browse the Samba server from your Network Neighborhood window. If you select *Entire Network*, you should see your server. If you don't see your server, check your Windows setup again.

 TIP If you are a real troubleshooter, the *tcpdump-smb* utility is for you. It gives you information about what's happening down at the packet level. It comes on the CD-ROM as an RPM package. Load it and read the documentation. But that goes way beyond the scope of this chapter.

Conclusion

You are now a troubleshooting expert, capable of commanding more than $100 per hour from your desperate customers. Okay, maybe not $100, but hopefully you have acquired the fundamentals of troubleshooting and a good measure of practical experience. I suggest that you view the simple system you have just set up as an invaluable laboratory. Before Linux, it was rare that an individual had the opportunity to work on a UNIX system without fear of destroying valuable data and hardware. In this Catch-22 scenario, you needed access to a UNIX system that you could configure if you were to learn UNIX Administration, but you had to know UNIX Administration before you could gain access to a UNIX system.

Summary

This chapter covers the following topics:

- Troubleshooting your network. I introduce you to the concept of troubleshooting. You should try to identify the problem and then work your way to the solution by first eliminating the simple causes and then the harder ones.

- Using the Fault Tree concept. This concept helps you to view a problem and its solutions in a graphical way, using a rooted tree to represent the relationship between a problem and its root cause.

- Using the Microsoft Network Troubleshooter as an example Fault Tree. I convert the menu-based Troubleshooter into pseudocode, to show how it helps you solve simple networking problems.

- Using My Troubleshooter. I use example problems resulting from setting up the client-server network in Chapter 1 to demonstrate real-world troubleshooting.

Part II

Background

Chapter 4

Looking Under the Hood

IN THIS CHAPTER

◆ Examining the Linux kernel's primary internal functions and its startup process

◆ Exploring the Linux file system

◆ Investigating the Linux File System Standard (FSSTND)

◆ Understanding the Red Hat configuration scripts

◆ Looking at networking protocols and the Open Systems Interconnect (OSI) model

◆ Discovering the Samba system's internal functions

◆ Looking at the Red Hat Publisher's Edition CD-ROM

◆ Understanding the General Public License (GPL)

◆ Working with the X Window system

I PLOWED THROUGH MY first installations of Linux and Samba in an impatient quest to get it all running as soon as possible. I always take that approach and probably always will. I don't care what I have to do to get what I want! The elderly, children, friends, and relatives, I sweep them all out of my way in a hungry lust just to get that first prompt:

```
[root@localhost /root]#
```

With this approach, I usually get to the prompt. But the dark side of this method — if I can even call it a method — is that I barely understand what I've done or how the system works after I get to the prompt. After I complete the installation, I painfully (and remorsefully) crawl toward competence. I have to take cold comfort in the prompt, because I no longer have any friends and my relatives won't speak to me.

I also find that I don't reach competence until I gain a fair understanding of the details — and if not the details, then at least the general concepts — underlying the prompt and all that makes the prompt possible. Similarly, even though I don't want to know how to repair my car's transmission, I do like knowing how it works. (Come to think of it, I did take the transmission apart in my first car. I fixed fifth gear but lived without third until the car finally rusted out. Did I miss a lesson in that experience?)

You don't need to know everything about Linux, but you should understand a few essential points. In this chapter, I describe the fundamentals of Linux, Samba, X and networking protocols. To manage your system effectively in the long term, you need to understand the basics of not only Linux and Samba, but also internetworking. Without an understanding of these fundamentals, you are like a racecar driver who doesn't know what a piston is. To get the most out of your vehicle — be it a car or a computer — you need to know a little about what happens underneath the hood.

Just What Is Linux Anyway?

The word *Linux* has several meanings. For example, it refers to the Linux kernel, which is the program that controls the interaction between the hardware and the application programs that you use and control. It also refers to everything that comes packaged on the Red Hat (or other manufacturer's) distribution CD-ROM — that is, all the software that works together as a Linux system. That includes the Linux kernel, system programs, the X Window system, and GNU (which stands for "GNU's not UNIX") programs. The term *Linux* also refers to us as a community of developers and users — as in "Linux is gaining market share."

In other words, the meaning of the term *Linux* generally depends on the context in which you use it. If I call up the Red Hat people and ask to purchase Linux, they will happily send me their CD-ROM. But if you are asked to "start Linux," you need to start the Linux kernel. Or if you say, "bring me the Linux box," I know to bring you the computer with a Linux distribution installed on it. After you digest the fundamentals of what makes up Linux, you should have no problem determining what people mean when they refer to Linux.

This theme carries through to other subjects. The Linux file system, for example, refers to information stored on a magnetic or optical disk that is organized in such a way that Linux can make use of it. Don't worry, all the terms and concepts that I introduce in this chapter make sense after some practice.

Exploring the Linux Kernel

The Linux kernel is a program that handles the following tasks:

◆ Determining when and for how long programs get executed

◆ Determining when and where to store programs and data in memory

◆ Refereeing the interaction among the devices that your computer comprises

Basically, when a process — user and system — asks for resources (such as when opening a file), the kernel receives the request and doles out the resources. The kernel does not actually control the processes directly. Because they depend on the kernel to respond to their requests, however, it controls them indirectly.

When a program gets executed, it is referred to as a *process* or a *task*. A *user process* has limited access to system resources such as memory. A *system process* has fewer limitations. The kernel imposes these limitations on processes to prevent them from interfering with each other and possibly crashing the system.

What does this master of the Linux universe look like? Log onto your Linux box and enter the following command from your shell prompt:

```
ls -l /boot
```

You should see a list of files similar to the example in Listing 4-1.

Listing 4-1: A sample /boot directory listing

```
total 4607
lrwxrwxrwx  1 root    root        19 Sep 26 15:58 System.map -> System.map-2.2.12-9
-rw-r--r--  1 root    root    182601 Jul 27 22:45 System.map-2.2.10-3
-rw-r--r--  1 root    root    200985 Sep 10 01:20 System.map-2.2.12-9
-rw-r--r--  1 root    root       512 Sep 26 08:45 boot.0300
-rw-r--r--  1 root    root      4544 Apr 12 22:19 boot.b
-rw-r--r--  1 root    root       612 Apr 12 22:19 chain.b
-rw-r--r--  1 root    root         0 Sep 10 01:23 kernel.h
-rw-------  1 root    root     10240 Sep 26 16:09 map
lrwxrwxrwx  1 root    root        20 Sep 26 15:58 module-info -> module-info-
2.2.12-9
-rw-r--r--  1 root    root     11773 Jul 27 22:45 module-info-2.2.10-3
-rw-r--r--  1 root    root     11773 Sep 10 01:20 module-info-2.2.12-9
-rw-r--r--  1 root    root       620 Apr 12 22:19 os2_d.b
-rwxr-xr-x  1 root    root   1431306 Jul 27 22:45 vmlinux-2.2.10-3
-rwxr-xr-x  1 root    root   1579349 Sep 10 01:20 vmlinux-2.2.12-9
lrwxrwxrwx  1 root    root        16 Sep 26 15:58 vmlinuz -> vmlinuz-2.2.12-9
-rw-r--r--  1 root    root    600514 Jul 27 22:45 vmlinuz-2.2.10-3
-rw-r--r--  1 root    root    651453 Sep 10 01:20 vmlinuz-2.2.12-9
```

The file *vmlinuz-2.2.12-9* is the Linux kernel; the *2.2.12-9* refers to the version number. The file *vmlinuz* is a link, which is simply a pointer to *vmlinux-2.2.12-9*. When you upgrade your system, the kernel file sometimes changes — for instance, from *vmlinuz-2.2.5-15* to *vmlinuz-2.2.12-9*. Everything else in this listing is just Linux housekeeping and is not discussed here. Overall, this list isn't too scary.

The kernel performs its magic by concentrating on a few things:

♦ **Multitasking:** Multiple programs can run at once.

♦ **Multiple users:** Multiple users can use the computer at one time.

♦ **Virtual memory:** Programs can use more memory than is available from just RAM.

♦ **The file system:** Your files are organized for you.

Understanding Multitasking

A multitasking operating system allows more than one program to run at once. Actually, multiple processes – or *programs* – execute sequentially; the operating system schedules their execution and allocates resources to them. As long as the number of tasks is kept to a reasonable number and the computer is fast enough, all the programs appear to be running simultaneously.

Linux is a *preemptive multitasking* operating system. Each process is given a time slice – generally about 20 milliseconds ($^{20}/_{1000}$ seconds) – to run within. Linux suspends the running process when its time slice expires and starts the next waiting process. This handling of time slices entails storing the environment – all the information that a process needs to run – of the current process in memory and loading the waiting process's environment from memory.

For comparison, MS-DOS is an operating system that allows only one program to run at once. MS-DOS has the Terminate and Stay Resident (TSR) feature, which gives the appearance of multitasking, but simply runs programs when you tell it to. Windows 3.X offers simple multitasking that doesn't always work. Windows 95, 98 and NT use preemptive multitasking that works.

For multitasking to work, the Linux kernel must coordinate the execution of all tasks. It also keeps track of all the details about each process that is running. However, the kernel does not start or stop any programs after it has been started at boot time. The *init* process and the programs themselves take care of that function. *Init* is the process that actually takes care of launching all the initial system and application programs at boot time. The *init* process is discussed further in the section, "Understanding the Linux Startup Process," later in this chapter.

A process table lists basic information about each process that is currently running. To see a typical process table (such as the example shown in Listing 4-2), log in as root and enter the following command:

```
ps x
```

Listing 4-2: A typical Linux process table

```
PID TTY         STAT    TIME COMMAND
    1 ?          S      0:04 init
    2 ?          SW     0:00 [kflushd]
    3 ?          SW     0:00 [kpiod]
    4 ?          SW     0:10 [kswapd]
    5 ?          SW<    0:00 [mdrecoveryd]
  255 ?          S      0:04 /usr/sbin/apmd -p 10 -w 5 -W
  282 ?          S      0:06 syslogd -m 0
  293 ?          S      0:00 klogd
  325 ?          S      0:00 crond
  341 ?          S      0:00 inetd
  366 ?          S      0:01 named
  382 ?          SW     0:00 [lpd]
  420 ?          S      0:00 sendmail: accepting connections on port 25
  459 ?          S      0:00 [smbd]
  470 ?          S      0:01 nmbd -D
  532 tty1       SW     0:00 [mingetty]
  533 tty2       SW     0:00 [mingetty]
  534 tty3       SW     0:00 [mingetty]
  535 tty4       SW     0:00 [mingetty]
  536 tty5       SW     0:00 [mingetty]
  537 tty6       SW     0:00 [mingetty]
  538 ?          SW     0:00 [prefdm]
  541 ?          S      0:00 update (bdflush)
 4124 ?          S    404:06 /etc/X11/X -auth /var/gdm/:0.xauth :0
 4134 ?          SW     0:00 [prefdm]
 6610 ?          S      0:00 in.telnetd
 6611 pts/0      S      0:00 login -- paul
 6630 pts/0      S      0:00 su -
 6631 pts/0      S      0:00 -bash
 6647 pts/0      R      0:00 ps x
 6648 pts/0      S      0:00 more
```

Linux uses a set formula to determine when each program is run, how long it runs, and which program takes precedence over the others. The formula tries to give each process its fair share of CPU time, based on a priority given to each process (you can manually change the priority with the *nice* command). The priority of a process is determined by a number of system parameters. The Linux kernel also transfers parts of or entire programs between disk and memory, keeping track of the details for each program. Thus, if you want to run a clock program and a nuclear reactor control program, the kernel should schedule the control program to run before the clock and for longer segments of time.

You can tell a lot from the process table. For example, the process table in Listing 4-2 shows that I am logged on as *paul* (Process Identifier – PID - 6611) from a Telnet connection (PID 6610). I have changed to the root (PID 6630), which is using a bash shell (PID 6631). There are several processes that have process identifiers (PIDs) greater than 6000, which implies that the computer has been running for a while or is heavily used, because PIDs are assigned sequentially starting at 1.

Understanding Multi-user Systems

Linux also allows more than one person to access the computer. By running programs (tasks or processes) that negotiate the logon process, the Linux box can handle more than one user at a time. In Listing 4-2, the process IDs (*PIDs*) 292, 293, 294, 297 and 298 are responsible for logging on users. The *mingetty* processes constantly monitor the virtual consoles waiting for you to log on (see the following Tip for further explanation). When you press a key on the console, the login program negotiates your authentication by prompting you for a user name and password. As you can see, I am logged on as *root*. (This generally isn't a good idea from a systems management perspective – see Chapter 10 for more on systems management.) From the console, I have also connected via the Telnet program, which enables you to use the network to connect from one computer to another without being physically present at the computer you're accessing. The *in.telnetd* process – PID 328 – is controlling my Telnet session. I have also changed to the *root* user via the switch user - su - command in my Telnet session. This change is made because the default Red Hat – and most Linux – distributions don't allow you to log on as *root* except from the console. (This is to increase security by forcing you to login as a normal user before switching to root. You have to know two passwords instead of just one. This also leaves a simple audit trail of which users switched to root.)

Each process that is associated with a user has file ownership and permissions associated with it. Any files that are created as a result of these processes will retain that file ownership and permissions. By those same permissions, the processes also will be limited in terms of which files they can access and use. Thus, Linux is a multi-user operating system.

By comparison, MS-DOS, Windows 3.X, Windows 95 and 98 are all single-user operating systems. Windows NT is a multi-user operating system.

Linux uses the concept of a virtual console or terminal to make life easier for you. It simply maps two or more terminal sessions onto a single physical monitor. Any Linux distribution comes configured for between four and eight sessions. By pressing the Alt key in combination with the first four to eight function keys (Alt+F1, Alt+F2, and so on), you toggle between independent sessions. This technique is equivalent to running several shells as windows and switching between them via the mouse.

Understanding Virtual Memory

Linux is also a demand-paged, virtual-memory operating system. By transferring (mapping) parts of a program or a data structure from memory to disk, the system can work with a program or data structure that is larger than the available memory. If you have 8MB of memory and you want to load a 10MB spreadsheet, the virtual-memory system takes part of that 10MB spreadsheet file and loads it into memory. If you access the part that is still on disk, part of the file that is currently in memory is stored to disk and the new segment is loaded into the freed-up memory. Using virtual memory slows down the system, but it makes your computer appear to have much more memory than it actually has.

Do you remember the hoops you had to jump through back in the 1980s to get MS-DOS to access more than 640K of memory? Not only was it limited to 640K, but it also did not have virtual memory, so a program had to use less than that amount to work. Linux does have virtual memory, so if you have only 8MB, you can load and run stuff that uses more than that amount. As you may recall from Chapter 1, during the Linux installation you set aside some disk space for a swap partition. Linux uses that space to store the memory contents when it "swaps out."

The Linux "File"

In the Linux (and UNIX) world, a file is not just an entity used to store information. It is also used as an abstraction to connect the kernel to each device, as well as a view into the kernel. In this way, Linux simplifies the access of devices by treating them like any other file. The directory */dev* contains many files that are used as the common connection points between the kernel and device drivers. The drivers contain the internal specifics of a device and the kernel knows about the drivers. The device file provides a convenient connection point that the administrator can easily view and modify.

For example, to use a mouse, it is not enough to have the device driver for the mouse installed (in the kernel itself); you also must have a device file associated with the mouse. I use a serial mouse connected to port ttyS0, so my system uses the file shown in Listing 4-3 to access the mouse.

Listing 4-3: The mouse device file

```
lrwxrwxrwx   1 root     root          4 Dec  8 14:00 /dev/mouse -> ttyS0
crw-rw----   1 root     uucp      5, 64 Dec  8 22:03 /dev/ttyS0
```

My kernel has the driver for a serial mouse and expects to find the device file as */dev/mouse*. As you can see in Listing 4-3, */dev/mouse* is a link, or pointer, to the first serial port device file – the device file to which my mouse is connected.

A device file is either a *character* or a *block* type, as specified by the first character on the listing (the c specifies that the mouse is a character device and a *b* specifies a block type such as a disk drive). A device also has major and minor numbers, which the kernel uses internally for its own bookkeeping. The major number, along with the device type, identifies the driver, while the minor number is passed to the driver to identify the device. The drivers themselves are contained either in Linux modules or compiled directly into the kernel.

You can create the */dev/ttyS0* device file by using the *mknod* command. For example, to create the mouse device file, log on as *root* and enter the following command:

```
/bin/mknod /dev/ttyS0 c 5 64
```

This command creates the file shown in Listing 4-3.

Linux has several file types:

♦ *Regular files* are the type you use all the time. In a long listing (which you produce by entering the command *ls -l*), a hyphen precedes the name of each regular file.

♦ *Directories* contain the names of files that are stored – or organized – as a group. The grouping is arbitrary; you can choose any combination you want. You also can change the grouping at any time. You create directories by entering the *mkdir* command. A lowercase *d* precedes the name of each directory in a long listing.

◆ *Character and Block device files* serve as the interface between the Linux operating system and the hardware devices. Character devices are accessed sequentially, a byte at a time; a serial port is a character device. Block devices — for example, disk drives — are accessed in chunks of bytes; you get a block (that is, 1,024 bytes) of data at one time. In a long listing, a lowercase *c* precedes the name of each Character device file, and a lowercase *b* precedes the name of each Block device file.

◆ The *named pipe* or FIFO (first-in-first-out) is a file that enables processes to communicate with each other. FIFOs are created with the *mknod* program and are designated by a *p* at the beginning of a long listing.

◆ The *pipe file* is an abstraction that enables processes to communicate with each other. Pipe files actually exist as sections of memory used to buffer the data going from one process to another. Pipe files are denoted as a vertical bar (|) and placed between two processes. For example, the command *ls -l / | more* lists the device directory one page at a time by piping the output of *ls* to the paging command *more.*

◆ *Sockets* facilitate communication between processes via the network.

◆ *Hard links* create additional names for a file. They are indistinguishable from the original file. The *ln* command creates hard links.

◆ *Symbolic or "soft" links* are files that contain the name of another file. They essentially point to that file. When a symbolic link is encountered by the kernel during the interpretation of a pathname, the pointer that the link contains is used as a new starting point. When you do a long listing — */bin/ls -l* — on a symbolic link you see it displayed with an arrow pointing to the target file, as follows:

```
mylink -> test.txt
```

For instance, if the file TEST.TXT contains the characters *xyz* and you enter the command **more mylink** you will see the string *xyz* displayed. This is because the symbolic link points to a text file TEST.TXT.

For another example, *gzip* is a GNU program used to compress data and files. If you want to decompress a file, you can use the command *gzip -d* or the command *gunzip*, which is a symbolic link to the command *gzip -d* (*gzip* looks at how it is called in order to determine its action).

Exploring the Linux File System

When I read technical discussions of Linux, I sometimes get confused about the meaning of the term *file system*. This is another one of those context-sensitive terms. It can refer to either how Linux organizes the raw bytes of data into files or how Linux organizes files and directories. The next two sections discuss these distinctions. The section after them explains how the Linux world is creating a standard for where to store standard and nonstandard Linux files.

Understanding How Linux Organizes Bytes of Data into a File

The Linux file system organizes the raw bytes that are stored on a disk into files. Linux does not impose any structure on the bytes that make up files; it simply enables processes to access all the bytes that belong to any given file. The methods that it uses to do that are described in this section.

The *Extended File System 2* (*ext2*) is the *de facto* standard Linux file system. However, Linux is capable of using many other file systems, such as MS-DOS, Minix (the earliest Linux was based on it), the original Extended File System, and ISO9660 (for CD-ROMs). When you create – or initialize – your disk partition, you have the choice of several different file systems. When you formatted your *root*, */home* and */usr/local* partitions in Chapter 1, you used the *ext2* system.

When you create an *ext2* file system, a data structure called an *inode* (index node) is folded into the disk format. When you format the disk, *inodes* are periodically placed on the disk. Unlike with MS-DOS, the number of *inodes* is fixed when you format the disk. (If you have a huge number of very small files, you can run out of *inodes*. That is unlikely in most circumstances, however.)

An *inode* is the essential element of a Linux file system. When you create a file an *inode* is allocated to it. It contains information on a file's ownership (*user* and *group*), access modes (*read, write*, and *execution*), time information (when a file was last accessed and modified, and when the *inode* itself was modified), the byte count, and the file's type (regular, special – that is, a device – or an abstract one such as those found in the */proc* directory). The *inode* contains the indexing information about the disk *blocks* where a file's data is located. However, an *inode* doesn't contain the name of the file; that information is stored in a directory file.

A *directory* is a *file* itself. It contains the name – or names – of the file(s) and its *inode(s)*.

Linux uses the information in *inodes* to access and work with files. For example, the file CHAP_4.DOC – which contains the text for this chapter – is physically stored on a hard disk that my Linux box controls. When I open this file, Linux tells the disk controller to go to specific locations to retrieve the raw data off the disk platter. Linux determines where to go by checking the information stored in the *inode* associated with the file CHAP_4.DOC. In other words, each file has an *inode* that points to data blocks scattered around on the disk platter. The kernel puts them all together into a form that humans can use. To obtain the *inode* information, I enter the long listing command *ls* and include the *-i* option (you can also use the synonym *--inode*):

```
ls -il /home/book/chap_4.doc
```

This command returns the following information about the specified file (including the *inode* — 106499):

```
106499 -rwxr-xr-x   1 root      root       124928 Sep  2 19:10 chap_4.doc
```

Listing 4-4 shows the listing of the Red Hat */etc* directory and the *inodes* associated with each file and directory.

Listing 4-4: A partial listing of the /etc directory and its inodes

```
total 919
    6046 drwxr-xr-x    3 root      root        1024 Sep 26 08:33 CORBA
    2034 -rw-r--r--    1 root      root        2045 Jul 28 20:51 DIR_COLORS
    2057 -rw-r--r--    1 root      root          19 Oct  3 16:48 HOSTNAME
    2300 -rw-r--r--    1 root      root          42 Sep 26 14:48 MACHINE.SID
    2272 -rw-r--r--    1 root      root        5468 Jun 22 14:35 Muttrc
    8035 drwxr-xr-x   14 root      root        1024 Oct  3 15:50 X11
    2051 -rw-r--r--    1 root      root          12 Jul 29 15:53 adjtime
    2279 -rw-r--r--    1 root      root         732 Jul  2 16:04 aliases
    2283 -rw-r--r--    1 root      root       16384 Oct  3 15:58 aliases.db
    2035 -rw-------    1 root      root           1 Jun 13 12:27 at.deny
    2029 -rw-r--r--    1 root      root         312 Sep 26 15:24 bashrc
    4264 drwxr-xr-x    2 root      root        4096 Sep 26 08:40 charsets
    4469 drwxr-xr-x    3 root      root        1024 Sep 26 08:41 codepages
    2263 -rw-------    1 root      root         263 Oct  1 07:11 conf.linuxconf
    2296 -rw-r--r--    1 root      root         105 Sep 26 08:45 conf.modules
    4262 drwxr-xr-x    2 root      root        1024 Jun  3 03:42 cron.d
    8072 drwxr-xr-x    2 root      root        1024 Sep 26 08:42 cron.daily
    6052 drwxr-xr-x    2 root      root        1024 Apr 15 08:00 cron.hourly
    6053 drwxr-xr-x    2 root      root        1024 Apr 15 08:00 cron.monthly
    6054 drwxr-xr-x    2 root      root        1024 Sep 26 08:39 cron.weekly
    2038 -rw-r--r--    1 root      root         255 Apr 15 08:00 crontab
```

A directory is itself a file whose data consists of filenames and *inode* pairs. The filename is a simple text string such as *bashrc* in Listing 3-4; it has an *inode* associated with it — in this example, 2035. When you do something to hosts, Linux looks at *inode* number 2035 to determine all the details about hosts, including where to access the data it contains.

The hierarchical directory structure is obtained by storing the names of other directories in a directory's *file/inode* list. Notice the directory *X11* (denoted by the *d* immediately after the *inode* number) in Listing 4-4. The *inode* 8035 points to a file that contains another list of file and *inode* pairs. And of course, any of those files can be directories that point to other files and directories.

 A file consists of an *inode*, the associated data blocks, and a filename stored in a directory file. Symbolic and hard links offer two different means for associating different names with a file. All hard links, however, will share the same inode with a file. A soft link does not share the inode.

The kernel knows where to look for *inodes* that make up any given file because it has a master table of file information called the *Superblock*. The Superblock contains the number of data blocks, the block size, the number of *inodes*, and the free and used *inodes* of the file system. The Superblock is loaded into memory at boot time. One of the reasons why you should perform a systematic shutdown (that is, *halt*) of your Linux computer is to write the updated Superblock to disk. (Linux generally is smart enough to reconfigure using the *file system check - fsck* — a Superblock after an unscheduled shutdown, but it is good administrative practice to avoid the risk of possible injury to your system.

The Virtual File System (VFS) — I've also seen it called the Virtual File System Switch — sits in between the low-level file system where the software drivers directly control the hardware and the high-level file system that works with the various formats such as *ext2* and *msdos*. It provides a layer of abstraction so that the system programs that deal with features like opening and closing files don't have to deal directly with the device drivers themselves. VFS translates the high-level operations into the language that the device drivers understand.

When you specify a directory path — for example, in the command *ls -l /etc/X11* — the kernel first looks in the *root* (/) directory file for the string *etc*. If the kernel finds this string, it uses the *inode* to access the */etc* directory file. The kernel then looks for the string *X11* and if it finds this string, the kernel uses the *inode* to find the */etc/X11* directory and list its contents.

Understanding how Linux organizes files and directories

The Linux file system also describes the structure that houses all the files that make up Linux. It is based on a *rooted-tree* model. The tree is made up of directories and files. Each directory can contain one or more subdirectories. Directories are used to organize files, and each directory or subdirectory can contain zero or more files. A file contains either information (data), an executable program or script, device information, or nothing.

As a system administrator, you need to be familiar with the file system organization, for troubleshooting as well as everyday management. The more you know it, the better. After you work with it for a while, you will come to instinctively know the locations of the most important files and generally where you find most of the other files.

The *root* directory is the mother of all directories. Listing 4-5 shows a listing of the *root* directory as Red Hat configures it (other distributions such as Slackware have somewhat different setups, but are basically the same). Its structure is important because the *root* directory is your starting point for the rest of the Linux file system.

Listing 4-5: Root directory listing

```
total 132
drwxr-xr-x    2 root    root        2048 Sep 26 08:42 bin
drwxr-xr-x    2 root    root        1024 Sep 26 16:09 boot
drwxr-xr-x    5 root    root       34816 Oct  3 15:58 dev
drwxr-xr-x   30 root    root        3072 Oct  3 16:01 etc
drwxr-xr-x    5 root    root        1024 Oct  3 05:37 home
drwxr-xr-x    4 root    root        3072 Sep 26 08:41 lib
drwxr-xr-x    2 root    root       12288 Sep 26 07:51 lost+found
drwxr-xr-x    5 root    root        1024 Sep 26 14:52 mnt
drwxrwxr-x    4 root    vm          1024 Oct  3 06:04 opt
dr-xr-xr-x   68 root    root           0 Oct  3 15:57 proc
drwxr-x---   13 root    root        1024 Oct  5 15:56 root
drwxr-xr-x    3 root    root        2048 Oct  5 14:59 sbin
drwxrwxrwt   10 root    root        1024 Oct  5 15:57 tmp
drwxr-xr-x   21 root    root        1024 Sep 26 08:38 usr
drwxr-xr-x   17 root    root        1024 Sep 26 08:39 var
```

Over the years, certain files have found homes in certain directories. For example, you can expect to find the password file, *passwd*, in the /etc directory. Run the following command and take a look:

```
ls -l /etc
```

It should be there (if it isn't, you probably weren't able to log on). The file systems used by the various UNIX versions have evolved differently from one another. You can easily recognize a System V or BSD file system. They look similar in general, but on closer examination you see significant differences, such as the location of the startup rc scripts. (System V puts them in */etc/rc.d* while BSD leaves them in */etc*.) However, the Linux community is striving to avoid this situation by creating standards.

Taking a look at the Linux File System Standard

The Linux community is working to standardize the Linux file system. Several Linux distributors – Red Hat and Caldera in particular – do a good job of following the Linux File System Standard (FSSTND). Because of evolving manufacturer standards and the whims of the marketplace, you can always find exceptions, but the FSSTND actually takes that into account and is a work in progress itself. To find more information about the FSSTND, go to the following URL:

```
http://www.pathname.com/fhs/
```

One essential FSSTND requirement is that the */usr* directory must remain read-only. Thus, it can be mounted from a CD-ROM or a remote networked disk (for example, via NFS or Samba). This capability is important for both small and large organizations that want to minimize management costs. One server can share its */usr* directory with many clients, which in turn require smaller (or no) disks. A read-only */usr* directory also means lower administration costs, because you can't clutter up and rearrange things. If you follow the standard and mount your own */usr* directory as read-only, you have to put your own stuff in the places where it belongs. Thus, this standard has the added benefit of minimizing your own confusion – no small gain.

By following the FSSTND, Linux vendors do themselves a big favor. In its nascent state, Linux needs to be as uniform as possible to gain momentum and acceptance in the business community. The more established FSSTND becomes, the more everyone will benefit.

Under the FSSTND, some of the more important directories contain the following functions:

♦ The */etc* directory contains local configuration files. Files that describe the network, and other standard configurations, all go here. You should not place any binary or executable files in */etc*.

♦ The */etc/X11* directory contains the *X11* configuration file.

♦ The */etc/skel* directory contains the basic configuration files for new directories.

♦ The */lib* directory gets all the library files needed by the programs in */bin* and */sbin*. Library files contain common functions and data – such as fonts – that many programs use dynamically. When you run a program, the program dynamically links to the necessary libraries.

♦ The */sbin* directory contains the programs needed to boot the system in addition to those in */bin* and should only be executable by *root*.

♦ The */var* directory is for variable stuff. Because */usr* is supposed to be read-only, you use */var* for storing files that change constantly, such as printer spool and system logging files. It has numerous subdirectories that I don't describe in detail but list for reference:

- ◆ */var/log:* log files
- ◆ */var/catman:* manual pages
- ◆ */var/lib:* library files
- ◆ */var/local:* variable local files
- ◆ */var/named:* name service files
- ◆ */var/nis:* network information services (Sun)
- ◆ */var/preserve*
- ◆ */var/run*
- ◆ */var/lock:* lock files used for process coordination
- ◆ */var/tmp:* temporary files
- ◆ */var/spool*: all spooling directories
- ◆ */var/spool/at*: prescheduled commands
- ◆ */var/spool/cron*: commands and scripts run automatically
- ◆ */var/spool/lpd*: print queue files
- ◆ */var/spool/mail*: mail files
- ◆ */var/spool/mqueue*: mail queues
- ◆ */var/spool/rwho*: rwho files
- ◆ */var/spool/smail:* smail queue files
- ◆ */var/spool/uucp*: UNIX to UNIX communication protocol
- ◆ */var/spool/news*: news spools
- ◆ The */etc/sysconfig* directory contains the Red Hat startup scripts.
- ◆ The */usr/lib/rhs* directory contains the Red Hat control panel and other systems administration programs.
- ◆ The */var/lib/rpm* directory has the Red Hat RPM files.
- ◆ The */usr* directory contains the files that can be shared across an entire LAN. It should have its own partition. According to the FSSTND, */usr* should be read-only.

The */usr* directory contains the following directories:

- ◆ */usr/X11R6* contains most of *XFree86* (the X Window system). This directory has the following organization:
- ◆ */usr/X11R6/bin* contains the executable programs.

◆ */usr/X11R6/doc* contains the documentation that is not part of the standard *XFree86* manual system (*man pages*). (*Note:* XFree86 man pages have the same format as standard Linux man pages.)

◆ */usr/X11R6/include* houses the *include* files. These files contain constants and other stuff that you *include* into a source code file during compilation.

◆ */usr/X11R6/lib* contains the libraries specific to *XFree86*.

◆ */usr/X11R6/man* houses the manual pages for *XFree86*.

◆ */usr/bin*, along with */bin*, has most of the programs that are considered standard Linux – everything from *clear* to *gcc* to *zip*.

◆ */usr/dict* has the Linux dictionary.

◆ */usr/doc* contains many useful documents, FAQs, HOWTOs, and so on. You can find more on those subjects in the CD1 chapter found on the companion CD-ROM.

◆ */usr/etc* is empty at this time. (*Note:* Slackware has a link to the *printcap* file, which configures the printers.)

◆ */usr/games* is where games are stored.

◆ */usr/ i486-linux-libc5* contains older libraries.

◆ */usr/include* has more include files.

◆ */usr/info* contains GNU info hypertext files on various topics. For more information on these files, see the man page on *info*.

◆ */usr/lib* contains more Linux libraries.

◆ */usr/man* houses most of the Linux man pages. It is divided into nine sections that reflect the Linux/UNIX convention. Table 4-1 details the organization of the Linux man pages.

◆ */usr/sbin* has system commands and daemons.

◆ */usr/share* is used to store general applications – *awk, ghostscript*, and so on – that are common to all users.

◆ */usr/src* is where you store the Linux or other important source codes.

◆ */usr/local* contains a hierarchy similar to */usr* and is used to store local programs and libraries. It is used to keep the */usr* as stable as possible. By following this convention, it is much easier to keep track of everything that you have installed on your system.

TABLE 4-1 LINUX MAN PAGE ORGANIZATION

Number	Contents
1	User commands and applications
2	System calls and kernel error codes
3	Library calls
4	Device drivers
5	File formats
6	The introductory man page
7	System and package descriptions
8	Network and system commands and utilities
9	Currently empty

 Although System V and BSD UNIX generally have similar structures, they differ in many details.

When you put all this together, you have an efficient, useful file system. As you use it over time, it will become a familiar, if somewhat dull, friend. I suspect that with time it will become the standard across the Linux world and you will be able to navigate a Linux system anywhere in the world.

Understanding the Linux startup process

The Linux startup process is fairly complicated. When the PC is turned on or restarted, a small bootstrap program located on the boot sector of the disk is executed automatically. The kernel is stored in a known location on disk, and the bootstrap program loads the kernel into memory and then starts it (you see a couple of lines of dots indicating the kernel is being loaded).

 If you want to read about the details of this startup process, the *Linux Systems Administrator's Guide* discusses the topic at:

http://www.redhat.com/mirrors/LDP/LDP/sag

After the kernel is started, it does an inventory of the computer's hardware configuration. As you watch the computer boot, you see information similar to the example shown in Listing 4-6. Notice how the kernel checks the memory, the floppy and hard disks, the CD-ROM, and the Ethernet adapters. It needs to know the parameters for these devices so it can manage their interaction with you.

Listing 4-6: The kernel determines hardware configuration during the boot process

```
Linux version 2.2.12-9 (root@porky.devel.redhat.com) (gcc version egcs-2.91.66 1
9990314/Linux (egcs-1.1.2 release)) #1 Fri Sep 10 03:16:15 EDT 1999
Console: colour VGA+ 80x25
Calibrating delay loop... 133.53 BogoMIPS
Memory: 62984k/65536k available (1072k kernel code, 416k reserved, 1000k data, 6
4k init)
Checking if this processor honours the WP bit even in supervisor mode... Ok.
DENTRY hash table entries: 262144 (order: 9, 2097152 bytes)
Buffer-cache hash table entries: 65536 (order: 6, 262144 bytes)
Page-cache hash table entries: 16384 (order: 4, 65536 bytes)
VFS: Diskquotas version dquot_6.4.0 initialized
CPU: Cyrix 6x86 2x Core/Bus Clock stepping 07
Checking 386/387 coupling... OK, FPU using exception 16 error reporting.
Checking 'hlt' instruction... OK.
Checking for popad bug... OK.
POSIX conformance testing by UNIFIX
mtrr: v1.35a (19990819) Richard Gooch (rgooch@atnf.csiro.au)
PCI: PCI BIOS revision 2.10 entry at 0xfdb91
PCI: Using configuration type 1
PCI: Probing PCI hardware
Linux NET4.0 for Linux 2.2
Based upon Swansea University Computer Society NET3.039
{...}
Adding Swap: 136512k swap-space (priority -1)
eth0: 3c509 at 0x310 tag 1, BNC port, address  00 20 af 38 6a aa, IRQ 11.
3c509.c:1.16 (2.2) 2/3/98 becker@cesdis.gsfc.nasa.gov.
eth0: Setting Rx mode to 1 addresses.
arpwatch uses obsolete (PF_INET,SOCK_PACKET)
device eth0 entered promiscuous mode
{...}
```

After the kernel completes the inventory phase, it starts the independent *init* process, which manages the launching of all user and system processes. From that point on, the kernel only manages the computer resources that user and system processes request.

Log on as *root* and run the now-familiar command:

```
ps x | more
```

The process table shown in Listing 4-7 (which is a subset of Listing 4-2) shows these processes in parentheses. The *init* process has the PID of 1 because it is always the first process to start. The (*kflushd*) and (*kswapd*) are really part of the kernel but are shown as separate processes so that the kernel can schedule them. All the processes after them are separate from the kernel.

Listing 4-7: The system or kernel processes

```
PID TTY      STAT   TIME COMMAND
    1 ?        S      0:04 init
    2 ?        SW     0:02 [kflushd]
    3 ?        SW     0:01 [kupdate]
    4 ?        SW     0:00 [kpiod]
    5 ?        SW     0:14 [kswapd]
    6 ?        SW<    0:00 [mdrecoveryd]
  278 ?        S      0:05 syslogd -m 0
  289 ?        S      0:00 klogd
  321 ?        S      0:00 crond
  337 ?        S      0:00 inetd
```

 You can see some of the internal details of these (or any) processes by looking in the */proc* directory. This special file system offers a window into the kernel. For example, if you display the contents of */proc/kcore*, you see the contents of all the memory in your system!

At startup, the *init* process first reads the */etc/inittab* file, shown in Listing 4-8. This file contains instructions for everything from staging the *run levels* of the kernel to starting the *getty* processes, which listen for terminal session logon attempts.

Listing 4-8: Run levels defined in /etc/inittab

```
#
# inittab     This file describes how the INIT process should set up
#             the system in a certain run-level.
#
#
```

```
# Author:        Miquel van Smoorenburg, <miquels@drinkel.nl.mugnet.org>
#                Modified for RHS Linux by Marc Ewing and Donnie Barnes
#

# Default runlevel. The runlevels used by RHS are:
#   0 - halt (Do NOT set initdefault to this)
#   1 - Single user mode
#   2 - Multiuser, without NFS (The same as 3, if you do not have networking)
#   3 - Full multiuser mode
#   4 - unused
#   5 - X11
#   6 - reboot (Do NOT set initdefault to this)
#
id:5:initdefault:

# System initialization.
si::sysinit:/etc/rc.d/rc.sysinit
l0:0:wait:/etc/rc.d/rc 0
l1:1:wait:/etc/rc.d/rc 1
l2:2:wait:/etc/rc.d/rc 2
l3:3:wait:/etc/rc.d/rc 3
l4:4:wait:/etc/rc.d/rc 4
l5:5:wait:/etc/rc.d/rc 5
l6:6:wait:/etc/rc.d/rc 6

# Things to run in every runlevel.
ud::once:/sbin/update

# Trap CTRL-ALT-DELETE
ca::ctrlaltdel:/sbin/shutdown -t3 -r now

{...}
```

Eight run levels exist. A *run level* defines the types of processes that the system will execute. Run level S, for instance, is the single-user mode and is used to perform tasks that cannot be interfered with. Run level 3 is the normal operating mode. The *init* manual page describes run levels in detail.

As shown in Table 4-2, Red Hat Linux has seven execution levels. For the startup phase, after the boot phase in the startup process, the kernel runs at the Single User level (level 1) so it can complete all the necessary startup tasks before the system turns on multitasking. (For example, the kernel does an in-depth disk check during this part of the startup process.)

TABLE 4-2 RED HAT LINUX EXECUTION LEVELS

Level	Function
0	Low-level system initialization.
1	Single User or Administrative. Performs tasks that can't be done after multitasking is turned on — such as detailed disk checks.
2	Multi-user but without NFS (and, I suppose, SMB). In other words, no networking (similar to Windows *Safe Mode*).
3	Full Multi-user. Networking, including NFS and SMB, turned on.
4	Not used.
5	X11. The X Window system that is run from system level. You log on and off from an X Window prompt rather than a shell prompt.
6	Reboot. First log off all users, stop all daemons, write all data waiting in memory to disk ("sync the disk"), and reboot the computer.

After the kernel hits level three (or five if you specify the system to run under X Window by default) where multieverything plus networking is enabled, it starts the general-purpose features such as the *getty* processes and the important *rc* scripts.

RED HAT CONFIGURATION SCRIPTS (RC)

Configuration scripts are used to configure Linux systems when they are started. They perform tasks such as setting up routing tables as well as starting Samba. They are similar in function to the DOS AUTOEXEC.BAT file but much more flexible and powerful.

Red Hat — as well as other distributions such as Debian — keeps the traditional UNIX System V-like */etc/rc.d* directory, but this directory contains mostly links to the actual scripts in other directories. In this way, Red Hat can provide the type of added value that it thinks is best while still ostensibly maintaining compatibility with the rest of the Linux world and, to some extent, the UNIX world. Listing 4-9 shows the basic structure of this directory.

Listing 4-9: The Red Hat configuration script directory

```
total 23
drwxr-xr-x   2 root      root         1024 Oct  5 14:59 init.d
-rwxr-xr-x   1 root      root         2722 Apr 15 07:53 rc
-rwxr-xr-x   1 root      root          945 Jul 15 14:54 rc.local
-rwxr-xr-x   1 root      root        10463 Jul 29 09:36 rc.sysinit
drwxr-xr-x   2 root      root         1024 Oct  5 14:59 rc0.d
```

```
drwxr-xr-x  2 root    root      1024 Oct  5 14:59 rc1.d
drwxr-xr-x  2 root    root      1024 Oct  5 14:59 rc2.d
drwxr-xr-x  2 root    root      1024 Oct  5 14:59 rc3.d
drwxr-xr-x  2 root    root      1024 Oct  5 14:59 rc4.d
drwxr-xr-x  2 root    root      1024 Oct  5 14:59 rc5.d
drwxr-xr-x  2 root    root      1024 Oct  5 14:59 rc6.d
```

Here's a quick rundown on the contents of the Red Hat configuration script directory:

◆ The *init.d* directory contains many of the rc scripts for doing a basic system configuration. The *init.d* directory contains the rc scripts that handle such basic tasks as configuring the name of the computer, mounting the disks, and configuring the network interfaces. Table 4-3 lists the scripts and the functions they configure.

◆ The rc script is responsible for setting up the very basic stuff such as your hostname on startup. Then it takes care of starting and stopping services as run levels change.

◆ You can add your own functions to the rc.local script as you deem necessary.

◆ The directories *rc0.d* through *rc6.d* contain the links to the specific scripts to be executed when changing to each run level. These links are ordered by their names to start up their respective scripts in sequence.

◆ The *rc.sysinit* is run only once when the system is booted; it starts the general network script and turns on the swap partition.

◆ The network script in */etc/init.d/network* executes scripts found in the */etc/sysconfig/network-scripts* directory and shown in Listing 4-10.The scripts listed in Listing 4-10 perform the functions of rc.inet1 — that is, setting up the network adapters and basic routing.

TABLE 4-3 THE RC SCRIPT RESPONSIBILITIES

Script Name	Function
atd	Starts the *at* daemon, which schedules one-time execution of commands or scripts.
crond	Starts the *crontab* daemon, which schedules and executes periodic tasks.

Script Name	Function
functions	Contains functions used by other scripts.
gpm	Starts the *gpm* program, to enable mouse use from a text screen.
halt	Gracefully and safely stops the computer for reboot or shutdown.
inet	Starts TCP/IP networking. Configures Ethernet adapter interface, and sets routing and other services.
kerneld	Automatically loads kernel modules when needed.
keytable	Maps your keyboard.
killall	Stops unnecessary daemons.
lpd	Starts and stops the *lpd* printing daemon.
network	Starts and stops networking.
nfsfs	Mounts and unmounts remote NFS file systems.
pcmcia	Initializes PCMCIA adapters for laptops.
random	Initializes a random number generator.
routed	Starts the *routed* daemon that uses the RIP protocol to automatically update the routing table.
rusersd	The *ruserd* daemon helps locate users on remote machines. (It must be allowed as a service on the target machine.)
rwhod	Lists the users logged into a remote machine. (It must be allowed as a service on the target machine.)
sendmail	Starts and stops the *sendmail* daemon, which transfers e-mail messages to their destination.
single	Sends computer into Single User (level 1) — also called Administrative state. It stops all daemons but retains all mounted partitions.
smb	Starts and stops Samba services (yeah!).
syslog	Starts system logging. This is very useful for security and other administrative functions.

Listing 4-10: Red Hat networking scripts — /etc/sysconfig/network-scripts

```
total 34
-rw-r--r--   1 root      root          125 Oct  3 16:48 ifcfg-eth0
-rwxr-xr-x   1 root      root          115 Oct  3 16:48 ifcfg-lo
lrwxrwxrwx   1 root      root           20 Sep 26 08:37 ifdown -> ../../../sbin/i
fdown
-rwxr-xr-x   1 root      root          267 Jul  7  1998 ifdown-post
-rwxr-xr-x   1 root      root         1199 Mar 15  1999 ifdown-ppp
-rwxr-xr-x   1 root      root          907 Jul  7  1998 ifdown-sl
lrwxrwxrwx   1 root      root           18 Sep 26 08:37 ifup -> ../../../sbin/ifu
p
-rwxr-xr-x   1 root      root        12968 Jul 26 08:52 ifup-aliases
-rwxr-xr-x   1 root      root         1072 Apr  6  1999 ifup-ipx
-rwxr-xr-x   1 root      root          724 Jul  7  1998 ifup-plip
-rwxr-xr-x   1 root      root          899 Jun 14 15:38 ifup-post
-rwxr-xr-x   1 root      root         3175 Jul 28 16:25 ifup-ppp
-rwxr-xr-x   1 root      root          349 Jun 18 15:23 ifup-routes
-rwxr-xr-x   1 root      root         1564 Jul  7  1998 ifup-sl
-rw-r--r--   1 root      root         1088 Apr  5  1999 network-functions
```

As you can see in Listing 4-11, *ifcfg-eth0* is simple. It just configures the shell network variables.

Listing 4-11: The ifcfg-eth0 script

```
DEVICE=eth0
IPADDR=192.168.1.254
NETMASK=255.255.255.0
NETWORK=192.168.1.0
BROADCAST=192.168.1.255
ONBOOT=yes
BOOTPROTO=none
```

The *ifup* script makes use of that basic information to set up the kernel routing table so the system can communicate with the network adapter interface. Listing 4-12 shows the script.

Listing 4-12: A sampling of the ifup script

```
#!/bin/bash
PATH=/sbin:/usr/sbin:/bin:/usr/bin

cd /etc/sysconfig/network-scripts
. network-functions
```

```
need_hostname

CONFIG=$1

[ -z "$CONFIG" ] && {
    echo "usage: ifup <device name>" >&2
    exit 1
}

[ -f "$CONFIG" ] || CONFIG=ifcfg-$CONFIG
[ -f "$CONFIG" ] || {
    echo "usage: ifup <device name>" >&2
    exit 1
}

if [ $UID != 0 ]; then
if [ -x /usr/sbin/usernetctl ]; then
        exec /usr/sbin/usernetctl $CONFIG up
    fi
    echo "Users cannot control this device." >&2
    exit 1
fi

source_config

{...}

exec /etc/sysconfig/network-scripts/ifup-post $CONFIG
```

Users and groups

A *user* is an account owned by an individual. You log on to a Linux system as a user — *root* is an all-powerful user — and you have access to certain files, depending on the access privileges that the system administrator defines for your account. Each user gets a home directory and a password; this information is stored in the */etc/passwd* file. You can read, write, and execute files depending on your access privileges. If you own a file, you generally can do anything you want to it.

Files also have a group membership. Each user belongs to one or more groups. Inclusion in a group gives you access to files belonging to that group. The file */etc/group* governs group membership.

Every file has permissions assigned to it. Three classifications of permissions exist: *user, group,* and *other*. The user permissions apply to the owner of the file. Group permissions apply to the group that the file is a member of. Other includes every user that is not either the owner or a member of the group.

Red Hat uses a new convention in which each user belongs to a User Private Group (UPG). Each user belongs to a unique group. When individual users need to share work, a new group is assigned to that project and the users get membership in the new group. In this way, people get common access to similar work and yet maintain their own privacy.

Networking and the OSI network model

The International Standards Organization (ISO) has developed the Open Systems Interconnect (OSI) networking model. This model logically separates higher- and lower-level networking functions into seven layers. In Figure 4-1, I reduce the model to four layers, to make it easier to understand.

1. Application	http, Telnet, FTP, SMB, etc.
2. Transport	TCP, UDP, ICMP
3. Network	IP
4. Physical/Data Link	Device Drivers (Ethernet, etc.)

Figure 4-1: The seven-layer OSI networking model, reconfigured as four layers

My four-layer interpretation of the OSI networking model has the following layers:

◆ The Application layer deals with high-level protocols, including SMB, NFS, FTP, SNTP, DNS, SNMP, and Telnet. Application programs that rely on these protocols access them directly. For example, the ftp program speaks the FTP protocol. If you write one of these programs, you are concerned with this layer.

◆ The Transport layer includes the Transmission Control Protocol (TCP), the User Datagram Protocol (UDP), and the Internet Control Message Protocol (ICMP). The Application layer protocols depend on these protocols to ensure that the packets they produce reliably get to their destination. By "reliably," I mean that either sooner or later – depending on the protocol – each packet is acknowledged or not, and the Transport layer protocol informs the Application layer as to the status of each packet.

   ■ TCP is called a connection-oriented protocol because it makes sure that when each packet is received by the intended host, it is acknowledged immediately and in sequence. Telnet uses TCP for the obvious reason that when you enter a character sequence (for example, *abcd*), you want each character to arrive in order and be acknowledged in a timely fashion.

- UDP is a connectionless protocol. It does not guarantee that a packet will reach its destination. The application is responsible for that. UDP is simpler than TCP, uses fewer resources, and is more efficient. Samba, for instance, uses UDP.

- ICMP is an auxiliary protocol used for troubleshooting and maintenance. PING uses it.

The UNIX/Linux ports (sometimes referred to as sockets) work at the Transport layer. You can connect to the TCP port 25 with Telnet, for example, and the *sendmail* daemon will talk to you. The Linux operating system provides this abstraction to ease the process of writing interprocess and internetwork communication.

◆ The Network layer contains the IP, or Internet Protocol, which deals with how to get each packet to its destination. It is responsible for encapsulating the higher-level packets (that is, a TCP packet) in an IP packet, which includes the destination and source addresses, the type of protocol, and several other chunks of information. If a packet is destined for a location outside of its LAN, routers down the line interpret this stuff and make their best guess as to where and how to forward the packet.

◆ The Physical/Data Link layer deals with the physical media such as the cable and the electrical bits that come into and out of the network adapter. (*Note:* If your only network connection is a PPP or SLIP link, you can think of that link as your network adapter.) In an Ethernet adapter, the circuits on the adapter know how to interpret the electrical signals coming out of the demodulator — the actual wire conducts radio frequency (RF) signals — and then turn them into binary bits. From there, the bits are compared to the permanent Ethernet MAC (Medium-Access Control) address and when they match, they are forwarded to the Network layer.

Each network adapter has a unique binary address. Each manufacturer gets a range of addresses so that no two adapters in the world should ever get the same address (who knows about bootleggers). Looking back at Listing 4-6, one line shows my Ethernet adapter's address in hexadecimal:

```
eth0: 3c509 at 0x310 tag 1, BNC port, address  00 20 af 38 6a aa, IRQ 11
```

To summarize, the OSI model logically breaks up the path that information — in the form of packets — takes in going from one computer to another as well as within the computer. The abstraction in this model enables you to ignore the messy details of whatever process you need to create or use. Regardless of the level on which you are working, this model enables you to understand how your LAN – as well as the entire Internet – functions.

Samba

The existence of Samba is the primary reason I am writing this book. It provides the straightforward and secure interface that NFS lacks, and it is considerably less expensive than Novell NetWare. Because Samba "speaks" the native Microsoft protocol, SMB, your Microsoft Windows PCs don't need any additional, expensive, or difficult-to-install software the way they do with NFS. Samba turns your Linux PC into a powerful Microsoft Windows file and print server.

NFS is more complex to set up than Samba. It is not terribly difficult, but you need more patience. But the real problem is purchasing and configuring the software that makes your Windows client speak the NFS protocol. If you want to use Windows 3.X or MS-DOS as a client, you have to purchase software such as PC-NFS from SunSoft, Inc. (http://www.sunsoft.com); Windows 95 and 98 require software such as DiskAccess from Intergraph Corp. (http://www.intergraph.com).

When you install Windows out of the box, it comes equipped with Microsoft Client and Microsoft TCP/IP. You have to choose to install TCP/IP, but it is part of the Windows package. Microsoft Client speaks the *Service Message Block (SMB)* protocol by default. That protocol is carried by the near-universal Internet Protocol (IP) or TCP/IP. TCP/IP is the default protocol for Linux, so Windows and Linux machines can converse. (Previously, with a UNIX/NFS server, you had to purchase additional software to install on the Microsoft Windows PC to make it speak NFS. This purchase was expensive because each PC client needed the software. Now, the single Linux PC already speaks the native Microsoft language.)

The Samba protocol

The SMB protocol is responsible for negotiating the use of remote files and resources such as printers. Figure 4-2 shows the file *A*, which physically exists on the Linux server – in SMB terminology, it holds the *share*. When the Windows client wants to use this file, the client must tell the server to make A available to it and then to transfer the file's contents across the network. SMB is responsible for handling the details of the transaction negotiation.

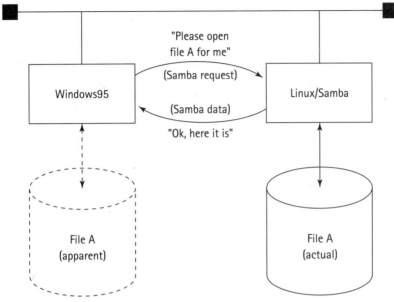

Figure 4-2: The server holds the file that the client needs.

For example, assume that I want to open the Microsoft Word file, CHAP_4.DOC, which is physically stored on the hard drive of my Linux server. I have the Linux directory containing CHAP_4.DOC mapped as the network *E:* drive. When I choose File → Open and then select E:\CHAP_4.DOC in Word, Windows sends an SMB request to the Linux box. Figure 4-3 shows a diagram of the process that occurs as the client asks for file access from the server.

After the server receives a valid SMB request, it accesses its own file system to get the information. Samba acts as the interface between the SMB packets arriving on the network and the Linux operating system.

THE SAMBA DAEMONS

The heart of Samba are the programs smbd and nmbd. They are usually run as daemons, which are processes that run all the time. Red Hat runs them as daemons by default. You have the option of launching them from *inetd* (a superdaemon of sorts that looks for requests for any programs it has control of—as defined in *inetd.conf*—and launches them as needed). But that method slows Samba down and the overhead of running smbd and nmbd as daemons is low, so the daemon method really does work best.

The nmbd process enables the Linux server to be browsed by other machines. The smbd daemon processes the SMB packets as they arrive on the network, and negotiates with the Linux kernel for access to its resources or shares. If a file is specified, the resource is a file; a printer request accesses a printer.

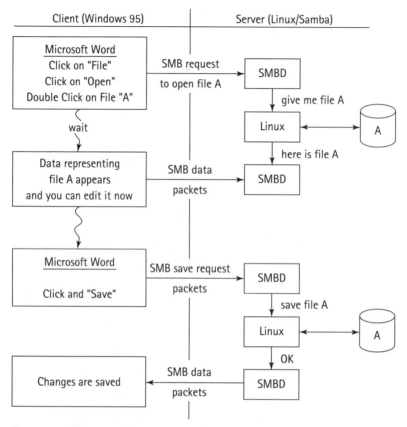

Figure 4-3: Client negotiates with the server for access to the file.

Actually, in the case of a printer, smbd stores the information to be printed in a print queue. For example, when I print CHAP_4.DOC to my network printer, Windows sends the document data to the Linux server; smbd saves the data to */var/spool/lpd* and launches a print request on that file. The *lpd* daemon (enter *ps - x | grep lpd* to view it) is the process that handles the print request.

In the case of a file, smbd sends the data to the kernel, which ultimately saves it to disk.

The file *smb.conf* stores all the configuration information that smbd and nmbd use. Listing 4-13 shows part of the *smb.conf* file that Red Hat uses as a default. It should be on your system already, if you configured your system as described in Chapter 1.

Listing 4-13: The Samba smb.conf file

```
# This is the main Samba configuration file. You should read the
# smb.conf(5) manual page in order to understand the options listed
# here. Samba has a huge number of configurable options (perhaps too
# many!) most of which are not shown in this example
#
# Any line which starts with a ; (semi-colon) or a # (hash)
# is a comment and is ignored. In this example we will use a #
# for commentry and a ; for parts of the config file that you
# may wish to enable
#
# NOTE: Whenever you modify this file you should run the command "testparm"
# to check that you have not made any basic syntactic errors.
#
#======================= Global Settings =======================================
[global]

# workgroup = NT-Domain-Name or Workgroup-Name
   workgroup = MYGROUP

# server string is the equivalent of the NT Description field
   server string = Samba Server

# This option is important for security. It allows you to restrict
# connections to machines which are on your local network. The
# following example restricts access to two C class networks and
# the "loopback" interface. For more examples of the syntax see
# the smb.conf man page
;    hosts allow = 192.168.1. 192.168.2. 127.

# if you want to automatically load your printer list rather
# than setting them up individually then you'll need this
   printcap name = /etc/printcap
   load printers = yes

# It should not be necessary to spell out the print system type unless
# yours is non-standard. Currently supported print systems include:
# bsd, sysv, plp, lprng, aix, hpux, qnx
;    printing = bsd

# Uncomment this if you want a guest account, you must add this to /etc/passwd
# otherwise the user "nobody" is used
;  guest account = pcguest
{...}
```

Unless you have configured your printer to work under this configuration, the only thing this sets you up to do is work in the *root* home directory. It's not terribly interesting except that it works! It's fascinating that my keystrokes are being converted into electrical signals, which are then converted into electrical signals in binary form, shunted through a complex piece of silicon (a mere Intel 486), sent to other complex slabs of sand, converted into radio frequency energy to reappear in another room, converted back to bits and stored as magnetic domains on a mechanically spinning disk, and so on. Sure, it's only my ranting, but lots of things have to happen to save this ranting on a spinning disk.

THE SAMBA UTILITIES

The utilities – *smbstatus, smbclient, nmbclient,* and so on – play an important role in configuring Samba. I showed you how to use them to perform basic debugging in Chapter 2. As you build a more complex – production – system in Chapters 6 and 10, they become increasingly important. The more shares, clients, and users you build into your system, the more you need the utilities. Table 4-4 gives a synopsis of their uses.

TABLE 4-4 SAMBA UTILITIES

Name	Description
smbstatus	Displays the shares (resources) currently exported by Samba.
smbclient	Acts as a Linux-based Microsoft (smb) client. Useful for debugging.
nmbclient	Acts as a Linux-based browser client. Useful for debugging.
smbfs	A file system that works with the SMB protocol. With it you can mount SMB shares on Linux computers.
smbmount	Used to mount an *smbfs* on a Linux system.

The Red Hat publisher's edition CD-ROM

The Red Hat CD-ROM itself is an invaluable resource. It contains not only the full Linux distribution, but also many other tools and documents. Table 4-5 lists the directories found on the CD-ROM.

Table 4-5 RED HAT CD-ROM CONTENTS

Directory	Contents
/RPMS/RedHat	The kernel and file system images installed directly onto hard disk.
doc	Red Hat and general documentation.
dosutils	MS-DOS programs and files used for creating Linux bootable floppy disks and creating or modifying hard disk partitions for installing Linux.
images	The kernel image that is copied directly to a floppy, which can then be used to boot Linux. This directory also contains supplemental floppy images used for PCMCIA disks.
live	The files, library, and programs as they exist on your disk after you install them. For example, you should be able to mount the *live/usr* directory from your CD-ROM and not need to have it on your hard disk. This is not a satisfactory way to work, because the CD-ROM is probably much slower than the hard disk, but it is possible.
misc	The *autoboot* program and source code.
rr_moved	Empty.

When you install the system for the first time, you use the MS-DOS program FIPS.EXE to repartition the hard drive in a nondestructive manner. You use the program RAWRITE.EXE to create a bootable Linux floppy disk; RAWRITE.EXE uses an image file from the \IMAGES directory.

When you install Linux for the first time (as I describe in Chapter 1), the installation program and the files it accesses are contained in the \DOSUTILS and \RPMS directories on this disk. If and when you upgrade or reinstall your system, you use the same programs.

The X Window System

Linux works just fine from a simple shell interface (that is, the *shell prompt*). An experienced administrator or user can do many things by entering commands at the shell prompts—this is analogous to working from the MS-DOS C: prompt. In fact, an administrator should perform a large percentage of tasks by entering explicit commands from the command line, to maintain an understanding of the underlying mechanics of the system. However, users of a Linux system – and administrators, to a lesser extent – greatly benefit from using a *Graphical User Interface (GUI)*. One reason is that you can do many things at once by separating tasks into different windows. Many tasks – for example, Web browsing – are best done graphically.

The X Window system – more commonly referred to as simply X – is a GUI just like Windows 95, 98 or NT in that it insulates you from the underlying operating system. However, it operates "on top" of Linux as an application. This is similar to the old Windows 3.X that uses MS-DOS as its base, while the Windows GUI is tightly integrated with its operating system. The Linux version of the X Window system is called *XFree86*, reflecting its allegiance to the Free Software Foundation. It is produced by the XFREE86 Project, Inc. (The Free Software Foundation (FSF) is described further in CD-ROM Chapter 2.)

XFree86 is stored primarily in the */usr/X11R6* directory. The executable programs and their libraries are stored in subdirectories. The configuration files, including XF86Config, are stored in the */etc/X11* directory. The *.xinitrc* file, which can configure the look and feel of your X Window main screen, is generally stored in your login directory.

If *XFree86* is anything, it is highly adaptable. You can configure it in so many ways that it is very confusing to the novice, and even to more experienced users. When I first installed it, I was lucky and actually got it working rather quickly with the help of the configuration program *Xconfig*. However, it quickly broke, and I spent the next few days trying to recover the system. Red Hat obviously recognizes this problem as a major hurdle to mass acceptance, because the Red Hat distribution includes the reasonably easy-to-use *Xconfigurator* program. It works well. I have used it to configure several systems with different VGA cards and each worked on the first try.

You can obtain more information about *XFree86* by visiting the following Web site: http://www.xfree86.org.

The GNU General Public License (GPL)

Linux uses the GNU General Public License (GPL). The Free Software Foundation developed the GPL as the key concept to its goal that software should be freely distributable. (For more information on the Free Software Foundation, see CD-ROM Chapter 2.) To that end, the GPL is designed to promote the freedom to distribute its software. The GPL does not necessarily mean that the software is free. Red Hat charges for the value it adds to Linux in the form of the CD-ROM and the configuration tools.

The GPL is printed at the end of this book, and I recommend that you read it. But here is a brief summary of its key points (I am not a lawyer; these are just my own opinions based on my reading of the GPL):

◆ Software published under the GPL is not in the public domain. The public does not own the software because it is copyrighted to the author(s) and protected by all international copyright laws. The author(s) choose(es) to allow you to use it in almost any way you want, but you do not own it.

◆ GPL published software is not shareware. Shareware authors own the copyright but ask you — without enforcement — to send them money after using their software.

◆ GPL software can be distributed for free or for a fee. When you get Linux off the Internet using anonymous ftp (see Chapter 5), the software is generally GPL and no charge is attached. When you buy a Linux distribution CD-ROM, you pay for the CD-ROM. Whatever GPL software comes on the CD-ROM, however, cannot be restricted. If I want to, I can give you the Linux source code, which I obtained on the Red Hat CD-ROM.

◆ GPL software can be modified and redistributed, but the new version must be covered by the GPL.

◆ GPL software must advertise that it is covered under the GPL.

This is an ingenious mechanism. First, it enables unhindered distribution of GPL software. Second, it enables those who add value to the base software and thus propagate it further to make money. Finally, it prevents any person or organization from gaining a restrictive hold on GPL software in the future.

Conclusion

I could cover much more in this chapter, but my goal is to outline the most important fundamentals in the way that I would want to be taught. As you read further in this book and gain hands-on experience building and managing a Linux/Samba network, you will pick up more details. This chapter offers a framework from which you can proceed with confidence.

Summary

In this chapter, some of the internal workings of Linux were revealed:

◆ Rushing to get a system running in Chapter 1 precludes gaining much understanding of what's under the hood. Administering a network in the long term requires you to understand how it works.

◆ Understanding the meaning of the term *Linux* is important when discussing its internal workings. The meaning of Linux depends on the context in which it is used. It can refer to the entire system, or the kernel, or some combination of the two.

◆ The kernel is the heart of the Linux system. It controls when and how long processes are processed by the microprocessor (for example, the Pentium). It also controls access to the file system.

◆ The Linux *file system* translates the raw bytes that exist on disk drives into the files and directories that you use every day. It is important to understand how Linux works in order to manage a Linux system correctly.

◆ Understanding the Linux startup process is important to gaining an understanding of the total system. The kernel is loaded into memory and determines what devices it can use. It starts the *init* process, which starts the computer in a single-user mode for safety and guides it to whatever user state (multiple user, X Window, and so on) is defined in the *inittab* file. It also starts the *rc* scripts that configure everything from what disks are mounted to the network setup.

◆ Understanding the OSI network model helps you to conceptually understand how networks work. It is a logical protocol and separates the different types of processes that need to occur in order for networks to work. It would be much more difficult to modularize network communications without its discipline. Although the programs that it codifies don't make the distinctions it does (because they would be unwieldy), conceptually, it is useful.

◆ If Linux is the heart of the system, then Samba makes it practical. It replaces NFS as an economical way of connecting Microsoft Windows computers. It "speaks" the Windows native language, whereas NFS does not and requires expensive software to communicate.

◆ Originating as a Microsoft networking protocol, the Samba protocol, *smb*, provides a powerful method for connecting Microsoft Windows clients to Linux servers. Samba provides the interface between networked resource requests from Windows machines and the Linux kernel.

◆ Processing Samba network traffic is the job of the Samba daemons — smbd and nmbd. They run continuously in the background on the Linux server.

◆ Using the Samba utilities provides a useful, if not essential, set of tools for building and troubleshooting your client-server network.

◆ The Red Hat CD-ROM contains much more than just the Linux system. It also contains a wealth of documents, manual pages, HOWTOs, FAQs, and utilities.

◆ The X Window system is the graphical interface similar in some respects to the Windows desktop. It provides the basis for many applications — including WordPerfect — and as a management tool. Without it, Linux would be a dull child.

◆ Linux and its GNU applications are copyrighted under the General Public License (GPL), which allows users to distribute it for free or for a fee but not to restrict its redistribution.

Chapter 5

Configuring Red Hat Linux

IN THIS CHAPTER

◆ Using the Red Hat Package Manager (RPM)

◆ Using the RPM query function

◆ Installing additional documentation and networking and compiler software with RPM

◆ Removing packages with RPM

◆ Upgrading packages with RPM

◆ Understanding the basic parts of the X Window system

◆ Configuring Linux using the Red Hat Control Panel

◆ Configuring Linux using LinuxConf

◆ Introducing Linux modules

◆ Exploring the concept of building a static or monolithic kernel

◆ Customizing your system by modifying the Red Hat startup scripts

THIS CHAPTER INTRODUCES some of the tools and techniques that you can use to configure Linux. Of course, you have been configuring Linux since installing it in Chapter 1. However, those chapters performed configuration on the fly, so to speak, in an ad hoc manner. In this chapter, you are shown how to configure Linux system in a more systematic fashion.

Red Hat provides three configuration systems that represent important evolutionary steps in the professionalization of Linux. Red Hat developed two of these systems, and the third is another proprietary system that Red Hat includes in its distribution. The first examples in this chapter discuss these systems and show you how to use them.

Another important aspect of Linux systems administration involves configuration of the kernel. The standard kernel that comes with Red Hat is a good base, but it doesn't include all the subsystems necessary for doing such things as establishing Point-to-Point Protocol (PPP) connections – that is, TCP/IP connectivity over a serial, or modem, line. One of the great features of Linux is that you can configure it on the fly. In other words, you can insert modules that include extra features such as PPP or other device drivers, while the kernel is running. You may use some of these extra features so often that you want to compile them permanently into the Linux kernel. You can easily recompile Linux, and I show you how to do so in this chapter.

Understanding the Red Hat Package Manager (RPM)

One of the great frustrations of systems administration is managing software packages and systems. Adding, deleting, modifying, and just plain inventory is a constant chore. I have several computers that I use on a daily basis. I have a good idea of what software I have and where to find the software that I use frequently, but my systems also have lots of software and configuration files that I have to rediscover when I find the need to use them. Add to that the necessity of changing a package, and I start getting really angry as I pick my way through endless directory trees and libraries. I'm not organized enough to make a formal database of the stuff — and doing so would take a lot of work. I just stumble along the best I can. There must be a better way.

The Red Hat Package Manager (RPM) goes a long way toward providing that better way of handling the complexities of systems administration. It automatically installs, uninstalls, and upgrades software. It operates like any other Linux command with the use of command-line options. RPM uses its database to keep track of what's what and where, and thus relieves you of that messy task.

RPM is a big improvement over distributions such as Slackware. In the past, I never hesitated to install a new package (How can you resist free software?), but I took deep breaths before upgrading those packages. Very often, I would completely delete stuff I knew I didn't have to delete, just to ensure that the upgrade would not stumble over its parents. Upgrading to significantly newer kernels entailed a number of disk formats! As you can imagine, I really appreciate the simplicity that RPM brings to the process of installing upgrades.

An RPM package consists of an archive of files and information describing its name, version, and contents. Packages are created to provide a particular Linux function. For instance, the Samba RPM package contains the Samba daemons, configuration files, manual pages, and other documentation.

RPM has 11 operational modes. (Red Hat says 10 but I include the upgrade as its own mode.) Five of these modes are most important to a systems administrator:

- ◆ **Install:** Install the package with the given options. Here's the syntax for this mode:

  ```
  rpm -i install-options package_file
  ```

- ◆ **Upgrade:** Install the upgrade package with the given options. You use the following syntax for this mode:

  ```
  rpm -U upgrade-options package_file
  ```

◆ **Erase (uninstall):** Erase or uninstall the package with the given options (removes all possible dependencies). This mode has the following syntax:

```
rpm -e erase-options package_file
```

◆ **Query:** Find out if a package is already installed and where the package may be located. Query mode has the following syntax:

```
rpm -q query-options
```

◆ **Verify:** Compare an installed package with the original, pristine package. The comparison includes size, a check sum, permissions, type, owner, and group of each file. Here's the syntax you use for verify mode:

```
rpm -V|-y|--verify verify-options
```

The last six modes are for software distribution and are of less interest to a pure administrator, but I mention them for completeness:

◆ **Build:** Create the RPM packages themselves. (This mode is mostly for software developers.) Here's the syntax for build mode:

```
rpm -bO build-options <package_spec>+ B
```

◆ **Rebuild database:** Rebuild the database with the package configuration information. You use the following syntax for this mode:

```
rpm --rebuilddb
```

◆ **Fix permissions:** Reset the original file permissions to the files belonging to a package.

◆ **Signature check:** Verify that a package's integrity and origin are correct. This mode checks the digital signature of a package to make sure that it has not been tampered with.

◆ **Set owners and groups:** Resets the original owner and group to the files belonging to a package.

◆ **Show RC:** Displays the values of the rpmrc file. The rpmrc file is used to set various parameters used by RPM.

'You can find additional information on RPM in the manual page man rpm. You can find additional technical information — file formats and so on — in the text files in the /usr/doc/rpm-2.4.10 directory.

To make use of the RPM operating modes, you use various options or parameters. Some parameters are general purpose and work with any of the functions. Table 5-1 describes the general RPM parameters and their functions. You can use these parameters with any of the modes that I describe in the preceding lists.

TABLE 5-1 RPM KEY GENERAL PARAMETERS (CAN BE USED WITH ANY MODE)

Parameter	Function
-vv	Print debugging information.
--quiet	Print as little as possible — normally, only error messages are displayed.
--help	Print a longer usage message than normal.
--version	Print the version number of RPM.
--rcfile <file>	Specify a different personal setup file, rather than $HOME/rpmrc or /etc/rpmrc.
--root <dir>	Use dir as the top-level directory for all operations.

Some parameters are specific to one mode or another. You can customize the install and upgrade functions to suit your needs. Table 5-2 lists the key parameters you use with install or upgrade.

TABLE 5-2 KEY RPM INSTALL AND UPGRADE PARAMETERS

Parameter	Function
--force	Force the replacement of a package or file.
-h, --hash	Print 50 dots, or hash marks, as a package is installed.
--oldpackage	Replace a newer package with an older one. Normally, RPM balks if it is asked to write over a newer package.
--percent	Print percentage to completion during installation.
--replacefiles	Force previously installed files from other packages to be replaced.
--replacepkgs	Force previously installed packages to be replaced.
--root <dir>	Use another directory as a start point or root.
--nodeps	Skip the package dependency check before installing a package.

Parameter	Function
--noscripts	Skip to pre- and post-installation scripts.
--excludedocs	Skip installation of documentation.
--includedocs	Install documentation files. Used with excludedocs to be more specific.
--allfiles	Installs, or upgrades all the files that belongs to a package.
--allmatches	Remove all versions of the specified package. You normally get an error message if there are multiple versions of a package.
--notriggers	Do not execute scripts that would normally be run as part of the package removal.
--ignoresize	Install a package without checking to see if enough file system space exists.
--test	Perform the installation without installing anything. Perform a "dry run."
-U, --upgrade	Install the new package over the old one. Remove the old package.

With RPM, you can specify that the package file is a URL. In other words, you can install or upgrade a package directly from your Internet connection!

The uninstall option is a variation of the install function. Table 5-3 shows the key options available for uninstalling RPM packages.

TABLE 5-3 KEY RPM UNINSTALL PARAMETERS

Parameter	Function
--noscripts	Skip to the pre- and post-uninstall scripts.
--nodeps	Skip checking dependencies before uninstallation.
--test	Execute the uninstallation steps without deleting anything.
--allfiles	Installs, or upgrades all the files that belongs to a package.
--allmatches	Remove all versions of the specified package. You normally get an error message if there are multiple versions of a package.

Continued

TABLE 5-3 KEY RPM UNINSTALL PARAMETERS *(Continued)*

Parameter	Function
--notriggers	Do not execute scripts that would normally be run as part of the package removal.
--ignoresize	Install a package without checking to see if enough file system space exists.
--test	Do not actually remove the package. Perform a "dry run" instead.

You use the query parameters to determine which packages are installed on your present system, which packages are available on CD-ROM, which files belong to a particular package, and other information about a package. Table 5-4 shows the parameters you use with query.

TABLE 5-4 RPM QUERY PARAMETERS

Parameter	Function
-a	Find all installed packages.
--whatrequires capability	Locate packages that require a particular capability.
--whatprovides virtual	Locate packages that require a virtual capability.
-f file	Locate packages that own a file.
-p package_file	Query an uninstalled package. The package_file can be a URL.

Information Selection Options

-I	Show various package information.
-R	List packages that this one depends on (same as --requires).
--provides	Show what a package does.
-l	List files in the package.
-s	Display the states of files in the package (implies -l). The state of each file is either normal, not installed, or replaced.
-d	List only documentation files (implies -l).

Parameter	Function
Information Selection Options	
-c	List only configuration files (implies -l).
--scripts	List shell scripts used for installation and uninstallation.
--dump	List dump file information as follows: path size mtime md5sum mode owner group isconfig isdoc rdev sym-link. This parameter must be used with at least one of -l, -c, -d.

You use the verify parameters to determine which parts of a package differ from the original package. This option is useful for determining the state of your system. For example, if you are having problems with an application and need to determine whether the configuration files have been changed, you can use this function to find out what has changed. Table 5-5 shows the parameters you use with verify.

TABLE 5-5 KEY RPM VERIFY PARAMETERS

Parameter	Function
--verify	Verify a package installation using the same package specification options as -q.
--dbpath <dir>	Use <dir> as the directory for the database.
--root <dir>	Use <dir> as the top-level directory.
--nodeps	Do not verify package dependencies.
--nomd5	Do not verify file md5 checksums.
--nofiles	Do not verify file attributes.
--setperms	Set the file permissions to those in the package database using the same package.

I leave it to you to investigate the package building functions. As always, the man page for RPM provides excellent documentation.

Now that you have an overview of RPM, some examples are in order. The Red Hat installation process, which I introduce in Chapter 1, uses the RPM system to install the default packages plus the Samba package that I had you specify. Consequently, you have RPM packages available that you can use for practice. The beauty of the RPM system is that if something goes wrong during your experimentation, you can easily recover. The RPM system takes care of the messy details.

Querying

Because you already have RPM packages installed, I start the examples with the Query function so you can see what's installed. I show you how to inventory the packages installed in Chapter 1 and then proceed to find details about the contents of an individual package.

FINDING ALL YOUR SYSTEM'S PACKAGES

Before you install any package, examine what the Red Hat installation process (which I describe in Chapter 1) has installed on your system. To display all installed packages, enter the following command with the -a option:

```
rpm -q -a
```

Listing 5-1 shows a sampling of the packages that you installed in Chapter 1. Recall that I had you choose only the default Red Hat packages plus Samba in the section "Installing Red Hat Linux" in Chapter 1. The remaining software that you use in this book will be installed manually.

Listing 5-1: A sampling of the default Red Hat installation packages plus Samba

```
setup-2.0.3-1
filesystem-1.3.4-4
basesystem-6.0-4
ldconfig-1.9.5-15
AfterStep-1.7.90-3
AfterStep-APPS-990329-2
aktion-0.3.3-2
AnotherLevel-0.9-1
glibc-2.1.2-2
chkconfig-1.0.6-1
mktemp-1.5-1
termcap-9.12.6-15
libtermcap-2.0.8-14
bash-1.14.7-16
apmd-3.0beta8-1
arpwatch-2.1a4-10
ncurses-4.2-18
info-3.12f-4
```

```
fileutils-4.0-2
grep-2.3-2
ash-0.2-17
at-3.1.7-10
```

This listing provides a good description of the Linux system. Every piece of software is treated as a package. This approach enables Red Hat to modularize its own installation process.

RETRIEVING INFORMATION ABOUT A PACKAGE

Examine the Samba package. Note that unlike the install, uninstall, and upgrade modes, the query mode does not require that you specify the full package name. Instead, you can use the generic name, as in the following example for Samba:

```
rpm -q -i samba
```

This command displays the general information about the Samba package, as shown in Listing 5-2.

Listing 5-2: The RPM Samba package information

```
[root@bart chap_7]# rpm -q -i samba
Name        : samba            Relocations: (not relocateable)
Version     : 2.0.5a               Vendor: Red Hat Software
Release     : 3                Build Date: Mon Jul 26 14:39:20 1999
Install date: Sun Sep 26 08:41:51 1999  Build Host: porky.devel.redhat.com
Group       : System Environment/Daemons  Source RPM: samba-2.0.5a-3.src.rpm
Size        : 5927864             License: GNU GPL Version 2
Packager    : Red Hat Software <http://developer.redhat.com/bugzilla>
Summary     : Samba SMB server.
Description :
Samba provides an SMB server which can be used to provide
network services to SMB (sometimes called "Lan Manager")
clients, including various versions of MS Windows, OS/2,
and other Linux machines.  Samba uses NetBIOS over TCP/IP
(NetBT) protocols and does NOT need NetBEUI (Microsoft
Raw NetBIOS frame) protocol.

Samba-2 features an almost working NT Domain Control
capability and includes the new SWAT (Samba Web Administration
Tool) that allows samba's smb.conf file to be remotely managed
using your favourite web browser. For the time being this is
being enabled on TCP port 901 via inetd.

Please refer to the WHATSNEW.txt document for fixup information.
This binary release includes encrypted password support.
```

```
Please read the smb.conf file and ENCRYPTION.txt in the
docs directory for implementation details.

NOTE: Red Hat Linux 5.X Uses PAM which has integrated support
for Shadow passwords. Do NOT recompile with the SHADOW_PWD option
enabled. Red Hat Linux has built in support for quotas in PAM.
```

As you can see in the sample listing, this command displays information about the version number, and the installation date and time. The type of package – Networking in this case – is shown, too. Recall that Samba was picked from the Networking group back in Chapter 1. An abstract of the package function is also displayed. This listing provides quite a lot of useful information. If you compare the output from Red Hat's query mode to that of the traditional tar file, you can see that Red Hat is a superior system.

 TIP A tar file is a good format for combining one or more files into one file or a pipe for storage or transport. You can use the tar command to copy files or directories from one place to another (including over a network), to a storage device such as a tape, or to a regular file.

LISTING A PACKAGE'S FILES
If you want to find out which files make up a package, you use the -l option. Enter the following command to examine Samba's files:

```
rpm -q -l samba
```

Listing 5-3 shows that Samba has quite a few files hiding in various places.

Listing 5-3: A sampling of the files that compose the Samba system

```
/etc/codepages
/etc/codepages/src
/etc/codepages/src/codepage_def.437
/etc/codepages/src/codepage_def.737
/etc/codepages/src/codepage_def.850
/etc/codepages/src/codepage_def.852
/etc/codepages/src/codepage_def.861
/etc/codepages/src/codepage_def.866
/etc/codepages/src/codepage_def.932
/etc/c
odepages/src/codepage_def.936
/etc/codepages/src/codepage_def.949
```

```
/etc/codepages/src/codepage_def.950
/etc/lmhosts
/etc/logrotate.d/samba
/etc/pam.d/samba
/etc/rc.d/init.d/smb
/etc/smb.conf
/etc/smbusers
```

Most of the files in this listing are document files, but just try keeping track of them without any help. You eventually get to know the structure of a system such as Samba because it is integral to your client-server network. But without the help of Red Hat's query mode, you would never remember where everything is located.

LISTING A PACKAGE'S CONFIGURATION FILES

Another system administration job is to configure a software package. The -c parameter lists just the configuration files for a package. Using Samba as the example package again, enter the following command:

```
rpm -q -c samba
```

Listing 5-4 shows the configuration files that RPM finds for you. Note that these files are stored in nine separate directories. It would take a lot of work to trace these files down, and you couldn't be completely certain that you had found all the files. RPM solves that problem.

Listing 5-4: The Samba configuration files found by RPM

```
/etc/codepages/src/codepage_def.437
/etc/codepages/src/codepage_def.737
/etc/codepages/src/codepage_def.850
/etc/codepages/src/codepage_def.852
/etc/codepages/src/codepage_def.861
/etc/codepages/src/codepage_def.866
/etc/codepages/src/codepage_def.932
/etc/codepages/src/codepage_def.936
/etc/codepages/src/codepage_def.949
/etc/codepages/src/codepage_def.950
/etc/lmhosts
/etc/logrotate.d/samba
/etc/pam.d/samba
/etc/rc.d/init.d/smb
/etc/smb.conf
/etc/smbusers
/usr/sbin/samba
```

The familiar smb.conf file is the main configuration file. The files in the rc.d directories are pointers to /etc/rc.d/init.d/smb, which is the start and stop Samba script. This listing of configuration files tends to be useful information for a systems administrator.

FINDING THE PACKAGE THAT OWNS A FILE

As the final query example, use the -f parameter to locate the package that owns a particular file. Maybe you are having a good time one Friday night looking through the /etc/rc.d/rc3.d directory, and you wonder what the S99local file is used for. You do a man on S99local and rc.local but don't find any entries. Hmmm, how do you find out what it is? No problem, enter the following command:

```
rpm -q -f /etc/rc.d/rc3.d/S99local
```

It tells you that the file belongs to the initscripts package. So you do a man on initscripts and all the variations you can think of, and you don't find a man-page entry for it. You hope that initscripts is a simple program to startup scripts but you don't know for sure — UNIX and Linux can be deceptive sometimes. So you decide to use the RPM system again. Enter the following variation of the query:

```
rpm -q -i initscripts
```

You get the information shown in Listing 5-5.

Listing 5-5: RPM shows which package a file belongs to.

```
Name         : initscripts          Relocations: (not relocateable)
Version      : 4.28                      Vendor: Red Hat Software
Release      : 1                     Build Date: Thu Jul 29 15:53:37 1999
Install date: Sun Sep 26 08:37:12 1999    Build Host: porky.devel.redhat.com
Group        : System Environment/Base   Source RPM: initscripts-4.28-1.src.r
pm
Size         : 184324                    License: GPL
Packager     : Red Hat Software <http://developer.redhat.com/bugzilla>
Summary      : The inittab file and the /etc/rc.d scripts.
Description :
The initscripts package contains the basic system scripts used to boot
your Red Hat system, change run levels, and shut the system down cleanly.
Initscripts also contains the scripts that activate and deactivate most
network interfaces.
```

Now you have enough information to confirm that it is what you thought it is. It was installed by Red Hat default in Chapter 1. Good job.

You can also determine what RPM package a file — for instance, bash — belongs to as follows:

```
rpm -qf `rpm -qla |grep -i bash`
```

The command string within the "backwards" quotes (`) indicates that the Linux shell — bash in most cases — is to execute the command(s) and feed the results into the overall command. The vertical bars (|) indicate a Linux pipe which is used to send the output of one command to the input of another. In this case, the commands in between the ticks extracts all of the files contained by all of the installed RPM packages and filters out all but those that contain the string "bash." That output is sent to the rpm –qf command which will tell you what package owns the file. The output of this example shows that several packages, including the bash-1.14.7-16 RPM, could own a file called "bash."

INSTALLING PACKAGES

One of the most common systems administration functions is adding and removing software packages to a computer. Adding and deleting software is a generally imprecise and often difficult administrative function, so get used to it. Fortunately, RPM makes this fact of systems administration life much easier.

There's not much to worry about with RPM. Just choose the package, enter the parameters, and hit the Return key. RPM tells you if have any problems. Generally, RPM stops execution if it encounters problems, but in some cases it prompts you for additional information and continues. The following examples cover many possibilities.

First, however, you should get an overview of which packages are available. You need to mount the Red Hat CD-ROM, if it is not already mounted. To mount the CD-ROM, log in as root and enter the following command:

```
mount -r -t iso9660 /dev/cdrom /mnt/cdrom
```

If you used a CD-ROM drive to install Linux, Red Hat created an entry in your /etc/fstab file — fstab stands for filesystem table and stores the mounting information for all drives on your system. You can save yourself some work when you mount disks by giving the mount command the name of the drive's mount point as a parameter. Therefore, you can mount the CD-ROM by entering the command: mount /mnt/cdrom.

Enter the following command to list the RPM packages on the CD-ROM:

```
ls -l /mnt/cdrom/RedHat/RPMS
```

You will see several screens of RPM packages.

 TIP If you are using Gnome and insert a CD-ROM, the Gnome RPM gui will be launched automatically. That gui performs all of the functions that the rpm command can do.

INSTALLING THE C COMPILER

In this section you are shown how to install some packages that you'll need in the near future – such as the GNU Make package and C compiler (gcc). The packages that you have used so far have come precompiled, but you often need to compile programs from their source. One huge advantage that Linux has over commercial UNIX is that it comes with source code without strings attached. While the RPM system is wonderful, it doesn't include everything you may need. Consequently, you will need to compile software directly into the kernel.

An essential utility to the compilers is the make facility. A make file is used to semiautomate the compilation – and often the installation – of a software package. It can be used not only to compile software but also to install it and keep book-keeping up-to-date. In this way, it is similar to RPM.

Leave it at that for now, and install the RPM make package by logging on as root and entering the following commands (note that the substituting the asterisk for the numeric version number precludes having to enter the full file name):

```
rpm -i -v -h /mnt/cdrom/RedHat/RPMS/make*
```

Many files created by the Make utility in Linux use the GNU C compiler (gcc), so you need to install gcc and its pre-compiler ccp. If you list the Red Hat CD-ROM RPMS directory and look for gcc, you can see that it is there (/mnt/cdrom/RedHat/RPMS/egcs-1.1.2-24.i386.rpm). Go ahead and install it by entering the following commands (note that the i, v, and h parameters have been combined):

```
rpm -ivh /mnt/cdrom/RedHat/RPMS/ccp*.rpm
```

```
rpm -ivh /mnt/cdrom/RedHat/RPMS/egcs-1*.rpm
```

Most C programs need some additional libraries. Enter the following command to install the following library:

```
rpm -ivh /mnt/cdrom/RedHat/RPMS/glibc-devel*
```

The glibc-devel package requires a library of common functions and gets the following message:

```
failed dependencies:
        kernel-headers is needed by glibc-devel-2.1.2-2
```

You install that package first and then the glibc-devel package by entering the following commands:

```
rpm -ivh /mnt/cdrom/RedHat/RPMS/kernel-headers*.rpm
rpm -ivh /mnt/cdrom/RedHat/RPMS/glibc-devel*.rpm
```

Many programs also make use of the Linux kernel header files.

TIP Compiling many Linux software systems, especially the kernel source, requires that their include files be located in a standard place — either the /usr/include or /usr/src/linux/include directories. Symbolic links placed in the /usr/include directory enable include files to be located in either location, so add them by entering the following commands:

```
cd /usr/include
ln -sf /usr/src/linux/include/asm-i386 asm
ln -sf /usr/src/linux/include/linux linux
ln -sf /usr/src/linux/include/scsi scsi
```

Now your Linux box can compile C programs using the Make utility.

UNINSTALLING
With multi-gigabyte disks now commonplace, there's no longer a need to worry about running out of disk space. That said, you don't want to keep unneeded stuff around just because you have room for it. You still can waste time figuring out what a particular package does, and if you never use a package, it is a drag on you and your system. You also may need to uninstall something because it is obsolete. In any case, uninstalling packages is very easy with RPM. I hesitate to say that any administration function is easy because so many little details can sneak up and bite you. But RPM keeps track and accounts for those little nasty details.

REMOVING A PACKAGE
Perhaps you've installed a package and experimented with it. But now you no longer need it and you want the disk space back.

I don't use the nfs-server-clients package that Red Hat installed by default, so I'll use it as an example of the remove command. Even if you find you want it in the future, you can always use RPM to install it. Enter the following command:

```
rpm -ev knfsd
```

No message is returned; RPM just goes ahead and erases nfs-server-clients. Enter the following command:

```
rpm -q -i knfsd-clients
```

You get the following message:

```
package knfsd-clients is not installed
```

This message verifies that the package was removed. That was simple as pie.

VERIFYING

The verify option takes the following form:

```
rpm -V|-y|--verify verify-options
```

RPM provides a way of checking, or verifying, the current contents of a package against the original pristine package as found on the CD-ROM or the Red Hat Web page. The verify option compares the size, MD5 sum (checksum), permissions, type, owner, and group of the current package files against the originals. That information can be used in a number of ways. It can provide simple information about what you have (similar to the query information), and it can help in debugging a problem by telling you which files have changed since the initial installation.

In the previous example, you simply removed the Samba package in order to completely restore its configuration information. This simple, brute-force method also removes a number of log files that you would not want to remove in a mature system. If you had used the RPM verify option as shown in the following command, RPM would tell you which files had been modified:

```
rpm -V samba
```

In my case, this command gives the following information:

```
S.5....T c /etc/smb.conf
```

The eight characters before the c—which means they are configuration files—identify each type, or attribute, of change that RPM recognizes. The S means the file size has changed, the 5 means the MD5 sum has changed, and the T means the modification time differs from the original. The dots (.) mean that a corresponding attribute has not changed (in this case, the L, D, U, G, and M attributes have not changed). Table 5-6 describes the meaning of each attribute.

TABLE 5-6 THE RPM VERIFY FORMAT

Character	Attribute	Description
5	MD5 sum	The file's checksum
S	File size	The file size in bytes
L	Symlink	The symbolic link
T	Mtime	The file's modification time
D	Device	Specifies that it is a device file
U	User	The file's user ID (the user ownership)
G	Group	The file's group ID (group ownership)
M	Mode	The file's permission and/or mode changed

To experiment, try changing the owner of /etc/smb to bin, as shown in the following command:

```
chown bin /etc/smb.conf
```

Run the following RPM command (rpm -V samba) and you get the following result:

```
S.5..U.T c /etc/smb.conf
```

The U specifies that the ownership of the /etc/smb.conf file has changed. Don't forget to change it back to root again!

UPGRADING

The upgrade function of RPM is useful in many ways. When the next version of Red Hat Linux comes along, you obviously will want to upgrade to some or all of the new packages. Linux is like any other operating system and some packages will have bug fixes that need to be applied; most packages will be improved and updated over time and will need to be replaced.

Upgrading is very simple. Identify the package that you want to upgrade, and use the -U option instead of the -i option. RPM automatically uninstalls the old package and installs the new one; it will, however, save your old configuration files (with the suffix .rpmsave) that are not compatible with the new package. Otherwise, upgrading works the same way as installation.

For example, instead of explicitly erasing and reinstalling Samba (as I describe in the section "Uninstalling and then Reinstalling a Package"), you could enter the following command:

```
rpm -Uvh --force /mnt/cdrom/RedHat/RPMS/samba*
```

The old files belonging to the Samba package will be deleted and the new ones installed. The old smb.conf file is saved as smb.conf.rpmsave.

INSTALLING LINUX SOFTWARE THE OLD-FASHIONED WAY

Traditionally, software has been distributed and transferred to Linux systems with tape archive – tar – files. With a tar file, one or more files can be stored in a single file, saved to a storage device, or transferred through a Linux pipe with the /bin/tar command. Anyway, the tar file offers a decent method for distributing software; this method is widely used throughout the Linux and UNIX world. (I have more to say about the tar command in Chapters 9.)

Tarball is common UNIX/Linux slang for a tar file.

To install a software system that is stored and distributed in a tar file, you should use the following guidelines:

1. Un-tar the file (this generally means saving the individual files in one or more directories on your computer). If the tar file is compressed (it is compressed if it has one of the following sufficestgz, gz, and Z), you can specify a tar option to uncompress it.

2. Most software systems come with a makefile, which contains rules for compiling and installing the software. Sometimes you need to explicitly modify the makefile or use it to create dependencies – in that case, enter the make depend command. See the manual page for make (man make) for more information.

3. The software is compiled. The syntax for doing this can be as simple as make or make all.

4. Optionally, the makefile installs the compiled software, configuration, and help files for you – typically by running a make install command.

That's it. If all goes well, you have your system installed. My experience is that most Linux tar systems compile and run with minimal difficulty.

I didn't realize until I started writing this book that Red Hat does not include a single tar file on its CD-ROM distribution. That is quite a shift in philosophy from traditional Linux and especially the Slackware distribution. If the Red Hat philosophy becomes the de facto standard, a large division could result between the Internet community and the commercial side. I imagine that many in the Linux/GNU community will continue to use the tar method while the commercial side migrates quickly to RPM. Whether that means anything negative in terms of the so-far successful software development cycle is anyone's guess.

There will be times when you can't use RPM. In Chapters 10 and 11 I use some security-oriented packages that are not available in the RPM format. They come in tar form and you will need to install and compile them manually.

Displaying simple help messages

Most Linux commands and utilities provide a simple and quick help system. Enter the string --help or -h as the only parameter and generally about one screen of options is displayed. For example, the command gzip --help displays the help information shown here:

```
gzip 1.2.4 (18 Aug 93)
usage: gzip [-cdfhlLnNrtvV19] [-S suffix] [file ...]
 -c --stdout      write on standard output, keep original files unchanged
 -d --decompress  decompress
 -f --force       force overwrite of output file and compress links
 -h --help        give this help
 -l --list        list compressed file contents
 -L --license     display software license
 -n --no-name     do not save or restore the original name and time stamp
 -N --name        save or restore the original name and time stamp
 -q --quiet       suppress all warnings
 -r --recursive   operate recursively on directories
 -S .suf --suffix .suf    use suffix .suf on compressed files
 -t --test        test compressed file integrity
 -v --verbose     verbose mode
 -V --version     display version number
 -1 --fast        compress faster
 -9 --best        compress better
 file...          files to (de)compress. If none given, use standard input.
```

Recall from Chapter 4 that the Linux File System Standard (FSSTND) specifies that the system administrator should use the /usr/local directory for local software. It is a good idea to install new packages — especially when not supported by the distribution — in a well-known area separate from the standard system software. That keeps your basic system relatively clean and distinct. In the long run, keeping new software separate reduces confusion and the possibility of mistakenly erasing or corrupting software.

Exploring the X Window System

It is important that you read this entire section carefully before working with the X Window System. (XFree86 is the Linux implementation of X Window.) You are manipulating physical monitor and video adapter settings that control high-voltage and high-frequency electricity. Some setting combinations are incompatible and can damage equipment and possibly you!

XFree86 comes without any warranty of any kind. Anything that you damage even after reading these instructions is your own problem.

The X Window system was installed as part of the Red Hat installation system. This section discusses a little about how the X Window system works.

Much of Linux administration can be handled through the Red Hat Control Panel and LinuxConf — both are Graphical User Interface (GUI) front-ends to several scripts and programs that configure system functions such as network interfaces and user modification. Both require the X Window System. Of course, the Control Panel is only one reason to install the X Window system. Dozens of other applications require X Window. Everything from Netscape to Xclock depends on it. It's hard to imagine a GUI-less world.

X configuration has always been the touchiest system to configure under Linux. It requires many different, and sometimes competing, parameters to work together. It is not always obvious how one parameter affects another. However, the continued maturation of the Xconfigurator program has made that chore much easier.

XFree86

XFree86 is the Linux version of the X Window system. It comes bundled with all Linux distributions. Its core is contained in the XFree86 package. It has matured since the middle 1990s into a robust and powerful system.

 You can access more information about XFree86 via the Web at
`http://www.xfree86.org`.

The X Server

The X Server is the interface between Linux and your computer's video adapter. You can use a generic version – SVGA – that works with any system, or special-ized ones that take advantage of one system or another – S3, for example. Several configuration packages come with Linux to assist you with configuring the X Window system on your computer.

Configuring the X Window system with Xconfigurator

The Red Hat distribution now includes the Xconfigurator system. It simplifies the difficult task of configuring the X Window system. I have found that it works across my fairly heterogeneous systems.

I presented you with the option to skip the X Window system installation in Chapter 1. If you did so, either to save resources or time, you can configure it now.

The following instructions describe the configuration process for XFree86.

1. **Log in as root.** Start the process by entering the following command

   ```
   Xconfigurator
   ```

   You get the Xconfigurator graphical setup window. Press OK to continue.

2. **Choose A Card.** The installation script runs the Xconfigurator program that lets you pick your video adapter and monitor from a large list of manufacturer's models as shown in Figure 5-1. Once you choose your card, the XFree86 server that works with that card is installed.

3. **Monitor Setup.** The second screen, shown in Figure 5-2, shows the available monitors. If your monitor is on the list then you simply select it and go to the next step. If it is not on the list, then I generally choose the Custom op-tion at the top of the screen and go to another window that explains the basics of choosing the monitor parameters.

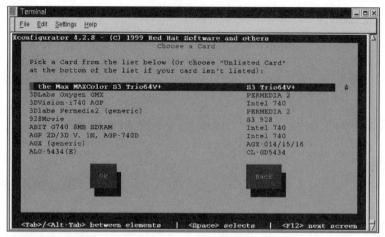

Figure 5-1: The Xconfigurator Choose A Card screen

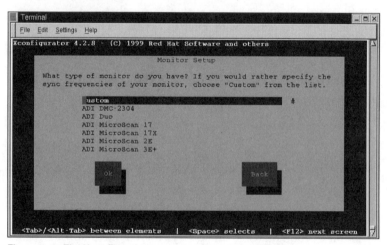

Figure 5-2: The Xconfigurator screen configurator window

4. **Monitor setup (Continued).** Figure 5-3 shows the second monitor setup screen, which lets you choose from ten generic monitor configurations. These include the horizontal and vertical resolutions as well as the horizontal sync rate. This information is contained in the manual that comes with your monitor. As the instructions point out, it is very important that you not pick a horizontal sync range that is greater than your monitor can handle. This is because a monitor can be damaged if you choose too high a value. If you are in doubt, then choose a conservative setting. The first choice, Standard VGA, 640×480 @ 60 Hz, is generally a safe one. My monitor can only handle 800×600 @ 60 Hz, which is the lowest value that I find useful with the X Window system. I recommend that you be careful and search through that pile of papers in your office for your manual.

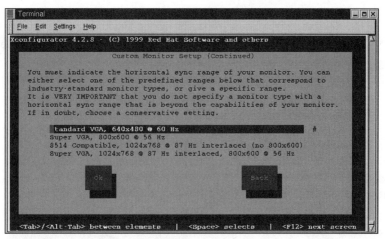

Figure 5-3: The Xconfgurator custom screen window

5. **Screen Configuration.** The next step is to probe or not probe your video card. If you successfully probe your video card, then it returns the exact values you can use. After those values are returned, you can let the system use them as the default or enter your own values. I generally use the return values as they are returned.

6. If you choose to probe, you are asked if it is okay to begin. Once it finishes, it displays the information that it acquires and either lets you select it as the default or enter it yourself. I select to use the defaults.

7. Start your X Window system by entering the following command

```
startx
```

You will see a bunch of libraries load and then you should have the X Window system running!

Introducing the GNOME graphical environment

When you start X after installing Red Hat, the window manager Enlightenment and graphical GNOME environment are started automatically. These are the software that give your desktop its look and feel. Enlightenment allows you to configure every aspect of the interface. You can access the Enlightenment configuration menu by clicking both mouse keys at once on the desktop background. A general menu pops up and you can then click on Enlightenment configuration menu.

GNOME (GNU Network Object Model Environment) provides applications and utilities for the X environment and includes applications like a calendar and a file manager. When you start up X, the Gnome help screen window appears. It provides a good tutorial and reference about GNOME. You can also refer to http://www. gnome.org for more information.

Several other window managers run on Linux. The KDE, tvm, lesstif-wm, fvwm95, and AfterStep are all included with the Red Hat distribution. You can install them during the installation process or anytime afterwards, manually.

USING THE START MENU

The little Gnome footprint (similar in purpose to the Windows Start button) in the lower left-hand corner of the screen, provides access to many applications and utilities. Click on the footprint and the menu shown in Figure 5-4 is activated. The menu is self-explanatory: click on the applications folder and choose an application from the submenu.

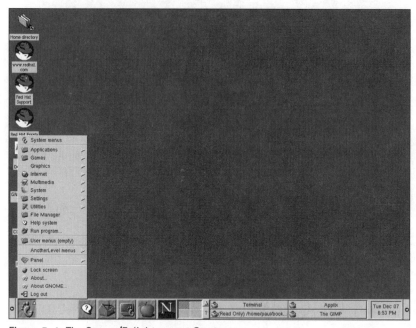

Figure 5-4: The Gnome/Enlightenment Start menu

The horizontal menu bar along the bottom of the screen provides access to commonly used functions. For instance, an icon for Netscape is included by default because Netscape itself was installed by default. You can add applications to this menu by clicking on the Gnome start button and clicking on Panel → Add new launcher. A window is displayed where you can enter the name of the icon and the location of the program to launch. For instance, to start the diald control program dctrl, you enter **/usr/bin/dctrl**. You can specify one of the generic Gnome icons or use one that you've provided yourself.

Viewing an X Client on an X Server

Recall that the X Window System is made of two parts: the X Client and X Server. The client and server can run on a single computer or on separate computers connected via a network. The following discussion briefly describes how to graphically view a remote process.

USING AN X CLIENT AND X SERVER ON THE SAME COMPUTER

First, display an X Client on your own X Server. Your X Server is the system that you started by running the `startx` program.

The terminology is somewhat confusing because the term *server* generally implies a computer that runs services for you while you are its client. In the case of X, the term *X Server* defines the software that takes care of displaying the graphical information generated by the X Client. Thus, when you start up X (literally the program `/usr/bin/X11/X`) you are starting up the X Server. The output of the X Client is displayed by the X Server.

You need to give permission to the X Clients to display on your X Server, so from a command line run the following program:

```
xhost +
```

This gives permission to any X Client on any network that has access to your X Server to display on your computer. This can be a security hazard so in the future use the more specific command like `xhost + somehost` to allow specific hosts or networks display access. Please refer to the man page on `xhost` for more information.

Using `xhost` can still present a security problem if you are displaying sensitive information on a computer that is used by more than one person. That's because any user who can log onto that computer can connect to the X Server. On the other hand, if you are the only person to work on a computer, then using `xhost` should not be a problem. However, if you are sharing a computer with others and work with sensitive information, use the `xauth` program rather than `xhost`. Please consult the `xauth` man page for more help.

Next, from a command line on your computer display the simple graphical clock by entering the command:

```
xclock -display :0
```

You should see the clock displayed. You've now allowed X client access to your local display and have run the X Client and told it to send its display to your local X Server. The :0 stands for the first display at the default network location.

DISPLAYING AN X CLIENT ON A REMOTE X SERVER

Once your local X Server has been told to display X Clients with the xhost command, you can expand the display variable to send the graphical information from an X Client running on a remote machine. If you are connected to a network that has another computer running X Window, then enter the following command from that machine (note that commercial products like Exceed give Windows machines the capability to do just that):

```
xclock -display chiva.paunchy.net:0.0
```

This command displays the graphical clock on the Linux box with the network address of chiva.paunchy.net (that is the IP 192.168.1.254 that was used for the Red Hat installation described in Chapter 1). Note that in the typical case where a computer has just one physical monitor, the 0. syntax is the same as 0.0. The second 0 means the first display or monitor attached to the X Server and can, in most cases, be abbreviated from 0.0 to just 0. It's confusing at first.

If you are sitting at the console of the remote machine then the clock is displayed on chivas. However, if you telnet to chiva from the remote machine and reverse the process, then you'll see the Xclock displayed on your machine. After you experiment with the system, it should become clear who is the server and who is the client.

Using the Red Hat Control Panel and LinuxConf

Red Hat Linux provides some useful tools devoted to systems administration. The X Window–based control panel and LinuxConf cover many administrative functions. Table 5-7 shows the functions that they cover.

TABLE 5-7 CONTROL PANEL AND LINUXCONF FUNCTIONS

Utility	Name	Function
Control Panel	Run Level Editor	Configures which services are started or stopped in various runlevels
Control Panel	Time & Date	Changes time and date

Utility	Name	Function
Control Panel	Printer Configuration	Configures local, remote, and Samba printers
Control Panel	Network Configuration	Configures network functions
Control Panel	Modem Configuration	Creates a soft link to a modem
Control Panel	Kernel Daemon Configuration	Manually loads and unloads modules into the kernel
Control Panel	System Configuration	Starts LinuxConf
Control Panel	Package Management	Adds and deletes RPM packages
LinuxConf	Network management	Configures network functions
LinuxConf	User management	Adds, deletes, and modifies user accounts
LinuxConf	File System management	Manages Linux, NFS, and swap file systems
LinuxConf	Boot Mode	Configures LILO
LinuxConf	Control panel	Manages system functions such as shutdown
LinuxConf	Control files	Configures system and application configuration files
LinuxConf	Logs	Manages various system and log files

Using the control panel

The Control Panel gives you a common graphical interface for performing basic system administration tasks. It handles package management, kernel daemon configuration, network configuration, printer configuration, user management, and many other tasks. In short, it handles everything you have done manually so far.

The Control Panel is an X application and can be accessed from several directions. You can start it from a command line, from the GNOME desktop, or from a remote X Window system machine. I'll just mention that if you set the DISPLAY environment variable to point to your remote X Window system's display (that is, DISPLAY=your_ip:0.0), you can interact with it as if you were sitting at the Linux box's console.

To run the Control Panel from a command line, first start the X Window system and open a shell window. Enter the following command and use the root password when prompted for one:

```
su -c control-panel
```

Alternatively, you can open a shell window and enter the following command along with the root password when prompted for it:

```
su -
DISPLAY=:0 control-panel &
```

Finally, and most conveniently, you can simply position the mouse cursor on any part of the Desktop and click the left mouse button. You'll see a generic fvwm95 menu, and if you click the Utilities submenu, you'll see the Control Panel option. Click it and you should get the main Control Panel window shown in Figure 5-5.

Figure 5-5: The Control Panel window

To select an option, click the module button that you wish to use. Note that if you position the mouse pointer over a button a short description appears.

PACKAGE MANAGEMENT

Click the Package Management button and you get its window. It is a graphical method for doing the same package management that you have just done with RPM. I suggest you retry some of the same examples described earlier to get a feel for it. In some cases, such as dealing with a lot of similar packages, a graphical tool like this one is superior to a simple text-based one. It generally boils down to personal taste.

KERNEL DAEMON CONFIGURATION

Red Hat includes a process called `kerneld` that dynamically loads kernel modules when application software calls for it. For example, when you fire up the `diald` program in Chapter 8 to establish an Internet connection, `kerneld` automatically loads the SLIP and PPP modules that diald depends on.

Some functions need to be explicitly specified to `kerneld` for it to work for them. Click the Kernel Daemon Configuration button in the Control Panel main window. The screen shows that `kerneld` knows about my Ethernet adapter, which I configured during the initial installation. Had I not configured it then, or changed to another adapter, I could use `kerneld` to do so now.

THE USER CONFIGURATOR

The User Configurator function handles user and group management in more detail than the simple adduser command. Click the Modules menu in the Control Panel shown in Figure 5-5. You get a submenu with a number of options. Click the User and Group Configuration button. This brings up the main User Configurator window showing the information for each user, which it gets from the /etc/passwd file.

If you open a window for Root, you get the Edit User Definition screen.

From here, you can edit any of the parameters shown. This method is nice because it does not let you do anything too foolish. Editing the /etc/passwd and /etc/group files by hand can wreak havoc, but you can do little wrong here. This method also provides you with choices you may not know exist. For example, the Password field has five choices – Original, Change, No Password, Lock, and Unlock. It's a useful system.

With the User Configurator, you can add, delete, deactivate, and reactivate a user. You can also add, delete, and edit groups.

THE RHS LINUX PRINT SYSTEM MANAGER

I haven't described editing the printer configuration very much yet. It is a good function to leave to the Control Panel. The /etc/printcap file is not too difficult to master except when you have unusual printers or a complex network printer. Open the Print System Manager from the Control Panel and you get the window shown in Figure 5-6.

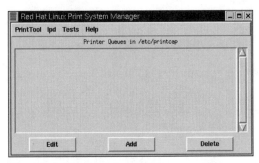

Figure 5-6: The Print System Manager window

Unless you have installed a printer already, choose PrintTool and then click the Add button. You get the three choices shown in Figure 5-7. Choose the Local Printer option if your printer is connected to your parallel port (this is the most common). Choose the Remote Unix option if you want to print to a printer connected to another Linux or UNIX computer over your network. Or choose the LAN Manager Printer (SMB) option if the printer is attached to a computer using the LAN Manager (Samba).

Figure 5-7: The Add a Printer Entry window

The last step is to fill in the fields in the Edit Local/Network/LAN Manager Printer Entry. The details vary depending on the type of printer you choose, but the completed screen will look something like the example shown in Figure 5-8.

Figure 5-8: The Edit Local Printer Entry window

The fields are used to store the following information:

◆ **Queue Name:** The name by which your printer is known. Note that it can be a pipe.

◆ **Spool Directory:** The location where the intermediate file is stored while it is printed. It is a good idea to use the name of the printer.

◆ **File Limit:** The maximum file size – zero for no limit – to be printed. While it is important to avoid filling up your root file system where the spool directory is normally kept (/var/spool), until you are dealing with a production system you aren't likely to have these problems.

◆ **Input File:** You have the choice of printing Regular, PostScript, TeX, GIF, JPEG, TIFF, or even RPM file formats. You get another screen where you need to choose the printer manufacturer and type.

If you chose the Network printer option, you need to specify the Remote Host and Remote Queue for Linux network printers or Printer Server Name, Printer Name, and Printer User if it is a printer based on LAN Manager (Samba).

THE NETWORK CONFIGURATOR

The Control Panel lets you configure most aspects of your network with the Network Configurator. From the Control Panel, click the Modules menu option and click the Network Configuration button and you get the screen shown in Figure 5-9. It displays the basic information about your current setup.

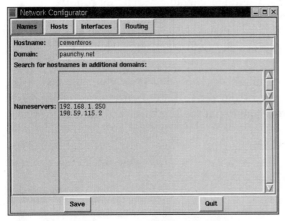

Figure 5-9: The Network Configurator window

In Chapter 8, you are shown how to set up your Internet connection, and you use this function in more depth to counterbalance the manual changes that you make. Chapter 10 shows you how to modify some of the LAN settings. The Network Configurator is used in both cases, so further discussion is left until those chapters. However, here is a list of the network functions that the Network Configurator handles:

◆ **Managing names.** You can set the host and domain name of your Linux box. It also shows you which name server is used to look up other computers on a network. It does not configure your machine as a name server. You must do that manually.

◆ **Modifying the /etc/hosts file,** which explicitly assigns IP addresses to names and their aliases.

◆ **Adding network interfaces.** It can add hardware adapters such as Ethernet, Token Ring, Arcnet and Pocket (ATP), as well as logical interfaces such as PPP, SLIP, and PLIP.

◆ **Configuring logical interfaces** with phone numbers, login names, and passwords.

◆ **Configuring hardware interfaces** with the device name, IP address, Netmask, broadcast address, a boot activate flag, and a BOOTP option. The boot activate flag indicates that you want the device to turn on when the system boots, and the BOOTP indicates that your computer gets its IP address from another source.

◆ **Adding, editing, or deleting static routes.** A route is an IP address to which you can send all packets meeting a certain criteria. The criteria are generally an IP address itself. For example, when you run `diald` in the next chapter, it sets up a default route to the PPP connection and thus the modem. All packets that cannot be directed to another route go to this connection. In your case, that means the Internet.

Obviously, this is another powerful tool that I need to show you more about. The preceding list just gives you a taste of the Network Configurator's capabilities. In the following chapters, I show you how to put the Network Configurator to work.

SETTING THE TIME AND DATE
Finally, you can set your system time and date from this window. The system time is not permanently set until you click the Set System Clock button.

TIP   The Control Panel is a dynamic system that shows only the options that are available to you. For example, the Package Configurator is actually a link to the GLINT system, which is an RPM package. If you remove that package and run the Control Panel, no Package Configurator option is displayed. Reinstall it, and the option returns. The options given depend on what packages were installed by the Red Hat installation process by default and what packages you have added yourself — whether by the initial installation process or individually since then. For that matter, so do the default menus you get by clicking the left mouse button against the window background. If you install a package such as XV, the next time you restart the X Window system and open the Applications menu you will see it there.

Using LinuxConf

When you login as root and run X, you can access the ControlPanel, shown in Figure 5-10, by clicking on the Enlightenment window manager and selecting Start → Programs → Administration → Control Panel. You must be logged in as root to perform most of the functions, however.

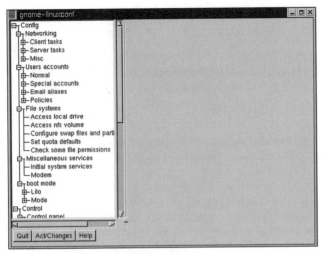

Figure 5-10: Control Panel Window

LinuxConf is a new system and its functions should grow with time. For now, it's useful for configuring several of the important Linux systems administration functions. LinuxConf is a GUI that ties together the Red Hat administrative utilities in one place. There is some overlap in functions between LinuxConf and control panel. You can use any of the overlapping functions as you see fit.

You can run LinuxConf from the command line, an xterm window, or a virtual console. Enter the command `LinuxConf` from a command line and you get a simple menu-based window. Use the Config menu item to select the LinuxConf program and the Control menu item to enter the Control Panel system. Use the cursor keys to navigate through either system.

Manually modifying user accounts

User login accounts are controlled by three files: `/etc/passwd`, `/etc/shadow`, and `/etc/group`. The `passwd` file contains the user name, an encrypted password if you choose not to use shadow passwords; the user and group numeric id (which are the same by default under Red Hat); the user home directory; a field for general information about the user; the user account home directory; and the type of shell used. The shadow password file contains the user name, encrypted password and access information about the account (note that system login accounts have no encrypted passwords because they cannot be logged into and thus do not have passwords). The `group` file contains the user name, a numeric group identifier, and zero or more user names that belong to the group (it can also contain a group password but that is rarely used); additional user names are separated by commas.

Continued

Manually modifying user accounts *(Continued)*

The passwd file can be edited by hand to add and modify users. It is generally okay to manually modify an existing user account but better to use either the useradd, userdel, and usermod command line programs or the LinuxConf GUI to add and delete users.

Red Hat creates a group for every new user. If you add the user paul, then the numeric user id might be 500. The group id for the group paul is set to 500 too. This method allows all of a user's files to be private unless the user wishes to share them. In that case, you add another user's or group's name to the user's group in the /etc/group file.

For instance, if you want to allow jorgito, ednita, lidia and aida to access jorgito's files, then edit the following line for the user jorgito in the /etc/group file.

```
jorgito:x:500
```

and add the users ednita, lidia and aida:

```
jorgito:x:500:jorgito:ednita:lidia:aida
```

This allows both of those users to access jorgito's files. The catch is that the other users can only access files with the group permissions that allow access. For instance, the following file

```
-rw-rw-r--  1 jorgito  jorgito   312 Sep 30 20:36 Xrootenv.0
```

belongs to jorgito and the group jorgito. The group access is read and write, so the other users can both read and write to that file.

You can create user accounts through the Control Panel or LinuxConf interfaces or manually edit the above mentioned files. That's a fairly difficult process. The intermediate way is to use the useradd program. Enter the following to add the new user jorgito.

```
useradd jorgito
```

If you examine the /etc/passwd, /etc/shadow and /etc/group files you see that the user jorgito has been added. Red Hat starts users with the user and group ids of 500. The home directory /home/jorgito has been created and the skeleton files copied over. Everything has the correct ownership.

You can delete user accounts by using the userdel program. To remove jorgito, enter the following command.

```
userdel jorgito
```

There are many options — for instance, to create a user home directory along with the user — available with usreadd and userdel. Please consult the man pages for more information.

Building a Custom Kernel

The Linux kernel is a dynamic beast. It can be configured to dynamically recognize new devices or systems or by recompilation. The kernel accepts the executable device code as modules. The beauty of this approach is that you can experiment with new stuff without the time-consuming recompilation process. The kernel is also far more efficient in terms of space utilization because only the drivers that are needed are loaded at any one time; they can also be unloaded. You can still compile in drivers that are used all the time, but it is your option.

Modularized kernels

Table 5-8 lists the Linux utilities that maintain and modify the kernel modules.

TABLE 5-8 LINUX KERNEL MODULE UTILITIES

Utility	Description
lsmod	Lists currently loaded modules
insmod	Inserts a module into the active kernel
modprobe	Loads a module or more than one module and their dependencies
depmod	Creates a dependencies file for a module (used by modprobe)
rmmod	Removes a currently loaded module

Adding a Module to Provide SLIP Support

In anticipation of Chapter 8, where I describe setting up a PPP connection to the Internet, this section shows you how to install the SLIP module. SLIP is short for Serial Line IP and is a simple method for establishing an IP connection over a serial (that is, telephone connection) line. It has been superseded by the Point-to-Point Protocol (PPP) but is still used by some good communications software to establish an IP connection.

Unfortunately, the base Red Hat kernel does not include SLIP support so you have to add it. That is not difficult with modular kernels. Log on as root and mount the Red Hat CD-ROM as usual. Install the package by entering the following command:

```
rpm -ivh /mnt/cdrom/RedHat/RPMS/slip*
```

You should have the SLIP system installed now.

Using the /proc file system to display Linux system internal information

You can check to see if SLIP has already been installed. The /proc file system is actually a view port into the kernel's internal tables. If you list the /proc directory, the numbered directories correspond to the running process IDs and contain information about each process. The other directories and files deal with major kernel systems. The /proc/net directory contains information about the network. If you list the contents of /proc/net/dev, all the network devices are displayed. Enter the following command:

```
cat  /proc/net/dev
```

The listing below shows the contents of /proc/net/dev.

```
Inter-|  Receive                       |  Transmit
 face |packets errs drop fifo frame|packets errs drop fifo colls carrier
   lo:    561    0    0    0    0     561    0    0    0     0    0
 eth0:  17684   12   12    0   12   13916    0    0    0     0    0
```

You can see my Ethernet adapter — eth0 — and the pseudonetwork lo device, but no SLIP devices.

Alternatively, you can see if SLIP is installed with RPM. To do this, enter the following command:

```
rpm -q -l slip
```

RPM tells you that no SLIP package is installed.

There is no RPM SLIP package to install. Red Hat installs the kernel package in its base configuration. Enter the following command to locate it:

```
rpm -q -l kernel |grep -i slip
```

It returns the location as follows:

```
/lib/modules/2.2.12-9/net/slip.o
```

Go ahead and install the SLIP module with the following command:

```
insmod  /lib/modules/2.2.12-9/net/slip.o
```

This command returns the message shown in Listing 5-6, indicating that you do not have all the necessary modules installed.

Listing 5-6: Insmod failed because slip.o is dependent on other modules.

```
slip.o: unresolved symbol slhc_free_R3787e5b9
slip.o: unresolved symbol slhc_remember_Rbc0f8a5e
slip.o: unresolved symbol slhc_uncompress_Ra2ca7e04
slip.o: unresolved symbol slhc_compress_R5d6838a9
slip.o: unresolved symbol slhc_init_R20741a64
```

No problem. The modprobe utility looks at the module to be loaded and determines if it depends on any other modules. Any dependent modules are loaded first. Enter the following command:

```
modprobe /lib/modules/2.2.12-9/net/slip.o
```

It does not return a message after it succeeds. Enter the lsmod command to make sure the modules were loaded:

```
lsmod
```

This command returns the information shown in Listing 5-7.

Listing 5-7: The lsmod shows that the SLIP module was successfully loaded.

```
Module:      #pages:  Used by:
slip            2            0
slhc            2     [slip]  0
3c509           2            1 (autoclean)
```

TIP You can list all the available modules by using the -l option with modprobe. You can be more specific by using the -t <module type> option to list all modules of a given type. For example, to list all the network modules, enter the command as modprobe -l -t net.

Static Kernels

It is almost easy to recompile a kernel. The source code is stored in the /usr/src/ linux directory. The README file located in this directory provides a good description of the necessary steps (about halfway through, look for the lines that describe make mrproper, make depend, and so on).

Use the following instructions to compile a kernel:

1. The GNU C compiler (gcc) must be ready. If you have not installed the necessary packages, login as root, mount the Red Hat CD-ROM and enter the following commands:

```
rpm -ivh /mnt/cdrom/RedHat/RPMS/binutils*
rpm -ivh /mnt/cdrom/RedHat/RPMS/cpp*
rpm -ivh /mnt/cdrom/RedHat/RPMS/egc-1*
rpm -ivh /mnt/cdrom/RedHat/RPMS/glibc-devel*
```

2. You also need the Make utility. If necessary, you can install it as follows

```
rpm -ivh /mnt/cdrom/RedHat/RPMS/make*
```

3. The Linux kernel source code directory must be installed. Install them as follows:

```
rpm -ivh /mnt/cdrom/RedHat/RPMS/kernel-headers*
rpm -ivh /mnt/cdrom/RedHat/RPMS/kernel-source*
```

4. To avoid confusion, the Red Hat kernel source package creates a symbolic link to your current Linux source code directory. Thus, /usr/src/linux-2.2.12 has a link of /usr/src/linux that is easy to remember and use. Keep in mind that if you manually upgrade your Linux version, you should delete and re-link to the new directory. This relinking can be accomplished by entering the following commands:

```
cd /usr/src
rm /usr/src/linux
ln -s /usr/src/linux-2.2-12 linux
```

5. Sophisticated source code tends to standardize the location of common functions. Include files store common variable and constant definitions and such in a file separate from the source code and therefore many different programs can use a common set of definitions. The Linux kernel source uses this method and looks in the /usr/include directory for such definitions. Therefore, symbolic links are used to point to these places and you must define them as follows:

```
cd /usr/include
rm -rf asm linux scsi
ln -s /usr/src/linux/include/asm-i386 asm
ln -s /usr/src/linux/include/linux linux
ln -s /usr/src/linux/include/scsi scsi
```

6. If you recompile your kernel more than once, make sure you start from a consistent point. The Linux kernel makefile provides a convenient mechanism for doing just that. The command make mrproper resets all configuration and definition files to a default state and deletes old compiled code. To perform this task, enter the following command:

```
cd /usr/src/linux
make mrproper
```

7. Next, you have to configure the kernel to be built. I still like to use the sequential, text-based yes/no system, but full-screen and the X Window system-based configuration systems are available for you to try — for example, make menuconfig and make xconfig. To use the sequential method, enter the following command:

```
make config
```

You get screen after screen (maybe I should learn the other systems) of yes-no questions. In most cases, you can simply press the Enter key to choose the default. Also, some questions have a third option — M — to choose a loadable module to be folded in at boot time. Listing 5-8 shows the section that deals with SLIP and PPP support. To use diald you must have SLIP, so enter Yes (y) to each.

For instance, if you answer yes to the PPP module, the questions about SLIP are asked. Otherwise, it is assumed you will not use it.

8. Create the dependency file.

make dep

9. Next, compile the new kernel. Modern Linux uses a compressed kernel, so use the zImage as follows:

```
make zImage
```

Listing 5-8: The Linux kernel configuration menu for SLIP and PPP

```
*
* Network device support
*
Network device support (CONFIG_NETDEVICES) [Y/n/?]
Dummy net driver support (CONFIG_DUMMY) [M/n/y/?]
EQL (serial line load balancing) support (CONFIG_EQUALIZER)
[M/n/y/?]
PLIP (parallel port) support (CONFIG_PLIP) [M/n/y/?]
PPP (point-to-point) support (CONFIG_PPP) [M/n/y/?] y
*
```

```
* CCP compressors for PPP are only built as modules.
*
SLIP (serial line) support (CONFIG_SLIP) [M/n/y/?] y
CSLIP compressed headers (CONFIG_SLIP_COMPRESSED) [Y/n/?]
Keepalive and linefill (CONFIG_SLIP_SMART) [Y/n/?]
Six bit SLIP encapsulation (CONFIG_SLIP_MODE_SLIP6) [N/y/?]
```

 TIP

If you chose any functions as modules, you have to run make again to first compile the modules and then to make Linux aware of them. Enter the following commands:

```
make modules
make modules_install
```

Further instructions are included in the /usr/src/linux-2.0.30/Documentation/modules.txt file.

10. Depending on the speed of your system, it could take hours to compile and link or else just five to ten minutes. The new kernel is placed in the /usr/src/linux/arch//i386/boot directory. You will need to make it bootable with the Linux Loader (LILO) system. I highly recommend you save your current kernel – which Red Hat places in /boot/vmlinuz – so move the new zImage to that directory without renaming it (for now)

```
mv /usr/src/linux/i386/boot/zImage    /boot
```

11. LILO consults a configuration file, /etc/lilo.conf, to get everything ready for booting. Listing 5-9 shows the default file, which still includes a reference to my original DOS partition.

Listing 5-9: The default /etc/lilo.conf file

```
boot=/dev/hda
map=/boot/map
install=/boot/boot.b
prompt
timeout=50
image=/boot/vmlinuz
        label=linux
        root=/dev/hda1
        read-only
```

12. Copy the last four lines and edit them to point to the new kernel image as shown in Listing 5-10.

Listing 5-10: The new /etc/lilo.conf file

```
boot=/dev/hda
map=/boot/map
install=/boot/boot.b
prompt
timeout=50
image=/boot/vmlinuz
        label=linux
        root=/dev/hda1
        read-only
image=/boot/zImage
        label=new_linux
        root=/dev/hda1
        read-only
```

13. Enter the LILO command to make the changes stick

```
lilo
```

14. When you next reboot your Linux box, the LILIO bootprompt is displayed after the initial BIOS messages. The timeout=50 gives you five seconds to choose the kernel to boot. If you press the Shift key and then the Tab key you get a list of the available kernels

```
LILO boot:  dos vmlinuz new_linux
```

15. Type in **new_linux** to get your new kernel loaded. Otherwise, enter **vm-linuz**, or simply press the Enter key to get the old version. If you wait more than five seconds, the old kernel is booted automatically. You can change that time to any value you want.

This process took a lot of instruction but is really quite straightforward with a little practice. It is a process that is much less necessary with the advent of loadable modules but is useful after you arrive at a stable kernel-module setup. When your system is in a production mode, you probably want to recompile the common functions for simplicity's sake.

Customizing the Red Hat Startup Process

The Linux startup process was introduced in Chapter 4. Recall that the rc scripts are used to start the various daemons and get the system running. The /etc/rc.d/rc.local script is provided so you can add instructions to start your own daemons. In the next chapter, I use it to launch a couple of daemons, but I want to mention it here because it is an important feature.

This script is executed after all the other startup scripts have been run. Therefore, your system should be fully functional by the time your scripts are started. For example, the network should be started and the disks mounted. Until you add your own functions, the rc.local script only sets the standard login screen that you see when you log on. Listing 5-11 shows this script.

Listing 5-11: The /etc/rc.d/rc.local file

```
#!/bin/sh

# This script will be executed *after* all the other init scripts.
# You can put your own initialization stuff in here if you don't
# want to do the full Sys V style init stuff.

if [ -f /etc/redhat-release ]; then
    R=$(cat /etc/redhat-release)

    arch=$(uname -m)
    a="a"
    case "_$arch" in
            _a*) a="an";;
            _i*) a="an";;
    esac

    NUMPROC=$[`cat /proc/cpuinfo | grep -i ^bogomips | wc -l`]
    if [ $NUMPROC -gt 1 ]; then
        SMP="$NUMPROC-processor "
        if [ "$NUMPROC" = "8" -o "$NUMPROC" = "11" ]; then
            a="an"
        else
a="a"
        fi
    fi

    # This will overwrite /etc/issue at every boot.  So make any changes you
    # want to make to /etc/issue here or you will lose them when you reboot.
```

```
    echo "" > /etc/issue
    echo "$R" > /etc/issue
    echo "Kernel $(uname -r) on $a $SMP$(uname -m)" > /etc/issue

    cp -f /etc/issue /etc/issue.net
    echo > /etc/issue
fi
```

You can modify other scripts if you need to, but it is a straightforward process to modify this one. You don't have to worry about ruining anything if you use it.

Summary

Linux configuration is a big topic. In this chapter, the basics of configuring Red Hat Linux are described by example. The Red Hat RPM system makes the task of adding, removing, and upgrading system functions, applications, and utilities very easy. The Linux system itself is modular and easy to modify. The following topics are covered in this chapter:

◆ The Red Hat Linux configuration tools are introduced in this chapter. Configuration issues were not discussed in order to get Red Hat Linux up and running as quickly as possible.

◆ The major installation and configuration topics this chapter covers include the RPM system, the X Window system, the Red Hat Control Panel, building a custom kernel, and the Linux startup scripts.

◆ The Red Hat Package Manager (RPM) provides a simple and sure method for installing, upgrading, uninstalling, querying, and verifying Linux packages. Linux packages are software stored in a format that works with RPM. They include the base Linux system, important Linux configuration files, and applications.

◆ Detailed descriptions of each of the RPM major functions (install, upgrade, uninstall, query, and verify) are given.

◆ Several examples that demonstrate how to use the RPM are given. In particular, you are shown how to use the query function in order to discover information about installed packages as well as ones available |on the Red Hat distribution CD-ROM.

◆ The first RPM installation example is used to install some documentation. This is a simple and straightforward example that also provides useful information.

◆ The second RPM installation example is more complex because it requires a package that in turn requires another package – so the installation order is important. It installs the basic networking support. The basic networking was not installed in Chapter 1 and is required if you are to remotely communicate with your Linux box.

◆ The last RPM installation example is quite complex. In anticipation of a number of systems that need to be installed and compiled in the future, I show you how to install the GNU C compiler (gcc) and the Make utility. The gcc compiler requires many libraries and the Linux kernel header files, so several other packages must be installed in the correct order.

◆ A verify example shows how to find out what package files have been changed. This is useful for debugging and as general information.

◆ Until the advent of RPM, most Linux subsystems were distributed through tar files. They were unpacked and semimanually installed. Installation often required compiling the source code. The Make facility helped the process by not only compiling the source code but also transferring it to its final destination.

◆ The manual – non RPM – installation of diald is used to show you how things were done before RPM, and still are in many places. You use the diald system in Chapter 8.

◆ The installation of XFree86, via RPM and the Xconfigurator system is described.

◆ With the X Window system installed, the Red Hat Control Panel GUI is introduced. This method is convenient for performing many administrative functions. Some of the functions are package management, user and group management, and printers and network management.

◆ The LinuxConf configuration system is introduced. It can configure an overlapping set of Linux systems with Control Panel.

◆ The concept of customizing the Linux kernel is introduced. You have the option of adding either modular functions or recompiling static functions indirectly. Modular functions, such as the SLIP module, can be added dynamically while your system is running. For example, when you want to establish an Internet connection with the PPP protocol (as described in Chapter 8) and you are using the base kernel from Chapter 1, you do not have to restart your system or even recompile the kernel; you simply have the SLIP module inserted.

◆ There is a brief description of the process for adding new functions to the Red Hat startup scripts. This is useful for customizing your system to meet your specific needs.

Part III

Expanding your Network Services

Chapter 6

Learning Samba by Example

IN THIS CHAPTER

- Reconfiguring Samba

- Understanding the Samba daemons

- Understanding the Samba configuration file

- Modifying the Samba configuration file

- Modifying Linux

- Configuring a Linux printer

- Adding Samba printer shares

- Authenticating Samba service requests

IN CHAPTERS 1 AND 2, you learned how to set up a simple client-server network. This network has all the essential ingredients to work as the foundation for a practical, useful personal or business system:

- The multiuser, multitasking, virtual memory, and TCP/IP network-ready Linux operating system.

- The resources exported to the network by the Microsoft network-compatible Samba server.

- A Windows 95/98/NT client that can connect to and use the services provided by the Linux-Samba server.

By adding some new parts to this foundation, you can create a powerful network. This chapter shows how to expand your simple network to create a Linux-Samba server capable of running a small business or your home office.

If you did not install Samba during the Red Hat installation process, in Chapter 1, then do so now.

1. Login to chivas as root.

2. Mount the Red Hat Publisher's Edition CD-ROM.

```
mount /mnt/cdrom
```

3. Install the Samba packages.

```
rpm -ivh /mnt/cdrom/RedHat/RPMS/samba*
```

4. There are several examples given later in this chapter that require modifications of the Samba configuration file /etc/smb.conf. It's a good idea to make a backup copy now.

```
cp /etc/smb.conf /etc/smb.conf.orig
```

This file will be used in all examples.

Starting with the basic recipe described in Chapter 2, you can add all the Windows clients you want until you overload the server. (Samba has no practical limits; the only limitation is that of your server.) You add Windows clients by modifying the Samba configuration file /etc/smb.conf. That file controls the following ingredients:

◆ Directories to be shared over the network. They are called shares or services.

◆ Printers to be shared over the network. These too are called shares or services.

◆ Who gets to use each directory. Access can be provided to an individual, specific individuals, groups, or everybody.

◆ Who gets to use each printer. Access can be provided to an individual, specific individuals, groups, or everybody.

◆ Miscellaneous parameters used for security, access, and tuning.

This chapter focuses on reconfiguring Samba. By modifying the Samba server, you can immediately transform what started as a simple example of Samba into a truly useable business or personal server. This chapter also describes how you can further expand your Samba system by adding some users and modifying permissions to the Linux system.

With the introduction of Samba 2.0 a graphical interface – SWAT – has been added. It simplifies the job of modifying Samba. However, it is important that you understand how the smb.conf file affects the behavior of Samba and how to modify it. The use of graphical interfaces can simplify your job in the long run but unless you understand the underlying system you will not sufficiently understand your system. Therefore, most of the examples show how to manually modify Samba.

Understanding Samba

In principle, the process for adding Samba clients is simple. By editing the smb.conf file, you can add, delete, and modify shares. A share is a resource – usually a directory or a printer — that the Samba server provides to the network. When viewed from the Samba configuration side — that is, in the `smb.conf` file — a share is known as a service. The `smb.conf` file is divided into sections that define the services.

You will modify the `smb.conf` file many times in this chapter, so make a backup copy of it before you begin the examples. At the beginning of every example, you are asked to restore `smb.conf` from the backup copy. Each example starts with the original `smb.conf` in order to minimize possible confusion. Enter the following command to create the backup copy:

```
cp /etc/smb.conf /etc/smb.conf.orig
```

Many parameters are available to configure Samba. Some are variations or synonyms of other parameters; others are used for fine-tuning the network. This chapter concentrates on the most important and widely used parameters. Because you can combine even just a few parameters in many ways, configuring Samba can be a complicated task.

Before you get into the mechanics of reconfiguring Samba, however, you need to understand Samba daemons. The following section offers a quick review of the Samba daemons, which make use of the configuration parameters.

Understanding the Samba daemons

Recall that at the heart of Samba are the two daemons — system processes that run continually in the background — `smbd` and `nmbd`. The `smbd` daemon monitors the network for share requests. When it detects a share request, `smbd` goes through Linux to get the resource that the share represents — that is, a directory or a printer — and makes this resource available to the Samba client(s) that requested it. The resource — a file, for example — stays on the Linux server, but the Samba client can make use of it just as if it were located on the client's disk.

The name server — `nmbd` — controls browsing done by Windows clients (such as when you open the Network Neighborhood), and responds to the Windows clients' requests to locate Samba servers. (A name server converts an IP name into its numeric IP address. Thus, `nmbd` converts `toluca.paunchy.com` into `192.168.1.1`.) Both daemons read the `smb.conf` file when they start up, to discover exactly which services to export.

You ask for a share when you open a directory, a file, or a printer from your Windows environment. In Chapter 1, for example, you access a share when you open the root directory from the Network Neighborhood.

The `smbd` daemon creates a copy of itself whenever it answers a share request. Try opening the root share from the Network Neighborhood on your computer by double-clicking the computer icon; you should see a window open with the contents — if any — of the `/root` directory. If you don't see anything, try copying a file

into the /root directory. Next, login to your Linux server as root and enter the following command:

```
ps x  |  grep smbd
```

You should see two smbd daemons (unless you have already started to experiment and have mounted other shares) as shown below. The process numbers you
see will differ from those in the listing. Note that the grep command you entered is
also shown, because it runs at the same time as the ps command. The question
marks after the process IDs (PIDs) indicate that these processes are not associated
with any IO device, which makes sense because they are daemons.

```
183   ?    S    0:00 smbd -D
3664  ?    S    0:00 smbd -D
3693  p0   S    0:00 grep smbd
```

Recall from Chapter 1 that you can start the smbd and nmbd daemons by running
the script /etc/rc.d/init.d/smb start. (You can run the same script to stop the
daemons, replacing the parameter start with stop.)

TIP   You can find complete descriptions of smbd and nmbd in their respective
man pages. To view these man pages, login to your Linux box and enter the
following commands: **man smbd** or **man nmbd**.

Introducing the Samba configuration file: smb.conf

The Samba daemons get all their directions from the smb.conf file. The smb.conf
file has a straightforward syntax and structure. The smb.conf file includes numerous – and in some cases, interdependent – commands. However, you can ignore
most of these commands at first, because they deal with specialized functions.

EXAMINING THE SMB.CONF SYNTAX

The smb.conf file has a simple structure (it's similar to Microsoft's WIN.INI file), as
listed here:

♦ The file is divided into sections. Each section contains parameters that define the shares Samba is to export and their operational details.

♦ A global section defines the parameters that control the general Samba
characteristics.

◆ Other than the global section, each section defines a specific service. Each section begins with a name enclosed within square brackets – for example, [home] – and continues until the next section appears or the end of the smb.conf file occurs. Sections define services.

◆ You specify a parameter with the following syntax:

name = value

The name can be one or more words separated by spaces. The value can be Boolean (true or false; yes or no; 1 or 0), numeric, or a character string.

◆ Comments are preceded by a semicolon (;) and can appear either as a separate line or after a name-value pair.

◆ You may continue lines from one to another by placing a backward slash (\) as the last character on the line to be continued.

◆ Section and parameter names are not case-sensitive. For example, the parameter browseable = yes works the same as browseable = YeS.

EXAMINING THE SMB.CONF FUNCTIONS

The smbd and nmbd daemons read the smb.conf configuration file when they are started (usually at boot time). The configuration file tells these daemons which shares to export, to whom the shares should be exported, and how to export them. The term *export* means to make available a service or share to one or more clients over the network. Because security is always a top priority, you must be specific about which computers can access a share. The smb.conf file offers tremendous flexibility for specifying precisely who has access to each service. As your Linux network grows, this control becomes increasingly important.

You may already be familiar with Novell or NFS networks. They both share, or export, directory and print services to clients on the network. In this way, their function is the same as Samba's.

EXAMINING THE SMB.CONF STRUCTURE

The smb.conf file has three main parts:

◆ The global parameters

◆ The directory shares section – including the standard [homes] section

◆ The printer shares section

The global parameters, as you may guess, set the rules for the entire system. The [homes] and [printer] sections are special instances of services. The term *services* is the Samba terminology for the directories and printers to be shared or exported with the network clients. The services define who should be able to access them and how. Listing 6-1 shows a summary of the Red Hat default smb.conf file.

Listing 6-1: The smb.conf structure

```
[global]
   workgroup = MYGROUP
   server string = Samba Server
   printcap name = /etc/printcap
   load printers = yes
   log file = /var/log/samba/log.%m
   max log size = 50
   security = user
   socket options = TCP_NODELAY SO_RCVBUF=8192 SO_SNDBUF=8192
   dns proxy = no

[homes]
   comment = Home Directories
   browseable = no
   writable = yes

[printers]
   comment = All Printers
   path = /var/spool/samba
   browseable = no
   guest ok = no
   writable = no
   printable = yes
```

In the global section of the example in Listing 6-1, the printers are the first shares to be described. This example specifies BSD – or Berkeley – style printing. (more is said about BSD style printing a bit later in this section.) The standard /etc/printcap is the printer definition file, and the Boolean variable (it can only be yes or no – true or false) load printers says that all printers can be browsed on the network. These three lines in the global section set the printing for the entire Samba system.

The /etc/printcap file contains the configuration information for the Linux printers. In Red Hat Linux, the lpd daemon reads the printcap file for its configuration information. Then it monitors the system for print requests and manages the printing process.

The [global] section also defines where the log and lock directories are located. The log files are useful for troubleshooting problems and for tuning your system. The lock files prevent multiple users from overwriting the same files.

The [homes] section defines the generic parameters for how an individual user's directories are exported. If your Windows 95/98/98 user name matches a Linux user name and you supply the correct password, you can double-click this icon in the Network Neighborhood and gain access to your home directory.

The [printers] section describes how printers are configured, of course.

You can expand on these special sections to create more specific services. They are useful in and of themselves, but you can also view them as templates.

The man page offers a complete description of smb.conf. To view it, enter the following command:

```
man smb.conf
```

Note: BSD printing is probably the most popular style of UNIX (and certainly Linux) printing. It uses the Berkeley model instead of System V. The daemon lpd and the program lpr both read the /etc/printcap file to learn about the printer definitions. The daemon lpd is started at boot time – and can be restarted at any time by root. It prints any leftover print jobs and then runs continuously in the background, listening for print requests from lpr. The program lpr is used to initiate the printing of a file. It copies the file to a spool directory – a temporary place to hold the file – and then signals lpd that a file is ready to be printed. The spooled file is then converted by filter programs to a printable form and then sent to the printer by lpd.

Introducing the Red Hat default smb.conf file

As you may expect, Red Hat provides a nicely preconfigured smb.conf file. Listing 6-2 shows a copy of the file that you install in Chapter 1. This is the standard configuration file that comes with the Samba system.

Listing 6-2: The Samba smb.conf file

```
# This is the main Samba configuration file. You should read the
# smb.conf(5) manual page in order to understand the options listed
# here. Samba has a huge number of configurable options (perhaps too
# many!) most of which are not shown in this example
#
# Any line which starts with a ; (semi-colon) or a # (hash)
# is a comment and is ignored. In this example we will use a #
# for commentary and a ; for parts of the config file that you
# may wish to enable
#
# NOTE: Whenever you modify this file you should run the command "testparm"
# to check that you have not made any basic syntactic errors.
#
```

```
#======================= Global Settings =======================================
[global]

# workgroup = NT-Domain-Name or Workgroup-Name
    workgroup = MYGROUP

# server string is the equivalent of the NT Description field
    server string = Samba Server

# This option is important for security. It allows you to restrict
# connections to machines on your local network. The
# following example restricts access to two C class networks and
# the "loopback" interface. For more examples of the syntax see
# the smb.conf man page
;    hosts allow = 192.168.1. 192.168.2. 127.

# if you want to automatically load your printer list rather
# than setting them up individually then you'll need this
    printcap name = /etc/printcap
    load printers = yes

# It should not be necessary to spell out the print system type unless
# yours is non-standard. Currently supported print systems include:
# bsd, sysv, plp, lprng, aix, hpux, qnx
;    printing = bsd

# Uncomment this if you want a guest account, you must add this to /etc/passwd
# otherwise the user "nobody" is used
;  guest account = pcguest

# this tells Samba to use a separate log file for each machine
# that connects
    log file = /var/log/samba/log.%m

# Put a capping on the size of the log files (in Kb).
    max log size = 50

# Security mode. Most people will want user-level security. See
# security_level.txt for details.
    security = user
# Use password server option only with security = server
;    password server = <NT-Server-Name>

# Password Level allows matching of _n_ characters of the password for
# all combinations of upper and lower case.
```

```
;   password level = 8
;   username level = 8

# You may wish to use password encryption. Please read
# ENCRYPTION.txt, Win95.txt and WinNT.txt in the Samba documentation.
# Do not enable this option unless you have read those documents
   encrypt passwords = yes
   smb passwd file = /etc/smbpasswd

# The following are needed to allow password changing from Windows to
# update the Linux system password also.
# NOTE: Use these with 'encrypt passwords' and 'smb passwd file' above.
# NOTE2: You do NOT need these to allow workstations to change only
#        the encrypted SMB passwords. They allow the Unix password
#        to be kept in sync with the SMB password.
;   unix password sync = Yes
;   passwd program = /usr/bin/passwd %u
;   passwd chat = *New*UNIX*password* %n\n *ReType*new*UNIX*password* %n\n
*passwd:*all*authentication*tokens*updated*successfully*

# Unix users can map to different SMB User names
;   username map = /etc/smbusers

# Using the following line enables you to customize your configuration
# on a per machine basis. The %m gets replaced with the netbios name
# of the machine that is connecting
;    include = /etc/smb.conf.%m

# Most people will find that this option gives better performance.
# See speed.txt and the manual pages for details
     socket options = TCP_NODELAY SO_RCVBUF=8192 SO_SNDBUF=8192

# Configure Samba to use multiple interfaces
# If you have multiple network interfaces then you must list them
# here. See the man page for details.
;    interfaces = 192.168.12.2/24 192.168.13.2/24

# Configure remote browse list synchronization here
#   request announcement to, or browse list sync from:
#        a specific host or from / to a whole subnet (see below)
;    remote browse sync = 192.168.3.25 192.168.5.255
# Cause this host to announce itself to local subnets here
;    remote announce = 192.168.1.255 192.168.2.44
```

```
# Browser Control Options:
# set local master to no if you don't want Samba to become a master
# browser on your network. Otherwise the normal election rules apply
;     local master = no

# OS Level determines the precedence of this server in master browser
# elections. The default value should be reasonable
;     os level = 33

# Domain Master specifies Samba to be the Domain Master Browser. This
# allows Samba to collate browse lists between subnets. Don't use this
# if you already have a Windows NT domain controller doing this job
;     domain master = yes

# Preferred Master causes Samba to force a local browser election on startup
# and gives it a slightly higher chance of winning the election
;     preferred master = yes

# Use only if you have an NT server on your network that has been
# configured at install time to be a primary domain controller.
;     domain controller = <NT-Domain-Controller-SMBName>

# Enable this if you want Samba to be a domain logon server for
# Windows95 workstations.
;     domain logons = yes

# if you enable domain logons then you may want a per-machine or
# per user logon script
# run a specific logon batch file per workstation (machine)
;     logon script = %m.bat
# run a specific logon batch file per username
;     logon script = %U.bat

# Where to store roving profiles (only for Win95 and WinNT)
#         %L substitutes for this server's netbios name, %U is username
#         You must uncomment the [Profiles] share below
;     logon path = \\%L\Profiles\%U

# All NetBIOS names must be resolved to IP Addresses
# 'Name Resolve Order' allows the named resolution mechanism to be specified
# the default order is "host lmhosts wins bcast." "host" means use the unix
# system gethostbyname() function call that will use either /etc/hosts OR
# DNS or NIS depending on the settings of /etc/host.config, /etc/nsswitch.conf
# and the /etc/resolv.conf file. "host" therefore is system configuration
# dependant. This parameter is most often of use to prevent DNS lookups
```

```
# in order to resolve NetBIOS names to IP Addresses. Use with care!
# The example below excludes use of name resolution for machines that are NOT
# on the local network segment
# - OR - are not deliberately to be known via lmhosts or via WINS.
; name resolve order = wins lmhosts bcast


# Windows Internet Name Serving Support Section:
# WINS Support - Tells the NMBD component of Samba to enable it's WINS Server
;   wins support = yes


# WINS Server - Tells the NMBD components of Samba to be a WINS Client
# Note: Samba can be either a WINS Server, or a WINS Client, but NOT both
;   wins server = w.x.y.z


# WINS Proxy - Tells Samba to answer name resolution queries on
# behalf of a non WINS capable client, for this to work there must be
# at least oneWINS Server on the network. The default is NO.
;   wins proxy = yes


# DNS Proxy - tells Samba whether or not to try to resolve NetBIOS names
# via DNS nslookups. The built-in default for versions 1.9.17 is yes,
# this has been changed in version 1.9.18 to no.
   dns proxy = no


# Case Preservation can be handy - system default is _no_
# NOTE: These can be set on a per share basis
;   preserve case = no
;   short preserve case = no
# Default case is normally upper case for all DOS files
;   default case = lower
# Be very careful with case sensitivity - it can break things!
;   case sensitive = no


#============================ Share Definitions ============================
[homes]
   comment = Home Directories
   browseable = no
   writable = yes


# Un-comment the following and create the netlogon directory for Domain Logons
; [netlogon]
;   comment = Network Logon Service
;   path = /home/netlogon
;   guest ok = yes
;   writable = no
```

```
;    share modes = no


# Un-comment the following to provide a specific roving profile share
# the default is to use the user's home directory
;[Profiles]
;    path = /home/profiles
;    browseable = no
;    guest ok = yes


# NOTE: If you have a BSD-style print system there is no need to
# specifically define each individual printer
[printers]
    comment = All Printers
    path = /var/spool/samba
    browseable = no
# Set public = yes to allow user 'guest account' to print
    guest ok = no
    writable = no
    printable = yes
```

Recall from Chapter 1 that Red Hat preconfigures Samba to export the Linux user's home directories. Root is the only user that you have on your system so far. If you open the Network Neighborhood and open (double-click) your Linux box icon, you should see the root share displayed.

The Samba configuration file contains the basic three services from Listing 6-2, but the file adds several examples services that are commented out with the semi-colon character (;). In the following examples comments are removed in order to show how Samba services work.

Configuring Samba to use encrypted passwords

To make Samba understand encrypted passwords, you must modify the smb.conf file and create an smbpasswd file. First, edit the /etc/smb.conf file, and make sure that the security setting reads security = user. Next, uncomment the following two lines:

```
encrypt passwords = yes
smb passwd file = /etc/smbpasswd
```

Next, create the smbpasswd file from your /etc/passwd file by running the following command:

```
cat /etc/passwd | mksmbpasswd.sh > /etc/smbpasswd
```

Introducing Bourne Again Shell Aliases

The Bourne Again Shell ("bash") that is standard to Linux and is automatically selected for you by Red Hat — and probably every other distribution — has the facility to associate a synonym, or alias, with a command or command string. Here's the form you use for setting an alias:

```
alias synonym=command
```

For example, to speed your ability to log out, you may set the following alias:

```
alias lo=exit
```

Or if you want to create an alias for a command and some accompanying parameters, enclose the command string in single quotes. For example, I like to use long listings but don't like to type, so I use the following alias:

```
alias l='ls -l'
```

You can enter an alias from the bash command prompt, but it is more useful to have aliases set when you login. The .bashrc file is executed every time you login and can be found in your home directory (~/.bashrc). Some aliases are already defined in this file, but I like to have the same aliases on all my accounts so I define them in /etc/bashrc, which .bashrc executes automatically. You can also define your own file (for example, user_aliases), place it anywhere, and then add a line to .bashrc to source your file. The file containing the alias definitions is not executed but is sourced. Therefore, you must remember to include a line such as this in your script:

```
source /etc/bashrc
```

Or, you can use this line in your script:

```
. /etc/bashrc
```

To remove an alias, use the unalias command. For example, to remove the lo alias, enter the following command:

```
unalias lo
```

You can list all aliases by using the alias command by itself.

The first few lines of the smbpasswd file look like the following (some of the X's have been deleted so that the entries fit onto the page):

```
#
# SMB password file.
#
```

```
root:0:XXXXXXXXXXXXXXXXXXXX:XXXXXXXXXXXXXXXXXX:root:/root:/bin/bash
bin:1:XXXXXXXXXXXXXXXXXXXXXX:XXXXXXXXXXXXXXXXXXXXXXXXXXX:bin:/bin:
daemon:2:XXXXXXXXXXXXXXXXXXXXX:XXXXXXXXXXXXXXXXXXXXXX:daemon:/sbin:
adm:3:XXXXXXXXXXXXXXXXXXXXXX:XXXXXXXXXXXXXXXXXXXXXXX:adm:/var/adm:
lp:4:XXXXXXXXXXXXXXXX:XXXXXXXXXXXXXXXX:lp:/var/spool/lpd:
```

Delete any lines that don't start with the username of a user on your system. Leaving the entries for the system users (root, daemon, bin) can create a security hole.

Next, you need to create a Samba password for each user that you want to provide with Samba access. Run the smbpasswd command as follows, where *iamauser* is the name of the user whose password you want to set:

```
smbpasswd iamauser
```

The smbpasswd program prompts you to enter the password twice. The iamauser entry in the /etc/smbpasswd should now look something like the following:

```
iamauser:500:834A03B3blahblahblahD80EBE5326::/home/iamauser:/bin/bash
```

Configuring Samba to Authenticate from an NT Server

Samba can also use an NT domain controller to authenticate requested shares. (The discussion of NT domain controllers are beyond the scope of this book.) In this case, you need to modify the /etc/smb.conf file to point to the NT controller. Change the security parameter to specify the use of an NT domain controller as follows:

```
security = server
```

Next, uncomment the following line:

```
;   password server = <NT-Server-Name>
```

Next, edit this line to include the name of the NT server, which in this case is called my_pdc:

```
password server = my_pdc
```

The name of your domain controller should convert into the IP address of your NT primary domain controller via DNS. Please take note that you could specify the IP address if you desire. For instance, if your controller address is 192.168.1.100, then you could enter the following line:

```
password server = 192.168.1.100
```

You must, of course, have an account on the primary domain controller.

The Xs have been replaced with the encrypted password. Next, you need to re-peat this process for each user.

Restart the Samba daemons:

```
/etc/rc.d/init.d/smb restart
```

Login to your Windows box and enter a user name and password that corre-spond to a user you have entered in the Samba password file. You should see that user's home directory in the Windows Network Neighborhood folder.

 TIP If you configure Samba to accept encrypted passwords, it still accepts plain text ones as well. When using encryption, Samba first tries to authenticate a share request against the encrypted version of the associated password. If that fails, Samba attempts to authenticate against the plain text password.

For further information on configuring Samba for encrypted passwords, read the ENCRYPTION.txt, Passwords.txt, Win95.txt, and WinNT.txt files in the /usr/doc/ samba-2.0.5a/docs/textdocs directory.

Creating Linux Users

The following Samba examples require the addition of user and printer shares. Adding user and printer shares requires that users and printers be known explicitly by Linux. Therefore, you need to know about some basic Linux administration tasks. This is a good time to address these tasks, because you have gone a long time without touching Linux.

Adding users to Linux

To make use of the standard [home] Samba shares, you must add one or more users to your Linux box. Users are defined in the /etc/passwd and /etc/group files.

Red Hat reasonably suggests that you use the User Configuration GUI from its Control Panel or LinuxConf administrative tool, or command line programs user-add and userdel, to add, delete, and modify users. All are good methods that you should plan to make use of in general. However, it is useful to manually create a user — at least once — in order to understand what goes on under the hood. So for now, I'll explain the password file, and give instructions for modifying the /etc/passwd and /etc/group files in order to add users.

All Linux distributions have the same /etc/passwd file format, with fields sep-arated by colons (:) in the order shown in Table 6-1. (The top item in this table cor-responds to the left-most item and the bottom item to the right-most item.)

TABLE 6-1 THE /ETC/PASSWD FILE FORMAT

Field	Description
Login name	The name with which the user logs into the system.
Encrypted password	If the user has no password, this field is blank. An asterisk identifies a nonlogin account. Otherwise, this field shows an apparently random jumble of characters representing the encrypted password. (If you use shadow passwords, the encrypted password is moved to the file /etc/shadow, which is not readable by anyone except root and thus is more secure.)
User ID	The user identification number. The number corresponds to the login name after it is set in the passwd file. The numeric user ID can be shown by using the -n and -l options with the ls command (that is, ls -n -l, or, ls -nl)
Group ID	The default group identification number. The number identifies the default group to which the user belongs; you can belong to multiple groups, however. Red Hat uses the individual group convention in which each user belongs to a unique and exclusive group. In the past, a user would belong to one or more general-purpose groups, which created problems. The groups are defined in the /etc/group file.
Name and/or comment	This optional field should contain the user's full name and other pertinent information such as office location, phone number, and pager number (especially important for systems administrators). Commas separate these pieces of information.
Home directory	The user's default directory. This is where you go when you log in.
Shell	Your default login shell. All Linux distributions, including Red Hat, use bash, which is the most commonly used in the Linux world. You can change the shell to ksh, csh, sh, or whatever you want or whatever you desire and want to have access to.

Listing 6-3 shows the default /etc/passwd file that Red Hat provides. Most Linux distributions use the same login names, user IDs, and group IDs through the first ten or so users (but vary in some of the directories). From there, the distributions vary according to their own needs. Don't worry, the details may vary, but they are for the system to use and don't affect your setup.

Listing 6-3: The /etc/passwd file defining all users

```
root:yTSdWTprhi7u6:0:0:root:/root:/bin/bash
bin:*:1:1:bin:/bin:
daemon:*:2:2:daemon:/sbin:
adm:*:3:4:adm:/var/adm:
lp:*:4:7:lp:/var/spool/lpd:
sync:*:5:0:sync:/sbin:/bin/sync
shutdown:*:6:0:shutdown:/sbin:/sbin/shutdown
halt:*:7:0:halt:/sbin:/sbin/halt
mail:*:8:12:mail:/var/spool/mail:
news:*:9:13:news:/var/spool/news:
uucp:*:10:14:uucp:/var/spool/uucp:
operator:*:11:0:operator:/root:
games:*:12:100:games:/usr/games:
gopher:*:13:30:gopher:/usr/lib/gopher-data:
ftp:*:14:50:FTP User:/home/ftp:
nobody:*:99:99:Nobody:/:
```

The next steps show you how to add a user.

Note: The names used in this example, such as lidia, for creating Linux user names and Samba shares are my own. Please feel free to use any names that you want to use.

1. Log in to the Windows computer toluca as the user lidia. If lidia is a new user, then you will be prompted to enter a password. Please enter the same password for lidia in the Windows machine as for lidia on the Linux computer.

2. Log in to the Linux server chivas as root.

3. Edit the /etc/passwd file and add a user name such as the one in the following example

   ```
   lidia::500:500:Lidia es muy bonita:/home/lidia:/bin/bash
   ```

   The format is what is important, so you can use your own name and other details. To be compatible with Red Hat, however, I suggest you use their user and group ID convention and stick with 500 and 500 (unless you have already added one or more users, in which case, you don't really need to add a user here).

4. For now, leave the password field blank — you can set it later with the passwd command.

5. Save and exit the file.

   Now you must — well, should — create a personal group. You do this by editing the /etc/group file shown in Listing 6-4.

Listing 6-4: The /etc/group file

```
root::0:root
bin::1:root,bin,daemon
daemon::2:root,bin,daemon
sys::3:root,bin,adm
adm::4:root,adm,daemon
tty::5:
disk::6:root
lp::7:daemon,lp
mem::8:
kmem::9:
wheel::10:root
mail::12:mail
news::13:news
uucp::14:uucp
man::15:
games::20:
gopher::30:
dip::40:
ftp::50:
nobody::99:
users::100:
```

6. First, add yourself to the users group (100) as shown in the following example (this is what Red Hat does when you use its Control Panel User Configuration process, and I want to stay consistent with it)

```
users::100:lidia
```

Notice the now-familiar nobody group that you have been using in the Samba configuration examples up to this point.

7. Next, add a line for your personal group at the bottom of the file, like the following example

```
lidia::500:lidia
```

8. Save and exit the file.

9. The next step is to create a home directory for your new user. Red Hat likes its users to live in the /home directory. I have no objection to this convention, so enter the make directory command, as in the following example

```
mkdir /home/lidia
```

10. You need to copy some supporting files, such as the bash initialization script — .bashrc — to the new home directory. You can use a skeleton

directory, /etc/skel to copy the new user's basic files from. Enter the copy command, as in the following example

```
cp /etc/skel/.*    /home/lidia
```

Don't worry about the messages omitting the directories. The directories "." and ".." are Linux's method of referring to the current and parent directories, respectively.

Linux uses the convention where support files, such as .bashrc, are hidden from normal directory listings such as ls -l. Linux does this because these files are generally of interest when you're configuring something. To show them, use the all (-a) parameter in the list command (for example, enter **ls -a**, or **ls -la**).

11. You need to change the owner and group for your new directory and configuration files. In the following two commands, the new user lidia is added

```
chown -R lidia /home/lidia
chgrp -R lidia /home/lidia
```

The recursive flag (-R) saves you from having to execute commands several times to account for all the subdirectories and files that your directory contains. Many commands recognize the recursive flag; it tells a command to descend through all subdirectories and perform the same task. This flag is very useful.

You can combine the chown and chgrp commands as follows:
```
chown -R lidia.lidia /home/lidia
```

12. You should change the permissions on /home/lidia. The permissions you choose depend on the requirements of the account. That depends on more variables than is reasonable described here. However, you'll want to give the owner complete access to the home directory, which includes read, write, and execute. For this example, read access is given to lidia's group and no privilege to everyone else (other). Enter the following command

```
chmod 640 /home/lidia
```

13. Finally, you need to set your password (no password is set at this point.). Root can do this via the passwd command. Enter the command **passwd lidia.** You are prompted for a new password. Enter a password and then the confirmation of that password. That's all you need to do. The user `lidia` has been added.

The first job the script does is to define your shell prompt, [root@chivas /etc]#, and then the alias which. If you wish to customize the way your shell is configured you will want to modify this script

A Source of Quick Help

When you enter the `--h` or `--help` parameter with GNU commands, they print a short help menu. For example, entering `chown --help` displays the screen. This help tool is more convenient than running a man page because it is quicker and more to the point.

```
Usage: chown [OPTION]... OWNER[.[GROUP]] FILE...
  or:  chown [OPTION]... .GROUP FILE...
  or:  chown [OPTION]... --reference=RFILE FILE...
Change the owner and/or group of each FILE to OWNER and/or GROUP.

  -c, --changes          be verbose whenever change occurs
      --dereference      affect the referent of each symbolic link, rather
                         than the symbolic link itself
  -h, --no-dereference   affect symbolic links instead of any referenced file
                         (available only on systems that can change the
                         ownership of a symlink)
  -f, --silent, --quiet  suppress most error messages
      --reference=RFILE  use the owner and group of RFILE instead of using
                         explicit OWNER.GROUP values
  -R, --recursive        operate on files and directories recursively
  -v, --verbose          explain what is being done
      --help             display this help and exit
      --version          output version information and exit

Owner is unchanged if missing.  Group is unchanged if missing, but changed
to login group if implied by a period.  A colon may replace the period.

Report bugs to <bug-fileutils@gnu.org>.
```

Take a moment to examine the `.bashrc` file. It contains a line, `. /etc/bashrc`, that tells the shell to source — or put into effect — the generic `.bashrc` script as shown below.

```
# /etc/bashrc

# System wide functions and aliases
# Environment stuff goes in /etc/profile

# For some unknown reason bash refuses to inherit
# PS1 in some circumstances that I can't figure out.
# Putting PS1 here ensures that it gets loaded every time.
PS1="[\u@\h \W]\\$ "
```

The bash shell treats any text after a pound symbol (#) as a comment, except when the first line begins with the combination #!. In that case, the bash shell treats the following string as the command interpreter. For example, #!/bin/bash, tells Linux to use the bash shell to interpret the script.

Creating Samba Shares

I like to learn by example, so the following sections give you some examples to try. The first examples require only minimal modifications to the `smb.conf` file. Subsequent examples require you to add a printer and a user or two to your Linux system. Even so, you don't have to do very much to your system to get some work out of it.

Please be aware that the Red Hat Linux distribution that comes with this book supplies a Samba configuration and also starts Samba when you boot your system. (See Chapter 1 for Samba installation instructions.) The Samba configuration uses what is called user level security and is specified in the `/etc/smb.conf` file by the parameter `security = user`. Using this type of security requires that in order to open a Samba share, you must supply a Windows 95/98 login name and password that matches an existing Linux user name and password.

As a system administrator, you should know how to send signals to processes. The Linux `kill` command is used to send signals to processes. The most widely used signals are `SIGHUP` (numeric value 1), which is generally used to signal a process to reread its configuration file, and `SIGKILL` (numeric value 9), which terminates a process.

The manual page on signals gives a complete list of Linux signals (as does the command `kill -l`). To access this man page, enter **man 7 signal**. (Note that nine divisions of man pages exist. That's why the `/usr/man` directory has nine subdirectories — `/usr/man/man1` through `/usr/man/man9`. For example, you find the manual pages on user commands in `/usr/man/man1`.

If you ask for a man page on a topic that exists in more than one area, the topic with the lowest number appears. That is why you need to specify the 7 in the preceding command — if you simply enter **man signal**, you get the same manual page as if you had entered **man 2 signal**.

Because you are going to be editing the configuration file a lot, you may want to set some aliases to make your life easier. My aliases are as follows:

```
alias sm='/usr/bin/smbstatus'
alias sn='/usr/bin/nmblookup'
alias smbstop='/etc/rc.d/init.d/smb stop'
alias smbstart='/etc/rc.d/init.d/smb start'
alias st='/usr/bin/testparm'
alias se='vi /etc/smb.conf'
```

Add these aliases to `/etc/bashrc`, or your own file, to retain them for successive logins. If you change them, you can make your system recognize the change by sourcing the file:

```
source /etc/bashrc
```

Note that `/etc/aliases` and `/etc/aliases.db` are not used for command aliases. They are, however, used by `sendmail` for its own purposes.

Starting and stopping Samba

As you proceed to create more complex client-server networks, you must be more careful about making sure that you keep Samba up-to-date. In the preceding example, the new smbd process reads the new configuration — that happens because each new share gets its own daemon. However, the original `smbd` does not know that `smb.conf` has changed. You have two Samba daemons running with two different configurations.

This situation can create difficulties as the number of `smbd` processes increases. Just imagine five or six `smbd` processes running at once as you experiment with new configurations. Trying to keep track of what's what becomes counterproductive — you can end up confused and traveling in circles very quickly. Of course, you can manually HUP all the Samba daemons — `kill -HUP` — but that can be confusing and time-consuming, too.

Here's an easier way to stay current. Because Samba daemons are a dime a dozen, it's simpler just to terminate all `smbd` processes and then start them up again. Red Hat, being the value-added Linux hero, provides an easy way of doing just that. It runs an `rc` script — `/etc/rc.d/init.d/smb` — at boot time to start the Samba daemons. You can also use this script anytime you want. Enter the following command (or the aliases, `smbstop` and `smbstart`, which are defined in a Tip in the preceding section) to restart the daemon:

```
killall HUP smbd nmbd
```

You may encounter irrecoverable errors if you stop and restart the Samba daemons while a share is being accessed. In my experience, if you restart Samba while you are reading or writing to a Samba share, you will lose your network connection. Most of the time, my Microsoft applications indicate that the connection was lost and prompt me to either try to make the connection again or cancel the attempt to reconnect. I generally click the Retry button and everything returns to normal; alternately, if I click the Cancel button, my data may be saved on my local disk or lost entirely. However, on occasion, I've received an unrecoverable error message, which led to my application closing and me losing the data. The answer is to be careful when you reset the Samba daemons. If you are working with other people, make sure that you reset the daemons when you are sure nobody is working on the system. You can use the smbstatus application to see if there are open shares. If there are, then ask the users to save their work and log out of their shares by closing any applications that are using the shares.

Any services that you had open will not be active because they were tied to the daemon you just terminated. However, they return as soon as you access them again. For example, if the computer icon `chivas` is opened from my `Network Neighborhood`, the same share becomes active again. If the window is still open, simply choose the Refresh option from the View menu, and that same share becomes active again; the `smbd` daemon has a new PID, however, because it is a brand-new process.

Accessing an individual user's home directory

Here's where things get interesting. In this section, you learn how to create a service out of the new user account, `lidia` (whose creation is shown in the preceding section of this chapter). After you create a new user account on the Linux-Samba server, you can automatically access its home directory from Samba. The default `smb.conf` file is pre-configured to export the home directory of Windows clients whose user names/passwords match the Linux user name/password. This is the same service that you use in Chapter 1, but the difference here is that a regular Linux user is created to make use of the service.

1. Log in to the Windows computer toluca as the user lidia.

2. Log in to the Linux server `chivas` as `root`.

3. Restore your original `smb.conf` file from the backup copy

   `cp /etc/smb.conf.orig /etc/smb.conf`

4. Restart the Samba daemons

   `/etc/rc.d/init.d/smb restart`

5. Double-click on the `chivas` icon in your `Network Neighborhood`.
   Double-click the `lidia` icon shown in Figure 6-1.

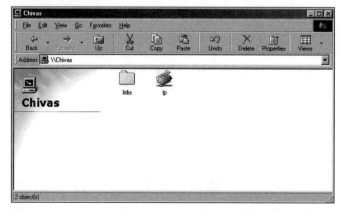

Figure 6-1: The contents of chivas, including the /home/lidia directory, are displayed.

You should see the contents of the `/home/lidia` directory.

6. Run the `smbstatus` command to see what Samba knows about your connection.

```
Samba version 2.0.5a
Service uid  gid  pid  machine
--------------------------------------------------
lidia lidia lidia 1190 toluca (192.168.1.1) Tue Oct 2 1999

No locked files

Share mode memory usage (bytes):
   1048464(99%) free + 56(0%) used + 56(0%) overhead =
1048576(100%) total
```

7. In this case, Samba sees the user — and group — lidia connecting from the machine toluca. The service `lidia` points to the `/home/lidia` directory, which not shown in the `smbstatus` output. The `[homes]` services has worked as advertised!

8. You can read and write to this share and use it just like a local disk!

Introducing Linux and Samba permissions

Linux file permissions play a controlling role in how Samba shares behave. Linux permissions supersede Samba permissions. Therefore, even if Samba says that you can do something, if Linux does not permit it then you cannot do it.

What are file permissions? File permissions control who can read, write, and execute a file. Every file has file permissions for the user that it belongs to, the group that it belongs to, and everyone else. If you do a long format listing of a directory or a file, you get a listing that includes the file's permissions — among other information — in the order just listed. For example, you may enter this command:

```
ls -l /etc/rc.d/init.d/smb
```

Here's the information that this command displays:

```
-rwxr-xr-x   1 root     root         1177 Sep 25 11:12 /etc/rc.d/init.d/smb
```

The characters `rwx` identify the permissions; as you probably have guessed, they stand for read, write, and execute — the hyphen (-) character means no permission. The order of their placement does not vary, so the hyphen in this example means no write permission.

These characters are grouped first as owner permission, then group, and finally other permissions. The owner is root in this case, as is the group (that information is, of course, shown to the right of the 1). The `other` group means any user who is not an owner or a member of the group — that is, other users.

UNDERSTANDING LINUX PERMISSIONS

Linux file permissions are important for Samba management because no matter what permission you set in the Samba configuration, it does not override the Linux file system permissions. For instance, if you set a share to be public but the directory that the share points to does not have the correct permissions set, that share will not be accessible to the public. The following example demonstrates this convention.

1. Log in to the Windows computer toluca as the user lidia.

2. Log in to the Linux server `chivas` as `root`.

3. Restore your original `smb.conf` file from the backup copy (if you have not already done so – as advised earlier in this chapter – reverse the process and make a backup copy)

```
cp /etc/smb.conf.orig /etc/smb.conf
```

4. Edit the `smb.conf` file and remove the comments (;) from the second [tmp] section.

```
[tmp]
    comment = Temporary file space
    path = /tmp
    read only = no
    public = yes
```

5. Save the changes, exit back to your shell prompt, and restart the Samba daemons with the following commands

```
/etc/rc.d/init.d/smb restart
```

6. Back on `toluca`, open the `chivas` share displayed in your Network Neighborhood. Double-click the `tmp` icon and you should see the contents of the /tmp directory similar to that shown in Figure 6-2.

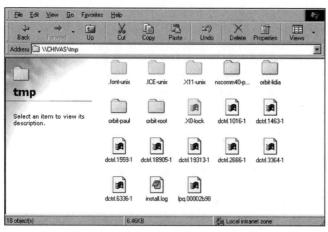

Figure 6-2: The contents of the /tmp directory are displayed.

7. Run the smbstatus command to see what Samba knows about your connection.

```
Samba version 2.0.5a
Service uid     gid    pid  machine
tmp     lidia lidia  5459 toluca (192.168.1.1) Thu Oct 2 1999
```

```
No locked files

Share mode memory usage (bytes):
1048464(99%) free + 56(0%) used + 56(0%) overhead =
1048576(100%) total
```

8. In this case, Samba once again sees the user – and group – lidia connecting from the machine toluca. The tmp service points to the /tmp directory, which is not shown in the smbstatus output.

9. You should be able to see the install.log file, which contains information on the Red Hat packages that you have installed. This file is owned by root. If you do a long listing on the install.log file – ls -l /tmp/install.log – you'll see that only root has the write privilege

```
-rwx------ 1  root    root      7710 Oct  2 03:36 install.log
```

10. Try opening install.log by double-clicking on its icon.

11. You get a dialog box telling you that you do not have the permission to open the file. That is because only the owner root has permission to do anything to the file. You can easily change that by changing the permissions as follows.

```
chmod 774 /tmp/install.log
```

12. Now you can open up the share from your Windows box by double-clicking its icon. (Depending on what version of Windows you are using you might be asked what application program you want to use to open it. You can select an editor such as Microsoft WordPad and then look at the contents of the file.)

13. Try modifying and then saving the file. Once again, you are told that you do not have permission. Even though you have marked the public Samba share pointing to /tmp as writable, you do not have the permission from Linux to do so.

14. Restore the original permissions to the install.log file.

```
chmod 700 /tmp/install.log
```

This proves that Linux permissions always supersede Samba's.

UNDERSTANDING SAMBA PERMISSIONS

In this next example, you once again export the /tmp directory. This time, however, you give world write permission on the install.log file so that you can modify it.

1. Login to the Windows computer toluca as the user lidia.

2. Log in to your Linux-Samba server as root.

3. Change the permissions on the /tmp/install.log file as follows.

```
chmod 777 /tmp/install.log
```

This gives world read, write and execute permissions to install.log.

4. Restore your original smb.conf file from the backup copy (if you have not already done so – as advised earlier in this chapter – reverse the process and make a backup copy)

```
cp /etc/smb.conf.orig /etc/smb.conf
```

5. Edit the smb.conf file and remove the comments (;) from the second [tmp] section and change the read only parameter to yes.

```
[tmp]
    comment = Temporary file space
    path = /tmp
    read only = yes
    public = yes
```

6. Save the changes, exit back to your shell prompt, and restart the Samba daemons

```
/etc/rc.d/init.d/smb restart
```

7. Back on toluca, double-click on the chivas icon in your Network Neighborhood. Double-click the tmp icon and you should see the /tmp directory.

8. Run the smbstatus command to see what Samba knows about your connection.

```
Samba version 2.0.5a
Service uid   gid   pid   machine
-----------------------------------------------
tmp     lidia lidia 1073 toluca(192.168.1.1) Tue Oct 1 1999

No locked files

Share mode memory usage (bytes):
   1048464(99%) free + 56(0%) used + 56(0%) overhead =
1048576(100%) total
```

9. In this case, Samba sees the user – and group – lidia connecting from the machine toluca. The tmp service points to the /tmp directory, which is not shown in the smbstatus output.

10. Do a long listing on the smb.conf file – ls -l /smb.conf – you'll see that the world has read, write and execute privilege

```
rwxrwxrwx   1 root      root      6549 Oct 12 20:19 smb.conf
```

11. Open up the `smb.conf` file from your Windows box by double-clicking the `smb.conf` file icon.

12. Modify the file in any way that you want. For instance, enter the widely used string `asdf`.

13. Try saving the changes. You are not allowed to do so. Even though Linux allows read, write and execute permission to the install.log file, Samba does not allow you to do so. You have set the read only parameter to yes.

14. If you wish to experiment, modify the `smb.conf` and change the `read only` to `no`. Restart Samba and this time you will be able to save any changes that you make. Be careful, however, and make only a trivial change. Once you have convinced yourself that it is possible, remove the changes.

15. Restore the original permissions on the `/tmp/install.log` file as follows.

```
chmod 700 /tmp/install.log
```

This example shows how Samba can manipulate share privileges when the underlying Linux privileges exist.

EXPORTING THE CD-ROM

Exporting the CD-ROM finishes this section up. By doing so, you can provide many useful functions to your network. For example, one very productive service is sharing software – say, your Linux distribution – or other material to your network. Exporting the CD-ROM cuts down on the number of CD-ROM drives you need (although CD-ROM drives are becoming ubiquitous, some of your older machines may not have them). Plus, it saves having to transport a CD-ROM disc from machine to machine.

The following example once again makes use of the default `smb.conf` file. The following instructions show you how to export the `/mnt/cdrom` directory.

1. Login to the Windows computer `toluca` as the user `lidia`.

2. Login to the Linux server `chivas` as `root`.

3. Restore your original `smb.conf` file from the backup copy (if you have not already done so – as advised earlier in this chapter – reverse the process and make a backup copy)

```
cp /etc/smb.conf.orig /etc/smb.conf
```

4. Edit the `smb.conf` file and find the `[tmp]` share section. Remove the comments, and then change the `[tmp]` share name to `[cdrom]` and the `path = /tmp` to `path = /mnt/cdrom`, as shown below.

```
[cdrom]
   comment = share CD-ROM
   path = /mnt/cdrom
```

```
read only = no
public = yes
```

5. Save the changes, exit back to your shell prompt, and restart the Samba daemons

```
/etc/rc.d/init.d/smb restart
```

6. Mount the CD-ROM that came with this book by entering the following command

```
mount -r -t iso9660 /dev/cdrom /mnt/cdrom
```

7. Double-click on the chivas icon in your Network Neighborhood. Double-click the cdrom icon and you should see the /mnt/cdrom directory, as shown in Figure 6-3.

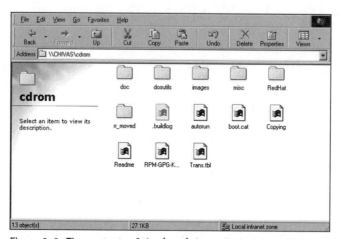

Figure 6-3: The contents of the /mnt/cdrom directory are displayed.

8. Run the smbstatus command to see what Samba knows about your connection.

```
Samba version 2.0.5a
Service    uid     gid      pid       machine
-------------------------------------------------
cdrom      root    root     1190      toluca (192.168.1.1) Tue Oct
12 22:58:40 1999

No locked files

Share mode memory usage (bytes):
    1048464(99%) free + 56(0%) used + 56(0%) overhead =
1048576(100%) total
```

9. In this case, Samba sees the user – and group – lidia connecting from the machine toluca. The cdrom service points to the /mnt/cdrom directory, which is not shown in the smbstatus output.

Exporting a service to two or more users

This section shows you how to use some of the user parameters, which were introduced in the preceding example. You can use this variable to allow any number of users access to a particular service. This access is not the same as group access, but it works in a similar fashion.

1. Login to the Windows computer toluca as the user paul.

2. Log in to the Linux server chivas as root.

3. Restore your original smb.conf file from the backup copy

   cp /etc/smb.conf.orig /etc/smb.conf

4. Edit the smb.conf file and find the [myshare] share section. Remove the comments, and then change the [myshare] share name to [lidia] and the path = /usr/somewhere/shared to path = /home/lidia and valid users = mary fred to valid users = lidia paul.

   ```
   [Lidia]
   comment = Lidia and Paul's stuff
   path = /home/lidia
   valid users = lidia paul
   public = no
   writable = yes
   printable = no
   create mask = 0765
   ```

5. Save the changes, exit back to your shell prompt, and restart the Samba daemons

   /etc/rc.d/init.d/smb restart

6. If you need to add the new user paul, follow the instructions in the section "Adding Users to Linux," earlier in this chapter, or enter the following command

   useradd paul

7. Set the password for paul by entering the following command

   passwd paul

8. Add paul to the lidia group in /etc/group

   lidia:x:500:paul

9. Change the group ownership of the /home/paul directory as follows

```
chgrp users /home/paul
```

10. Change the permissions on /home/paul to allow group access.

```
chmod 770 /home/paul
```

11. Add paul's password to the /etc/smbpasswd file.

```
smbpasswd paul
```

12. On toluca, double-click your Linux-Samba computer icon – chivas – in your Network Neighborhood. Double-click the lidia icon and you should see the /home/lidia directory.

13. Run the smbstatus command to see what Samba knows about your connection.

```
Samba version 2.0.5a
Service uid    gid    pid  machine
------------------------------------------------
lidia   paul paul 1267 toluca (192.168.1.1) Tue Oct 12 1999

No locked files

Share mode memory usage (bytes):
   1048464(99%) free + 56(0%) used + 56(0%) overhead =
1048576(100%) total
```

14. In this case, Samba sees the user – and group – paul connecting from the machine toluca. The [lidia] service, which points to the /home/lidia directory (not shown in the smbstatus output), is active. The fact that the user ID is paul is important because the service points to lidia's directory, which is fully owned by the user lidia. Thus, Samba has indeed allowed multiple users to access a single share.

 If you had not set the others permission on lidia's directory to read and execute, you would not be able to access lidia's share. Remember, Linux supersedes Samba's permissions and you are recognized as the user paul and the group paul here. So you will only gain access there from the other permissions.

You can avoid this problem by changing the group of /home/lidia from lidia to users. Both lidia and paul belong to that group, which has read, write, and execute permissions on /home/paul.

15. Unlike with the previous examples in this chapter, you can read and write to this share. You can use it just like a local disk!

Using Samba's macro capability

Samba can substitute macros for service parameters. Upon connection, it dynamically allocates its resources according to which machine, user, or other is asking for each resource.

You designate a macro by adding a percent (%) symbol as the first character of any of several predefined names. Table 6-2 shows the macros.

TABLE 6-2 SAMBA MACROS

Macro	Description
%S	Current service or share if it exists (if any exists)
%P	Root directory of the current service or share (if any exists)
%u	User name of the current service or share (if any exists)
%g	Primary group name of %u
%U	Session user name the client requested, but not necessarily the one received
%G	Primary group name of %U
%H	The home directory of the user given by %u
%v	Samba version number
%h	Host name of the Samba server
%m	NetBIOS name of the client computer
%L	NetBIOS name of the Samba server
%M	Internet name of the client computer
%d	Process ID of the current server process
%a	Architecture of the remote server
%I	IP address of the client computer
%T	Current date and time

Experiment with the %u macro in the following example. Note: The names used in this example, such as lidia, are optional. Please feel free to use any names that you want to use.

1. Log in to the Windows computer toluca as the user lidia.

2. Log in to the Linux server chivas as root.

3. Restore your original smb.conf file from the backup copy

   ```
   cp /etc/smb.conf.orig /etc/smb.conf
   ```

4. Edit the smb.conf file and find the [pchome] share section. Remove the comments and then change the path = /usr/pc/%m to path = /home/%u, as shown below. Notice that smb.conf uses the %u macro, which expands into the user name of the Windows user — lidia in this case — connecting to it.

   ```
   ; The %m gets replaced with the machine name that is
   connecting.
   [pchome]
       comment = PC Directories
       path = /home/%u
       public = no
       writeable = yes
   ```

5. Save the changes, exit back to your shell prompt, and restart the Samba daemons

   ```
   /etc/rc.d/init.d/smb restart
   ```

6. On your Windows box, double-click your Linux-Samba computer icon in your Network Neighborhood. Double-click the pchome icon and you should see the /home/lidia directory, as shown in Figure 6-4.

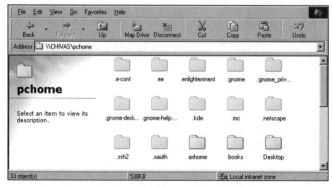

Figure 6-4: The contents of the /home/lidia directory are accessed by lidia as pchome.

7. Run the `smbstatus` command to see what Samba knows about your connection.

```
Samba version 2.0.5a
Service uid    gid pid machine
----------------------------------------------------
pchome  lidia lidia 964 toluca(192.168.1.1) Tue Oct 28 1999

No locked files

Share mode memory usage (bytes):
    1048464(99%) free + 56(0%) used + 56(0%) overhead =
1048576(100%) total
```

8. In this case, Samba sees the user – and group – lidia connected from the machine toluca. The `[pchome]` service, which points to the /home/lidia directory (not shown in the smbstatus output), is active.

This Samba macro-based service attempts to connect every Windows client that comes down the pike. If a valid Linux user name exists, this service will automatically connect a matching Windows client to it. Using macros really simplifies the `smb.conf` file setup, because you can adapt one service section to numerous situations. If you have numerous shares to distribute (or are just plain lazy like me), this option is for you.

Adding network printers using Linux and Samba

No client-server network is complete without a shared printer. Sharing printing gives you a lot of bang for your client-server buck. If you fold the services of just five $200 printers into one $1,000 printer, you come out ahead. You have less maintenance, lower overhead costs, maybe less initial cost, and probably better overall performance. It's a win-win situation.

Before you can configure Samba to share a printer you must first configure a printer. The following section describes how to use Samba's Printtool to do just that.

CONFIGURING A LOCAL PRINTER

Configuring a printer that is attached to a Linux computer is a straightforward process. The following instructions describe how to do it.

1. Log in to the Linux server `chivas` as `root`.

2. Attach a printer to your Linux computer's parallel (printer) port.

3. Start the `Control-Panel` by clicking on the GNOME `start`'`System`' `Control Panel`. The GNOME start button is the little footprint in the lower left-hand corner of your screen. It is similar in function to Windows' Start button.

4. Next, click on the Printer icon, which is the third from the top, and you see the window shown in Figure 6-5.

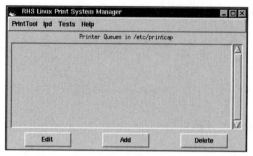

Figure 6-5: The RHS Linux Printer System Manager window

5. If you have not already configured a printer, then you'll get a blank screen. To add a printer, click on the Add button and you'll get the Add a Printer Entry window shown in Figure 6-6.

Figure 06-06: The Add a Printer Entry window

6. The Local Printer radio button should already be set. Choose OK and the printer port(s) that is detected is shown.

7. Click on OK and you are given the Edit Local Printer Entry window shown in Figure 6-7.

Figure 06-07: The Edit Local Printer Entry window

The default values for the printer name, spool directory and file limit fields should all be acceptable. (You can choose any name for the printer that you want but by convention the default name is lp. You can assign multiple names to a single printer.) If your printer port is detected, it should show up in the Printer Device field; if it doesn't, then choose the port yourself. Click the Input Filter Select button and you'll get the window shown in Figure 6-8.

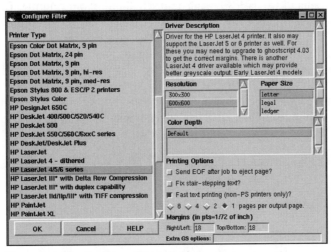

Figure 6-8: The Configure filter window

8. Highlight and select the printer type that you are using and click OK, and control will be sent back to the Edit Local Printer Entry window.

9. Click OK and you are sent back to the RHS Linux Printer System Manager window and your new printer is displayed.

10. Test your new printer by first restarting the print daemon and then use the Tests->Print Postscript test page. Enter the command lpr /etc/printcap

11. Finally, from the Red Hat Print System Manager window, click on the Tests->Print Postscript test page (you can also choose to print a plain text file). The PostScript, or text file, should be printed. You can try a more complex job by using an application like Netscape (included on the companion CD-ROM).

USING SAMBA TO SHARE A PRINTER

Samba, of course, makes network printer sharing easy. You can use a printer that is already connected to your Linux box. All you have to do is configure Samba to use the Linux printer setup. The Linux setup is simple unless you have an unusual printer or some other irregularity. So give it a try. In the following section, I use the existing Red Hat printer configuration to give you a quick tutorial on configuring Linux.

The last example in this chapter shows you how to use a printer over the network. It is perhaps superfluous to extol the virtues of using a printer over the network, but I want to do it anyway. This function alone makes the a network worthwhile. My old company wasted a great deal of time and money purchasing and sharing printers. Until we got our NFS network, we shared printers by means of switch boxes and long serial cables, by physically moving printers, and with a floppy-disk/sneakernet. No method sufficed and we basically ended up self-limiting our printing. This setup severely impaired our productivity, and we didn't realize the extent of the productivity drain until we could all access a common fast laser printer.

The following instructions show how to configure your Linux-Samba server to work as the printer server for your network.

Note: The default `smb.conf` file that comes on this book's CD-ROM does not require any editing to work. The following instructions that refer to it are for instructional purposes only. I continue to use the names found on my system – such as the HP LaserJet 5L (PCL) – and you should make the appropriate substitutions for your system.

1. Login to the Windows computer `toluca` as the user `lidia`.

2. Login to the Linux server `chivas` as `root`.

3. Restore your original `smb.conf` file from the backup copy

   ```
   cp /etc/smb.conf.orig /etc/smb.conf
   ```

   Do not restart the Samba daemons just yet, however.

3. Edit the `smb.conf` file and find the `[global]` share section, as shown below.

   ```
   [global]
   ;  printing = bsd
      printcap name = /etc/printcap
      load printers = yes
   ```

This section gives Samba the following information

- The printing entry specifies which printer daemon Linux uses. (BSD is the default, but Linux also uses `sysv`, `hpux`, `aix`, `qnx`, and `plp`. Linux works well with BSD; the others are mentioned for the sake of being complete.) It also tells Samba the default values for the `lpr` and `lpq` commands that Linux uses to perform the actual printing.

- The `printcap name` parameter defines where the Linux printer configuration file printcap is located.

- The load printers parameter indicates whether to load all the printers defined in the printcap for browsing.

4. Next, find the [printers] share section, as shown below.

```
[printers]
    comment = All Printers
    path = /var/spool/samba
    browseable = no
# Set public = yes to allow user 'guest account' to print
    guest ok = no
    writable = no
    printable = yes
```

This section gives Samba the following information

- A comment describing what it is set up for.

- If browseable is yes, you can browse all the printers defined in the printcap file from a Windows client.

- If printable is yes, it allows nonprinting access to the spool directories associated with the print service. If printable is set to no, it does not prevent you from printing, it simply denies you direct access to the printer spool directories – /var/spool/lpd/lp, for instance.

- If public is set to no, those Windows clients that are not authenticated by a Linux user name (the guest account, for example) will not be able to use the Samba print services.

- If writable is set to no, you will not be able to write directly to the printer spool directory. You will still be able to print, however.

- The create mode determines which default permissions the printer spool files will have.

5. Exit from the smb.conf file and edit the /etc/printcap file. It contains the Linux printer configuration information, and Samba reads this information when it starts. I have a Hewlett Packard LaserJet 5L attached to my Linux computer. The following shows my printcap file.

```
#
# Please don't edit this file directly unless you know what
you are doing!
# Be warned that the control-panel printtool requires a very
strict format!
# Look at the printcap(5) man page for more info.
#
# This file can be edited with the printtool in the control-
panel.

##PRINTTOOL3## LOCAL ljet4 600x600 letter {} LaserJet4
```

```
Default 1
lp:\
        :sd=/var/spool/lpd/lp:\
        :mx#0:\
        :sh:\
        :lp=/dev/lp0:\
        :if=/var/spool/lpd/lp/filter:
```

Here's an explanation of the file's contents

- Anything after a pound sign (#) is treated as a comment.

- Colons (:) bound variables and their parameters.

- A backslash (\) specifies that the parameter continues on the next line.

- The first line after the comments defines the printer name and any aliases (not shell aliases) by which Linux knows the printer (it can have zero or more aliases). The printer name lp (line printer) is standard.

- The sd=/var/spool/lpd/lpd line identifies the location of the printer spool directory. Recall that the lpd daemon spools a print file to a temporary directory. The effect is to buffer the print file so the processor does not have to wait for the much slower printer.

- The mx variable specifies the largest file that can be printed. The pound-zero (#0) makes it unlimited.

- The sh variable is a flag that prevents the printing of a burst page (header page) before each print job. This feature is only useful if you have many users printing to a single printer.

- The lp=/dev/lp1 line defines the device file (in this case, lp1 points to the first parallel port, which would be lpt1 in MS-DOS parlance).

- The if=/var/spool/lpd/lp/filter specifies my input filter. It is used to translate various file formats to a printer. It translates everything from straight text to PostScript into PCL, which is what the HP printer understands.

6. Save the changes, exit back to your shell prompt, and restart the Samba daemons

```
/etc/rc.d/init.d/smb restart
```

The preceding changes to your smb.conf file make all your printers available over your network, which in this case means that you can print to the LaserJet from any of the Windows clients. You can explicitly set parameters (such as where the spool directories are located), but I prefer to keep that information in the printcap file as much as possible.

Red Hat provides a printtool (via its Control Panel) that asks you most necessary questions and translates your responses to a printcap file. Because the Control Panel requires the X Window system, I defer further description until the section "Configuring the Print Server" in Chapter 10 where I show you how to configure the X Window system.

TIP One very useful thing that the Control Panel printtool does is set up printer filters for you. A printer filter can enable you to do things such as print PostScript files to a non-PostScript printer by translating from one protocol to another.

7. Windows may not recognize the new printer when you try to mount it. If you have not configured the printer on your Windows PC, you have to do so. You will get a dialog box asking if you want to configure a printer. If you click the Yes button, the Windows Wizard guides you through the process with minimal confusion. You most likely need your Windows or printer CD-ROM to get the print driver.

8. After you have Windows configured for your Samba printer, open the Network Neighborhood icon. You should see a Samba share 1p, along with any other shares that you have as shown in Figure 6-9.

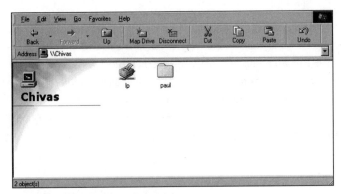

Figure 6-9: The Samba printer share

9. Double-click the lp icon and you get the Windows HP LaserJet 5L (PCL) queue dialog box.

10. To test your Samba print service, click the Printer menu. Next, click the Properties menu item and you get the Windows HP LaserJet 5L (PCL) Properties dialog box.

11. Click the Print Test Page button and a test page is printed for you. In fact, if you keep an eye on the HP LaserJet 5L (PCL) queue dialog box (shown in Figure 6-10), you can see the progress of your print job. Figure 6-10 shows the first stage in which Windows processes the job before sending it to the Linux-Samba server.

Document Name	Status	Owner	Progress	Started At
veracr.eCiLLb	Printing	paul	0 bytes of 2...	10:30:51 PM 10/28/99

1 jobs in queue

Figure 6-10: The test print job being processed by Windows

12. After the print job has been processed by Windows 95/98, it is copied as a file to the Linux-Samba server. The file is then processed as a Linux print job.

13. The test page is finally printed on your printer. It is a marvelous system.

 You can print directly with Linux by redirecting output to the device driver of a printer. For example, if you have a printer connected to your parallel port — the common PC method — you can print the content of a file as follows:

```
cat /etc/smb.conf > /dev/lp1
```

This method is occasionally useful — usually for troubleshooting purposes — but unadvisable in general. Linux uses a spooling system to print. Recall from Chapter 3 how the daemon process, lpd, and the user program, lpr, work in tandem to send a print job to a spool directory and then to the printer. This method efficiently and safely shares a resource among many users and processes. The /etc/printcap file contains the configuration information for each attached printer (both physically and via a network).

Introducing SWAT

The Samba team has introduced the *Samba Web Administration Tool* (SWAT) in the Samba 2.0 distribution. SWAT is a Web-based tool that enables you to use your Web browser to configure Samba. This tool was introduced during the writing of this book. It appears to be a good tool and should only get better with time.

SWAT uses a specialized version of the `httpd` daemon to act as the interface to your Web browser. When you open SWAT with your browser, the `inetd` daemon kicks off the `swat` daemon.

The `inetd` daemon is used for kicking off other daemons on a per-use basis. The `inetd.conf` configuration file controls the action of `inetd`.

Start up your Web browser and enter the `http://localhost:901/` URL in the Location window. You are prompted to enter a user name and password. Enter root as the user name and enter the root password. You are then presented with the SWAT interface window shown in Figure 6-11.

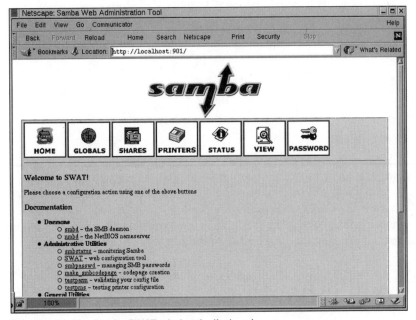

Figure 6-11: The Samba SWAT window is displayed

SWAT is in an a relatively early phase of development. It currently enables you to do all the things that you can do by manually modifying the `smb.conf` file. It allows you to modify the global parameters; add, modify, and create shares (printer shares too); and view the status of open shares. For instance, to modify the Samba workgroup, click GLOBALS, change the name from WORKGROUP to MYGROUP, and then click the Commit Changes button.

Next, look at the /etc/smb.conf file and you see that SWAT not only has changed the workgroup parameter, but it has completely rewritten the file.

```
# from localhost (127.0.0.1)
# Date: 1999/03/30 12:15:12

# Global parameters
        workgroup = MYGROUP
        server string = Samba Server
        log file = /var/log/samba/log.%m
        max log size = 50
        socket options = TCP_NODELAY
        dns proxy = No

[homes]
        comment = Home Directories
        read only = No
        browseable = No

[printers]
        comment = All Printers
        path = /var/spool/samba
        print ok = Yes
        browseable = No
```

SWAT replaces the original smb.conf file with one that does not include all the comments. Any changes that you make with SWAT are written into this new file.

One of SWAT's best features is that you can return any parameter back to its default value by clicking the Set Default button to the right of the field. It also prevents you from specifying incompatible parameters. You can display help on a subject by clicking the Help button to the left of the field.

Troubleshooting

If you have trouble getting Samba to work, please review the steps described in this chapter. Remember that if you are using Windows 98, NT or newer versions of Windows 95, then you need to configure Samba to accept encrypted passwords. Troubleshooting Samba was also discussed in Chapter 3.

Summary

The examples in the previous sections give you an overview of Samba configuration. The variables you use to set the configuration are some of the most widely used ones. In Chapter 10, I give even more detailed examples. These examples cover – in essence – most of the situations you should encounter in setting up a business network. For instance, you can take the steps for allowing two users access to one service and easily expand to a dozen users by including their names in the valid users variable.

This chapter covers these topics:

◆ By working on the Samba configuration first, I show you how to expand the client-server network. This approach offers the most efficient method for obtaining a working system because modifying a simple text file is all that is required.

◆ I review the roles of the two Samba daemons: smbd and nmbd. Together they form the heart of Samba.

◆ I describe the process for restarting the Samba daemons. A new smbd process is started with every new share that is exported. Even so, it is advisable to restart these daemons when configuring Samba to make sure everything works the way you intend it to.

◆ I describe the smb.conf file: the global section, directory, and printer shares.

◆ The first set of examples concentrate on services that do not require any Linux modifications. Shares that are public or guest types are very easy to make and serve as good starting points. Some are useful in the real world.

◆ The first example shows how to make the entire Linux disk visible (but not writable) is the subject of the first example. This is a very simple way to demonstrate a working Samba share.

◆ You are shown how to start and stop Starting and stopping the Samba daemons with the /etc/rc.d/init.d/smb script is the subject of the second example. This is an easier and safer method than doing it manually.

◆ Further examples show you how Linux permissions take precedence over Samba permissions is the subject of the third example. This example demonstrates how even if you have Samba's permission to do something you cannot do it if Linux does not let you.

◆ Another example shows you how Samba permissions work along side Linux permissions. If you have the proper Linux permissions, then you can use Samba to further tune your user's access.

◆ An example is give showing how to export your CD-ROM. Because the CD-ROM is a read-only device, it can be made publicly available and provide a valuable network service.

♦ I describe the process for manually adding a user to Linux. This process entails adding a line to the `/etc/passwd` and `/etc/group` files and creating a home directory for each new user.

♦ Another example shows how to allow multiple users to access to a single shareIn the example, the `allow users` parameter is used to provide that service.

♦ Using Samba's macro capability enables you to automate many services. Samba provides a set of macros that expand to match things such as the Windows machine name.

♦ The chapter concludes by showing how to configure a Linux printer. The Red Hat printtool, which is accessed via the Control-Panel, is used to configure the printer. Samba is then used to provide network access to that printer.

♦ You are shown how to use the graphical user interface SWAT to configure Samba shares. It allows you to modify Samba shares without touching the `smb.conf` file.

Chapter 7

Connecting to the Internet

IN THIS CHAPTER

- ◆ Connecting your Linux computer to the Internet
- ◆ Understanding SLIP and PPP
- ◆ Choosing an Internet Service Provider (ISP)
- ◆ Understanding the role of the Linux pppd daemon
- ◆ Connecting to your ISP with help from the dip program
- ◆ Automating the PPP connection process with the diald daemon
- ◆ Using the Red Hat Network Configurator to make a PPP connection
- ◆ Monitoring PPP and SLIP connections

YOU ARE PROBABLY FAMILIAR with logging on to a remote computer via a modem. If you use a service provider such as America Online (AOL), CompuServe (now owned by AOL), AT&T, or a university account, you probably use a terminal emulator. However, if you use a protocol such as PPP (Point-to-Point Protocol) or SLIP (Serial Line Internet Protocol), you actually become a part of the Internet — you become a node or a LAN. I refer to this type of connection as a node connection.

An important difference exists between a terminal session and an Internet node connection. A terminal session is like riding on a bus — you control where you go by choosing the particular route, but then leave most of the control to the driver and the bus schedule. Using an Internet node connection is like using your own car — you have far more control over where, how, and when to go someplace, plus the responsibility for your decisions.

With a terminal session, you make a connection to a computer that is connected to the Internet. The session works the same as if you were physically sitting at that computer's monitor and keyboard, except it is slower. With a node connection, however, your computer becomes part of the Internet. It is the same as if your computer is physically connected to an Internet Service Provider (ISP) network, except the connection is slower. Figures 7-1 and 7-2 show diagrams of the two connection types.

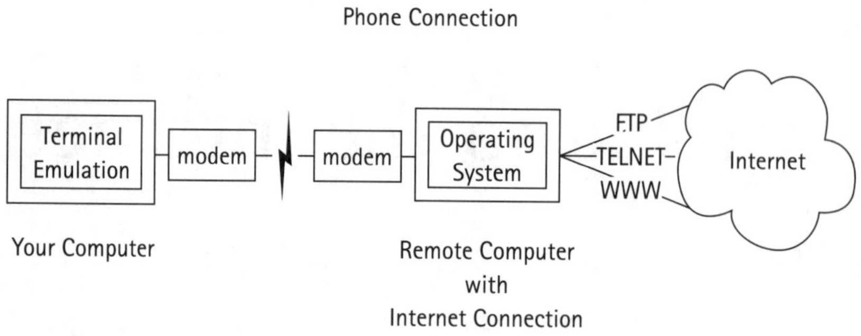

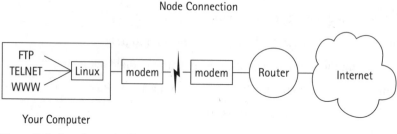

Phone Connection

Figure 7–1: A terminal session

Node Connection

Figure 7–2: A node connection

At first glance, the node connection may not seem to offer a great advantage over the terminal connection. Companies such as CompuServe and AOL offer software that provides good Web browsing and file transfer capabilities. However, the capability of your computer or LAN to seamlessly become part of the Internet is a powerful one. It removes a layer of software to deal with. It removes your dependence on a particular service provider's proprietary software and service. It enables you to tap into a vast reservoir of software and gives you more control over your own destiny. Most important, you can run multiple applications over the serial connection at one time. For example, you can run a Web browser, a Telnet session or two, and an FTP job, all at once. The only limitation is the speed of your connection.

This chapter describes the mechanics of making node connections. To establish a foundation for managing your connection, I also describe the Internet and LAN protocols that are the basis of these types of connections. And to help you better manage your connections, I address management and security concerns.

Node Connections

Two protocols are currently used to make node connections. Both the Serial Line Internet Protocol (SLIP) and the Point-to-Point Protocol (PPP) provide a method for using the telephone network to speak IP to remote places. Both protocols encapsulate IP packets in order to deliver them over serial connections.

SLIP

SLIP is a simple method for delivering an IP packet over a phone line. It simply adds a control character to the beginning and end of every IP packet. The control characters are SLIP-END and SLIP-ESC. They are decimal values 192 and 219 in the ASCII 7-bit definition.

SLIP-END marks the end of an IP packet. SLIP-ESC marks SLIP-ESC and SLIP-END characters embedded in the IP packets. If data contained in an IP packet coincidentally matches the value of either of the control characters (192 or 219 decimal), the addition of a SLIP-ESC tells the other end of the connection not to treat it as a control character. Figure 7-3 shows a hypothetical SLIP packet encapsulating the message hello world.

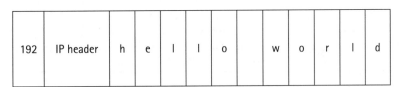

| 192 | IP header | h | e | l | l | o | | w | o | r | l | d |

Figure 7-3: A SLIP-encapsulated message containing hello world

The SLIP-END is something of a misnomer because it starts as well as ends each packet. The SLIP-START character is not needed, because the SLIP-END acts to frame the IP packet.

TIP SLIP is defined in RFC 1055, "A Nonstandard for Transmission of IP Datagrams over Serial Lines: SLIP" (Ronkey, 1988). This is a de facto standard and not an official Internet protocol. (The term RFC stands for Request For Comment — this is the method by which Internet standards are introduced and discussed.) You can find RFC 1055 at http://www.landfield.com/rfcs.

I prefer simplicity whenever possible. Unfortunately, SLIP is just a bit too simple. It doesn't do anything other than signal the start and end of an IP packet. This limitation presents several problems:

◆ No IP address negotiation is possible. Each end of the connection must know the other end's IP address from the outset of the connection. The IP address can be determined outside of SLIP, but connections would be more efficient if SLIP could handle that task rather than relying on yet another protocol.

◆ Each IP packet must be the same size. If one packet is smaller, it must be padded with extra, meaningless characters to make up the size. If a packet is larger, it must be broken up (and maybe padded, too) to match the size that the other end of the connection expects.

◆ The underlying packet type (IP can handle several types) is invisible until the SLIP packet is unpacked, which makes connection less efficient.

My own experience with SLIP attests to these shortcomings. Many years ago, I wanted to connect my company to the Internet without paying the steep price of ISPs at the time. I placed an inexpensive MS-DOS 386SX PC in a colleague's office at the University of New Mexico, and connected it to his LAN, which was routed to the Internet. At my office, I connected a Sun workstation to the 386SX via a modem. The PC ran under MS-DOS, the Sun ran with SunOS UNIX, and both had SLIP. I could establish a connection, and SLIP allowed IP connections to run, but only for a few minutes or seconds before SLIP would crash. Almost as soon as I got that far, the administration rejected — for several reasons that I had to agree with — my formal request for using that type of connection, and I ended that quest for the Holy Grail.

I am sure that with time it would have worked much more reliably. I have no doubt the problems were more the result of my being low on the learning curve than of the stated shortcomings with SLIP. However, PPP has established itself as the protocol of choice and SLIP is quickly fading. I don't have any hesitation in recommending the use of PPP for all your Internet needs.

 CSLIP, which compresses the IP header but not the data, is defined in RFC 1144, "Compressing TCP/IP Headers for Low-Speed Serial Links" (Jacobson, 1990). You can find it at http://www.landfield.com/rfcs.

PPP

The PPP packet contains information that facilitates the establishment of not only the serial connection, but also the encapsulated packet type. Consequently, PPP is more complex than SLIP.

PPP uses the `Link Control Protocol` (LCP) to establish a connection, and to configure and test it. This is an increasingly important feature, as modems become faster and more complex. Other connection technologies, such as ISDN, further complicate your telecommunications landscape, and thus increase the importance of controlling things via your connection protocol.

PPP uses the internationally recognized `High-Level Data Link Control` (HDLC) protocol. It uses bit patterns as opposed to control characters to distinguish the start and end of packets. The receiving end looks at each bit coming in and if it recognizes a pattern, it starts passing the data to the next stage. (For more information on HDLC, see the discussion on page 216 in *Data Communications, Computer Networks and Open Systems,* by Fred Halsall; published by Addison-Wesley Publishing Company, Inc., Reading, MA, 1992.)

The Network Control Protocol (NCP) defines several network level packets that PPP can encapsulate. The most popular ones are IP, IPX (Novell's IP-like protocol), and Microsoft's `Network BIOS Extended User Interface` (NetBEUI). If your LAN speaks any or all of these protocols, they all get to go through your PPP connection to the outside world. Figure 7-4 shows a diagram of a PPP packet.

Flag 1 byte	Address 1 byte	Control 1 byte	Protocol 2 bytes	Data 14989 bytes (max)	Flag 1 byte

Figure 7-4: A PPP packet contents

The sequence for making a PPP connection is as follows:

1. You make the modem or other (for example, ISDN) connection.

2. The computer making the connection sends LCP packets to the receiving computer. These packets establish a data link, which exists at the Network level, according to the OSI network model that I describe in Chapter 4.

3. The sending computer sends NCP packets to tell the other end what type of protocols are to be carried by PPP.

4. You have a full-fledged Internet connection. Any protocols that are mentioned in Step 3 are now usable until another PPP connection is established.

 PPP is defined in RFC 1661, "The Point-to-Point Protocol" (Simpson, 1994). You can find this official Internet standard at `http://www.landfield.com/rfcs`.

Making the Connection

Now comes the problem of making a PPP connection. I want to concentrate most of my attention on modem connections because they are the easiest, least expensive, and certainly the most popular method currently available.

However, I should mention a couple of the other widespread technologies. If you intend to run a business with any significant amount of Internet traffic, you are going to need more than a modem or two. (Linux does allow multiple modems to be used in parallel, however.) Frame Relay and ISDN are the most common high-speed methods widely available. Frame Relay is expensive but almost universally available, while ISDN is inexpensive, relatively fast, but less available; ISDN is much easier to get in metropolitan areas than outlying ones. The low-end Frame Relay connections run at only 56 kilobits per second (Kbps) – kilobits per second, not kilobytes per second (KBps) – and are only somewhat faster than today's high-end modems, cost several hundred dollars to establish and also per month to maintain. By spending roughly four times more per month, you can get a 1.5 megabit-per-second (Mbps) connection (called a T1 line), which is 28 times as fast, giving you a better price-performance ratio. ISDN is widely available in some locations but not in others, and still has the reputation for being difficult to set up.

TIP   Theoretically, you can lease a 45Mbps connection called a T3. Unless you plan to be the next AOL, however, this is an expensive option.

Introducing Leased Lines, Frame Relay, and ISDN

If you need or want a continuous connection to your ISP, you literally need to lease a wire from the phone company. In most cases, you end up using a wire to connect from your physical location to the nearest phone company switching station, where they send your packets to your ISP via their leased line. This system, called Frame Relay, is a very common system in the industry and is the one that I have used.

Frame Relay gives you a virtual circuit to your ISP that is also continuously connected so you have immediate access to the Internet. A device called a Channel Service Unit/Data Service Unit (CSU/DSU) converts the binary format of your network into that of the phone network; the phone company also uses the CSU/DSU to troubleshoot its network up to that unit. The packets or frames travel from your computer, through a router (a Linux computer can serve as one) to the CSU/DSU and into the phone company's cables. From there, the phone company switches your information stream through their system until it ends up at your service provider's CSU/DSU. The service provider converts it back into IP form and routes it to the Internet.

TIP Most consumers' and many businesses' telephone connections start from the customer's premises as DS0 connections, which operate at 64Kbps. A DS0 travels over a physical pair of wires (twisted-pair) to the nearest Telco switching station, where the wires enter a Channel Bank. Each Channel Bank can handle 24 DS0s and convert the analog signals to digital. The Channel Bank multiplexes all the DS0s into a DS1, which has a 1.45Mbps capability; it is also known as a T1 circuit. All the DS1 circuits carry digital frames or packets. The DS1 circuits go to the local telephone company's main switching center, where each packet is routed to its final destination.

ISDN is generally available in most locations in the United States but it is more readily available in some places than in others. It is probably an acceptable alternative if it is actually marketed in your area. It is a fairly difficult service to set up, both from your point of view and the phone company's.

ISDN can cost less than $100 per month and in many places less than $50 (unfortunately, Albuquerque is not one of those places). Linux is becoming more compatible with it as well. Linux kernel drivers are available to ISDN, and you can purchase ISDN PC adapters that plug directly into your PC. For more information about ISDN, consult the Howto file in `/usr/doc` as well as the following ISDN-related URL:

`http://www4.zdnet.com/wsources/content/current.featsub2.html`

Introducing Cable TV modems

Cable TV companies are introducing cable modems in many areas. Even little ole' Albuquerque is scheduled to get them. I'm not holding my breath but if and when they are introduced I will get one and post instructions on my web page: `www.swcp.com/~pgsery/rhlntk2e`.

Cable modems offer speeds of several hundred kilobits per second and just as important, they offer instantaneous connection. With a cable modem you have essentially full-time Internet connection.

Cable modems work in much the same way analog modems do. However, instead of converting your computer's digital information into an analog form, they convert it into another digital form that the cable TV system can handle.

Introducing DSL

Digital Subscriber Line (DSL) uses existing copper telephone cables to achieve speeds up to 1.5 Mbps at this time. Your speed depends on many factors such the distance to your phone company's central office and the condition of your line. You also get a continuous Internet connection.

Using modems

A modem converts digital data to the analog form that your average telephone line carries. As of this writing, modems theoretically capable of return speeds of 56Kbps are the state of the art. However, the phone system itself has bottlenecks. If even one link in the chain can't handle the higher speed, the entire system is slowed down.

 56Kbps modems are rated up to that speed only for data returning from the remote connection to your modem. Your outgoing data is limited to a lower rate. This limitation is generally tolerable because many Internet functions such as browsing the World Wide Web require much more bandwidth for downloading graphics or other data than for your outgoing keystrokes.

Problems like this crop up with any technology. It took a while for consumers to accept 1200Bps.

 A common acronym used in and out of the telephone industry for the analog phone system is POTS, which stands for "plain old telephone system (or service)."

Your problem – at any speed – is to use a modem to connect your network to the Internet. Linux provides both a manual and an automatic method for making connections.

If you want an Internet connection, you can't go wrong with a modem. Modems are the workhorses of the Net, and ISPs are configured to handle them.

The more recent Linux distributions and the GNU software that comes bundled with them have simplified the connection process. The programs for dialing an ISP and negotiating the PPP connection are included with Linux and have become progressively more sophisticated; the associated documentation also has improved. The explosion of demand for node connections and the desire of ISPs to meet the demand have made connecting progressively easier as the necessary knowledge permeates the market. Many ISPs use Linux, which makes connecting easier still.

Obtaining an ISP

Whichever method you choose for making the connection, you need to have an ISP to which you can connect. I recommend obtaining service from a local company, which is my method. In my opinion, a local company will give you better service than a national one. If the ISP is properly managed, your service will come from a small number of technical people who know their system and will become familiar with you and your needs. This is a big "if" and you may need to try more than one ISP before you find the right one. Personal recommendations are very important; that's how I found my ISP.

Of course, nothing is wrong with a national or international ISP, but you will not get consistent personal attention. A central service group generally processes your questions. Even worse, the people who handle typical calls are accessing a question-answer database rather than relying on their own experience. Your call may eventually reach an engineer or technician who knows the system, but you have to thread your way through the system first. For this reason, I think the local ISP is the way to go.

Most ISPs give you the choice of several different kinds of accounts. The traditional login account is still one possibility, but as I mention earlier in this chapter, this type of account will not be part of this discussion.

Configuring your PPP account

Okay, one way or another you find a good ISP, so what's next? The ISP should supply you with the login information for your account. You need to pay attention to the PPP account information and the corresponding phone numbers. The PPP account will supply you with either a static or a dynamic IP address. A static address is one that is permanently assigned to you by your ISP; whenever you make a connection, you will be known as the same IP address. A dynamic address is one that your ISP picks out of a pool of addresses whenever you connect and thus will generally be different every time. Dynamic addresses are becoming more common, if not dominant, because they give ISPs more flexibility with their allocation of IP addresses.

You need several Linux utilities to establish the connection:

♦ The pppd daemon is a program that transfers IP packets across the PPP connection.

♦ The pppd, chat, or dip program establishes a PPP connection.

♦ The chat program helps you automate the negotiation of your PPP connection. Typically, you write a chat script that contains the username and password of your PPP account and supplies them as needed.

The following sections provide more details on using and installing these programs.

THE PPPD DAEMON

The pppd daemon converts your local network packets into PPP format, and sends them out to the Internet via the PPP connection. The pppd is an RPM package and was installed as part of the default installation. Log on as root and enter the following command:

```
rpm -ivh /mnt/cdrom/RedHat/RPMS/ppp-*.i386.rpm
```

You can manually start the pppd daemon and supply it with command-line parameters to show it how to make a connection. I prefer to use the dip application — which I describe in the following sections of this chapter — to make manual connections. Usually, I use the diald utility to connect automatically. (Subsequent sections of this chapter describe how to connect with diald and both dynamic and static addresses.)

TIP   If you recompile the kernel with SLIP support, it will indeed show up as in this listing. However, you also can add it dynamically as a loadable module. In that case, it doesn't show up here until you establish a PPP connection. Also, the SLIP and PPP modules will be loaded by the kerneld daemon if you are using it and dip or diald calls for them.

Consult the pppd manual page for more in-depth information.

INTRODUCING DIP AND CHAT

The Dial-up IP Protocol Driver — dip — utility is a program that you can use interactively or automate with a script to dial the modem, authenticate your PPP or SLIP connection, and then fire up the pppd daemon. Chat is a script interpreter that the on-demand diald application uses.

You can use either of two primary dip command-line types. First, you can invoke dip in an interactive mode by including the -t option, as follows:

```
dip -t
```

I want to show how to use dip interactively only — the following two examples describe how to use dip with both static and dynamic IP addresses. I skip any script file examples because I show how to use diald via a script in the section "Finding the Package that Owns a File" in Chapter 5, and via the Red Hat Control-Panel in the section "Installing the Howto Documents," also in Chapter 5. The diald daemon is ultimately far more powerful than a manual dip script. However, the dip command examples are easily converted to scripts if you want to use dip that way.

Connecting with dip

You can use dip to create a PPP connection. The following instructions describe how to make the connection:

1. Log on as root.

2. Enter the following line again to start dip in its interactive form:

```
dip -t
```

3. You get the DIP> prompt as shown below.

```
DIP: Dialup IP Protocol Driver version 3.3.7o-uri (8 Feb 96)
Written by Fred N. van Kempen, MicroWalt Corporation.
DIP>
```

4. From the DIP> prompt, use the port command to tell dip where to find the modem. In this case, the modem is connected to the second serial port /dev/ttyS1. You do not need to specify the full pathname /dev/ttyS1. If you have a soft link /dev/modem you can substitute modem for tty: S1DIP> port modem. (Note: The Linux serial ports /dev/ttyS0, /dev/ttyS1, /dev/ttyS2 and /dev/ttyS3 correspond to MS-DOS ports COM1:, COM2:, COM3and COM4):

```
DIP> port ttyS0
```

5. Change into interactive terminal mode as follows:

```
DIP>term
```

6. You should see the following information.

```
[ Entering TERMINAL mode.  Use CTRL-] to get back ]
```

7. You can enter the at command to make sure that you are connected to the modem. The at command means attention.

```
at
OK
```

8. Dial your ISP by using the atdt command followed by your ISP's phone number:

```
atdt5555309
```

9. You should hear the modem negotiate the connection (unless you have your volume turned off) and then see a prompt like the following.

```
CONNECT 38400
Welcome to Paunchy's cyberport.  You're jacked in on dpm2:s33

Iamisp login:
```

10. Enter your PPP account login name. Note that the convention that my ISP uses is to append a capital P before my user name. Your ISP may use a different convention.

```
Your_isp_login: Piwantppp
```

11. Enter your PPP password at the next prompt.

```
Password: popwilleatitself
```

12. If your PPP login name and password is accepted, you will see some garbled-looking text. This is the ISP pppd daemon trying to connect to your pppd daemon.

13. You need to return to the interactive dip mode. Press the Ctrl and right square bracket (]) at the same time. You will see the DIP> prompt again.

14. From the DIP> prompt, enter the following command:

```
DIP> get $local 0.0.0.0
```

This command tells dip to get its local IP address from your ISP. ISPs almost universally assign IP address dynamically. (You can purchase a static IP address but this command will still work.)

16. Tell dip to use the assigned IP address as your computer's default route. Actually, dip tells pppd to use the IP as its default address.

```
DIP>default
```

17. Finally, tell dip to start the pppd daemon. Enter the following command and you automatically exit from dip and the pppd daemon will be started. After a few seconds your Internet connection should be complete.

```
DIP> mode PPP
```

TIP

Recall from Chapter 1 that you were directed not to assign a default route during the network configuration. You do not want to have two default routes. However, if you have permanent network connection — either to your own LAN or the Internet — you can still have it all. If you omit entering the default command, and go directly to mode PPP, then a route to your ISP's network will be created. For instance, if your ISP assigns your connection the IP 192.168.115.54, then a route to the 192.168.115.0 network (class C) will be created by dip. All network traffic for that subnet will be directed — routed — through the PPP connection that dip sets up.

If all goes well, your pppd daemon is launched and connects with your ISP's pppd daemon. Once they understand each other, you get a connection to the Internet. You can look at the process if you enter the ps x | grep ppp command.

```
729  a0 S    0:00 pppd -detach defaultroute crtscts modem 192.168.5.8:...
733  p0 S    0:00 grep ppp
```

Once the connection is established, you can enter the netstat -r -n command. The resulting information indicates that your default route is set to the ppp0, which in turn is connected to your modem and then your ISP:

```
Kernel IP routing table
Destination     Gateway         Genmask         Flags Metric Ref    Use Iface
198.168.5.8     0.0.0.0         255.255.255.255 UH    0      0        0 ppp0
192.168.1.0     0.0.0.0         255.255.255.0   U     0      0        9 eth0
127.0.0.0       0.0.0.0           255.0.0.0     U     0      0        1 lo
0.0.0.0         198.168.5.8       0.0.0.0       UG    0      0        0 ppp0
```

Try making a connection to someplace outside your own LAN — I sometimes try to Telnet to an account I have at the local university, as shown in the following example.

```
telnet 192.168.111.84
```

TIP If you have not configured your own nameserver — described in the section "Creating a Simple DNS Server" in Chapter 8 — or pointed your network towards your ISP, then you need to use raw IP addresses. You can configure your computer to use your ISP's nameserver by creating the /etc/resolv.conf file like that shown below.

```
search paunchy.net
nameserver 192.168.169.250
```

The namesever IP address is fictitious of course. Substitute the IP address supplied by your ISP.

Connecting to your ISP login computer is a good bet. You already know the IP of its PPP server and that may even double as the login device.

To disconnect the PPP connection, enter the following `dip kill` command:

```
dip -k /dev/modem
```

It may take a few seconds to disconnect and clean up its lock files. Ten years ago I would have killed for such convenience. But I'm spoiled now and still it gets better! The `diald` system described in the next section automates the PPP connection.

Using diald to establish a PPP connection

Red Hat supplies a simple and effective way to connect to the Internet via its Control-Panel, which I describe in the section "Using the Network Interface Window to Establish a PPP Connection" later in this chapter. However, I highly prefer using the `diald` system, which automates the entire process. It monitors your computer for any communication going to the Internet. When it sees a packet destined for the outside world it dials your ISP and negotiates a PPP connection.

Red Hat does not include a `diald` RPM package on its CD-ROM. However, it does have an RPM `diald` package on its Web (and Anonymous FTP) server in the `contrib` directory. (You can also find it on the SunSITE in the `linux/distributions/redhat/ contrib/i386` directory.) I have included a copy on the companion CD-ROM in the diald directory.

1. Log on as root.

2. Mount the IDG supplemental CD-ROM.

3. I've had problems getting the current PPP rpm to work correctly. However, the previous version – from Red Hat 6.0 – works quite well. There is no functional or performance penalty, so go ahead and install the previous version which is found in the supplemental disk:

   ```
   rpm -ivh /mnt/cdrom/diald/ppp*.rpm
   ```

4. Install the `diald` package by entering the following command:

   ```
   rpm -ivh /mnt/cdrom/diald/diald*.rpm
   ```

5. A sample `connect` script is provided on the supplemental CD-ROM. It contains the information that `diald` needs to connect to your ISP. Enter the following command to copy it to its proper location:

   ```
   cp /mnt/cdrom/diald/connect /etc/diald
   ```

6. Modify the `/etc/diald/connect` script to match your ISP's configuration. The essential parameters are the phone number, user name, user password and prompt. Pay particular attention to the `PROMPT` option. If you do not match the expected value with the actual one, then your connection might fail. This information is not necessarily supplied by your ISP. It might be necessary to ask for it explicitly; you can also use the `dip` program to login and record the information directly. The sample `connect` script is listed below.

   ```
   # The initialization string for your modem

   MODEM_INIT="ATZ&C1&D2%C0"

   # The phone number to dial
   PHONE_NUMBER="555-5309"

   # The chat sequence to recognize that the remote system
   # is asking for your user name.
   USER_CHAT_SEQ="ogin:"
   ```

```
# The string to send in response to the request for your user
name.
USER_NAME="Piwantppp"

# The chat sequence to recongnize that the remote system
# is asking for your password.
PASSWD_CHAT_SEQ="word:"

# The string to send in response to the request for your
password.
PASSWORD="freewayscarsandtrucks"
# The prompt the remote system will give once you are logged
in
# If you do not define this then the script will assume that
# there is no command to be issued to start up the remote
protocol.
PROMPT="PPP session"
```

7. A generic configuration file also exists in the same directory. This file contains the rules about how `diald` will operate. The standard `diald` expects this file to be found in the `/etc` directory, so enter the following command to copy it over:

```
cp /mnt/cdrom/diald/diald.conf /etc
```

8. Modify the `/etc/diald.conf` script to match your own computer and ISP's configuration. The sample script is shown below. This script should work without modification. (The difference is that if you use the `diald.conf` script that comes with the `diald16` RPM instead of the one on the supplemental CD-ROM, you must change the `connect "sh /etc/ppp/connect"` line to `connect "sh /etc/diald/connect"`.)

```
fifo /etc/diald/diald.ctl
mode ppp
connect "sh /etc/diald/connect"
device /dev/modem
speed 115200
modem
lock
crtscts
local 127.0.0.2
remote 127.0.0.3
dynamic
defaultroute
pppd-options asyncmap 0
include /usr/lib/diald/standard.filter
```

```
###Ignore the following lines. They are used in chapter 11.
###ip-up /usr/local/etc/ipchains.rules
###ip-down /usr/local/etc/ipchains.reset
```

9. Create a link to your modem port. If, for instance, the port is port /dev/ttyS1, then enter the following command.

```
ln -s /dev/ttyS1 /dev/modem
```

10. Finally, if you wish diald to start every time you reboot, you need to copy its startup script to the /etc/rc.d/init.d directory and create a link to it in the startup run-level directories. (Otherwise, simply enter **diald** and you will start it manually.)

```
ln -s /etc/rc.d/init.d/diald /etc/rc.d/rc3.d/S91diald
ln -s /etc/rc.d/init.d/diald /etc/rc.d/rc5.d/S91diald
```

11. The default /etc/rc.d/init.d/diald startup script expects to see the diald.conf script in the /etc/diald directory. You should see the following line in the script.

```
[ -f /etc/diald/diald.conf ] || exit 0
```

However, the diald program itself expects to see the /etc/diald.conf file. Change the script to reflect that difference.

```
[ -f /etc/diald.conf ] || exit 0
```

12. Start diald by running its startup script.

```
/etc/rc.d/init.d/diald start
```

13. Run the **ps x | grep diald** command and you should see the diald daemon.

```
324 ?        S       0:07 diald
```

The diald program runs in the background as a daemon and appears as a SLIP device — sl0 — to your network. The SLIP device is, in general, the default route to the external Internet. When packets appear on the SLIP device, destined for an outside network, diald starts up the chat script that dials the modem and negotiates the login process with the remote server. The diald daemon can set up either a SLIP or a PPP connection, but is most often used with PPP.

diald gives your network a functional, effectively continuous Internet connection. Of course, there is a fairly long latency between the time the packets are generated and the time they finally get delivered, but at least you do not have to deal with making the connection manually. It is a good compromise between a costly full-time connection and having to do it manually.

TIP The diald daemon is responsible for setting up your default route — the route that handles all packets that cannot be routed explicitly. Using the defaultroute option is a good idea if your LAN has no other Internet connections. (This is why I recommended that you leave the default route blank during the network configuration in Chapter 1.) Any packets not intended for your network you probably want going to the Internet. Many possible exceptions exist, but this is a good rule of thumb.

Nothing happens until a packet hits the default route. Try using a network program such as Telnet to access an outside machine — that is, one not on your LAN. Your ISP login computer is a safe bet. If you are in X Window, open another terminal window or go to an alternate screen and run the ps|grep command again. As shown in the resulting output, diald has spawned a chat script to dial the modem and log in to your ISP's PPP server:

```
1030   ?   S    0:00 diald
1045   ?   S    0:00 sh /etc/ppp/connect
1049   ?   S    0:00 chat -r /var/log/connect REPORT CONNECT TIMEOUT 45 ABORT NO
```

The modem fires up and dials your ISP. After it establishes a connection, it sends your login name and password to the ISP pppd daemon, and you're in! To see that the pppd daemon is running, run the following command:

```
ps -x | grep ppp
```

You see the pppd daemon as shown in the following line (note that the line is cut short):

```
1132  S0 S    0:00 /usr/sbin/pppd -detach modem crtscts mtu 1500 mru 1500 asyn
```

If you are fast enough (or just lucky), you can see the kerneld daemon load the ppp.o kernel module in anticipation of the pppd daemon. Here's what this information looks like:

```
1203   ?   R    0:00 modprobe -k -s ppp
```

TIP Of course, it can be dangerous to leave your PPP login name and password in plain text in your chat script file. There may be ways of encrypting it that I am unaware of, but at the very least you should only give root permission to read the file.

Using Network Configurator to establish a PPP connection

The Red Hat Network Configurator window provides another method for establishing a PPP connection. With the Network Configurator you can configure a PPP connection and then activate it simply by pressing a button. However, it does not automatically connect you on demand like diald does.

1. Log in as root.

2. Open the Control-Panel by clicking on the GNOME Start button (the little Gnome footprint in the lower left corner of the screen). Click the System menus→Control Panel buttons. When the Control Panel is activated click the Network Configuration button, which is second from the top. The Network Configurator, shown in Figure 7-5, is started.

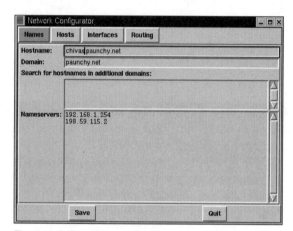

Figure 7-5: The Network Configurator window

3. Click the Interfaces menu button at the top middle of the Network Configurator window. The Choose Interface window activates, as shown in Figure 7-6.

4. Click the PPP radio button, and the Create PPP Interface window appears. Enter your ISP account information, as shown in Figure 7-7.

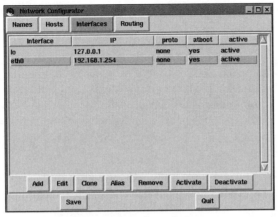

Figure 7-6: The Choose Interface window

Figure 7-7: The Create PPP Interface window

5. If you need to tweak any of the hardware, the communication interface (that is, serial port), or the networking settings, click the Customize button, and you get the customization window (titled Edit PPP Interface) shown in Figure 7-8. Otherwise, click the Done button to finalize your PPP interface setup.

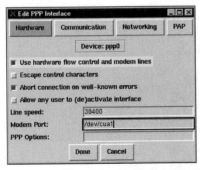

Figure 7-8: The customization window for the serial port

6. If you have not set the symbolic link from the serial device file to the modem file (either manually with the `ln` command or via the Modem Configurator from the Control Panel), you should set the serial port in the Customization window. For instance, the port is set to `/dev/ttyS1` in Figure 7-8. This is the most likely setting if you have a mouse attached to `/dev/ttyS2` (`COM1`in MS-DOS), but your system may be different. You should not have any problems if you just experiment. You most likely want to keep the hardware handshaking, which is how the modem and the computer signal each other when one has filled its data buffer and needs time to process it.

7. Click the `Networking` button next, and the window shown in Figure 7-9 appears. This window is where you may have to change such things as your default route.

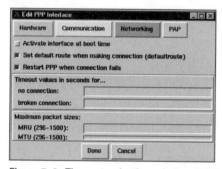

Figure 7-9: The customization window for the network settings

8. Finally, click the Communication button and the window shown in Figure 7-10 appears.

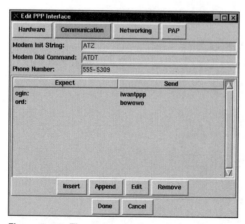

Figure 7-10: The customization window for the communication settings

9. Click the Done button and another window appears asking you whether you want to save or cancel the edits that you just made.

10. Click the Save button and you return to the `Network Configurator`.

You have configured the PPP connection, and you can activate it by clicking the `Activate` button. If your modem is connected properly and turned on, the `pppd` daemon is started and a `chat` script is run.

The internal process is very similar to that of the `diald` example. The shell script `/etc/sysconfig/network-scripts/ifup-ppp` is run when you click on the `Activate` button. It was created from the choices you just made in the `Network Configurator`. If you run the **ps x | grep ppp** command you should see the scripts being run.

```
714   1 S    0:00 sh /etc/sysconfig/network-scripts/ifup-ppp daemon /etc/sysc
716   1 S    0:00 /usr/sbin/pppd -detach lock modem crtscts defaultroute /dev
718   ? D    0:00 modprobe -k -s ppp0
```

Notice that the `kerneld` daemon is inserting the `pppd` into the kernel with mod-probe. The `chat` script to dial your ISP is run next.

```
636   1 S    0:00 /usr/sbin/pppd -detach lock modem crtscts defaultroute /dev
641   1 S    0:00 /usr/sbin/chat -f /etc/sysconfig/network-scripts/chat-ppp0
```

Finally, the chat process finishes and the `pppd` daemon is left controlling the connection.

```
636   1 S    0:00 /usr/sbin/pppd -detach lock modem crtscts defaultroute ...
```

You again have a full TCP/IP network connection. You are an Internet node. To disconnect, just click the `Deactivate` button in the `Network Configurator`.

When you establish an PPP connection, as described in this chapter, you can communicate with the Internet only from the machine. (If you have an InterNic registered network address, then you can turn the connecting computer into a gateway. However, this book assumes that you do not have registered addresses and use the public address system described in Chapter 3.) The connecting computer can be turned into an Internet gateway (router) if you use IP masquerading, which is also known as `Network Address Translation` (NAT). Chapter 11 describes how to do that.

Using dctrl

The dctrl script is a nice GUI-based interface to diald. It is part of the diald RPM and can be found in the /usr/bin directory. To run it, log in as root and run the following command:

```
dctrl -dstatus -tload -gload -pqueue -dlog
```

That command starts up dctrl and activates all of its display functions. You should see the interface shown in Figure 7-11.

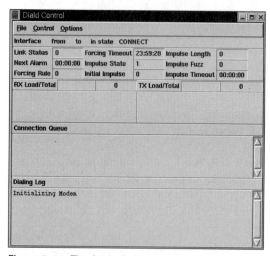

Figure 7-11: The dctrl window

If you click Control → Forced up, diald connects to your ISP and remains connected until you click on Control → Forced up again. At that time, if there are no more open connections, then diald takes down the connection. The open connections are displayed in the Connection Queue sub window.

If you click Control → Up, then diald also starts up a connection. This connection, however, remains up only while there is an open connection present.

By clicking Control → Down, you remove any open connections from the connection queue and if the Forced Up item is not active, then your connection is broken.

Selecting the Control → Block connection choice kills any open connections and prevents any new ones from being started.

Controlling diald manually

You can also control the diald connection manually. diald monitors the /etc/diald/diald.ctl file, which is a First In First Out (FIFO) queue. You can send signals to that file and diald acts as appropriate.

The signals are `block`, `unblock`, `force`, `unforce`, `up`, and `down`. They are similar to the menu selections and are mostly self-explanatory; see the `man` page `diald-control` for more information.

For instance, to start up a PPP connection enter the command:

```
echo "up" > /etc/diald/diald.ctl
```

To stop it do the following:

```
echo "down" > /etc/diald/diald.ctl
```

Troubleshooting

This troubleshooting section is divided up according to the sections of this chapter.

Fixing modem problems

If you have trouble getting your modem to connect, then there are several things you should check.

If you have an external modem, then make sure that it's connected properly. Can you see the Light Emitting Diodes (LED) flicker when you interact with it? For instance, if you use `dip -t`, then you should be able to see the LEDs flicker when you enter keystrokes.

If you have an internal modem, check that it is seated properly on the system board. Can you manually communicate with it via a program like `dip`? If not, then it might have an IRQ or IO port setting that is conflicting with another device. You can check its current settings against the other installed devices by looking at the /proc/ioports and /proc/interrupts files (for instance, `cat /dev/ioports`). You also can check the device file that it is supposed to be using. If, for instance, you have a soft link pointing to /dev/ttyS0, then check to see if that is correct. You might have to change the link to /dev/ttyS1 for instance. Try using the `dip` command to communicate directly with another device (`DIP>port ttyS1` for instance). Keep in mind that if you have a PnP modem, then you might have to turn that feature off to make it work with Linux. A `WinModem` will not work with Linux.

Using dip to connect to the internet

The good aspect of `dip` is that you can see everything that is going on. Any problems that occur are immediately visible. If you are having problems connecting via `dip`, turn on its debug mode. You can do that by using the verbose mode: `dip -t -v`:

```
DIP: Dialup IP Protocol Driver version 3.3.7o-uri (8 Feb 96)
Written by Fred N. van Kempen, MicroWalt Corporation.
DIP: name=root home=/tmp
```

```
         host=atlas.paunchy.net IP=192.168.1.250
         prot=SLIP MTU=296
Modem set to "HAYES".
DIP [0   ]>
```

The output shows information about what computer you are working on. Set the port to the modem and you see information about the modem: `DIP [0 ]>port mo-dem`.

```
PORT: terminal port set to "modem".
DIP: tty_open: /dev/modem (3) DIP: tty_open: IBUF=1024 OBUF=1020
DIP: tty: set_speed: 38400
DIP: tty: set_databits: 8
DIP: tty: set_stopbits: 1
DIP: tty: set_parity: N
DIP [0   ]>
```

You'll enter into terminal mode as usual. Try dialing your ISP and then authenticating your PPP as usual too. Escape back to your `DIP>` prompt and proceed as described before. If there is a problem with any of your settings, then you receive more information about the problem.

If you continue to have problems getting your PPP connection to work, then make sure that you don't already have a default route set up. If you have `diald` running, then that can also create problems. You can also check the `/var/log/messages` file for any messages about `dip`.

Connecting automatically to the internet with diald

`diald` is the most complex of all connection methods described in this chapter. It uses two systems, both `diald` and `chat`, to make connections. It also works non-interactively and problems are not as obvious.

If you are having problems getting it to work, then it is best to start from the beginning. Make sure that you can connect to your ISP by using either Network or `dip` methods to verify your connection. Next, make sure that the information in the critical `/etc/ppp/connect` and `/etc/diald.conf` files are correct. Pay particular attention to the prompt string fragments like `USER_CHAT_SEQ="ogin:"`, `PASSWD_CHAT_SEQ="word:"` and `PROMPT="PPP session"`. It is essential that each one match up with the strings that your ISP sends you. For instance, if `diald/chat` is expecting the PPP session prompt (as defined in `/etc/ppp/connect`) but your ISP sends the string `XYZ session`, then `diald/chat` never finishes up the connection process and you don't get your PPP connection.

You should also check the /var/messages log file for dialog from the diald startup process. It shows the progress of each diald session and might include insights into your problem. For example, if you have set up diald and everything looks okay but no connection is occurring, then take a look at the end of the messages file.

```
tail -20 /var/log/messages
```

It might show something like the following:

```
Apr 18 atlas diald[1312]: Specified device '/dev/modem' not a
character device.
```

There's something wrong with the soft link file /dev/modem. In this case, the link is pointing to the /dev/ttyS0 device file. Use the following command to find out what serial ports are in use.

```
cat /proc/tty/driver/serial
```

It returns the following information.

```
serinfo:1.0 driver:4.27
0: uart:16550A port:3F8 irq:4 tx:0 rx:0
1: uart:16550A port:2F8 irq:3 baud:1200 tx:8 rx:59382 brk:5 RTS|DTR
2: uart:16550A port:3E8 irq:4 baud:115200 tx:359592 rx:8684037
RTS|CTS|DTR|DSR|CD
3: uart:unknown port:2E8 irq:3
```

The first port (0) looks like it is unused. The second port, (1) is probably a serial mouse because 1200 baud modems have not been in use for years. The third one, however, has a 115,200 baud, which is a high bandwidth connection (for a serial port device). Modems don't run at that speed but they do communicate with the computer at that rate. It's a good bet, so change the soft link to refer to the new device.

```
ln -s /dev/ttyS2 /dev/modem
```

In this case, that was the problem. Restart the diald daemon (/etc/rc.d/ init.d/diald restart) and it now works.

If you have trouble with dctrl, then make sure that you have read/write privilege with the /etc/diald/diald.ctl file. You also need to be able to display to the X Window so make sure that you have run xhost +atlas and export DISPLAY=:0.

Using the control panel to connect to the internet

If you have set up your modem correctly, then most problems that you encounter using the `Network` GUI in `Control panel` probably result from the misconfiguration of your ISP settings. If you have problems getting a connection going, then check that your ISP PPP login name and password are set correctly. You might also need to check that your ISP is not using unusual settings: go through the options in the `Network Interfaces` window and make sure that each one is correct.

Summary

This chapter describes how to connect your network to the Internet, which is the last important step to completing your client-server network. After this chapter, you have all the components necessary to run your internal and external network.

I cover the following topics in this chapter:

- Understanding the difference between a terminal and a node connection to the Internet is important to understanding the power that is available to you and your network. A node connection offers comprehensive Internet access, giving your network the functionality that a terminal session cannot provide.

- It is important to have a basic understanding of the PPP and SLIP protocols. PPP has become the standard, providing the stability and flexibility required for consistently using phone connections for Internet access.

- The type of connection you use to carry your PPP or SLIP packets to the Internet depends on your needs and budget. If you have high bandwidth requirements, you need a Frame Relay or ISDN connection. Otherwise, the traditional modem offers the best compromise. Note that Linux can combine multiple modems in parallel – load balancing – to increase bandwidth.

- Frame Relay offers medium to high bandwidth connection to the Internet but is expensive. It is generally carried, in part, over a leased telephone wire and provides continuous service. Although specialized equipment is required, it is reasonably priced.

- ISDN is an intermediate alternative to modems and Frame Relay. It is reasonably priced and gives several times the bandwidth of a modem. However, it is not universally available.

- You must obtain an Internet Service Provider (ISP) to serve as your gateway to the Internet. Your PPP or SLIP packets ultimately get routed through your ISP.

◆ Your ISP provides you with the information you need to connect your system. Most often, it is just a phone number, account name, and password if dynamic IP addresses are used. Otherwise, ISPs give you your IP address and theirs.

◆ The Linux `pppd` daemon is used to encapsulate your network's IP packets and send them across the serial connection to your ISP, where they are decoded.

◆ Several methods are used to establish a PPP connection via the `pppd` daemon. `Dip`, `chat`, `diald`, the Control Panel, and even `pppd` can be used to dial up your ISP, negotiate the PPP connection, and set your local routing tables.

◆ `Dip` is a utility that you can run interactively or from a script to establish PPP and SLIP connections.

◆ To show you in detail how a PPP connection is established, I provide several examples using interactive `dip`. Both static and dynamic IP addressing are used.

◆ The `diald` daemon, which you install in this chapter, monitors your network traffic and automatically establishes a PPP connection when necessary. It makes your network look like it is continuously connected to the Internet. It does take a few seconds, however, to make the connection after outgoing packets are detected.

◆ Examples are given to show how to make `diald` connections using both static and dynamic IP addresses. I show you how to enter the `diald` commands interactively, and how to put them into a script file, which you can add to the rc.local script. This script is run at boot time so `diald` is loaded at that time.

◆ The Red Hat `Network Configurator` is used to establish a PPP connection. It is a GUI and simplifies making a connection by using point-and-click methods. It is a good one-time connection alternative to both `dip` and `pppd`.

◆ Several methods (programs) exist to help you monitor your PPP and entire network connection. The programs `ifconfig`, `route`, and `netstat` are used to configure and monitor your network. The `statnet` program provides a concise method for continuously monitoring your important network statistics.

Chapter 8

Creating NFS, NIS, DNS, and E-mail Servers

IN THIS CHAPTER

- ◆ Creating an NFS Server
- ◆ Creating an simple NIS server
- ◆ Configuring automount
- ◆ Creating a simple DNS server
- ◆ Creating a simple e-mail server

RED HAT LINUX CAN PROVIDE many resources in addition to Samba. For instance, Linux can share files and directories via the Network File System (NFS). The Network Information Service (NIS) makes it possible to automatically share many common resources across your network. The Domain Name Server (DNS) centralizes the job of sharing network host names and addresses. You can also create an e-mail server that will take care of all of your internal messaging as well as communicate with external e-mail systems.

Creating a New Red Hat Linux Computer

The services described in this chapter require that you use a Linux computer (or a UNIX computer if you have one) to make good use of them. You can simply use the Linux server `chivas.paunchy.net` as a client to itself, but that arrangement will only demonstrate the services. This chapter makes use of the new Linux computer `cementeros.paunchy.net`. Go ahead and build the new box and give it the IP address 192.168.1.200. Don't worry about answering the questions about NIS — step 5 in the section "Continuing the Configuration" in Chapter 1 — because this chapter describes how to configure it manually.

Creating a Simple DNS Server

It is convenient, but not necessary, to configure a local DNS server. If you set one up, then every machine on your Private Network can find the IP address of any other machine on the Private Network without having to include every host name/IP address in every Linux /etc/hosts file or every Windows lmhost file. By configuring one local DNS server, you save having to duplicate the same address information on every computer on your private network.

Configuring a DNS server from scratch can be very difficult at first. DNS is a complex system and requires several configuration files to work together. Rather than go through the instructions for setting up the simple system needed by the paunchy.net, the configuration files for paunchy.net are included on the companion CD-ROM.

1. Login into chivas as root.

2. Mount your Red Hat Publisher's Edition CD-ROM.

   ```
   mount -r -t iso9660 /dev/cdrom /mnt/cdrom
   ```

3. Install the caching-nameserver and bind RPM packages:

   ```
   rpm -ivh /mnt/cdrom/RedHat/RPMS/bind-8*
   rpm -ivh /mnt/cdrom/RedHat/RPMS/caching-nameserver*
   ```

4. Unmount and eject the Red Hat CD-ROM.

   ```
   umount /mnt/cdrom
   eject
   ```

5. Mount the IDG supplemental CD-ROM.

   ```
   mount -r -t iso9660 /dev/cdrom /mnt/cdrom
   ```

6. Copy the example DNS configuration files as follows:

   ```
   cp -f /mnt/cdrom/IDG/dns/named.conf /etc
   cp -f /mnt/cdrom/IDG/dns/named.ca /var/named
   cp -f /mnt/cdrom/IDG/dns/named.local /var/named
   cp -f /mnt/cdrom/IDG/dns/named.paunchy /var/named
   cp -f /mnt/cdrom/IDG/dns/named.reverse /var/named
   ```

7. Take a look at the /etc/named.conf file. It should look like this:

   ```
   // Boot file for paunchy.net name server
   options {
           directory "/var/named";
   };
   zone "." {
       type hints;
       file "root.hints";
   };
   ```

```
zone "0.0.127.in-addr.arpa" {
        type master;
        file "named.local";
};
zone "1.168.192.in-addr.arpa" {
        type master;
        file "named.reverse";
};
zone "paunchy.net." {
    type master;
    file "named.paunchy";
};
```

The first section tells named to use the /var/named directory as its home directory. The section defining the named.local file is used to set up name resolution for the localhost network. The paunchy.net section deals with converting IP names to numeric addresses for the paunchy.net-based devices. The 1.168.192 zone (named.reverse) provides reverse lookups — numeric IP addresses to names — for the paunchy.net.

8. Start the named daemon by using the start-up script.

   /etc/rc.d/init.d/named start

9. Modify your /etc/resolv.conf file to look as follows:

   ```
   domain paunchy.net
   nameserver 192.168.1.254
   nameserver 192.168.32.2
   ```

   where the 192.168.32.2 name server entry is a fake one and should be replaced the IP address of your ISP's name server.

10. Test its operation by starting the nslookup program. At the nslookup prompt, enter a network name like atlas.

    nslookup>atlas

11. The nslookup utility should return the numeric IP address of atlas:

    ```
    Name:    chivas.paunchy.net
    Address: 192.168.1.254
    Aliases: chivas
    ```

If you enter an address that is not found within the named files in the /var/named directory, then your system will attempt to access your ISP name server — 192.168.32.2. In the case where you enter a name of a network device on your own network, the lookup fails. You should enter the device name and address information in your local named configuration files.

Creating a Simple NFS Server

NFS is similar in function to Samba. It provides Linux-to-Linux file sharing (it provides UNIX-to-Linux sharing too). NFS is a simpler protocol than Samba, however, and is part of the Linux kernel. Samba runs as an application. When you configure your Linux computer to act as an NFS server, NFS modules are loaded into the kernel and provide all NFS services.

Exporting file systems

The /etc/exports file configure all NFS exports. A sample exports file is shown that configures the /mnt/cdrom drive to be exported. Please see the exports man page for more information.

```
/mnt/cdrom
```

The exportfs command is used to tell the NFS server which file systems can be mounted. If you run the exportfs -a command, it will export all the file systems listed in /etc/exports. Run the exportfs command without any parameters to view the exported file systems.

Mounting file systems

The mount command is used to – what else? – mount NFS file systems. You can mount NFS file systems across a network or even locally. For instance, you can use the following command to mount the CD-ROM mentioned in the /exports file from the computer called nfs_server.

```
mount -t NFS nfs_server:/mnt/cdrom /mnt
```

The NFS file system is mounted on the /mnt directory. If you run the df command you see the NFS file system.

TIP NFS does not work with Windows systems without additional software. You can mount Linux file systems from Windows machines with software like PC-NFS.

Configuring an example NFS server

The following instructions guide you through the process of installing NFS on your Linux file and printer server chivas. Your server will be capable of exporting NFS to other Linux computers on your network.

NFS uses Remote Proceedure Calls (RPC) to work. When used with NFS, RPC accesses a server's operating system to use its file systems. NFS works along with the portmap program. portmap allocates ports to all RPC services.

 TIP NFS is runs as part of the Linux kernel. When you start NFS several kernel modules are loaded. NFS is a simpler system than Samba and thus can be included in the kernel. It also does not suffer from having to keep up with the Microsoft "enhancements" that keep the Samba team on its toes.

1. Login to chivas as root.

2. Mount your Red Hat CD-ROM.

   ```
   mount -r -t iso9660 /dev/cdrom /mnt/cdrom
   ```

3. Create the user lidia. This example user will provide a platform for testing all of the examples in this chapter.

   ```
   useradd lidia
   ```

4. Give lidia a password.

   ```
   passwd lidia
   ```

5. Install the NFS and portmap packages in the following order:

   ```
   rpm -ivh /mnt/cdrom/RedHat/RPMS/portmap*
   rpm -ivh /mnt/cdrom/RedHat/RPMS/knfs*
   ```

6. Start the portmap program.

   ```
   /etc/rc.d/init.d/portmap start
   ```

7. Start the NFS server.

   ```
   /etc/rc.d/init.d/nfs start
   ```

8. Edit the /etc/exports file to include the following line. This file is used by NFS to export file systems to the network. In this case, the user lidia is exported to the local network — the asterisk is used as a wildcard and the mount will be both readable and writable.

   ```
   /home/lidia 192.168.1.*(rw)   # example NFS export
   ```

There are many NFS exports options. The most commonly used ones are read-write (rw) and read-only (ro). It is beyond the scope of this book to describe exports in detail. Please consult the exports man page for more information.

9. Activate the NFS exports as follows.

```
exportfs -a
```

You can unexport NFS shares by using the -u option with exportfs. For instance, to unexport the lidia user share use the command exportfs -u /home/lidia. All shares can be unexported by using the command exportfs -ua.

10. You can check the export that you just created by running the exportfs command without any options. You should see the following output.

```
/home/lidia        paunchy.net
```

11. Next, mount the lidia home directory.

```
mount chivas:/home/lidia /mnt
```

12. Run the df command to see your new NFS mount.

```
Filesystem          1k-blocks    Used   Available  Use%  Mounted on
/dev/hda1               54416   33367       18240   65%  /
/dev/hda8              995115  317206      626503   34%  /home
/dev/hda7             1856990   13857     1747147    1%  /opt
/dev/hda5             1011928  611008      349516   64%  /usr
/dev/hda6             1856990  176081     1584923   10%  /usr/local
/dev/hda9              202220    9965      181815    5%  /var
chivas:/home/lidia     995115  317206      626503   34%  /mnt
```

You now have an NFS server. It is a self-serving server at this point so the next step is to make it more useful. The next section describes the process of configuring an NFS client on your new Linux box veracruz.

You can stop all of the NFS services by running the /etc/rc.d/init.d/nfs stop script.

Configuring an example NFS client

This section describes configuring a Linux box to act as an NFS client. First you need to construct another Linux computer. Use the process described in Chapter 1 to build a Red Hat Linux computer. The first section in this chapter Creating a New Red Hat Linux Computer describes the network parameters you need to use. Next, you need to first configure an NFS server. That process is described in the previous section, "Configuring your NFS Server."

The following instructions describe how to mount NFS shares across a network.

1. Login to `veracruz` as `root`.

2. Mount the Red Hat Publisher's Edition CD-ROM.

   ```
   mount -r -t iso9660 /dev/cdrom /mnt/cdrom
   ```

3. Install the NFS client package.

   ```
   rpm -ivh /mnt/cdrom/RedHat/RPMS/knfs-clients*
   ```

4. Mount the `lidia` user.

   ```
   mount chivas:/home/lidia /mnt
   ```

5. Run the `df` command and you should see the new mount.

You can now access the user's files from the `/mnt` mount point. However, just as with Samba, the Linux file permissions take precedence over the ones that you declare with NFS.

Creating a Simple NIS (yp) Server

Once you use more than a couple of Linux (or UNIX) computers on a network, the job of managing users and their files becomes more difficult. The life of the user also becomes more difficult when more than one computer is used. One solution is to use the Network Information System (NIS).

 Please do not confuse your DNS domain name with the NIS domain name. They are two different animals. The DNS domain name is the name that your private network — for instance, paunchy.net — is called.

Introducing nsswitch.conf

The `/etc/nsswitch.conf` file controls if, and when NIS is used. It contains a list of services and where the configurations are found. For instance, the `passwd` line in `nsswitch.conf` controls how logins are performed. If you look in the default configuration, you see that first the password file is consulted, then `nisplus` and finally `nis`. Since NIS+ only works on Sun Microsystems Solaris and SunOS, it is never actually used (you can take out the reference if you wish). If a user account password is not found in the `/etc/passswd` file, then NIS is consulted.

```
passwd:     files nisplus nis
```

The important services that `nsswitch.conf` controls are as follows:

◆ Passwords

◆ Host names

◆ Group names

◆ Auto mounts

The sequence that this book uses is files first and then NIS. You can use any sequence that makes sense for you. However, when it comes to passwords, it is best to leave the sequence: files and then NIS. This sequence allows you to login in case your network isn't working.

NIS was originally called Yellow Pages, or simply YP, when Sun Microsystems created it. However, that term was already trademarked and NIS was used instead. However, the YP legacy lives because the actual program names such as ypbind and ypserv are still used.

NIS consolidates many different resources into a common pool. The consolidation takes the form of maps, which are exported, from the NIS server to the clients via the network. For instance, instead of each Linux computer using its own local copy of `/etc/passwd`, `/etc/shadow`, `/etc/hosts` and such, they use a single copy from the server.

The copy of NIS that comes with Red Hat maps a common set of system files. This book makes use of a few of them and it is left to you to examine the other ones.

1. Login to `chivas` as `root`.

2. Mount the Red Hat CD-ROM.

   ```
   mount -r -t iso9660 /dev/cdrom /mnt/cdrom
   ```

3. Install the NIS packages.

```
rpm -ivh /mnt/cdrom/RedHat/RPMS/yp*
```

3. If you have not already done so, create the user lidia. This example user will provide a platform for testing all of the examples in this chapter.

```
useradd lidia
```

4. Give lidia a password.

```
passwd lidia
```

5. NIS uses the concept of the domain name. A domain name does not refer to the name of your network – for instance, paunchy.net. It is tied to NIS. You can set a domain name as follows.

```
domainname tiburones
```

6. Make sure that portmap is started.

```
/etc/rc.d/init.d/portmap restart
```

7. Start the NIS server and client.

```
/etc/rc.d/init.d/ypserv start
```

TIP You can create master/slave servers within a single NIS domain. The single master server pushes its maps to the slaves. The slaves then act as master servers in every way. Please consult the ypserv man page for more information.

8. You need to create the /var/yp directory and the NIS databases for the server to work from. Run the following command.

```
/usr/lib/yp/ypinit -m
```

A subdirectory called tiburones is created in the /var/yp directory. The NIS databases – or maps – are stored there. The ypserv daemon distributes those maps to all of the NIS tiburones clients.

9. ypinit prompts you for the name of the hosts to use as a server. The machine that you are working from is used as the default so you don't have to enter any host names. Press the Ctrl-D keys and then press the Return key to finish the process. The databases will be constructed.

10. Start the NIS client.

```
/etc/rc.d/init.d/ypbind start
```

11. NIS is now configured. You should be able to view the maps now. Run the `ypcat passwd` command and you should see the contents of your `/etc/passwd` file.

```
lidia:$1$VIwBfONk$F/r1KkG1ZE0:502:502::/nethome/lidia:/bin/bash
```

12. You can test your NIS server from the server itself as follows.

```
su - lidia
```

13. If you run the `whoami` and `pwd` command, you'll see that you've indeed logged in as the user `lidia` and that your current working directory is `/home/lidia`.

Using Automount

The `automount` system allows you to access resources, such as your home directory, from any Linux (or UNIX) computer on a network. When combined with NFS and NIS you can use automount to specify any directory or file system to be automatically mounted on a Linux computer.

Using automount locally

You need to tell automount which directory will be used to mount the resources. For instance, if you want to automatically mount your home directory, then a typically convention is to use the `/nethome` directory. Any directory that you declare as a mount point will be a virtual one. That is, you do not have to physically create such a directory with the `mkdir` command.

You also need to give automount a map of the resource to be mounted. Maps contain the information about the resource to be mounted. For instance, automount must know about where a user's home directory resides if it is to be mounted. Maps can be a local file(s), a NIS database or a command. The local file will be typically be something like `/etc/auto.home`; an NIS map will be distributed by `ypserv` and `ypbind` and reside in a computer's memory; a program map will be created by running a script or program.

1. Login to `chivas` as `root`.

2. Mount the Red Hat CD-ROM.

```
mount /mnt/cdrom
```

3. Install the `autofs` (automount) package.

```
rpm -ivh /mnt/cdrom/RedHat/RPMS/autofs*
```

4. If you have not already done so, create the user lidia.

   ```
   useradd lidia
   ```

5. Create a password for lidia.

   ```
   passwd lidia
   ```

6. Modify the /etc/passwd file to change the home directory from /home/lidia to /nethome/lidia.

   ```
   lidia:$1$XyYsQZKt$us6/:504:504::/nethome/temp:/bin/bash
   ```

7. Create the file /etc/auto.home and enter the following line into it.

   ```
   lidia   chivas:/nethome/lidia
   ```

8. Manually start the automounter.

   ```
   automount /nethome file /etc/auto.home
   ```

   The first parameter /nethome tells the automounter where to mount the directories. The second parameter is the map type and in this case specifies that the map will be a file. The third option tells automount where to find the mount map. (If the map type is yp, then the third parameter will specify an NIS database.)

9. Now try changing to the new automount directory.

   ```
   cd /nethome/lidia
   ```

10. If you run the pwd command, and everything has worked correctly, then you will see your new automount directory.

    ```
    /nethome/lidia
    ```

11. Next, if you log in as the user lidia, you will find yourself in the user's home directory. That directory is mounted as an NFS directory on chivas. You do not need the network in this case but it does demonstrate what is happening.

    ```
    su - temp
    ```

12. Once again, you should be placed into the temp's home directory.

Using automount remotely

The previous example demonstrated how automount works. The example was only useful for demonstration purposes. The real benefit comes when you use automount remotely. The following example shows you how.

1. Log on to cementeros as root.

2. Mount the Red Hat CD-ROM.

   ```
   mount /mnt/cdrom
   ```

3. Install the NIS `ypbind` package.

   ```
   rpm -ivh /mnt/cdrom/RedHat/RPMS/ypbind*
   ```

4. Set your NIS domainname.

   ```
   domainname tiburones
   ```

5. Edit the `/etc/yp.conf` file to look as follows.

   ```
   Domainname     tiburones
   ypserver       chivas.paunchy.net
   ```

6. Start the NIS client.

   ```
   /etc/rc.d/init.d/ypbind start
   ```

7. Check to see that it's running.

   ```
   ypwhich
   ```

   The name of the NIS server `chivas` should be returned.

TIP

If `ypbind` is not running then repeat steps 4 and 5. If that doesn't work, then check the `ypbind` man page and the documentation in `/usr/doc/ypbind*/README`.

8. You can use `ypcat` to look at any of the NIS maps. For instance, the `yp-cat passwd` command will show the password map.

9. Now, try logging in as the user `temp`. If all works correctly, you should be placed into the user `temp`'s home directory on the server `chivas`. Use the `pwd` and `df` commands to prove it to yourself.

Configuring an E-mail Server

Configuring e-mail systems is one of the more complex tasks that you can do. There are numerous e-mail servers and clients and getting them all to interact can best be described as a non-trivial task.

In order to simply your e-mail configuration, this chapter uses two types of e-mail systems. One is simple and easy to configure but is not very flexible and the other is not so easy to set up but is somewhat more flexible. You can choose the best solution for your operation.

Using the Netscape e-mail client

Once you have subscribed to an ISP and connected to the Internet, you can use your ISP as your e-mail server. This is quite simple in concept and execution: your ISP gives you a login account and that login account comes with an e-mail address. Your ISP also provides `Post Office Protocol` (POP) and `IMAP` protocol capabilities, which means that you can download and/or view your e-mail from your `Private Network`.

The POP and IMAP protocols are designed to allow access to e-mail via an external network or connection. Traditionally, you would have to log into an account and access e-mail directly from that machine, but the introduction of the POP and IMAP protocols makes that unnecessary.

Netscape provides an e-mail client that is capable of using either POP or IMAP. You can configure the Netscape e-mail client to access your remote ISP account to send and retrieve e-mail. You pay your ISP to manage your e-mail, and don't have to worry about anything other than configuring the Netscape client. Figure 8-1 shows an e-mail system based around an ISP server. Connections are made through the Linux gateway `chivas`, and local workstations send and receive mail through the ISP.

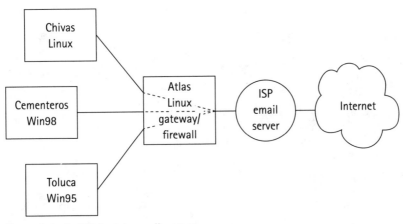

Figure 8-1: An ISP–based e-mail system

You are not limited to Netscape as your e-mail client. There are other clients available that work with POP and IMAP. For instance, the simple, text-based PINE client can be used. The Netscape client is used as the example in this chapter because it is included in the Red Hat distribution included on the companion CD-ROM, and it is also easy to use and powerful.

1. Netscape is installed as part of the Red Hat installation process. Log in as any user and click on the Netscape (N) button on the Main menu panel. When the Netscape window opens up, click Edit→Preferences. The Preferences screen is displayed.

2. Click Mail and Groups, then click Mail Server. Enter the information about your user name (as it exists on your ISP's mail server) and the names of your outgoing and incoming servers.

3. Click on either the POP3 or IMAP4 radio buttons depending on what protocol your ISP provides you.

   - POP3 is a two-way protocol. It is used to send and retrieve e-mail. It is an older protocol and is not as secure as IMAP. If you want increased security, then use IMAP.

   - IMAP4 is a two-way protocol. You can use it to both send and receive e-mail. It is the newer of the two protocols and has reached a state of maturity where you should not have any problems with it.

   Your entries should look something like the window shown in Figure 8-2.

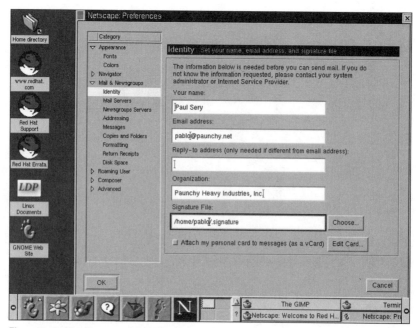

Figure 8-2: The Netscape Mail Server window

4. Next, click on the Identity item and enter your full e-mail address, and optionally your real name, organization, and signature file.

5. Click OK and try to send yourself some e-mail. You should be able to click on the Get messages button and receive your e-mail.

The drawback to this method is that each user on your network will need an e-mail address provided by your ISP. That typically costs some money, but not much, and is quite reasonable for even the smallest business. Also, since all of your e-mail is queued through your ISP, you have to have a PPP connection activated in order to access it. So if users on your Private Network want to communicate with each other, then they have to all go out to the ISP to do so. This will probably not be a problem until your operation grows beyond a dozen people or so.

> Another advantage to this method is that you can retrieve e-mail from any location. As long as you have a way to connect to your ISP, then you can retrieve your e-mail. For instance, if you have a lap top with a modem, then you can configure it to retrieve your e-mail and all you have to do is dial in to your ISP to get it.

Even if you have a lot of e-mail traffic this method still might make sense as long as you have a fast connection to your ISP. For instance, if you have a T1 (1.54 Mbps), then you very likely will not have any problems. However, if your little modem has to manage megabytes of e-mail traffic every day, then you need either a bigger Internet pipe or you need to reduce the load by keeping local traffic within your network. The next section, "Configuring a Local E-mail Server," describes that process.

Configuring a local e-mail server

If you have a significant amount of e-mail traffic — especially local traffic — then using your ISP as your e-mail server might not be practical. This section describes a hybrid system where your chivas acts as the local e-mail server using the send-mail, fetchmail and IMAP software. Clients send their e-mail destined for locations outside of your network to IMAP on chivas. sendmail then takes over and forwards the e-mail to your ISP and then to their final destination. Incoming e-mail is retrieved from your ISP via fetchmail. fetchmail feeds the retrieved e-mails to IMAP, which distributes it to the local network. sendmail directs all internal traffic to IMAP for internal distribution. Figure 8-3 shows the configuration of the local e-mail system. The Linux IMAP server chivas downloads all e-mail from the ISP's mail server. The local workstations send and receive e-mail via chivas. (If atlas is acting as the Internet gateway/firewall atlas, then it funnels the e-mail to the ISP. If chivas is acting as the gateway, then it sends the e-mail traffic to the ISP.)

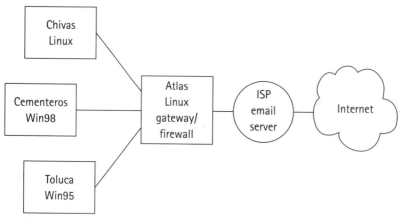

Figure 8-3: A locally-based e-mail system

There are four parts that need to be configured together to make this system work: the e-mail client, local delivery, external delivery and external retrieval. They are described in that order.

The fictitious user `rodbush` will be used in the examples for this configuration. Log in as root and create the user by running the commands:

```
adduser rodbush
passwd rodbush
```

CONFIGURING THE NETSCAPE E-MAIL CLIENT

This e-mail system depends on the use of the Netscape mail client on each computer on `paunchy.net`. Netscape should be configured to use IMAP4. You can use the instructions previously given in the section "Using the Netscape E-mail Client."

However, instead of entering the name of your ISP as the incoming and outgoing server, you should enter `chivas.paunchy.net` instead. The Linux e-mail server `chivas` directs all local e-mail traffic and forwards or retrieves e-mail destined for or coming from the Internet via the ISP server.

CONFIGURING SENDMAIL FOR LOCAL E-MAIL

The default `sendmail` configuration requires all the names that your e-mail server is known as to be listed in `/etc/sendmail.cw`. Modify the file as follows.

```
# sendmail.cw - include all aliases for your machine here.
bart
paunchy.net
```

Your ISP must know what name you are known by too. That process is discussed in the section "Registering your Domain Name" later in this chapter.

The /etc/sendmail.cf file must be modified too. Modify the paramter #Dj$w.Foo.COM as shown below.

```
Dj$w.paunchy.net
```

This line tells sendmail what the local domain name is.

CONFIGURING SENDMAIL FOR EXTERNAL DELIVERY

To send mail from your network to the outside world through your ISP, you need to make a another modification to the /etc/sendmail.cf file. Log in as root and edit the sendmail.cf file. Find the section that looks as follows:

```
# "Smart" relay host (may be null)
DS
```

Modify the DS parameter to DSmyisp.com which tells sendmail to deliver external mail to your ISP.
The modified configuration file should look like the following.

```
# "Smart" relay host (may be null)
DSmail.myisp.com
```

Next, comment out the following line to allow your messages to be relayed to your ISP. This line can be found at, or around, line 1033 in the /etc/sendmail.cf file.

```
# anything else is bogus
###R$*                    $#error $@ 5.7.1 $: "550 Relaying denied"
```

RESTART THE SENDMAIL DAEMON TO ACTIVATE THE CHANGES

You need to restart the sendmail daemon in order to put the changes into effect. Use the sendmail startup script to restart the daemon.

```
/etc/rc.d/init.d/sendmail restart
```

You should be able to test your system. While logged on as root, enter the command:

```
mail rodbush@myisp.com
```

This is a simple e-mail client. Type whatever you want on the subject line, and then everything that you type in is part of the message that you are composing. Finish the message by entering a period (.) as the first character on a line and then press the Enter key. Press the Enter key once more at the CC: prompt.

If your have a PPP connection to your ISP, then your message should be delivered immediately. Otherwise, your diald program will make the connection and your message is delivered. Log on to your ISP account and check for your message. If it works, then great, but if not, check the Troubleshooting section in this chapter.

Restart the `sendmail` daemon to make it reread its configuration files.

```
/etc/rc.d/init.d/sendmail restart
```

INSTALLING IMAP

The `imap` RPM package needs to be installed in order for the Netscape clients to access the e-mail distributed by `sendmail`. Login as `root` and add it as follows:

```
rpm -ivh /mnt/cdrom/RedHat/RPMS/imap*
```

The `imapd` daemon is kicked off by the `inetd` daemon. If you look in the `/etc/inetd.conf` file, then you see that there is an entry for `imapd`. Whenever Netscape, or any other IMAP-based e-mail client, queries `chivas` (the e-mail server) the `imapd` daemon is started and negotiates the delivery of the e-mail.

 You could use the `Post Office Protocol` (POP) for this function. However, POP does not deliver outgoing mail, and that would require you to setup `sendmail` on each client workstation. That is not terribly difficult but it enhances security if you remove `sendmail` completely from every Linux workstation except `chivas`. Also, Windows machines do not run `sendmail` and so the only site-wide solution is to use `imap`.

CONFIGURING FETCHMAIL FOR EXTERNAL RETRIEVAL

`fetchmail` can be used to retrieve e-mail queued up for an individual user on a remote account. When used for a single user it works in much the same way that you can use your Netscape e-mail client; it uses POP or IMAP to download your e-mail to your local e-mail client.

`fetchmail` can be used on an individual basis to download each user's e-mail. This is reasonable if your network has only a few people. Please see the section "Configuring fetchmail for a Single User" for instructions.

`fetchmail` can also download e-mail for multiple local users from a single remote account. This is called `multidrop` mode and is the method used here. Please consult the section "Configuring fetchmail for Multiple Users" for instructions.

In order to make use of `multidrop` mode you must have a registered domain name. The domain name must be registered so that more than one individual can receive e-mail. For example, if you have just a single ISP login account, then only that user name can receive e-mail. However, if you have registered domain name such as paunchy.net, then any user that you give an account on your own network (`paunchy.net`) can receive e-mail from the Internet.

The following section describes the process of registering your domain name.

REGISTERING YOUR DOMAIN NAME

The local e-mail server as described in this chapter relies on funneling all e-mail through a single e-mail account at your ISP. This means that you need to register a domain name with the `InterNIC`. This is a simple process if you pay your ISP to process the paperwork for you. It costs $45-70 (as of fall, 1999) for two years of registration. You can have your ISP create an alias in its own e-mail system to map your registered domain name to your single e-mail address.

The alternative to registering a domain name and routing all of your user's e-mail through a single account is to pay your ISP to create an e-mail account for every user on your system. You need to create a separate `fetchmail` process to retrieve each of your users' e-mail.

Once you have registered your domain and had your ISP configure its system for you, then any mail addressed to that domain should show up at your ISP login account. For instance if your login account name is `widget_inc@isp.com` and someone sends e-mail to `rodbush@paunchy.net`, then that message shows up in the mail queue for `widget_inc`.

The trick is to download that mail queue to your local server and then distribute it to the appropriate individual mail queues. The following sections describe how to do that.

CONFIGURING FETCHMAIL FOR A SINGLE USER

`fetchmail` gets its configuration from the `.fetchmailrc` file in a user's home directory. The `fetchmailconf` program provides an interactive configuration GUI. However, a sample configuration file is provided here that can be used with the `paunchy.net` network. It is used in this example for the example user `rodbush`.

To configure your own `fetchmail`, log in as root, mount the CD-ROM and install `fetchmail`.

```
rpm -ivh /mnt/cdrom/RedHat/RPMS/fetchmail*
```

Copy the configuration file from the companion CD-ROM.

```
cd /home/rodbush
cp /mnt/cdrom/IDG/email/fetchmailrc.sampleuser  ./.fetchmailrc
chown rodbush.rodbush /home/rodbush/.fetchmailrc
```

Change it to include your ISP login name and password.

```
# Configuration created Fri Apr  9 22:28:57 1999 by fetchmailconf
set postmaster "root"
poll mail.myisp.com with proto POP3
user "rodbush" there with password "iwantmail" is rodbush here
options fetchall
```

◆ The set postmaster parameter informs the sendmail program that any un-recognized or such messages should be forwarded to the root user.

◆ The poll mail.myisp.com with the protocol POP3 tells fetchmail to go to your ISP's mail server and use the POP3 protocol (IMAP and other protocols can be used too).

◆ The user line tells fetchmail that your ISP user name and password are rodbush and iwantmail and that any e-mail in that account should be sent to the local user Rod Bush.

◆ The fetchall option tells fetchmail to download all messages in the widget_inc e-mail queue.

Your .fetchmail file contains your ISP password, so change the permissions so that only the user can read and write to it.

```
chmod 0600 .fetchmailrc
```

Once fetchmail is run and the e-mail for rodbush is downloaded, then the Netscape e-mail client (or any e-mail program that speaks POP or IMAP) can be used to view the e-mail.

You can modify the .fetchmailrc file to get the e-mail for another user by changing the local user name. For instance, to use that script to get the e-mail for garagon just change the user line as follows (you should also create the account - adduser gabe_aragon).

```
user "rodbush" there with password "iwantmail" is garagon here
```

The problem with this method is that everyone who wants to receive e-mail needs a separate e-mail account at the ISP. This can certainly be arranged and should not be prohibitively expensive. It works in much the same way as when you use Netscape to go directly to your ISP as described earlier in the section "Using the Netscape E-mail Client."

The advantage of using fetchmail on an individual basis is that it automatically downloads the e-mail for a particular user without configuring your local sendmail, fetchmail and procmail systems. When you receive e-mail from mailing lists, delivery can become a problem. Mailing lists typically do not have your explicit e-mail address. Using `fetchmail` on an individual basis solves that problem because every message is directly downloaded to each user's local account.

CONFIGURING FETCHMAIL FOR MULTIPLE USERS – MULTIDROP

`fetchmail` can be run by `root` to retrieve an entire Private Network's e-mail. This is called `multidrop` mode. In `multidrop` mode, fetchmail is configured to read the e-mail's destination fields and convert it to a local domain's users. If the two fields do not match up completely (for instance, I receive e-mail from the list `samba@samba.anu.edu.au`, which does not match up with my ISP user name), then the mail will not be delivered to your local account. Instead, it is sent to the postmaster which, in this example, is root.

Copy the sample multidrop `.fetchmailrc` file to the `root` home directory.

```
cp /mnt/cdrom/IDG/e-mail/fetchmailrc.multidrop /root/.fetchmailrc
```

Your `.fetchmail` file contains your ISP password, so change the permissions so that only the user can read and write to it.

```
chmod 0600 .fetchmailrc
```

The `fetchmail` configuration file with multidrop is shown below.

```
# Configuration created Fri Apr  9 22:08:58 1999 by fetchmailconf
set postmaster "root"
poll mail.myisp.com with proto POP3
    localdomains paunchy.net
       user "widget_inc" there with password "iwantemail" is * here
options fetchall
```

- ◆ The `localdomains` line is added to tell `fetchmail` that the Private Network's domain name that it is serving is `paunchy.net`. This tells `fetchmail` to transfer e-mail from one domain to another. For instance, e-mail that shows up for `rodbush@paunchy.net` at your ISP account `widget_inc` is transferred to the local e-mail account for `rodbush`.

- ◆ The user line substitutes the asterisk metacharacter (*) for an individual user name. That informs `fetchmail` that any e-mail that shows up with a paunchy.net domain name is to be downloaded and converted to the appropriate local e-mail account.

- ◆ The `fetchall` option tells `fetchmail` to download all messages in the widget_inc e-mail queue.

Now try and get your e-mail via your multidrop `fetchmail`. Log in to your ISP user account and send e-mail to two or more of your local users.

From your Linux e-mail server — chivas — log in as root and run fetchmail. Your diald should dial your ISP and make the PPP connection.

SCHEDULING FETCHMAIL FETCHES

You can configure fetchmail to automatically retrieve your company's e-mail in couple of ways.

One way is to run fetchmail in daemon mode and have it periodically download mail. It must be run as root and must be run in multidrop mode. For instance, if you run it as fetchmail -d 300, then fetchmail downloads your e-mail once every 5 minutes (or 300 seconds). If you run fetchmail in this mode, then you need to start it automatically every time you boot your Linux box. A good way to start up a system that does not have a startup script in the /etc/rc.d/init.d directory is to use the /etc/rc.local file. Log in as root and add the following lines to the rc.local file.

```
if [ -f /etc/fetchmail ]; then
    /usr/bin/fetchmail -d 300
fi
```

Another method is to have cron kick off a fetchmail process. Log in as root and run the crontab -e command. It starts up vi (or whatever your default text editor is) and edits the crontab file for the user root. Add the line like the following:

```
# Fetch mail from mail.myisp.com
0,20,40 * * * * /usr/bin/fetchmail -v
```

Cron starts the fetchmail process as the user root every 20 minutes. Please refer to the crontab man page for information about the scheduling details.

Finally, you might want to opt to download mail whenever you connect to your ISP. You can modify the /usr/local/etc/ipfilter.rules to include the following line at the end of the file.

```
/usr/bin/fetchmail -d 60 -v
```

Once the PPP connection is made, diald/chat kicks off a fetchmail daemon that checks for e-mail once every 60 seconds (you can choose any interval you want).

Add the following rule to the /usr/local/etc/ipfilter.reset script to stop the fetchmail daemon when PPP is disconnected.

```
killall -9 fetchmail
```

You can use this method by itself or in conjunction with the previous two methods. There is no reason why you shouldn't download your e-mail every time you connect. It doesn't cost you anything other than the filling up of your PPP connection with the e-mail coming across.

Troubleshooting

Designing and maintaining an e-mail server can be a very complex job. Fortunately, the default Red Hat installation provides a ready made sendmail system that works for a small network. You can readily construct a complete e-mail system by adding fetchmail to get remote e-mail. Please test your new e-mail system before using it as your primary e-mail system.

However, keep in mind that if you have problems configuring it, you can always configure e-mail clients like Netscape to send and receive e-mail directly from your ISP.

Using the Netscape e-mail client

If your Netscape e-mail client refuses to read your mail queued up at your ISP, then first check that you have a PPP connection. Next check that your ipchains based firewall has rules set to allow POP or IMAP (depending on which protocol you use). A quick and potentially dangerous (if you happen to get attacked during the time your firewall is turned off) way to do this is to simply turn off the filtering rules. If you can then get your e-mail, then you know that a modification of your firewall is in order; consult Chapter 12 for a discussion of filtering rules.

If you still can not get your e-mail, then make sure that your Netscape preferences are set correctly. Look at the server name and protocols as well as check that your user name and e-mail address are correct. Consult the /var/log/messages and /var/log/maillog files for any hints to your problems. You might also consult with your ISP for its advice.

In the case where you are running your own e-mail server and your e-mail client can not access it, first check that your network connection is functioning correctly; Chapter 7 discusses network troubleshooting. If your network is okay, then check to see if the sendmail daemon is running correctly. That can be tested with a simple ps x | grep sendmail or /etc/rc.d/init.d/sendmail status commands as well as by logging into your server and running Netscape. Change the preferences to use Move-mail and if you get your mail, then sendmail is fine. Change back to POP or IMAP and try again. If e-mail still fails, then check the /etc/services and /etc/inetd.conf files to make sure that they have POP and/or IMAP entries. Use RPM to check that POP or IMAP is installed (rpm -qa | grep -i pop). Also check your /var/log/messages and /var/log/maillog for any hints that you might glean. Finally, check out the Usenet news groups like comp.mail.sendmail for advice and information on your problem.

Fixing problems with local e-mail

The `sendmail` daemon is configured out of the box by Red Hat to serve a small Private Network. If you never need to go outside your own network and you are not getting e-mail, then check first that `sendmail` is running. Second, check the `sendmail` installation with the `rpm -V sendmail` command. If it still does not work, then consult your `/var/log/messages` and `/var/log/maillog` for insights. The last step is to consult the Usenet news groups like `comp.mail.sendmail`.

When a message fails to get sent, it is returned to the sender or the postmaster; in the case where it cannot be delivered to either, a message will be written to the `/var/log/maillog` file. The return message has information about why it failed. It is beyond the scope of this book to discuss the many reasons this might happen. Please refer to the `sendmail` man page as well as the FAQ and other documents in the `/usr/doc/sendmail` directory for further information.

FIXING PROBLEMS WITH EXTERNAL DELIVERY

Configuring sendmail to forward e-mail destined for the outside world is a simple matter of modifying one parameter in the `/etc/sendmail.cf` file (see the section "Configuring Sendmail for External Delivery" in this chapter for details). If you cannot get your e-mail delivered, then the problem most likely lies in either your Internet connection or your sendmail installation. Use the troubleshooting techniques described in Chapters 11 and 12 to investigate the former. You can check the latter using the `rpm -V sendmail` command; don't hesitate to reinstall `sendmail`, because you only have three parameters in the sendmail.cf to change.

FIXING PROBLEMS WITH EXTERNAL RETRIEVAL

`fetchmail` is another system that depends on your ISP PPP connection being in place and your firewall filtering rules correct. If you are having problems getting it to work then use all the network and firewall troubleshooting hints given in Chapters 11 and 12 to verify your Internet connection. You can use the verbose flag to see how the connection and downloading process is going by using the `fetchmail -v` command. Pay attention to the login and authentication process. When `fetchmail` has authenticated with the POP or IMAP server you should see it saying that it is downloading the text or data of each message. Once that is done, then you should see `sendmail`-related handshaking messages displayed. Any errors are displayed during this process. When all else fails, check with your ISP and the Usenet `comp.mail.sendmail` group.

Summary

- A description of building a simple DNS server. DNS is used to convert Internet domain names into numeric IP addresses. By running your own internal DNS system, you can avoid having to enter all the host names on your Private Network into every machine. Scripts are provided that allow you to set up a simple DNS server. The scripts are oriented around the `paunchy.net` network used in all examples in this book.

- Using your Netscape e-mail client to directly access e-mail queue at your ISP. This is a simple and nearly bulletproof method. Your ISP takes delivery of e-mail addressed to you. Netscape is configured to pull your messages across your PPP connection via POP or IMAP. Each user on your network requires a separate account for this method to work.

- Using your Linux server to handle local e-mail delivery while forwarding or fetching external e-mail from your ISP. This requires four separate functions: local deliver, external forwarding, external fetching and domain name registration.

- Obtaining an Internet domain name if you want to run your own e-mail system. This is necessary so that your ISP can forward messages to to your sendmail server. Your ISP can handle the registration process for a small fee.

- Configuring your Linux box to act as a local e-mail server. Messages destined for people on your network can be handled by the Red Hat default `sendmail` installation. No modification of the `/etc/sendmail.cf` configuration file is necessary.

- Modifying one parameter in your `/etc/sendmail.cf` file takes care of the e-mail forwarding process. That line simply points to your ISP's e-mail server.

- Using `fetchmail` to retrieve external messages queued at your ISP finishes your Linux e-mail server configuration. There are several ways to configure `fetchmail` — either on an individual retrieval basis or for your entire domain. The individual method is straightforward but the group — maildrop — method is not much more difficult.

- Troubleshooting e-mail problems. Much of the troubleshooting is based on basic network and PPP connection methods. Beyond that you can use the log information that `sendmail`, `fetchmail` and `procmail` produce.

Part IV

Managing your Network

Chapter 9

Introducing Systems Administration

IN THIS CHAPTER

◆ Creating and interpreting administration policy

◆ Creating and maintaining backups

◆ Creating and maintaining security

◆ Creating Internet firewalls

◆ Using cron to automate repetitive jobs

◆ Using shell scripts

◆ Starting and stopping a Linux system

◆ Maintaining your computer network system

◆ Recovering from disaster

THIS BOOK DESCRIBES how to build individual Linux computers and networks. In previous chapters, you are given the basics for constructing a network and configuring both your clients and servers. Along the way, the subject of systems administration is briefly introduced. The subject will now be treated at greater length.

Introducing Systems Administration

Because an entire book is required to discuss administration in any detail, this chapter is intended only as an introduction to the subject. You are given just enough information to get started. Consider this a starting point on the systems administration journey.

The job of an administrator is to serve the needs of the computer user. To this end, an administrator must address human as well as technical concerns. In my experience, the technical side of systems administration is the simpler of the two. In other words, systems administration is as much an art as a science. Much, if not most, administration work takes the form of interpreting problems in terms of the technical implementation of their solutions.

Every administration job is completely different in its details. I can't possibly quantify the sum of the tasks, equipment, and people involved. However, most organizations – from a home office to a Fortune 500 corporation – share essentially the same set of core functions. My intention in this chapter is to describe them. The human factor is, of course, more difficult to describe, but I offer comments and advice wherever I can.

Systems administration is a complex, amorphous subject. No two administrative jobs are the same. Throughout this chapter, and the rest of the book, I try to provide you with the tools you need for devising solutions to the unique problems that you will encounter in your role as a systems administrator.

Understanding the Essentials

In some cases, systems administration is a purely part-time job; in other cases, you may inherit (or create) the administrator's job as a system grows, or it may be a specific, full-time job to begin with. In any case, the essential functions are the same, but they vary in terms of size, interaction, and complexity. The following list summarizes those functions:

◆ Creating, modifying, interpreting, and enforcing policy. This is the most important philosophical aspect of any administrator's job. All the other functional duties stem from it. The administrative policies you create and inherit will rule your life. They can be in the form of company law or they may be completely verbal. Even if you do not set the rules, your interpretation of them will be the effective law. Because the nature of administration is managing chaos, your policy road map is essential for keeping everything under control.

◆ Creating and maintaining backups. This is the most important single function of a systems administrator. You need secure, reliable backups of your servers and possibly the client computers.

◆ Creating and maintaining an effective security system. Security is both a technical and a human concern. Technically, it spans everything from individual computer configurations to your firewall design. The human side encompasses everything from how you set up and enforce password policy to people's feelings.

◆ Managing users. It is your responsibility to add, remove, and modify user accounts.

◆ Maintaining file systems. It is your responsibility to add, remove, and modify the various file systems on your servers. (I introduce the topic of file systems in Chapter 3.)

- Modifying and maintaining hardware. Unless you work for a large company (and even if you do, in some cases), you are responsible for the installation and maintenance of computers and peripherals.

- Modifying and maintaining software. The need here is obvious. Computers must have their operating systems installed and upgraded. Applications such as databases, word processors, and spreadsheets need to be installed and maintained, too.

- Troubleshooting. This is an everyday task. When something goes wrong — big or small, real or imagined — you get called. This responsibility generally requires that you carry a pager.

- Ensuring reliability. This is your ultimate goal. Ensuring reliability is both a specific job and a general goal. It is achieved by properly doing your job as outlined in the preceding items as well as planning and designing for the unforeseen problems as best you can.

- Crawling under floors and through ceilings, answering the phone, and taking out the trash.

As you can see, the administrator's responsibilities are wide-ranging and complex. The following sections describe these responsibilities in more detail.

Creating and interpreting policy

Any computer system and network needs a roadmap to operate reliably and efficiently. With this book I aim to give you the tools you need to operate a network. The tools are introduced in a systematic way, in order to bring you to the point where you have an overall understanding of a complete, albeit simple, system.

The policy that you set and the policy that you enforce often are two different things. You may determine certain things yourself — for example, the backup policy discussed later in this chapter. Outside of your own business or home office, many administration and security issues generally cross into policy areas that management determines. You may collaborate in the establishment of these policies, or they may be completely out of your hands. It's up to you to implement such policies as best you can and be willing to draw a line if a policy becomes impossible to enforce.

If you have a personal home network, you need to know which tasks you need to perform to keep your system up and running. You do not need to write a manual of rules you want to follow, but you do need to perform certain tasks at specific times. You certainly need to back up your valuable data regularly and in such a way that you know how to recover lost files. It is okay to keep such tasks on an informal level; however, you may find it helpful to write down the instructions for performing more complex processes. You may need only to write down the exact instruction that you use to create a backup, but that can be invaluable information and it doesn't take much effort to write it down on a slip of paper and stick it in the cassette case.

If you manage a small to medium network for someone else, you must systematically write things down. At this level, the line between policy and pure instructions begins to blur. A page or two of backup instructions can serve as both the policy and the instructions. The instructions may say first do step A, then B, and finally C, three times a week. That is your company's policy.

For larger operations, you most likely inherit policy. The exception is when a takeover or a major reorganization occurs. In most cases, you still have a great deal of power in the way you interpret and implement the rules given to you. The number of people who ultimately depend on you determines the importance of a job.

Another purpose of writing policy and procedure down is to make yourself dispensable. Your goal should be to enable someone else – with the appropriate level of computer experience – to come in cold and perform the basic system administration. The more administration functions that I systematize, the better I am doing my job.

Part of your general policy should be to document both your everyday tasks and your occasional ones. The more you write down and diagram procedures, the easier your job will be and the easier it will be for your successor. Also, documenting a process can lead to that process becoming policy. If you do a job a certain way and you can document it in a reasonable way, it's likely to become the way it is done all the time. By writing it down, you can make it the official method by default.

Web browsers can make the job of documentation easier. By placing all or most of your documents on a private (Intranet) Web page, you make them easy to find and view. If you make part of the documentation into a FAQ, you may even reduce your workload after you educate your users to access it for everyday problems. If you possess an artistic streak, you can actually relieve the drudgery of documentation by using HTML as your brush and palate.

The rest of this chapter discusses the distinct functions of systems administration. Each function is governed by a policy, written or not.

Creating and maintaining backups

Your backup policy determines your single most important job as an administrator. If you have good backups, you can recover from any catastrophe. At one end of a catastrophe (even if all your computers burn to the ground or a disk crash destroys your data), if you have reliable, complete backups, you can recreate your system. At the other, less ominous, end of the catastrophe spectrum, backups enable you to recover individual files or groups of files that have been accidentally erased. Therefore, you must have a system to make backups and follow it religiously.

You need secure, reliable, multiple backups of your servers. Do not trust just one or even two backups. Whatever your method, make multiple, overlapping backups, and keep at least one, but preferably two, backups offsite. By offsite, I mean in another building separate from your normal working location. At one job, I took backups home because we only had one office. In another job, I took the backups to another company building. Having offsite backups helps you to sleep well at night.

You should periodically test your backup system. By practicing restoring data, you keep yourself confident and also test for data integrity. Periodic testing should be an essential part of your backup policy.

You can use various utilities to create backups. The standard Linux (and UNIX) tools are the tar, cpio — and now — dump utilities:

♦ The tar utility creates an archive file and has the advantage of being nearly universal. The GNU tar now enables you to specify compression as an option. It also provides for making incremental backups (an incremental backup includes whatever files have been created or modified since a full backup was last made; a full backup includes every file in the directory or file system that is specified to be backed up). In my opinion, tar is the easiest system to use.

♦ The cpio utility also creates an archive file, with fewer restrictions in terms of the depth of a directory structure that it can traverse and also the length of a filename it can handle. It also handles localized tape errors by skipping over them.

♦ The dump program is oriented toward backing up entire file systems and then keeping track of changes in order to provide incremental backups. It also provides a hierarchy of incremental backup levels (ten levels) that gives you a convenient system to use on weekly and monthly intervals. (dump is not described in this book.)

USING THE TAR UTILITY

The tar utility archives directories and files to a tar file. A tar file can be a tape, a pipe, or a normal file. The first parameter specifies one of the primary functions — such as create, list, or extract — for tar to perform. The next parameters are optional modifications to the primary function. The last parameters are files or directories to archive (note that when a directory is given, it and all its subdirectories will be archived).

It is a simple program to use. For example, to create a tar file of the example user lidia that you created in Chapter 6, enter the following command:

```
tar cf lidia.tar /home/lidia
```

You can also use a hyphen (-) to specify command-line parameters. For example, you would run the previous command as follows: `tar -cf lidia.tar /home/tar`.

All the files in the `/home/lidia` directory are stored in the tar file `lidia.tar`. The f parameter specifies that the next argument will be the tar file. The following command lists the contents of `lidia.tar`:

```
tar tf lidia.tar
./
.Xclients
.Xdefaults
.bash_logout
.bash_profile
.bashrc
.xsession
.bash_history
```

 You can get more information displayed by using the verbose — v — parameter. If you use it while creating or extracting an archive, each file is displayed as it is copied or extracted. Using it with the listing option t produces a listing like the one you would get with the long format of the `ls` command (`ls -l`).

To restore those files, use the extract option as shown in the following command:

```
tar xf lidia.tar
```

The extracted files are placed in your current directory unless you specify that `tar` use the absolute path — -P — option, in which case `tar` attempts to restore the files to their original location at `/home/lidia`.

 The `tar` version that comes with the Red Hat Linux distribution is smart enough not to include the archive in itself. That is, if you are copying to a tar file that happens to be in the directory from which you are saving, the tar file that you are creating will not be included in the tar file. However, older versions will happily include themselves in the tar file they create.

The more recent versions of GNU `tar`, such as the one that comes on this book's CD-ROM, now have gzip compression included as an option. The previous examples for creating and extracting tar files can include gzip compression by using the `gzip - -z -` option, as shown in the following commands:

```
tar czf lidia.tgz /home/lidia
tar xzf lidia.tgz /home/lidia
```

Note that I use the `.tgz` filename suffix to indicate that the file is a gzipped tar file. Please refer to the `tar` man page for more information.

Throughout this book, I use the `gzip` program to compress a file or files and pipe its output to `tar`. This is the traditional combination, but is no longer necessary with the modern `tar` with the `gzip` and `ungzip` options. In some circumstances, I have continued to use the old combination because it shows the use and operation of pipes as well as the `gzip` and `tar` programs.

USING THE CPIO UTILITY

The GNU `cpio` utility creates `cpio` archives to store files in. It is more complex to use than `tar` because you must feed it the files that you want it to process. That extra step, however, makes it extremely flexible for picking files and directories to archive. Because it archives whatever filenames you pass to it, you can archive complex directory trees.

Creating a `cpio` archive is referred to as copy-out mode and is specified by using the `-o` parameter. Here's a simple `cpio` process to archive the files in the `/home/lidia` directory to a cpio archive called `lidia.cpio`:

```
find /home/lidia | cpio -o > lidia.cpio
```

Here, the `find` command simply sends the name and path of each file in the `/home/lidia` directory. (In this case, `/home/lidia` does not have any subdirectories so you could simply use the `ls` command to send the filenames to `cpio` and it would work as it does in this example.) `cpio` converts the contents of each file into its own format. If you do not redirect it to a file or device, the contents of each file are sent to standard output and you'll see them flash by.

Extracting files from a `cpio` archive is referred to as copy-in mode and is specified by using the `-i` parameter. If you want to extract the files, omit the t option and `cpio` attempts to recreate the files in the current directory. Enter the following command to recreate the files relative to the current directory:

```
cat lidia.cpio | cpio -i
```

TIP You can take advantage of bash's capability to redirect standard input and output by substituting the following single command, which is more elegant and efficient than the previous example:

```
cpio -i < lidia.cpio
```

In this case, cpio balks because the files it has archived already exist in the current directory. If you redirect its output to another directory, it will happily create them at that location. The following command redirects them to the /tmp directory (Red Hat removes all files from /tmp that are older than ten days):

```
cat lidia.cpio | (cd /tmp ; cpio -i )
```

You can list the files in a cpio archive by using the following command:
```
cat lidia.cpio | cpio -it
```

TIP Unlike the tar utility, cpio requires that you prefix all option parameters with a hyphen (-). For example, the previous command does not work if you enter it as cpio it.

cpio also has the capability to copy files from one directory tree to another. This capability — called copy-pass — combines the function of copy-in and copy-out but does not create a cpio archive. The following command copies the files in /home/lidia to /tmp:

```
find /home/lidia -print | cpio -p /tmp
```

The cpio operating modes are copy-in, copy-out, and copy-pass. They enable you to create, delete, list, or modify cpio archives. The archives can be stored to a file, a pipe, or a device (such as a tape). Please refer to the cpio man page for more details.

Using the tar utility for low-volume backups

If you have a simple network — such as a home office or small business — then you may not even need a dedicated backup system. In my own home network, I simply do not have much data to back up. I have several megabytes of word processing files, some spreadsheets, a few HTML files, and my Linux configuration files. Because I store all my data files on my Linux server, my Microsoft Windows workstations have zero data — aside from their own configuration files and application software — stored on them. I keep a backup of some of their configuration files and application software on the Linux server. I use the tar application to back up the critical directories, and the `gzip` application to compress the `tar` file and then back up the resulting file to floppies and also my ISP account. This system is neither elegant nor sophisticated, but it is — most importantly — effective and cheap.

The following example illustrates the simple command I use to make my personal backups:

```
tar cvf - /etc /home | gzip > /tmp/backup.tar
{copy tar file to floppy, Zip, Jaz, tape or other media}
{copy tar file to ISP or other offsite location}
```

TIP The Linux `tar` command has the option to compress the data without piping it explicitly to the `gzip` or `compress` utilities. The `-z` or `-gzip` parameters invoke the `gzip` utility; the `-gunzip` calls the `gunzip`; and the `-Z` or `-compress` invokes the compress command, while `-uncompress` calls for the `uncompress` option.

Making backups this way is simple and effective. To save time and limited bandwidth, I also make incremental backups. During critical periods such as while writing this book, I make frequent full backups to a floppy disk during the day and then an incremental backup to my ISP account at the end of the day. Here's the command I use for the incremental backup that uses the newer — `-N date` — feature of `tar` where the date is a simple four-digit month-day format. Note that in this case I use the compression — `z` — feature of tar in place of putting gzip in the pipeline:

```
tar -czvf /tmp/incr.tgz -N 0128 /etc /home
```

For my personal network, I use this simple system, which simply does not require a log. At this level, the work involved in keeping a log would probably reduce the number of times a day I back up my work. Now if I were administering a small system for someone else, I would certainly keep a log. When you do work for someone else, you need to be as systematic as possible so that more records exist about the system than just what is in your own memory.

TIP Actually, I do keep a minimal log. On a slip of paper that I keep with the floppy disk, I write a quick date and time at the end of the day when I copy my files to it. Of course, I have been making copies to it all day, but the end-of-day notation helps me to remember when my last backup was if I leave my work for a day or two.

Performing intermediate-volume backups

For larger networks – including most small- to medium-sized businesses, or a home office where you happen to use lots of data – a more substantial backup system is necessary. If you need to store several gigabytes (GB) of data then you need some sort of backup mechanism. You can choose from several technologies: PC tape drives, ZIP, JAZ, Digital AudioTape (DAT), Digital Linear Tape (DLT), writable CD-ROMs, and additional, removable hard disks. Tapes are good because of their high capacity, durability, compact size, and ubiquitous nature. I recommend making several overlapping full backups every month. I also recommend that you create long-term archive tapes of particularly important information. You could use a portable hard disk, but it would be too expensive and cumbersome to carry around. Tapes are the way to go.

Although I think PC tape drives and DAT drives are the best general choices, the others can fit specialized needs. For instance, a writable CD-ROM is reliable and reasonably inexpensive, but fairly slow, and only has about 650MB of storage. I recommend that you invest in an SCSI interface and a 4mm DAT drive. They are fast and reliable, they can store between 2 and 4GB of data, and the tapes are inexpensive. In my opinion, it is important to keep at least a dozen tapes in order to maintain multiple overlapping backups, spread wear and tear, and keep several tapes offsite. Note that it is also important to follow the manufacturer's tape-cleaning guidelines, because DAT drive mechanisms are complex and more prone to failure if not cleaned properly.

The BRU2000 (backup and restore) backup utility provides a reasonable solution for medium sized backups. It gives you a GUI interface that simplifies the job of making and reading backups. It sold by Enhanced Software Technologies, Inc., and provides device-independent operation as well as verified backup and restore operations. I used `bru` with a Silicon Graphics workstation years ago and found it superior to `tar`.

You can also use the inexpensive PC Travan tape drives. Drivers are available for drives such as Iomega Ditto Tape Insider 3200 or the Colorado drives. They use either inexpensive proprietary interfaces or the parallel port. The high-end drives can back up gigabytes of data at reasonable speeds. However, the tapes themselves are expensive at around $35 apiece. At that price, they have never been attractive to me because I like to keep a dozen or more tapes.

It is also important to keep detailed and accurate logs. Figure 9-1 outlines the format for such a log.

Date ___/___/___

Computer name _____ IP address ____-____-____-____
Location _____

Backup device _____ Capacity _____

Date	Directories	Command	Notes
___/___/___	_____	_____	_____
___/___/___	_____	_____	_____
___/___/___	_____	_____	_____
___/___/___	_____	_____	_____
___/___/___	_____	_____	_____
___/___/___	_____	_____	_____
___/___/___	_____	_____	_____
___/___/___	_____	_____	_____
___/___/___	_____	_____	_____
___/___/___	_____	_____	_____
___/___/___	_____	_____	_____
___/___/___	_____	_____	_____
___/___/___	_____	_____	_____
___/___/___	_____	_____	_____
___/___/___	_____	_____	_____
___/___/___	_____	_____	_____
___/___/___	_____	_____	_____
___/___/___	_____	_____	_____

Figure 9-1: Your tape backup log

If you have large backups, you should consider making incremental backups at frequent intervals. Remember that if you need to restore a file or files from an incremental backup, you will need to start the restoration from the most recent full backup and supply the incremental backup or backups in chronological order.

TIP

There is now an alternative to manually creating backups. The Arkeia system provides automated backups over the network. Chapter 10 describes its use.

Handling high-volume backups

When you get to the point of backing up many gigabytes of data you can expect that your organizational problems will skyrocket. Just consider the difficulty of keeping track of numerous 4mm DAT tapes and you will realize that the possibility of making errors is significant. Keeping the tape sequence in order while doing the backups, correctly labeling the tapes, and storing them over time all require unerring consistency. Making just one mistake at the wrong time could jeopardize your entire operation.

What is the solution? The solution is probably a tape library or optical disk jukebox. They are expensive and difficult to set up, but in the long term they pay for themselves. Add commercial software that further automates the process and you end up needing to do nothing other than monitor the process and occasionally add and remove tapes.

If you must use many tapes, your top priorities are systematically labeling your tapes and keeping precise logbooks. (Alternatively, you can solve that problem by purchasing a tape library that uses a bar code reader.) Your job is further complicated if others perform the backups. In either case, but especially the latter, you should systematically conduct your own data integrity tests. This testing involves choosing some data to restore, finding the appropriate tape, and checking to see if the data is really there. The last thing you want to have happen is to need to restore some data and find out that it was never saved in the first place due to some foul-up.

Automating backups

Making manual backups appears to be an inexpensive process. You only have to purchase relatively inexpensive tape drives or tape libraries. However, the appearance is deceptive. In the long term, labor costs are high and it's almost certain that you'll make a mistake.

You should seriously consider automating the entire process. Automated backup software is expensive but worth the cost in the long run. Chapter 10 describes the commercial Arkeia system by Knox Software, Inc. The company has provided a demonstration license for this book so that you can experiment with its system.

Creating and Maintaining Security

The problem with any rating system is that you have to come up with a methodology and adhere to it. As much as I would like to have two most important items, I can't honestly do that (I wish that my management would be as kind!). Therefore, I have decided to put the subject of security second, after backups. It is a very close second. My reasoning is as follows: Security is much more complex than the issue of maintaining proper backups and therefore more prone to imperfections and breakdown over time. It is also highly dependent on the participation and belief of other people; it is very easy to become complacent if you do not see a direct threat and especially if you do not understand the underlying issues. As an administrator, you are at the mercy of variables over which you have less than perfect control. Therefore, any system you design will be less than perfect. Ultimately, if you have a reliable backup, you can recover from most security failures.

The drawback to that reasoning is that if your security is breached in a subtle manner, the breach may go undetected and propagate over time. If your system is broken into and subtly changed over time, then your backups may become worthless because they will eventually contain only the corrupted files. If your work is compromised over time, your efforts may become worthless or worse – you may become liable in other ways. In that case, my ranking system breaks down. Perhaps it would be better not to rate things like this. In any case, it is best that you be aware of the potential and decide for yourself.

The difficult nature of security makes it as much a function of vigilance and constant education as of the policy itself. Security is a day-in, day-out grind that you simply have to do. An effective system makes itself appear to be unnecessary. If you lock your house every time you leave it and you never have been robbed, it may appear to be an unnecessary task. But if you start leaving your house unlocked, the one time you are broken into will drive home the necessity of having to do it without fail.

Security is also part of every task you do. For instance, while I have listed backups separately, backups are actually the last bastion of your security policy because they enable you to recover from malicious activities. Security should be viewed as integral to every aspect of systems administration.

You should concentrate on several security areas:

◆ **Human Factors.** All security starts with the people who use the system. Unless you are the only user, you must depend on other people to adhere to your security policy. Your users have the ability to make your system safe or not. Unfortunately, dealing with people is a lot messier than dealing with computers because people have silly things like lives, free will, and such. We all tend to lose enthusiasm for what seems like unnecessary work with time. Therefore, you must be oriented toward that messy reality. Education is an important factor in this equation. Your own attitude will affect how seriously others view the issue.

◆ **Passwords.** Your passwords are your first line of defense. They are the locks on your doors. If you do not demand good passwords and their consistent use, all your other security measures will be compromised.

◆ **Firewalls.** They are your primary defense from unauthorized Internet connections. A firewall must be transparent enough to allow effective and efficient use of the Internet and also prevent unwanted outside access. The type and level of effectiveness depends on what you use the Internet for.

◆ **Internal network security.** You must consider the internal threat. If you have valuable information, then people with valid access to it might actually compromise it. Your network configuration and layout determine much of your security structure. If you have varying security requirements within your own organization, you can, and probably should, arrange your network topology to reflect those realities. This arrangement can divide your network into subnets to isolate the functional areas of your network, and it can specify file permissions to further divide your network.

◆ **External network security.** Your firewall will be the first line of defense against the barbarians. You should also be careful not to advertise how your network is configured and what security measures you use.

◆ **Layered security.** All the previous items should be constructed to work together. One layer should back up another and vice versa. If your firewall is breached, you should still have all your user accounts protected with effective passwords. Even if you are not sure about all your passwords, you still have your firewall. If a burglar is attempting to break in and a user happens to notice something amiss, that person should have enough security education to know to inform you about the suspicious activity. When you put all this together, it works well enough to strengthen each individual measure.

◆ **Vigilance.** You should regularly test your system. You can do this with a number of helpful software systems, such as Tripwire, Satan and COPS. Testing should be done regularly and with the attitude that prevention is the best policy.

Addressing human factors

If you have more than one person involved in your system, you have to concern yourself with managing people. Systems administrators must walk the fine line between requiring too much and too little security. If you are too harsh, your users will actively and passively find ways around your measures. On the other hand, if you are too lax, the users will not respect your system and you leave yourself open to external threats.

What is the fine line? I'll take the easy way — actually, the reasonable way — out. It depends on your situation. If you are the systems administrator for a bank, you must take more precautions than if you run a hobby shop. However, any operation must take a core group of measures, and I concentrate on those core measures here.

The most important measure you should strive for is the respect and education of your system's users. The average person respects the need for basic security measures. If the users know the basics of how passwords are used and why they are important, you can count on a higher level of consistency in their use. Otherwise you can expect far more problems.

An important aspect of education should be a simple, straightforward usage policy that everyone signs in order to obtain access. You should emphasize the essential rules that are most important to your organization. Include other policy statements, but restrain yourself from cluttering this essential document. If you end up with more than one page and can't reduce it, I suggest dividing it up into two documents: one essential and the other important items.

Individual or group classes should also be considered. They are unpleasant but can greatly help in the long run. For instance, even though a new user signs the usage policy, you still do not know whether it has been fully read and understood. Even if the policy has been read and understood, a short tutorial will reinforce it and hopefully emphasize that you take security seriously. If the person has not understood it fully, such a lesson will clear things up. In the long term, an occasional refresher class or meeting can put people back on the right track.

The occasional person who simply doesn't take security seriously presents a difficult issue. I can't offer much advice other than to suggest that a patient, consistent, and firm direction from you may help over time. The difficult people I have run into in my career were relatively benign in that they generally refused to follow policies such as logging off when leaving the small building where we worked. It was frustrating because I didn't have the clout to force adherence but I accomplished it by default when I installed automatic computer locks (Linux and Windows screen locks) during operating system upgrades. Dealing with people who actively eschew security measures is a difficult issue. The best advice I can offer is to have management establish a standard and make it clear that anyone who doesn't maintain it will be fired. What constitutes the standard is for each organization to determine. A reasonable starting point is a zero-tolerance policy concerning the malicious use of the organization's computer resources (such as sending threatening e-mail). I have never had to go close to such measures, but I would be willing to do so if pushed far enough.

Devising a password policy

A good password is a difficult animal to define. On one hand, a good password should not be crackable with a standard cracking program, which compares passwords against dictionaries and also uses heuristics to guess at them. However, if a password is too complex, it will either not be used or it will be written down and become almost as dangerous as no password at all.

Cracking programs work like this: The Linux password-encrypting algorithm is publicly known. So a cracker starts with an already encrypted password and works backward by encrypting words and making a comparison. If your password is apple and its encrypted form is al2sdjf, the cracking program goes to a dictionary and encrypts each word in order until it comes to apple and finds that its encrypted form matches the string found in the password file. At that point it has broken your password.

The idea is to find a compromise between too much simplicity and too much complexity. It should work over the long term, too. The method I prefer is to choose two short names or things and combine them. That type of password is easy to remember, does not have an entry in any dictionary in the world, and is not connected to you directly. A password should adhere to the following points:

♦ It should not exist in any dictionary found in the world. An apparently obscure word is only obscure to you because you are not a computer. However, a computer essentially has instant access to – and knowledge of – any word that is in a database to which the computer has access. The same goes with any place or proper name because they may be in an encyclopedia somewhere. You should assume that if you can locate it, anyone else can, too.

Note: The use of trivial passwords is a moot point on most new systems. For instance, the `passwd` program shipped with Red Hat uses the `Pluggable Authentication Modules` (PAM) and does not allow you to use words that can be found in a dictionary anymore. It also prevents you from using slight variations on dictionary words. Older versions do not make such checks, so beware.

♦ It should not have any direct connection to you. For obvious reasons, you should not use numbers or words that are related to your personal situation such as a date of birth or an address. Conversely, avoid using things that could be used against you if guessed, such as PIN numbers.

♦ Simple variations of words or common phrases should be avoided, too. Modern computers are capable of a huge number of operations per second. Therefore, programs using heuristics – rules that define methods for guessing – can perform enough permutations of existing words so variations can be discovered. For instance, if your name is Big Blue and you choose a password such as BiBlue, a burglar knowing you can readily program a crack to start with Big Blue and variations thereof until the correct one is discovered. The lesson is, do not depend on changing a word or a personal number slightly because it can be cracked. Again, the password may seem obscure to you but to a mindless computer it is no problem at all.

♦ On the other side of the spectrum, random strings generated by password-generating programs are difficult to remember. People tend to write down things that are difficult to remember. Things that are written down can be left lying around. Passwords that are left lying around are of no protection to you. Even if you do not leave them lying around, the fact that your shop generates random passwords is a hook for a determined burglar. If I wanted to break into a computer system and I knew that it used such passwords, I would plan on looking for such a list. A determined burglar could probably find the list one way or another. Is this a little paranoid? Yes, unless your system is valuable enough to somebody. That depends on your situation.

The solution I like avoids those pitfalls. First I'll describe the algorithm and then I'll explain it.

Choose two simple words and combine them. The words should be short enough so that together they do not add up to much more than eight characters. The words should not be normally used together. I use a non-alphanumeric linking character such as the tilde (~) character. Here's an example of such a password:

`radi~road`

Why did I make such a choice? I just looked out my window and saw the road in front of my place. I am also listening to the radio. Put together, they are not in any dictionary. Any cracking program will have to check nearly as many combinations as if the password were a completely random string of characters.

Note: Because only the first eight characters are significant, the effective password is

`radi~roa`

This password is actually better because `road` becomes the essentially random string `roa`. Nobody knows that your linking character is ~, which is also good. It is not truly a random string, but a cracker program will have to attempt a large number of permutations of all the words in a dictionary. It is not perfect, but even though it is a compromise, it is a good one in my opinion.

An alternative to the preceding method is to use one of the random or pseudo-random password generators and keep generating passwords until one appears that you like. If you like it, then that implies you can remember it, too. I used this method to get such classics as `gglujoy` and `shoeboe`.

After you choose a password, you must decide how long to keep it. The extremes are changing too often or never at all. If you change it too often, your password will be difficult to remember. If you never change it, you run the risk of having your password become common knowledge. Personally, I think changing every six months to a year is best. Keeping a password longer than a year is dangerous, in my opinion, but I cannot quantify a precise time-frame other than to say that a year seems like a long time to keep the same password.

Shadow passwords

Even with correctly conceived passwords, you are still vulnerable to attack. The fact that the encrypted (technically they are referred to as encoded) passwords are contained in the /etc/passwd file makes them vulnerable to attack. That file must be world readable (recall that three sets of permissions exist for a file: owner, group, and world) because many application programs need to check it. If a burglar gains access to your system, files can be retrieved to another machine and cracked at leisure.

The way around this problem is to use shadow passwords. When used, shadow passwords store the encrypted passwords in another file — /etc/shadow — that only the system can read. Therefore, a burglar must gain root access to your machine to access the shadow password file, which would be a superfluous act at that point. Shadow passwords add another layer of security.

The Red Hat installation system uses shadow passwords by default. However, if you choose not to use the default, then you can convert to shadow passwords as follows:

1. Log on as root.

2. Enter the following command to change to the /etc directory

   cd /etc

3. Enter the following command to convert your /etc/passwd file to use shadow passwords

   pwconv5

4. The encrypted passwords are now contained in the /etc/shadow file. The original /etc/passwd file is renamed to /etc/passwd- and also contains the encrypted passwords. These files are only accessible by root and thus nobody else can attempt to crack your passwords.

The pam_pwdb.so module will automatically detect that you are using shadow passwords and will make all necessary changes to your system to use shadow passwords.

Choosing a firewall

The job of a firewall is to filter communications from the Internet into and out of your internal network. Firewalls are divided into two main types: filtering and proxying. This book concentrates on filtering firewalls because they are simple to construct and provide good protection for simple networks. The firewall used in this book is described in Chapter 11.

Internal network security

Unless you are the only user of your system, you need to consider internal security. People who work together expect their colleagues to respect their privacy, but sometimes that doesn't happen and extra measures are needed. For instance, locking a file cabinet with sensitive financial information is considered standard and acceptable policy. Although I discuss passwords in terms of external security, they also are a form of internal security. Passwords offer a form of internal security by protecting valid users from each other as well as nonusers. No one feels slighted by such measures because they are expected.

Using Subnetworks

Briefly, subnetworks (subnets) divide IP network address spaces into smaller groups. The smaller groups can only communicate directly with other group members. Otherwise, for one subnet to communicate with another, it must be explicitly routed.

This is accomplished via the subnet mask that you may recall configuring at the end of Chapter 1. The 32-bit IP address is split into a network address and the host address. The class C address uses the first 24-bits for the network address and the last 8 for the host address. Recall that you have used the public class C addresses 192.168.1.1-3 throughout this book. The network address is 192.168.1 and the host address has been 1, 2, and 3 (out of a total possibility of 254).

The subnet mask for a class C address is 255.255.255.0. When packets from a particular host first arrive at your network interface, their IP address is masked by the subnet mask and compared with your own network address. (The masking process is carried out by the mathematical AND process, which means that if one bit is 1 and the other bit is also a 1, the result is a 1. Otherwise, for a 1 and a 0, a 0 and a 1, or a 0 and a 0, the result is 0. You may want to think of a 1 as true and a 0 as false.) So if you have an IP address of 192.168.1.3, your network address is 192.168.1. Combine the network address with the subnet mask of 255.255.255.0 and the resulting masked network address is still 192.168.1 and any packets with a network address of 192.168.1 are accepted.

However, if you divide your LAN into two subnets, your subnet mask becomes 255.255.255.128. Only IP packets with addresses of 192.168.1.129-254 will be accepted.

To provide further internal security, you may want to divide your network into subnetworks and set different file protections on different user groups to prevent casual snooping.

If you split your LAN into two or more subnets, you keep the subnets from interacting directly with each other. You may put the accounting people on one subnet and the development people on another. Each subnet can be on the same physical network or on separate ones. The idea is to place client computers along strategic divisions of your network in order to enhance security.

TIP Splitting your network into subnetworks can also improve performance. The network packets of one subnetwork stay on that subnetwork unless they are routed to another subnetwork. In other words, packets stay within their own segment and don't clog up other segments unnecessarily.

You can also accomplish separating client computers along natural divisions by making use of Linux groups and file permissions. The division will not be as clear-cut as with subnets because the client computers will be able to communicate, but the idea is the same.

Red Hat Linux creates individual groups for each user. But by editing the /etc/group file as root, you can create any groups you want. Individual users are provided access to a group by adding their name after the group.

```
root::0:root
bin::1:root,bin,daemon
daemon::2:root,bin,daemon
sys::3:root,bin,adm
adm::4:root,adm,daemon
tty::5:
disk::6:root
lp::7:daemon,lp
mem::8:
kmem::9:
wheel::10:root
mail::12:mail
news::13:news
uucp::14:uucp
man::15:
games::20:
gopher::30:
dip::40:
ftp::50:
nobody::99:
users::100:
floppy:x:19:
console:x:101:
gdm:x:42:
utmp:x:102:
pppusers:x:230:
popusers:x:231:
slipusers:x:232:
slocate:x:21:
xfs:x:233:
lidia:x:500:
```

To add a group for the accounting department, edit the /etc/group file. Enter the following line to give the accounting group the arbitrary group number 200:

```
account::200:lidia
```

You now have a group called accounting and only lidia has access. To add users to a group, append each user name separated by a comma. A program called useradd automatically performs this operation. The Control Panel also provides a User and Group Configuration GUI.

You can instruct Samba to limit access to shares by including the group parameter in the share. Recall from Chapter 6 that writing to a share could be limited with the write list parameter. You can go further and limit all access to users in a group by devising a share as shown below.

```
; A publicly accessible directory, but read only, except for people in
; the staff group
[public]
    comment = Public Stuff
    path = /home/samba
    public = yes
    writable = yes
    printable = no
    force group = accounting
;   write list = @staff
```

The force group parameter forces all new or renamed files to that group – as determined by the Linux user and group information. It's that simple.

There are many tools that you can use to enhance your internal security. For instance, tripwire is a system that informs you when files have changed. Files that change unexpectedly can spell trouble. Chapter 12 describes how to use tripwire.

External security

The best general advice that I can give here is to keep your doors locked and be careful about discussing details of your network to people outside your organization. Don't be paranoid – *if I tell you about our firewall, I'll have to kill you* – but keep in mind that the more someone knows about the construction of your network and security, the more he or she can use that information against you. If someone is out to compromise your security, and you have done a good technical job of security, then the obvious way to attack is to look for ways around your system.

One job that I worked on involved work on a sensitive environmental waste site. It was informal company policy not to casually discuss our work with people unfamiliar with it. There were no explicit restrictions, but we reasonably believed that there were people who would "monkey wrench" us if they could. We simply did not want to make targets of ourselves and thus did not advertise what we were doing. I certainly did not want to make more work for myself by giving anyone a hook into our system.

Layering security

After you put all the separate items together to form your security system, you should view them as a whole as well as separately. You should not depend on your firewall alone, just as you should not depend on your passwords alone. One system depends on the other and vice versa.

To this end, some useful utilities can assist you in looking for security loopholes in one system or another:

◆ The nmap port scanning and operating system. Use this system to probe your own network in order to check it for weaknesses.

◆ The password-discovering tool crack. Use this system to discover weak or non-existent passwords.

◆ Tripwire. This suite of programs monitors your computer network and computers for possible intrusions by checking such things as file size and date against known good values.

These systems are described in Chapter 12.

Maintaining Your System

The more you plan ahead and maintain your system, the fewer problems you'll have in the long term. Maintenance requires you to look at both hardware and software. It requires you to know what is on your system and where it is located. This may sound trivial, but over time a computer network is like any living thing and changes in both subtle and not-so-subtle ways. Especially as a network grows, it is very easy to forget where software applications and equipment are located. You can also easily forget when it is time to do such tasks as cleaning tape drives.

The solution is to divide your system into functional areas such as hardware and software. Within these divisions you can keep lists and logs that will help you keep your computer network running smoothly and reliably. The following list shows how I like to divide a system:

◆ **Vigilance.** You must perform boring tasks reliably and consistently.

◆ **Network.** You should view your network separately from the individual machines. Computers and devices will be added to and deleted from your network and you need to know what and where they are.

◆ **User accounts.** Users will be added to and deleted from both your server(s) and the client machines. You need to know who is on your system.

◆ **Hardware.** Computers and other devices will be added to and deleted from your system. Sub-components will be added to and deleted from individual computers and devices. You must know what you have and where everything is.

◆ **Software.** System and application software will be added to and deleted from your system. You need to know what you have and where it is located. This is especially important for keeping track of software licenses because the lack of a license can have severe legal ramifications.

Part of your job, as an administrator, is to do boring jobs consistently and reliably. This means checking such things as the log of Super User (root) logins — users changing into root — and your firewall logs on a daily basis, including weekends. Backups also come under this heading.

It's hard to do something a million times when nothing ever happens. But something may happen on the one-million-and-first time, and you want to know when it does.

The best advice I can give is to just do it. It becomes habit after a time and is worth it in the long run. Plus, when something does happen, it can become very interesting and challenging.

It also helps to have a small notebook with lists of tasks and logs of those tasks. Lists of daily, weekly, and monthly tasks should be included.

The following list offers examples of tasks that recur on a daily basis, showing the time, the job, and a description of each task:

◆ 08:00. tail -100 /usr/adm/sulog. Check root logins for possible security violations.

◆ 08:00. tail -100 /usr/adm/syslog |more. Check system log for problems.

◆ 08:00. tail -100 /usr/adm/messages |more. Check system messages for problems.

◆ 08:00. mail root. Check root's mail for tripwire (file integrity) early morning check.

◆ 04:00. mail root. Check root's mail for general messages.

It is impossible to account for every task, or even most of the tasks that occur daily, but the idea is to account for as many as you can.

The following list shows sample tasks that may occur on a weekly basis:

◆ Monday: mail root. Check root mail for status of full system backup (Monday, 4 am).

◆ Monday: tripwire check. Check Tripwire's database against original stored on floppy.

◆ Monday: offsite backup. Take last week's system backups to another location for safety.

◆ Tuesday: job 1. Do company's job number 1 (that is, pull point-of-sales data from remote stores).

◆ Wednesday: tripwire check. Check Tripwire's database against original stored on floppy.

◆ Friday: tripwire check. Check Tripwire's database against original stored on floppy.

Notice how tasks are listed in a more general fashion – no explicit command to run. This is because not every recurrent job is exactly defined; many are amorphous in nature.

Finally, the following list shows examples of jobs that occur on a monthly basis:

◆ 1st of the month: tripwire. Manually check Tripwire database against read-only, offsite copy.

◆ 1st of the month: offsite backups. Take older tapes to offsite storage location and return current offsite backups for recycling.

◆ 15th of the month: offsite backups. Take older tapes to offsite storage location and return current offsite backups for recycling.

If you keep accurate logs of all such tasks, you will have little doubt about whether you're doing your job right.

Maintaining Your Network

Maintaining the network is another amorphous job. You need to know both the physical and logical configuration of the network topology. You need to fix and replace broken cables, network adapters, and computers. Maintaining the network also involves adding and deleting computers and other devices – such as network printers – from the network.

It is a good idea, if not essential, to keep both a tabular list and a representative graphical diagram of your network. If you have that information, you do not have to guess at what devices are where in the network. A simple diagram showing the layout of the network can also be helpful both in understanding how your system is constructed and the tabular list provides a good equipment and user reference.

A list of network devices is also useful. If your network has more than two or three devices, such an inventory system will help you in the long run. Table 9-1 shows the layout for a simple inventory system. I recommend that you keep the number of fields to a minimum so that each device needs only one line. You can use the computer name or IP address to peg each device to a more complete inventory.

TABLE 9-1 THE NETWORK INVENTORY

Number	Computer Name	IP Address	Description
1	chivas	192.168.1.254	Linux file, print, (nfs, nis, etc) server
2	atlas	192.168.1.250	Linux Internet gateway
3	toluca	192.168.1.1	Windows workstation
4	veracruz	192.168.1.2	Windows workstation
5	puma	192.168.1.100	Linux workstation
6	cementeros	192.168.1.101	Linux workstation
7	tigres	192.168.1.240	printer

The idea is to have a complete overview of your network. As time passes and your system changes, the network inventory will help you remember how your system is constructed. Having that information will save you time in the long run.

Maintaining user accounts

The mechanics of maintaining user accounts are straightforward, especially if you use the `useradd` script or the `Control Panel` GUI, which I describe in previous chapters. However, other concerns exist that you should carefully consider.

First, if you have more than a few users, you need a system for keeping track of them. My personal preference is a simple paper and spreadsheet system. You give a new user, or one asking for modification, a simple application form such as the example in Figure 9-2. You then enter that information in a spreadsheet or a database. This simple system should keep confusion to a minimum while not presenting any big hurdles to obtaining an account. You may even add a disclaimer or policy statement on the application.

Dog House Computers, Inc.
34 Barkers Lane,
Albuquerque, NM 87110

Last name _____ First name _____ M.I. _____
Location _____
City _____ State _____ Zip _____
Office phone ___-___x_____ Pager (optional) ___-___-_____ Home phone ___-___-___

Policy: By signing this form, you agree to adhere to the corporation's computer usage policy on the opposite side of this application form.
Signature _____ Date _____

Figure 9–2: A sample user account application form

The computer usage policy statement should be a legal document and clearly describe your company's expectations and requirements. I am no fan of paperwork, but this is one place where it is appropriate and useful. Knowing what is expected of you up front is very important and where the line(s) are drawn is even more important.

Maintaining hardware

The process of maintaining hardware spans new systems and old. For new systems, you can go in two general directions: purchasing turnkey, retail systems or creating your own by purchasing a component system. With the former approach, you simply purchase the computer from a mail-order or local company (generally at retail prices). With the latter approach, you purchase one or more components – case, power-supplies, system boards, disks, and so on – and slap them together yourself. Unless you need more than a dozen or so all at once, this method gives you more control over your destiny, at a lower price than purchasing a turnkey system. The added benefit is the familiarity you obtain, which helps with your troubleshooting skills down the line. I prefer this method.

Modifying existing systems is an ongoing job, too. Disks need to be replaced or upgraded, memory added, power supplies replaced, and so on. Get used to it.

Your choice of peripherals is important, too. Spending money up front on a network laser printer instead of a less expensive desktop one will ultimately save you money both in terms of maintenance as well as productivity if you have more than a handful of users.

Finally, you should keep track of all your equipment. It is one of those boring, thankless jobs that only pays off occasionally. But knowing what you have is important. If you can consult a simple paper folder or a spreadsheet or a simple database to see what equipment user XYZ has, then your day-to-day management will be easier. For instance, if you want to install Linux on a client computer and also know what kind of video and Ethernet adapters it has, you look like you know what you're doing when you immediately install the system. The value of such a database really is apparent when you need to troubleshoot a problem. The information is helpful especially if the problem system is remote.

Figure 9-3 shows a sample form that you can use for both your paper file as well as a spreadsheet. I maintain both types. As much as I like and use computers, I still like being able to open a file cabinet and put my hands on a piece of paper. (Especially if my computer is giving me problems and I need to find out what hardware it contains!) The spreadsheet or database, however, has the advantage of taking up less physical space – important for large systems with many users – and being able to summarize data for you. Obviously, you will want to customize your own. The point is to maintain a systematic inventory.

Computer name _____ Domain name _____ IP address ____-____-____-____
Location _____ User phone # _____
Manufacturer _____ Brand name _____ Type _____
Video adapter _____ Monitor _____
Network adaptor _____
CD-ROM drive _____
Hard disk make/model _____ Capacity _____
Floppy _____
Memory _____
Notes _____

Figure 9-3: A sample hardware equipment inventory form

Maintaining system and application software

Software installation and maintenance is generally more difficult than maintaining hardware. Almost no limit exists to the amount of software you can have on a computer. Installing software can be a challenge at best. The Microsoft world is getting a little better with system registries and such, but the onus is still on you to figure things out when problems occur. With the RPM system, the Linux world is definitely getting better.

Keeping track of software is a more involved job than keeping track of hardware. You can only have a few adapter cards in a computer, but the only real limit on software is determined by the available disk space. You can have almost limitless software installed. This presents both maintenance and legal problems.

Maintenance is difficult for several reasons. First, everyone has individual preferences, which could involve lots of different packages and variations. You also face the problem of software creep, in which some workstations get updated and others do not. The result is a plethora of different versions of the same package. Last, you must face the problem of obtaining proper licenses. The advent of CD-ROM distribution makes it easy to make illegal copies of software and it is your job to prevent such acts.

You need to create and maintain a software inventory. Doing so requires lots of work but ultimately minimizes your trouble. I suggest that you maintain both a paper and an electronic inventory. Figure 9-4 shows a sample organizer at the computer workstation level to give an overview of all the packages on one machine.

Computer name _____ Domain name _____ IP address ____-____-____-____
Location _____ User phone # ____-____-____ ext _____
Primary OS _____ License # _____ Date installed ___-___-____
Secondary OS _____ License # _____ Date installed ___-___-____
Software package _____ License # _____ Date installed ___-___-____
Software package _____ License # _____ Date installed ___-___-____
Software package _____ License # _____ Date installed ___-___-____
Software package _____ License # _____ Date installed ___-___-____
Software package _____ License # _____ Date installed ___-___-____
Software package _____ License # _____ Date installed ___-___-____
Software package _____ License # _____ Date installed ___-___-____
Software package _____ License # _____ Date installed ___-___-____

Figure 9-4: A sample computer software inventory form

You can't keep all the important information on each individual package on one form, so use the sample form shown in Figure 9-5 for each package.

Computer name _____ Domain name _____ IP address ____-____-____-____
Location _____ User name _____
_____ Phone # ___-___-____
_____
Primary OS _____ License # _____ Date installed ___-___-____
Secondary OS _____ License # _____ Date installed ___-___-____
Software package _____
License # _____ Date Registered _____
Manufacturer _____
Address _____
Phone ___-___-____ ext _____ Contact _____
Notes _____
_____
_____

Figure 9-5: A sample individual software package inventory form

You should keep one folder per computer with one of the general inventory forms and as many of the individual forms as necessary. I also recommend that you make a copy of the registration form, note the date you submitted the form, and keep the copy in this folder. (Yes, I really do send in the registration form.)

People will believe that you are organized when they come to you for information and you whip out the appropriate folder. It really does help to minimize confusion, too.

Ensuring reliability

All the preceding topics are really aimed at making your system reliable. The dream of any administrator is a completely reliable system. Of course we'd all like to win the lottery and be skinny. The reality of life has never prevented me from dreaming the impossible dream. However, you can do some things to make the world safer for your system.

The first thing you can do is to think in terms of reliability. The attitude you take has a lot to do with how things work. If you have the luxury of designing your system from the ground up, you can do many things to fold reliability into its core. If you inherit a system, you can still do many things – from your system management policies to the replacement components you purchase. By thinking in terms of reliability, you are more likely to make big and small choices that point in that direction.

Your policy decisions can have a significant effect on reliability. If you give users too much privilege, they can – and will – delete files that they should not. If you do not schedule regular maintenance downtime, your system will gradually degrade and eventually fail altogether. If you do not protect your network with a firewall, your system will fail when a malicious person breaks in to it and wrecks havoc. These are somewhat extreme examples, but they illustrate the fundamental role that your policy decisions play in terms of reliability.

Whether you design your own system or simply maintain an older one, your component selection plays an important role in the system's overall reliability. For example, purchasing computer power supplies with ball-bearing-based fans, for a few dollars more, can have a significant long-term impact on your system up-time. If you have 100 workstations, and two power supplies per year fail, you may have two users down for a half day each while you identify and fix the problem. Add to that the extra trouble if remote troubleshooting and travel are involved. By spending a few dollars more initially, you very likely will get zero to one failure per year, and end up saving as much as a full user-day of work and frustration.

Following that line of reasoning, think about the cost of network wiring connectors. The individual component cost is a few cents for BNC (10base2) connectors. But if one fails, the whole network goes down. The costs can be huge even for small operations. The cost to you as an administrator is large: your time taken away from the fun tasks and your reputation, for instance. If you are a part-time administrator, your problems are only amplified, as any problems will probably take you away from your real job.

RAID SYSTEMS

Linux supports Redundant Arrays of Inexpensive Disks (RAID). RAID provides a mechanism for increasing disk storage reliability and performance.

Of the six standard RAID levels, only four are commonly used today:

♦ Level 0 – Disk striping only. This increases I/O bandwidth and storage capacity.

♦ Level 1 – Disk mirroring only. The same data exists on two or more disks. Disk failures do not result in lost data.

♦ Level 2 – Rarely used in practice.

♦ Level 3 – Disk striping with parity. Data is split across multiple disks on a byte-to-byte basis. An additional, dedicated disk is used to store parity information, which enables all data to be reconstructed if a disk fails.

♦ Level 4 – Rarely in practice.

♦ Level 5 – The same as level 3 but the parity information is split across multiple disks. This is done to increase I/O performance by splitting the parity information storage across multiple controllers.

It is beyond the scope of this book to describe how to use RAID. Please consult the `/usr/doc/HOWTO/Root-RAID-HOWTO` document for more information.

UPS SYSTEMS

One of the simplest things you can do to increase reliability is to use an uninterruptible power supply (UPS) for your server(s). They vary in price from approximately US $100 to many thousands of dollars for commercial systems. They provide your computers and other equipment with several minutes to more than an hour of power after a blackout. The advantage is that at least part of your operation can continue at all times.

A UPS offers other advantages, too. For example, it acts as a great filter. Your equipment is isolated from not only blackouts, but also brownouts (reduction of voltage) and lightning strikes. If you live in a place with marginal or "dirty" power, a UPS will smooth it out for you. In the long run, it can save you money on component replacements because of the isolation from the vagaries of your electrical supply, which may otherwise find their way into your PC bus.

KEEPING SPARE DISKS

In my last job, our Sun server failed one Saturday afternoon. I had been planning on shifting from the old Sun server to a Pentium PC running Linux for some time. However, at the time the Sun failed, its capacity had exceeded that of the PC's disk. I had held off asking my boss for more money for my experiment when I thought the Sun still had more life in it. So when it did fail, I did not have the spare disk ready at the time and had to run out to the nearest chain electronics store and purchase a new IDE disk. It actually only took me an hour and a half to go to the store, find and purchase the disk, and get back to the office. Then it took another two hours to install Slackware Linux and set up the Samba file server and copy over the old file systems (the Sun did not completely fail but instead would run for between one and several hours before rebooting itself). I was lucky that no one was busy on a project at that time, so the pain was minimal and not having a ready disk turned out to be okay. But I could have saved myself the worry of having a downed system during that interval if I had a spare disk. (Over the next couple of days, I purchased an SCSI controller for the PC and got the old Sun SCSI disk running on it.)

So you can see that if you can afford it, you should keep one or more disks on your premises. The number of disks, of course, depends on your situation. If you are a large operation, you need more disks. Even the smallest operation, however, benefits from keeping one handy. The idea is to be able to replace a disk when it fails in the minimum amount of time. It is more important to have a spare disk if you have an SCSI system than if you have an IDE. This is simply because they are less immediately available — you cannot simply go to any store and purchase one.

KEEPING SPARE SERVERS

The need for a ready server is more problematic than the need for a ready disk. The ease of Linux installation makes it quick and simple to reconfigure the operating system. It is also quite easy to replace any PC subsystem. If your PC-based server stops functioning, in all likelihood, you need only replace a power supply, a controller or even the system board. Because none of the hardware components except the system disk affect the server's function, the problem is a matter of identifying the malfunctioning component and then finding a replacement.

This solution breaks down if you can't find the culprit or if you are using proprietary hardware. The reason I replaced the Sun with the PC (in the example I describe in the preceding section) was that it was proprietary and expensive to maintain. I knew how to work with each component on a PC but only a few on a Sun. I did not need a maintenance contract for a PC but I did for a Sun. With the advent of Linux and Samba (or NFS under Linux), I was sure I could duplicate the function of the Sun server.

Some operations could benefit from keeping a spare server. If your server is based on a proprietary system or if you cannot afford any downtime, you should carefully consider this option. The spare can be in the form of a computer normally used for another function that will substitute for your primary server when necessary or a computer that is specifically set aside for that purpose.

You need to know how to substitute your ready server. Without going into the details, you need a plan for implementing your spare. The main problem is how to synchronize your file system. In some cases you should be able to place your old disk in the ready server. If that is not possible, you either have to use your backups or transfer the file system directly — that is, over the network with `tar`, `cpio`, or another program. The idea is to make the change to the new system as transparent to the user as possible.

After you decide how to make the switch, it is best to practice for it. The amount of practice you need depends on the complexity of your entire network. When I practiced to switch the PC for the Sun, I started by constructing an experimental file system that mimicked the Sun's file system. Later, I switched a couple of our non-critical word processing directories from the Sun to the Linux PC and found that it did not create any problems when used by their owners. I left the file services split between the Sun and the PC until the Sun failed , whereupon I switched over to the PC with little trouble. (I had not used the network printer via Samba, so that actually caused me some worry, but it worked with fewer problems than the Sun had in the end. I should have tested it first, of course.)

Using cron

cron is a system for scheduling and executing systematic Linux system and user tasks. When you start your system, the crond daemon is started and reads the system and user configuration files in the /etc/crontab and /var/spool/cron directories. The /etc/crontab configuration file contains the system cron jobs reconfigured by Red Hat and can only be edited by a privileged user (generally root). The user crontabs are limited to things the users can normally do — for instance, a normal user cannot schedule cron to erase another user's files.

This system is useful for doing system maintenance as well as anything that you want to have done regularly. For instance, Red Hat configures the default crontab to rotate the log files found in the /var/log directory on a daily basis.

```
SHELL=/bin/bash
PATH=/sbin:/bin:/usr/sbin:/usr/bin
MAILTO=root

# run-parts
01 * * * * root run-parts /etc/cron.hourly
02 1 * * * root run-parts /etc/cron.daily
02 2 * * 0 root run-parts /etc/cron.weekly
02 3 1 * * root run-parts /etc/cron.monthly
```

To create, edit, list, or remove a user crontab, you simply run the crontab command with the appropriate option. Whoever you are logged in as determines what user crontab is accessed. A privileged user (generally root) can use the -u option to edit other users' crontabs. Table 9-2 lists the user crontab editing options.

TABLE 9-2 THE USER CRONTAB EDITING OPTIONS

Option	Description
crontab –e	Edits your crontab (uses your default editor)
crontab –l	Lists your crontab entries
crontab –r	Removes (deletes) your crontab
crontab - u username	Edits, lists, or removes another user's crontab

The crontab utility uses the vi editor (you can specify another editor by setting the VISUAL or EDITOR environmental variables) to edit the crontab file (see the instructions in Chapter 1 for the basic vi commands). For example, to edit your crontab — the first time you do so you create it — enter the following command:

```
/usr/bin/crontab -e
```

 You are put into command mode immediately upon execution of this command, and you must enter the i, a, or o command to start editing. After you finish editing, you need to press the Escape key and enter the character sequence :wq to save and then quit from the editor.

To send yourself the message "Hello from Cron" simply add the following line:

```
* * * * *    echo "Hello from Cron"
```

The message will be mailed to you every minute. To examine the crontab file, enter the command crontab -l and you'll see the listing of your crontab as shown in Listing 10-5.

```
# DO NOT EDIT THIS FILE - edit the master and reinstall.
# (/tmp/crontab.1018 installed on Sat Jul 19 14:36:03 1997)


# (Cron version -- $Id: crontab.c,v 2.13 1994/01/17 03:20:37 vixie Exp $)
* * * * *        echo "Hello from Cron"
```

I doubt that you'll want to have such a trivial message mailed to you every minute. To delete that example cron entry, enter the following command:

```
crontab -r
```

The formats of the /etc/crontab and the user crontabs differ somewhat. The two formats use the same time format as well as the file or program to execute. However, the /etc/crontab file includes the user name (as found in /etc/passwd) and first describes the time and day to run the job, then the user name to execute as, and finally the file name, including the directory, to execute. Table 9-3 shows the details of each field.

TABLE 9-3 THE CRONTAB FORMAT FIELDS

Field Number	Function	Range	Notes
1	minute	0–59	The asterisk (*) means every minute, hour, day, and so on
2	Hour	0–23	
3	day of –month	0–31	
4	Month	0–12	Or names such as jan
5	day of –week	0–7	0 or 7 is Sun, or use names
6	user name and then command or file to execute		Only for the /etc/crontab file
7	command or file to execute		

The tasks that can be accomplished via cron extend far beyond simply cleaning up your /tmp directory. Any job that you want to be run regularly without having to manually run yourself you can have cron run for you. For instance, if you want to have some or all of your backups run at a time of day when the system is not being used or is used only lightly, execute the backup via cron. For example, if you have a 4mm DAT drive attached to an SCSI interface at /dev/rmt0 and you want to run a full backup of your system at 4:00 a.m. every Monday (Sunday = 0, Monday =1, and so on), log in as root and add the following crontab job (crontab -e):

```
0 4 * * 1 /bin/tar czvf /dev/rmt0 /
```

At 4:00 a.m. on Monday, tar will copy all files from the root (/) directory to the device attached to /dev/rmt0. It will compress each file using gzip and produce a listing as it works. The listing will be mailed to root, giving you the opportunity to examine the backup on Monday morning. Of course, you could use cpio or dump to do the same job.

USING SHELL SCRIPTS

Shell scripts are generally simple text files that contain shell commands, variables, and conditional statements. They provide programming capability to the system without the complexity of compilers. However, even while lacking the sophistication of programming languages such as C, they are powerful enough to do much, if not most, of your systematic, day-to-day chores.

One of the most common uses of shell scripts is to have `cron` run them. If you have a job that requires more than a one-line command but is not complex enough to require subroutines, a shell script is the way to go. For instance, if you need to compress and then transfer files from one machine to another, it is better to create a script than to force a single command to do too much.

I summarize some of the more important bash functions and conditional statements in Chapter 1. In Chapter 11, I describe the script that comes configured with tripwire to check your file system integrity on a nightly basis — `cron` is used to start it every morning. It is a simple script but descriptive of the type of job that can be readily automated with a little knowledge of shell scripting.

SHUTTING DOWN AND STARTING LINUX

Linux keeps a dynamic file system. If you turn off the power without having it shut down gracefully, then parts of the file system will need to be reconfigured when you start it up again. Generally, this simply increases the time it takes to boot, but why risk possible problems? The file system is also buffered — that is, data to be written to disk are first stored in memory before actually being written to the disk. You may lose those data if you simply power the computer off.

The preferred method for shutting down a Linux system is to use either the `halt/reboot` or `shutdown` commands. The `/sbin/shutdown` command performs a systematic termination of user and system processes, writes the buffers to disk (syncs), and informs the `/sbin/init` process to put the system into runlevel 0, 1, or 6. Runlevel 0 is a complete halt; runlevel 1 is a single user administrative state; and 6 reboots the system. Logged-on users are given a specified amount of time to log off (default of 1 minute). Here's the syntax for the `/sbin/shutdown` command:

```
shutdown [-t sec] [-rkhncf] time [warning-message]
```

Table 9-4 shows the options to the shutdown command. Note that you can also reboot your Linux computer by entering the reboot command as root or simply pressing the `Ctrl+Alt+Del` key sequence long familiar to DOS users.

TABLE 9-4 THE /SBIN/SHUTDOWN COMMAND OPTIONS

Option	Description
-t S	Wait S seconds before changing the run level.
-k	Execute the other shutdown options without actually shutting down the system.
-r	Reboot the system after shutting down.
-h	Halt the system after shutting down.

Continued

TABLE 9-4 THE /SBIN/SHUTDOWN COMMAND OPTIONS *(Continued)*

Option	Description
-n	Do the shutdown yourself (don't use init). Use of this option is discouraged because it can have unpredictable results.
-f	Do a fast reboot. The normal startup process skips such time-consuming tasks as disk checks (fsck).
-c	Cancel a shutdown already in progress.

Minimizing wear and tear

You can do a couple of things to reduce the wear and tear on your system. The following information is based on common sense:

♦ Keep your systems powered on. The thermal expansion and contraction of turning your systems off at night wears them out faster than leaving them on. Also, most nonportable hard disks have heads that "land" on the disk platter. This is worse than the wear and tear on the bearings.

♦ Minimize shaking and bumping. The most delicate system is your hard disk. It spins at several thousand rpm with a delicate head floating on a cushion of air. If it is bumped too hard, it can physically impact the disk platter and fail. Even if it is not bumped hard enough for immediate failure, the ill effects simply add up over time.

Disaster Recovery

Disaster comes in many forms – for example, a fire, an earthquake, or a flood. But anything that catastrophically destroys or renders your operation unusable is a disaster. It is essential that you make recovery plans commensurate with the value and the importance of your operation.

Your plan can be as complex and expensive as contracting with a company that specializes in such things. You can pay someone to maintain a computer or computers compatible with your own system. They should be in another geographical location, to remove the possibility of a local event rendering them inoperable. However, you should consider the likely travel time and means of travel, too. If you choose a location on the other side of the continent, you eliminate the possibility of a common natural disaster but you may not be able to get there in a reasonable amount of time. However, if they are too close, a common event may affect everybody. A location reached by an airline shuttle may be a good benchmark. A few tens to a thousand miles (one Albuquerque company that I worked for had a disaster site near Seattle) appears to be reasonable to me.

On the other end of the spectrum – a small business or home office – you probably do not need a formal contract. You should have a simple plan of action, however. First, the offsite backups are obviously essential. If your shop burns down, you are going to live off your backups. Having stored them in another location, your plan will go something like this:

1. Assess your physical damage.

2. Restore the minimal network necessary to run your operation.

   - Use computers and equipment that were not damaged significantly.

   - Borrow or purchase the additional equipment necessary.

   - Set up your network in the most convenient location.

   - Restore your file systems.

   - Restore your Internet connections.

3. Systematically restore customer or your own services as quickly as safety allows.

Obviously, the specifics of your situation will determine the details of these steps, but the process of acting instead of reacting is the essential factor. Even if you end up doing everything completely different from how you planned to, the fact that you planned at all will probably save you.

I should state that training is also essential. In my present job, we do at least two practice recoveries a year, including the travel and complete restorations of our essential services. However, I realize that may not be possible for you. In that case, I recommend that you do as many of the subsets of disaster recovery as possible. Even "paper runs" are helpful – go through the plan by talking it through with your peers and management. Any practice is better than no practice.

TIP A small operation that handles life-and-death matters or has people depend on it for their livelihood is another matter. If you run an organ donor database or an ambulance service, for instance, then you need a formal contract as well as a plan even though you may have only one or two computers.

Summary

In this chapter, I describe the basic elements of systems administration. Systems administration is a large topic that would take an entire book to cover in any detail. As a result, I can only cover the essential aspects in this chapter. It is to your advantage, though, to investigate the subject in more detail.

This chapter covers the following topics:

♦ Setting policy. This is the road map that is essential to navigate in your system. If you have the luxury of setting it, you are a step ahead. If the policy is set for you, your interpretation still gives you considerable power.

♦ Reliably making backups. Backups are used for recovering misplaced or accidentally deleted files as well as for recovering from disaster. You should devise a system that accounts for both possibilities. To that end, you need to decide on what method to use to make backups and how often to make them. This generally depends on the size of your operation. I divide backups into three camps: small, medium, and large. Each has its own requirements and limitations:

  ■ Small backups can be performed using media as ubiquitous as floppy disks. You can also make use of the Internet as a storage system. Your records can be minimal.

  ■ Medium-sized backups generally require specialized media such as 4mm DAT tapes. They also require that you use formal, regimented scheduling and record keeping.

  ■ Large backups are a world apart from smaller ones. If you are backing up more than a gigabyte a day then highly specialized media such as jukeboxes are often required.

♦ Ensuring security. This responsibility is next in importance to your backups. It is a very large field and no one book, much less a single chapter, can cover it in detail. You can do several specific things from the start, however, that will greatly improve your network's security. If you learn the basics, you can learn about security as an ongoing process. Those basic tasks are outlined.

♦ Administering users. You are generally responsible for adding, deleting, and modifying user accounts.

♦ Administering file systems. Adding, deleting, and modifying them is an everyday job.

♦ Administering software. This is generally one of the more difficult administrative tasks. So many combinations of operating system and application programs are possible that installing, maintaining, and upgrading software is an art in itself. This is one of those areas where you have to experiment.

◆ Maintenance. This is a constant and ongoing job. The more you can anticipate hardware and software problems, the less trouble you have. I outline some areas that you look at in order to do just that:

   ■ Keeping some spare equipment in a ready state can minimize downtime due to equipment failure.

   ■ RAID systems enable you to build redundancy into your disk drives. Linux supports RAID.

◆ Troubleshooting. This is another constant of the systems administrator's job. This is an art and must be learned well. Experience and logical thought are the keys.

The systems administrator must learn to wear many hats. I have done everything from answering phones to squeezing through crawl spaces in my work. I do, however, draw the line at woodwork (one of the people I worked with wanted me to fix his chair once).

Chapter 10

Automating Network Backups

IN THIS CHAPTER

◆ Introducing the advantages of automated, network-based backups

◆ Introducing the Arkeia backup software

◆ Installing the Arkeia software

◆ Configuring Arkeia backups

◆ Monitoring your backups

◆ Troubleshooting backup problems

THE PROCESS OF MAKING local backups is introduced in Chapter 6. Making local backups is a complex process because although the mechanics are important, the human factors are even more so. Managing the whole process at the minimum requires a large amount of your time as a reluctant system administrator.

Understanding Backups

The solution to your time management problem is an automated, network-based, client-server backup system. Until recently such software was either very expensive or unavailable on Linux. However, there are now numerous companies vying for your business. One such company, Knox Software, produces a network backup product called Arkeia. Their system works on platforms such as Linux and Windows and is included on the CD-ROM.

 Another backup system is called BRU2000. It's made by Enhanced Software Technologies and more information about it can be found at http://www. estinc.com. The taper program also provides another backup system, and comes as part of the Red Hat distribution.

Introducing Arkeia

Arkeia is based on the client-server model. The Arkeia server controls the backup media and the backup schedule. The media can be simple floppy disk(s), disk file(s), a single tape device or a tape library. The schedule can be daily, weekly or monthly; and a backup can be of the total file system(s) or only files that have changed since the last backup. A client is any machine that you want to have backed up and the server can be a client to itself.

 Tape libraries, also known as autoloaders or jukeboxes, combine one or more tape drives, multiple tape slots, and a robotic arm mechanism to transfer the tapes from the slots to a drive. The whole system is generally contained within a simple box with a door on the front. (The biggest libraries have a slot for inserting and removing individual tapes without opening the front door). Tape libraries are generally connected to their server but can also be connected by other methods.

The Arkeia backup server maintains indexes (databases) of what client backups have been done and where they exist. The indexes allow you to interactively browse the existing backups. Additionally, the indexes keep track of which tapes were used for each backup. This relieves you of the burden of keeping manual logs of the data located on each tape. You can use the browser to retrieve any backups via a GUI.

Both the backup server and client agents run daemons. The server daemons are responsible for starting the scheduled backups, telling the client daemons to start their backups, and maintaining the backup indices.

The server maintains a schedule of what to back up and when. When the server determines that a client has reached its scheduled backup time, the server daemon communicates with the client daemon to initiate the backup. The two sides manage the transfer of the data corresponding to the file systems being backed up across the network. The data is received by the server and written to the storage media.

Knox Software allows their software to be downloaded from their Web site to help you facilitate upgrades and patches and you can also download a time-limited demo or a home-use shareware version.

Knox Software Corp has provided a demo version of Arkeia (with a limited use license). They provide four RPM packages that run under Linux, including a client, server, a command line and X Window interface. They also provide a Windows client that is packaged in a Zip format. All of the Arkeia software is included on the supplemental CD-ROM in the /mnt/cdrom/Arkeia directory.

Knox Software maintains a web site, at www.knox-software.com, which provides general information about the company. More information on their Arkeia product can be found at www.arkeia.com.

To understand Arkeia you need to understand its underlying premise. The idea is to break down the backup process into component parts, which are then used as building blocks to "build" your backup. By decomposing the backup process into parts, Arkeia achieves system flexibility and scalability. The parts are called the Drive(s), drivepack, Tape Pools, Tapes, savepacks, and Libraries, respectively, and they are configured by the Server Administration GUI.

Server administration

The server administration screen is the central control system for Arkeia, and the place where all other components are reached. This screen, broken down into four major areas, includes system menus, server/job status, message area, and the icon bar. The system menu area allows you to access all features and function, while the icon bar provides shortcuts to the most frequently used functions. The server/job status area, (center of the screen), shows the backup server you are attached to, user id/user class, and the current date and time. It also shows the active backup or restoration jobs that are running. When nothing is running, it indicates that too. The message area shows general system status messages.

Drive management

The `Drive Management` component is used to logically define the read/write device(s) (typically the tape drive) to Arkeia. The `Drive Management` screen allows you to define one or more tape drives according to their specific characteristics, as well as providing the connection between Arkeia and the tape drive(s). By using logical drive definitions, Arkeia refers to the tape drive by its own internal logical name without needing to know how it is defined by the operating system. This allows you to change the drive definition, if required, without changing any other Arkeia settings.

Drivepack

The drivepack is used to group one or more tape drives into a single processing group, which allows Arkeia to determine how many drives to use during a backup. On a system with one tape drive, this isn't important since the drive can only be used for one task at a time. However, on a backup server with multiple tape drives, or with libraries that have multiple tape drives, this feature lets you easily perform independent operations (like simultaneous backups and restores) very easily. For example, on a backup server with a library that contains four tape drives, a drivepack can be defined with just two of the four drives, leaving the other two drives available for other backups. When the backups run, only the two drives in the drivepack will be used, which leaves the other two drives available for performing restore operations. Because of its multi-processing design, Arkeia can simultaneously backup data from one client while restoring data to a different client.

Savepack

savepack specifies which client machines, file system(s), or individual files are to be backed up.

When you configure a savepack, you might tell the Arkeia server that you want to back up XYZ files on client C. Savepack is meant to provide the necessary flexibility to back up a diverse network of computers, which allows you to back up several client-related computers as a single unit. Your grouping could be anything from all machines in the company to just those in a certain department or on a certain floor.

Pools Management

The Pools Management screen is used to define a general-purpose storage pool. A pool is a set of one or more tapes, and so, by using separate tape pools, you can control where your data is saved. For example, you might perform a total backup once a week and an incremental backup every other night during the week. By using different pools, you can assign different retention periods to the backup. This allows you to retain, and keep valid, your total backup for, say, 12 months, while letting the incremental backups expire after just one month. Tape pools can be used to separate data in whatever fashion makes sense for your company. A default "scratch" pool is provided and can be used to hold tapes in reserve in case you run out of logical definitions in your regular pools.

Dividing your tape volumes between pools can also separate the types of data by the person who generates the data. This generally makes sense for several reasons. One reason is that computers used for different tasks generally generate different amounts of data. For instance, if you use your Linux machine as a file server to your Windows machines, then your Linux server probably will need to store much more data than the client Windows machines. By creating different pools, you can assign more volumes to the server pools than your client pools. When you advance to the point of using tape libraries, this capability becomes advantageous. Because a library has a fixed number of slots, you can put more tape in the more heavily used pools than the lesser used ones. Thus, the tape library doesn't run out of tapes as frequently as if it had only one pool of tapes.

Tapes Management

The Tapes Management screen is where you create the logical definitions of the tapes that will be used during backup and restore operations. Again, Arkeia uses logical definitions of the tapes so that the backup and restore processes don't have to consider the underlying attributes of the media.

Libraries management

Libraries combine volumes into either actual tape libraries or virtual ones. A tape library is a device that, under control of the backup software, automatically mounts one tape from a selection of many tapes into a tape drive. A virtual library mimics the action of a tape library, but creates volumes on a disk drive instead of on tapes. Using virtual libraries is a good way to experiment and learn about making backups. Arkeia can select volumes from both real and virtual libraries.

Installing Arkeia on the Linux Server

The installation process is simplified by the use of the RPM format. You need at least 50MB of free space on the file system you install it on.

1. Log in as `root` on `chivas`.

2. Mount the IDG supplemental CD-ROM.

3. Run the following command

   ```
   rpm -ivh /mnt/cdrom/Arkeia/arkiea*
   ```

   Most of the files are stored into the `/usr/knox` directory. The Arkeia manuals are stored into the `/usr/doc/arekeia-server/html` directory and can be viewed with your browser.

 The FSSTND, as do I, suggests that all third party software be installed in the `/usr/local` directory. However, to keep it simple, I will use the default Arkeia installation directory of `/usr/knox`. If you want to follow the FSSTND guidelines, or if you don't have enough space in your root (/) partition, I suggest first creating the `/usr/local/knox` directory and then creating a soft link to `ln -s /usr/local/knox /usr/knox` and finally installing the RPM packages.

Configuring the Arkeia Server

When the savepacks, the drivepacks, and the Pools are combined by Arkeia, you are able to automatically back up a network of almost any size. The packs and pools can be used to build both interactive and scheduled backups. Once the component parts are built, the Arkeia takes care of the detailed administration and your function becomes the much more high-level one of monitoring the process. You need to make sure that previous night's backups ran successfully and, if not, then either run them again or troubleshoot the cause. You also need to maintain the system by supplying new and recycled tapes, but the worry of keeping track of the individual files on the individual tapes is removed.

Creating a null backup

The Arkeia configuration documentation recommends configuring a null device to begin with. This is a good idea because it eliminates the need to deal with actual devices and their messy details, thereby letting you focus on overall system installation and configuration. It's also an excellent way to learn the system. A null device in this case means the Linux device /dev/null. This is a standard mechanism that UNIX systems send output to when the output is not to be saved or otherwise acted upon. The binary stream copied to the /dev/null file is simply discarded.

 You can obtain help information at any time by clicking the information icon in the extreme upper left of the Arkeia GUI. It provides help related to the window that you are currently viewing.

1. Log in as root on chivas.

2. Run the following command to start the Arkeia GUI

   /usr/knox/bin/arkx

 When you install the arkeia-gui RPM it installs the shell script /usr/bin/ARKEIA. You can start the GUI by entering ARKEIA from the command line.

3. Next you'll see the introduction window as shown in Figure 10-1. Please note that in the Arkeia interface, the green checkmark button serves the same purpose as Windows' Ok button — it indicates that you want to accept what you've entered in the window and move on. The red X button is the same as a Windows Cancel button — it indicates that you want to close the window and discard your changes.

Figure 10-1: The Welcome to Arkeia window

4. The first time that you start the arkx GUI there is no Arkeia-based password for the root set yet. Leave the password field blank this time and click on the checkmark button. The next window is the Server administration window shown in Figure 10-2.

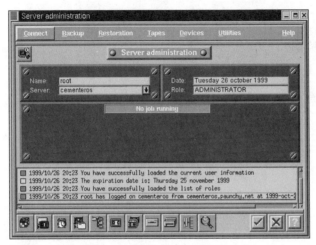

Figure 10-2: The Server administration window

5. Now is a good time to set a password for the Arkeia root user, which is different from the Linux root user. You should make the Arkeia root user's password different from the Linux root user's; this permits other users to manage the Arkeia system without knowing the Linux root password. Click on Utilities 'Users Management and you should see the user root displayed in the right half of the window. Click on it and control is passed to the Users management window. Click on the root user with the right mouse key and select the change password option (click with the left key on that item to select it). Leave the old password blank; enter the new password in the new password field, and enter the same password in the Confirm password field. Click on the checkmark and your password becomes active. Exit from the // window and control returns to the Server administration window.

6. Create a Null Drivepack. Back in the Server administration window click on the Devices 'Drives management. The Drives management window shown in Figure 10-3 is displayed.

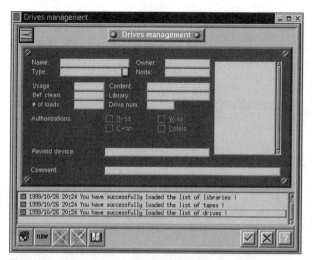

Figure 10-3: The Drives Management window

7. Click on the New button near the lower left hand of the window. A window similar to the Drives Management window is displayed. Fill in the entry field itemsuse the name **NullDrive** for the drive name, NULL for the drive type, and **/dev/null** for the rewind device, as shown in Figure 10-4.

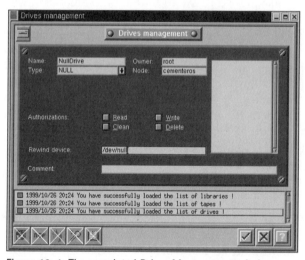

Figure 10-4: The completed Drives Management window

The information entered in this window is

- Name: The name that you want to call the device.

- Type: The device type of the drive that you are using. In this case it is a NULL device, which is not an actual device.

- Rewind device: The device files are found in the /dev directory. When you use a tape drive or a tape library, the rewind device specifies that the tape gets rewound after every access to it.

- The Authorizations section enables you to configure the drive as a read-, write-, clean- and delete- capable device. Again, this is really unnecessary because nothing is being saved to the device, but it is indicative of what options you have to set for a real backup device.

8. Click the checkmark twice and you return to the Server administration window. Click on Devices'Drivepacks. The Drivepacks window is opened as shown in Figure 10-5.

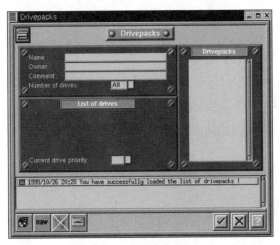

Figure 10-5: The Drivepacks window

9. Click the New button. Enter the drivepack name **NullPack** and click on the NullDrive drive as shown in Figure 10-6. (Clicking on the NullDrive drive button associates that drive with the new drivepack.)

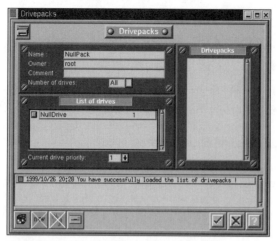

Figure 10-6: The completed Drivepacks window

10. Click on the checkmark again and the NullPack Drivepack shows up in the Drivepacks window at the right of the screen. Click on the checkmark once more and control is returned to the Server administration window.

11. Create a Null Pool. Click on Tapes ' Pools management. The window shown in Figure 10-7 is displayed.

Figure 10-7: The Pools Management window

12. Click on the New button and the Pool creation window is activated. Enter a name, and optional comments as shown in Figure 10-8. The name NullPool is used for this example.

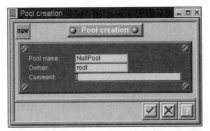

Figure 10-8: The completed Pool creation window

13. Click the `checkbox` in the `Pool creation` window and you go back to the `Pool management` window. Next, click on the `checkbox` in the `Pools management` window and control returns to the `Server administration` window.

14. You need to create a null tape for the null pool. Click on the `Tapes` `Tapes management` menus. You'll get the `Tapes management` window shown in Figure 10-9.

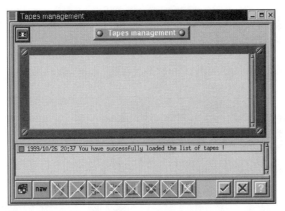

Figure 10-9: The Tapes management window

15. Click on the `New` button to get the Create tapes window.

   Because multiple tapes are used, the tape name that you specify becomes the prefix for all the tapes that you use for your backups. That is, if you use a tape name of `XYZ`, then tapes 1 through 3 are labeled as `XYZ1`, `XYZ2`, and `XYZ3`. In this case, the name (prefix) `NullTape` is used and the five virtual tapes used in this example are labeled as `NullTape1` through `NullTape5`.

   Leave the Bar Code field empty. For this example, enter 1 and 5 respectively for the First number and Last number fields. Specify the NULL tape type by pulling down the submenu in the Type field.

16. You must also associate tapes with a pool. To do so, click the down arrow next to the Current pool field, and select the NullPool. The Create tape(s) window is shown in Figure 10-10 with the information entered as described.

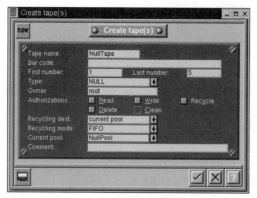

Figure 10-10: The completed Create tape(s) window

17. Click on the checkbox to save the settings. The Tapes management window is returned as shown in Figure 10-11. It now contains the 5 tapes, from NullTape-1 through NullTape-5, that you just created. Click checkmark to return to the Server administration window.

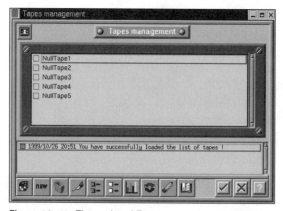

Figure 10-11: The updated Tapes management window

18. Create a savepack. Back in the Server management window, select Backup ' savepackes. The savepackes management window is displayed.

Create a new savepacke by clicking on the New button. A window appears asking for the name of the savepack. Enter **Testsp** as the name for this savepack and click on the checkmark. The savepacks management window shows your new savepack as shown in Figure 10-12.

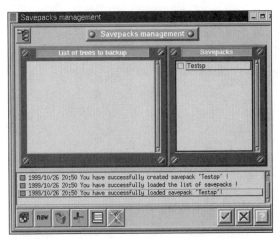

Figure 10-12: The Savepacks management window

19. The next step is to associate Testsp with a file system(s) to backup. Click on the button to the left of the Testsp menu (the button turns orange). Next, click on the navigator button – the fourth button from the left (the one with the arrows) at the bottom of the Savepack management window.

The Select via navigator window is displayed as shown in Figure 10-13. This is a graphical display of your file system.

Figure 10-13: The Select via navigator window

20. If you click on the button to the left of the machine name chivas, then the entire machine will be backed up. Otherwise, if you double click the machine icon you see a display of your root-level directories. For this example, the /etc directory is chosen to be backed up by clicking on the selection box to the left of the /etc directory icon as shown in Figure 10-14.

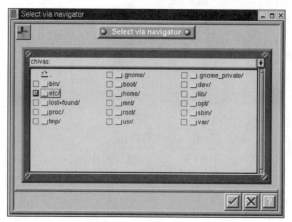

Figure 10-14: Selecting to back up the /etc directory

21. The next step is to choose the files to backup. Click on the checkmark and control is returned to the Savepack management window. This window now contains the files to be backed up in the List of trees to backup subwindow. Click on the checkmark and you go back to the Server administration window.

Making an interactive backup

Now that you have set up a drivepack, a Pool, and a savepack, you can test your system by running an interactive backup. Remember that nothing is going to be backed up because the null device discards the backup data that it is fed.

1. From the Server administration window click Backup → Interactive backup menus. Then you'll enter the Interactive backup window shown in Figure 10-15.

2. Now you'll see the names of the savepack, drivepack, and Pool that you just configured. Other information such as the backup type is displayed too. Later, when you have other backups defined, you can select them from this window.

Figure 10-15: The Interactive backup window

3. Test the system. Start by clicking on the checkbox. If everything is set up properly, then you see the status window shown in Figure 10-16.

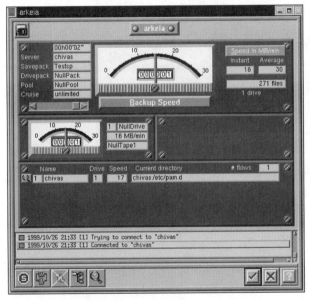

Figure 10-16: Arkeia status window

The speed in megabytes per second is displayed prominently, along with other progress indicators. You have the option of stopping the backup by clicking the Stop backup button in the lower left-hand corner of the screen.

One informative aspect of running a null backup is that it gives you a good indication of the maximum throughput of your machine. Since the data is not being written to any mechanical device, the speed that you see is pretty much the maximum that your computer is capable of. Everything happening on the storage side (data is, of course, being read from a mechanical disk) is electronic with no mechanical tape or disk drives slowing up the process.

Schedule an automatic backup

Next, try scheduling a backup.

1. From the Server management window click Backup ' Periodic backup. The Periodic backup window is displayed, as shown in Figure 10-17.

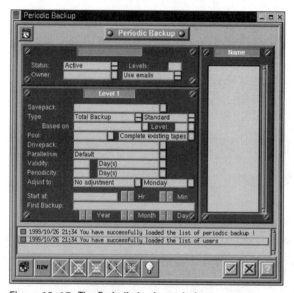

Figure 10-17: The Periodic backup window

2. To create a periodic backup click the new button. Enter the name **NullBackup** for the new backup.

3. Click the checkbox and control returns to the Periodic backup window.

4. You need to specify the savepack, pool, and drivepack to use. You also can change the default start time to any time that you want. Click on the plus (+) and minus (-) buttons on the Start and First backup menus to change the start time.

Arkeia provides a periodic backup assistant to help you create an automatic backup. From the Server administration window, click Help → Assistants → Periodic backup. The assistant walks you through the process of setting up a schedule by giving some predefined examples.

In this example the savepack, pool, and drivepack values are Testsp, NullPool, and NullPack respectively. Fill in the dialog box in the Periodic backup window as shown in Figure 10-18.

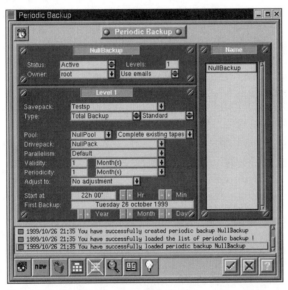

Figure 10-18: Creating a periodic backup

You can optionally change from a total backup to an incremental one (a total backup copies every file, while the incremental backup copies files created or changed since the last full backup — or variations on that theme). Consult the Arkeia documentation for information on these and other optional periodic backup topics.

Using real backup media

Running a backup to a null device is an excellent method for learning the Arkeia basics and testing the software. The configuration process requires some attention and patience; but if you set up a null backup two or three times, you'll begin to understand how things fit together. The knowledge that you've gained can now be used to create a real backup.

Arkeia provides the ability to use a disk drive as the backup media. The disk can be a floppy or Zip disk as well as a hard disk (it is possible to use other types of disks as well). When a disk is used it is referred to as a file. Under Arkeia, a file is an abstraction for a physical storage medium. (Most backups today make use of tapes. So the file concept is added to provide a generic method for accessing a disk).

CONFIGURING A ZIP DRIVE BACKUP

The following example makes use of a Zip disk (sometimes referred to as a Zip diskette). Zips do not store much data compared to DAT or DLT tapes, but can be useful for small operations and are certainly well suited for learning the Arkeia system. They are fairly common and thus provide another learning tool that almost everyone will have access to.

You can also use a hard drive to store data. A hard drive is generally not a good place to save long-term data, but it does provide another good mechanism to learn how to set up your backups.

In some cases, a hard drive is a good backup alternative. For instance, a medium-sized retail chain in Albuquerque, New Mexico, with 70 stores, uses a UNIX server for each store, with an extra hard drive installed in each machine for backups. The backups are made daily and are recycled on a monthly basis. In this case, hard disks work better than tapes because they are cheaper and do not require as much maintenance. The backups are made with a simple `tar` command that is executed from `cron`. Arkeia would make sense for this retail chain because it has more functionality than `tar` and is inexpensive.

The previous example showed almost every graphical menu that you'll encounter while running Arkeia. The method is used to make the example easier to follow the first time. The following example, however, is given in list form without any illustrations.

MOUNT A ZIP DISK

Arkeia requires that a mounted file system be used in conjunction with the File media type. For this example you must mount a blank Zip disk.

1. Log in as `root` on `chivas`.

2. Insert a Zip disk into the drive and enter the following command

```
mount /dev/hdb /mnt/zip
```

The /dev/hdb is used in this example. An IDE Zip drive device can be /dev/hda, /dev/hdb, /dev/hdc or /dev/hdd.

3. If you want to use a DOS formatted Zip disk, then use the following command

   mount -t msdos /dev/hdb4 /mnt/zip

   To use a floppy disk the command should be

   mount /dev/fd0 /mnt/floppy

4. Create a File drive. Open the Drives management window, and then, from the Server administration window, click Devices ' Drives management. Create the new drive called FileDrive. From the Drives management window, click on New, enter the name FileDrive, and the type FILE. Click on the checkbox and the new drive name appears in the menu on the right. Click the checkbox again to return to the Server administration window.

5. Create a drivepack. Open the Drives management window, and then, from the Server administration window, click Devices ' Drivepacks. Create the new drive pack called FileDrive. From the Drivepacks window, click on New, enter the name **FilePack**, and click on the FileDrive in the List of drives menu. Click on the checkbox and the new drivepack name appears in the menu on the right. Click the checkbox again to return to the Server administration window.

6. Create a new Pool. Open the Pools management window, and then, from the Server administration window, click tapes ' pools management. Create the new file pool called FilePool. From the Pools management window, click on New, enter the name **FilePool**, and click on the checkbox. Click the checkbox in the Pools Management window to return to the Server administration window.

7. Add tapes to pool. Open the Tapes management window. Then, from the Server administration window, click Tapes ' Tapes management.

8. Open the Create Tape(s) window. From the Tapes management window, click the New button and enter the following values in the Create tape(s) window

   - Tape name: **FileTape-**
   - Bar code: **/mnt/floppy/FileTape- (/mnt/zip/FileTape-** for a Zip drive)
   - First number: **1**
   - Last number: **5** (Five simulated tapes for a Zip drive)
   - Type: FILE 20MB (100MB for a Zip drive)
   - Current pool: **FilePool**

9. Click the checkbox button. If you were using a tape drive or library that allows bar codes, then you would specify it here. Bar code labels can be placed on tapes so that they can be identified and inventoried automatically. In this example, however, the bar code field is used to specify the device being used as the backup media. No bar code is used in this case. You should see five tapes in your pool corresponding to 20MB of space on your Zip disk.

If you list the contents of your floppy disk (**ls /mnt/floppy**), then you should see directories corresponding to those new files (/mnt/floppy/ FileTape-1 through /mnt/floppy/FileTape-5).

10. Create a file library. A file library is not used for a null drivepack. However, any backup that uses the file drive/file tape abstractions requires that a library be defined. The file library is used as a virtual library to facilitate the file tape/file drive concept. When you use a disk drive (floppy, Zip, hard disk) as your storage media, the directories appear as a library containing individual tapes. (Backups done using a stand alone tape drive do not need a library to be defined. If you have a tape library for your tape drive, then you will need to define and configure the library before doing any backups.)

11. Open the Libraries management window. From the Server administration window, click Devices ' Libraries management.

12. Create the new library called FileLib. From the Libraries management window click on new button, enter the name FileLib and click on FILE in the Type menu. Click the checkbox and the new library name appears in the menu on the right.

13. Click the Drive Options button, which is the sixth button from the left on the bottom. The Drive of libraryFileLib window appears.

14. Click the Attach Drive button, which is in the lower left-hand corner of the window. The Attach drive in libraryFileLib window activates.

15. Click on the checkbox and Arkeia attaches, or associates, the Zip disk drive (FileDrive) with the library.

16. Click the checkbox button and control returns to the Libraries management window.

17. Click on the Slot usage button, which is the seventh button from the left (to the right of the Attach drive button). The Slots in libraryFileLib window should appear. There should be 100 slots listed, each with the No Tape indicator set in the Tape field. Click on the button in the Slot field

for each of the first five slots. (If your X Window color mapping is correct, then the buttons should turn orange when set.)

18. Click on the Set tape button, which is in the lower left-hand corner of the window. The Tapes management window should activate with the tapes (FileTape-1 through FileTape-5).

19. Select tapes 1 through 5 by clicking on the button to the left of each tape name; you can also use the Select All button which is the fifth button from the left at the bottom of your window. If your X Window color mapping is correct, then the buttons should turn orange when set.

20. Click on the checkbox button. You return to the Slots in libraryFileLib window and should see tapes FileTape-1 through FileTape-5 in the Slots in libraryFileLib window (they should also be listed as /mnt/zip/FileTape-1, /mnt/zip/FileTape-2).

21. Click the checkbox to return to the Library management window and again to return to the Server administration window.

22. Create a savepack. Open the Savepack management window. From the Server administration window click Backup ' Savepacks.

23. Create the new savepack called FileSave, and then from the Savepacks management window click on New, enter the name **FileSave**, and click the checkbox.

24. Attach a file system(s) to the savepack. From the Savepacks management window click on the box next to the FileSave item in the Savepacks submenu (the box should become orange). Click on the Navigator button, which is the fourth button from the left on the bottom of the screen.

    Remember that before you selected to back up your server's entire file system by clicking the button to the left of your server icon (chivas in this case). However, since in this example we're using a floppy, it's not possible. Instead, double click the chivas icon and you'll see all the top-level directories displayed. Click on the /etc directory and then on the checkbox and control returns to the Savepacks management window.

25. Click on the checkbox and the Server administration window returns.

Make a test backup

1. Open the Interactive backup window. From the Server administration window, click Backup → Interactive.

2. The Interactive backup window appears. The original Testsp should appear in the savepack submenu. Click on that menu and select the FileSave savepack.

3. Click on the `checkbox` and the Arkeia window. It displays the information on your backup as before. The backup should run quickly with information on the results appearing at the bottom of the window.

Please take note that when configuring the interactive backup you have the choice of associating different savepacks with different drivepacks and also different pools. This provides you with a flexible way of using your resources.

 Arkeia offers a command line interface called `arkc`. You can install the `arkc` package by logging onto `chivas` as root and entering the command **rpm –ivh /mnt/cdrom/Arkeia/arkc***. Please consult the `arkc` documents in the `/usr/knox/arkc` directory for more information.

Using a SCSI tape drive or tape library

To make better use of this backup system, you are most likely going to need a device(s) capable of storing gigabytes of information. The most common medium is a DAT tape drive.

This book does not describe the process of using a DAT drive, or a real tape library, in any detail. The following paragraphs provide some information on how to find information on a DAT drive if you have one. It also points out what parts of the previous example you should change in order to accommodate such drives.

If you don't want to purchase a tape library, you can use a 4mm or 8mm DAT drive. They are generally SCSI devices. It is best to purchase a good SCSI controller to work with a DAT. (Technically, tapes used for data storage are referred to as DDS, but they are commonly referred to as DAT.)

If you want to use a SCSI DAT drive, then consult the `/usr/doc/HOWTO/HARD-WARE-HOWTO` for details on installing it. Linux comes with numerous SCSI drivers. Once installed and configured the DAT device shows up similar to `/dev/st0` or `/dev/st1`.

Arkeia provides installation and configuration information in its on-line documentation. Use your browser to look at the `file:/usr/doc/arkeia-server-4.2.1/html/install/setup.htm` and `file:/usr/doc/arkeia-server-4.2.1/html/install/setup.htm` for detailed information on configuring Arkeia for DAT tapes, tape libraries and other devices.

Configuring a Windows client

Arkeia provides a Windows 95 client. It is stored in the windows.zip file in the `/mnt/cdrom/Arkeia` directory on the companion CD-ROM. To install the Windows client, proceed as follows.

1. Log in as `root` on `chivas`.

2. Mount the Red Hat Publisher's Edition CD-ROM (optional).

3. Install the `unzip` program (`gunzip` does not work on .zip files) and unzip with the following commands (optional)

```
rpm -ivh /mnt/cdrom/RedHat/RPMS/unzip*
```

4. Create a temporary directory.

```
mkdir /var/tmp/arkeia
```

5. Unzip the Windows client to the temporary directory.

```
cd /var/tmp/arkeia
unzip /mnt/cdrom/IDG/Arkeia/client
```

You could copy the unzipped files to your Windows machine and then run the installation program. However, a more elegant method is to leave a single set of files on the Linux server, mount that directory on your Windows computer, and then run the installation program. This method is efficient because you do not make multiple copies of the file. If you install this, or any program, on more than one machine, then you do not end up with copies on multiple machines.

6. Edit the `/etc/smb.conf` file by hand or with SWAT and add a share for the `/var/tmp` directory.

```
[Arkeia]
        path = /var/tmp/arkeia
        public = yes
```

7. From your Windows computer, mount the Arkeia share by opening your Network Neighborhood, double-click the `chivas` icon and then double-click the Arkeia share. You should see the Setup.exe program. Double-click that icon and the software installs itself. (You need to have the Microsoft Virtual Machine, available at `http//www.microsoft.com/java/vm/dl_vm32.htm`, installed for the Java based Arkeia GUI to work under Windows 95 or Windows 98.) The MS Java VM must be installed before installing the Arkeia Windows client and GUI software.

8. Next, locate the Knox software submenu in the Start → Programs menu. Click on the `Arkeia` selection. The Arkeia server GUI is functionally the same as the `Linux Server Administration window`.

9. Create a `savepack` for your Windows client. Use the same process as for creating a Linux `savepack`. Finally, go to the Interactive Backup and select the new `savepack` and one of the existing `drivepacks`. Click on the `Ok` button and the backup should start.

Restoring data

You can restore data to a computer by using the Restoration → Restoration menu in the Server administration window. Double-click the client icon that you want to restore.

The files and directories that have been backed up are displayed. Click any or all of the icons that you want to restore. Click the `checkbox` and the Restoration window activates.

This window displays all the files and directories that are scheduled to be restored. It is often advisable to restore files and directories to a different location than they were originally stored on. This is because you often want to manually sort through restored files to choose what you want to use; it is also good to restore to a temporary location while you are learning the new system. Enter the new directory by entering the path name in the Redirection box towards the lower half of the window. You can also search for files by clicking on the Search button, which is the 8th button from the left.

Click on the `checkbox` and the restoration begins.

Troubleshooting

Arkeia is a sophisticated system. A full troubleshooting manual is beyond the scope of this book. However, this section provides an overview of the Arkeia system plus a few specific hints. If you understand the system as a whole, then it is easier to overcome problems when they occur.

 Keep in mind that Knox Software maintains considerable documentation on their Web site in addition to the text provided on the companion CD-ROM. The Arkeia GUI also contains context-sensitive help screens. You can obtain 30 days of free support by filling out their registration form on the `http://www.arkeia.com/download.html` page.

The Arkeia client-server backup system consists of three parts: the client, the server, and the interface GUI. The client daemon and server daemon can operate on the same machine as in the case of the backup server. The client can also operate on computers that are on the same network as the server.

When the Arkeia client is on a different machine from the server, then you need to make sure that all the normal connectivity works. That is, if a client workstation cannot communicate with the server (ping, telnet, etc.) then the backup will not work. If you are having problems making a backup work then make sure the network is okay before you look to the backup software as the problem.

The Arkeia server has five components that must all work in order for backups to succeed. Arkeia uses the concept of Pools, Tapes, Drives, drivepacks, and savepacks. These components separate the hardware from the software. The computer(s) backups do not need to know anything about the underlying hardware that the data is to be stored to.

The Pool concept logically combines one or more backup media — such as DAT tapes — into a single object. The object is controlled by Arkeia, which maintains all the bookkeeping details on what volume(s) belong to it, what files and directories from which clients are contained on each volume and where those volumes can be found. A volume is an abstraction for physical media; a volume can be a tape, a disk file, a floppy file, a Zip file or any number of other devices.

When creating tapes of the File type, you must follow the following rules. The file device, such as a Zip drive, must be mounted and have a Linux ext2 file system. The value that you enter in the Bar code field in the Create tape(s) window must include the mount directory and the name of the simulated tape (for instance, `/mnt/zip/FileTape-`). Otherwise, the simulated tapes are created in the same directory as the mount directory. If you use the Bar code value of `/mnt/zip`, then the simulated tapes are created in the root directory file system as `/mnt/zip/FileTape-1`, `/mnt/zip/FileTape-2`, etc. In that case, your data is written to your hard disk and not the Zip disk.

Drivepacks link together one or more backup devices. The drivepack is another logical device. You must define at least one drive before you can create a drivepack.

Libraries define where a volume or volumes can be accessed. If you have a tape library, the library management system controls it. (A tape library is a device that combines multiple tapes, one or more tape drives, and a robotic arm to load and unload the tapes, into a single case.) Otherwise, the library management system logically divides a volume such as a Zip disk into directories that mimic individual volumes in separate slots.

savepacks combine the client's file systems to be backed up with a drivepack. A savepack makes it easy to make a client backup. For instance, to back up your server chivas you simply specify that, for instance, the directory XYZ on chivas uses drivepack W. You can then execute the savepack manually or schedule it to run at some specific time.

The log files contain a good source of information that can be useful for debugging purposes. Click Utilities ' Log management from the Server administration window and you are given a choice of five logs. The logs cover the backups finished, general information and the drives, and tapes and restorations that you have done. Log information is displayed in all the windows that you access from the Server administration interface.

Once you have configured the four Arkeia systems, then it becomes a simple process to back up any computer with the software. You are divorced from having to execute, verify and maintain manual systems as you would with tar. Arkeia runs the show and you are left to monitor it and keep it fed with volumes.

If you have problems configuring the system or making backup, then there are several places that you can look for help. As mentioned there are numerous documents available to you—both locally (for instance, `file://usr/doc/arkeia-server-4.2.1/html/install/solving.htm`) and at the Arkeia web site. There is also the information that is displayed on the Server administration GUI. Arkeia also maintains several log files that can be accessed from the Server administration window by clicking on the `Utilities ' Log management` menus.

Summary

This chapter provides you with the information to get a simple Arkeia client-server backup system working, with two examples highlighted. The first is trivial, but excellent for learning the basics of the system and how to get it working. The second is a real-world example everyone should be able to get working. The more complex process of using a SCSI DAT tape drive system and even a robotic tape library is discussed in general terms. Other general topics such as scheduling are described.

- ◆ An introduction to the Arkeia client-server backup system. Arkeia is an automated system (it can also be run manually) that allows you to step back from the details of making backups.

- ◆ A description of its installation. Arkeia is contained on the companion CD-ROM and is in RPM format.

- ◆ A description of the configuration and operation of a null backup. This backup makes use of the Linux `/dev/null` device which exists solely in the mind of the operating system. The null backup writes to the null device, which simply discards the data. This is the simplest method for verifying and learning the backup system.

- ◆ A description of the configuration and operation of a file backup. The file can be any kind of Linux disk drive. A floppy is used in this case because it's the only device that nearly every reader is guaranteed to have—the floppy can readily be transferred to Zip, hard disk, or other device. This example allows you to create actual backups and is a good way to practice. In some cases, it might be all that you need to use (I used a Zip drive for the daily backup of this manuscript).

- ◆ Most operations of any size require at least a single DAT tape drive. The details of doing so are not discussed in this book but the best places to research this are discussed. You should be able to configure a DAT or a tape library, if you use the examples and change the details to reflect the new equipment.

- ◆ A discussion of installing and configuring a Windows client. With this client you can back up your Windows machine to your Linux server.

- ◆ A discussion of the recovery of data. Arkeia makes it a simple process to restore files and directories.

◆ A brief discussion of scheduling backups. Total backups are performed less frequently than the incremental ones. Incremental backups include files and directories that have changed since the total backup (incremental backups can also be referenced to other incremental backups). Total back-ups can be scheduled on various schedules. There are other scheduling operations that you are encouraged to investigate on your own.

◆ A general discussion of troubleshooting. Arkeia is a complex system to configure at times. Since it is beyond the scope of this book to discuss the many things that are interrelated, the general, overall logic is described. Arkeia also provides free help for 30 days if you register with them. They also provide considerable help systems both online and at their Web site.

There are many more functions that Arkeia can perform. You are encouraged to work with the simple examples described in this chapter and then experiment with the more advanced features.

Chapter 11

Building a Firewall

Introducing Firewalls

A firewall is a computer, router, or a dedicated device that is configured to prevent unauthorized access to one network from another network. For the purposes of this book, a firewall is a Linux computer set up to protect your simple business network from troublemakers on the Internet.

This book uses terminology that is somewhat different than what you'll find in the technical literature. The local network that we have been working with is referred to as the private network. (What I call the private network is often referred to as the protected network when reading about firewalls in the technical literature.). The Linux-based firewall is called the firewall server; in other circles that machine is often referred to as a screening router or Bastion Host. (An optional firewall system is described where a separate network is created to isolate the firewall server from the private network. The separate network is typically referred to as the DMZ network. That convention is used here too.) Hopefully, the terms used here are descriptive and clear.

Firewalls come in two primary flavors: filtering and proxy. Filtering firewalls look at each IP packet and decide whether to pass or reject the packets based on a set of rules that you set; they work at the OSI Network layer (see the section "The

337

OSI Network Layer Model" in Chapter 4 for more information). Proxy firewalls act as an intermediary between a program client and its server by replicating the communication and performing other security functions. They work at the OSI application layer.

There are several strategic places to put a firewall within a network. Two common configurations put a firewall either directly on the private network or on a separate network dedicated to security. The former allows a simple firewall to be easily constructed and, depending on what services the firewall provides, can be reasonably safe. The latter is more difficult to configure but provides a higher degree of safety; this book refers to the latter as a firewall network, but the general term is the DMZ.

IP Filtering Firewalls

Filtering firewalls look at each packet coming into and going out of them, and compare the source IP and port as well as the destination IP and port to a set of rules. The packet is either permitted to pass or not depending on these rules, which you, the network administrator, choose.

Red Hat Linux comes with the `ipchains` package, which provides filtering capabilities. This package allows the filter rules to be configured dynamically and also can perform numerous levels of logging. The `diald` program described in Chapter 7 can automatically set up the `ipchains` rules. This allows you to completely automate both your Internet PPP connection and firewall.

Filtering firewalls are relatively easy to configure. They are also efficient; an Intel 486 firewall server can easily handle a medium-sized network (dozens of computers) connected to the Internet through a T1 frame relay connection (1.54 Mbps). They also are safe as firewalls when providing one-way communication to the Internet.

The knock against IP filters is that once you start to allow incoming connections from the Internet you are poking holes in your firewall. For instance, if you want to interactively connect to your private network from your home computer (assuming that they are not one and the same), then you need to set a rule(s) that allows incoming Telnet connections. There are tools (for instance `nmap`, which is discussed in the section "Using nmap" in Chapter 12) that can potentially find those holes and use them against you.

Proxying Firewalls

Proxying firewalls allow you to add application-level authentication to permit incoming connections. For instance, if you want to connect to your private `network` from your home computer, a proxying firewall forces you to provide a password before allowing you through. Using one-time passwords makes it very difficult for unauthorized users to gain access to your system.

Hybrid firewalls

This book assumes a networking model where most, if not all, of your Internet traffic is outward bound to the Internet. Chapter 12 describes using Secure Shell as an external communication path into your network. However, you might want to use another method for external communication – a hybrid firewall.

This book uses a hybrid firewall designed to minimize your work while maximizing your safety. After all, as a new administrator, you should have a firewall that you can put into place quickly. Once you are protected, then you have a window of time to learn security more fully and make decisions on how much additional protection you need. You might very well never require anything more than what is described here.

The hybrid firewall uses IP filtering to allow one-way communication from your Private Network to the Internet. You allow incoming communication by placing a one-time password system on the dial in the PPP connection described in Chapter 8. By separating the two channels, you use the strength of the IP filtering system to its maximum. The semi-private phone system provides limited (you need to know a phone number before an attack can even be made) access to your network that is further supplemented by a tough authentication system. Put together, this system provides the best of both worlds.

Note: If you do not require incoming connections, then you're that much better off. The IP filtering still works in its best mode (one-way). Plus, you do not have to worry about providing any incoming protection. Most individuals (for instance, an aspiring writer) and many small businesses only need functions such as e-mail and Web browsing.

The problem with proxying firewalls is that they are relatively difficult to set up. They are somewhat inefficient, and are vulnerable to software bugs and new attack methods.

Configuration is difficult because each application that you want to proxy requires its own configuration. (The SOCKS system, however, only has one configuration.) It is inefficient because the communication processing is doubled for every application because every packet has to be rewritten as it passes through the proxy.

It's somewhat vulnerable to new attacks because any attack that finds an opening can only be fixed by the programming of the proxy itself. For instance, when Denial of Service (DoS)attacks first appeared, any proxy that fell victim to them had to be reprogrammed. Unfortunately, this isn't something that a pressed administrator can do easily, if at all. (Filtering firewalls, while not immune to new attacks, can readily be reprogrammed to simply deny the IP packets that carry the new attack.) The fact that a proxying firewall is often sitting out on the Internet means that potentially everyone on the Internet can pound away at your firewall. The more attempts made on your firewall the higher the probability that a weak spot can be found.

Don't assume that proxying firewalls are inadequate for the job; the potential hazards are pointed out only for completeness. Proxying firewalls are not used in this book because the filters described here work well when a network only (mostly) accesses the Internet and does not (mostly) allow anyone to come in.

One of the most widely used proxy firewall systems is the TIS Firewall. It is freely available for US citizens by way of the Internet. Please check the www.tis.com web page for license and download instructions. The alternative is SOCKS www.socks.nec.com, which provides the same function.

Please refer to the Firewall-HOWTO in the /usr/doc/HOWTO directory for more information on proxying firewalls.

Introducing ipchains

The ipchains RPM package provides IP packet filtering for your Linux gateway. You can configure it to accept or deny each IP packet going into and out of your Linux gateway. The ipchains package should be installed by default during the Red Hat installation process. However, if it has not for any reason been installed then proceed as follows:

1. Log in to atlas as root.

2. Mount the IDG supplemental CD-ROM.

   mount /mnt/cdrom

3. Install ipchains.

   rpm -ivh /mnt/cdrom/RedHat/RPMS/ipchains*

You can get a short informational listing by entering the command **rpm -qi ipchains.**

The ipchains has replaced the ipfwadm system with the introduction of the Linux 2.2 kernel. ipchains is similar to ipfwadm but has several improvements (please refer to the ipchains HOWTO document for a full account). If you have an older Red Hat, or other Linux distribution, that uses an older kernel, then you should download ipfwadm from a Red Hat mirror site.

Creating a Filtering Firewall

If you have built the Linux Internet gateway described in Chapter 7, then you'll need to protect it with a firewall. The following section describes how to set up simple filtering rules. You should keep in mind that until you construct the full firewall described in this chapter, you are potentially vulnerable to attack while connected to the Internet. This is probably a reasonable risk right now, because you are connected via a dial-up phone connection, which is invulnerable when not connected. Also, the system constructed in this book has no valuable information on it other than the passwords (unless you have put information and data on it yourself). You can judge the potential danger for yourself.

Figure 11-1 shows the layout of the network.

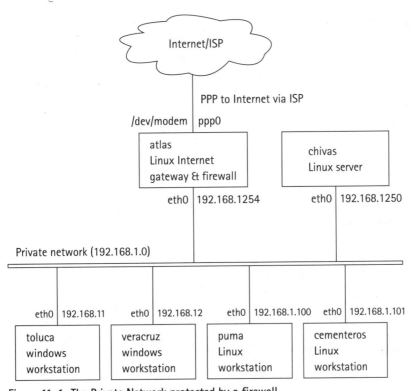

Figure 11-1: The Private Network protected by a firewall

In order to test and build the chains described in this chapter you need to be connected to the Internet (a chain is simply a series of filtering rules). If you are experienced with IP filtering, then you can translate the rules to apply to an internal connection; a good idea if you don't want to risk being unprotected.

Building a simple filter

You can make a simple filter as follows. The Linux computer `atlas` is used as the firewall in this example. To enhance security it is best to use a separate computer for your firewall. By using a dedicated machine you can reduce the services and software that it provides in order to minimize potential vulnerabilities.

1. Log in to the Internet gateway `atlas` as root.

2. Connect to your ISP

   ```
   echo "force" /etc/diald/diald.ctl
   ```

 The following instructions should be carried out from your Linux server's console. The rules initially shut off all network communication. If you are working on `atlas` remotely, then your remote session will freeze when you set up the initial rules. You can run the `/mnt/cdrom/firewall/ipfilter.reset` script, on the IDG supplemental CD-ROM, to turn off the filters.

3. Flush out any existing rules

   ```
   ipchains -F
   ```

4. List all the filtering rules

   ```
   ipchains -L
   ```

5. You should see the following results if you have not configured any filtering rules yet.

   ```
   Chain input (policy ACCEPT):
   Chain forward (policy ACCEPT):
   Chain output (policy ACCEPT):
   ```

   The results show that there are no input, output, or forwarding rules set and that the default policy is to accept any IP packet to come into or out of your network. Your system is completely open.

6. Setup your default filter policy to deny all network traffic.

   ```
   ipchains -P input   DENY
   ipchains -P output  DENY
   ipchains -P forward DENY
   ```

   Those rules set your output, input and forwarding rules on `atlas` to deny any IP packets in any direction; the following list shows the ipchains filter commands. You now have a very, very safe firewall. However, it does not allow you to access the Internet either.

7. Setup the input and output TCP rules. (The following rules set your firewall to allow you to browse the World Wide Web.)

```
ipchains -A output -p TCP -j ACCEPT -i ppp0  -d 0.0.0.0/0 www
ipchains -A input  -p TCP -j ACCEPT -i ppp0 ! -y -s 0.0.0.0/0
www
```

- The destination and source addresses - 0.0.0.0/0 - indicates the entire Internet address space.

- The first command sets up a filter that only allows TCP packets originating at the PPP connection (within the Linux gateway atlas) to go out to any location.

- The second command allows only the return packets from connections that originate from within the private network by using the ! -y parameter. For instance, if you Telnet to an external computer, for every outgoing Telnet packet that you send a response packet comes back to you. That response packet has its SYN (for synchronize) flag set. Thus, with this filter rule set, only the return packets can get back through the firewall. It is highly unlikely that any bad guy can take advantage of this arrangement.

Note that these rules apply to your first PPP (-i ppp0) network interfaces and will act on network traffic to and from your Linux server via the Internet. You can apply ipchains rules to any network interface by using the -i parameter. For instance, to apply rules to the first Ethernet interface you should use the option -i eth0. If you omit the -i parameter, then the rules will apply to all network interfaces.

8. Setup the input and output UDP rules. The following rules configure the firewall to allow DNS queries to go out to the Internet and the response to come back in. DNS uses UDP and is identified as the domain service.

```
ipchains -A output -p UDP -j ACCEPT -i ppp0 -d 0.0.0.0/0
domain
ipchains -A input  -p UDP -j ACCEPT -i ppp0 -s 0.0.0.0/0
domain
```

UDP is a simpler protocol than TCP and requires less configuration. Outgoing and incoming UDP packets of the type domain (used by DNS) are allowed. This will permit DNS to work.

The first filter rule specifies that UDP packets of the type domain can leave the firewall and go anywhere. This rule allows you to access external DNS services.

The second rule allows the return UDP domain packets from anywhere to come back in with the DNS information.

These rules create a simple but quite effective firewall. The more advanced filtering rules described in the next section, Building a Working IP Filter, give you a more complete firewall.

 It is often quite useful to turn off all your IP filters and set them to accept mode. The script /mnt/cdrom/firewall/ipfilter.reset is shown here, and does just that.

```
/sbin/ipchains -F
/sbin/ipchains -P input   ACCEPT
/sbin/ipchains -P output  ACCEPT
/sbin/ipchains -P forward ACCEPT
```

Once the connection is established, enter the following command to see the status of your IP filters.

```
/sbin/ipchains -L
```

The primary ipchains modes, parameters, and options

As you've seen in this exercise, ipchains is a powerful utility. Here I've provided a quick rundown of the most common ipchains modes, parameters and options. Let's start with the primary ipchains modes:

-A	Append one or more rules to a chain
-D	Delete one or more rules from a chain
-R	Replace a rule from a chain
-I	Insert a rule into a chain
-L	List the rules in a chain
-F	Flush a chain — all rules are lost
-N	Create a new chain
-P	Set a policy for a chain
-M	Masquerading rules to follow

Please consult the `ipchains` man page for more information (`ipchains --help` will display the same information too).

Here are some of the more frequently used `ipchains` parameters:

- ◆ `-p` Set the protocol (for instance, tcp, udp, icmp) for the rule or packet to check. The rules in a chain only apply to packets that match the protocols. The available protocols can be found in the /etc/protocols file.

- ◆ `-s` Determines whether to allow or deny packets through the filter depending on the source address. Every IP packet has a source and destination address; they also have a corresponding source and destination port. Any packet with a source address that matches an `ipchains` rule is then checked against the rule to determine whether it passes through the firewall or not.

- ◆ `-d` Determines whether to allow or not deny packets through the filter depending on the destination address. Every IP packet has a source and destination address, as well as a corresponding source and destination port. Any packet with a destination address that matches an `ipchains` rule is then checked against the rule to determine whether it passes through the firewall or not.

- ◆ `-i` Sets filtering rules for an indivdual or type of interface. You can optionally specify an interface to configure rules on.

- ◆ `-h` Display a help screen.

Finally, here are some of the most commonly used `ipchains` options:

- ◆ `-b` Forces a rule to work in both directions. For example, in the previous steps, the two rules for the UDP protocol could be replaced by one rule. This does not work if you wish to limit incoming packets with the SYN (`! -y`) parameter.

- ◆ `-v` Sets the verbose mode. If you use this option with the `-L` list command, more information about each chain is displayed.

- ◆ `-n` Sets the numeric output mode. Display IP numbers instead of names.

- ◆ `! -y` Only allow packets with their SYN bit set through. Typically used for limiting network traffic to only the return packets of existing, outgoing connections.

Building a working filter

There are two approaches that you can take in designing filters: deny everything and add rules to allow specific access, or allow everything and write rules to deny specific access. The latter can make sense if you want to provide public-service access to your system. However, the former mode is used in this book in order to provide the maximum security.

The filter script used for this firewall can be found in /mnt/cdrom/firewall/ipfilter.rules on the companion CD-ROM. Most of its rules are listed here, but some of the comments and the Type of Service (TOS) rules, which are used for optimizing the modem connection, have been omitted for brevity's sake.

```bash
#!/bin/bash
# i------------- Define variables --------------
# High (non well-known ports)
HI="1024:65535"

# Define the default network address
ALL="0.0.0.0/0"
# Define the private network's address
PRIV_NET="192.168.1.0/24"
# Define localhost address
LOCAL_HOME="127.0.0.1"
# Get dynamic PPP IP address (your ISP assigns this to you at connection time
PPP_IP=`/sbin/ifconfig ppp0 |grep 'inet addr'| awk '{print $2}'| \
    sed -e "s/addr\://"`
echo $PPP_IP
# ------------- General Rules ------------------
# Flush out all existing rules
/sbin/ipchains -F
# Flush out any existing chains
/sbin/ipchains -X

# Set default filters to deny everything
/sbin/ipchains -P input    DENY
/sbin/ipchains -P output   DENY
/sbin/ipchains -P forward DENY

# Allow all internal network traffic
#/sbin/ipchains -A input   -i lo -j ACCEPT
#/sbin/ipchains -A output -i lo -j ACCEPT

# Allow all internal network traffic
#/sbin/ipchains -A input   -i eth0 -j ACCEPT
#/sbin/ipchains -A output -i eth0 -j ACCEPT

# Deny spoofed packets
/sbin/ipchains -A input   -j DENY -i ppp0 -s $PPP_IP -d $ALL
/sbin/ipchains -A output -j DENY -i ppp0 -s $PRIV_NET    -d $ALL
# --- TCP ----
```

```
/sbin/ipchains -A output -p tcp  -j ACCEPT -i ppp0      -s $PPP_IP -d $ALL
/sbin/ipchains -A input  -p tcp  -j ACCEPT -i ppp0 ! -y -s $ALL     -d $PPP_IP
# --- UDP ----
/sbin/ipchains -A output -p udp -j ACCEPT -i ppp0 -s $PPP_IP   -d 0.0.0.0/0
/sbin/ipchains -A input  -p udp -j ACCEPT -i ppp0 -s 0.0.0.0/0 -d $PPP_IP
# --- Masqurade (Network Address Translation) ----
# Masquerade your private network
# (see the section "Configure Linux Networking for Masquerading"
# in this chapter for more information.)
# (all local IPs appear on the Internet as your PPP IP address)
###/sbin/ipchains -A forward -j MASQ -s 192.168.1.0/24 -d 0.0.0.0/0
```

MAKING CUSTOM RULE SETS (CHAINS)

This filter does not make use of the nice ipchains feature – chains. A chain is simply a list, or chain, of common rules. The previous script only uses the two built-in chains: input and output. You can create custom chains, however, by running the following commands:

```
ipchains -N xyz
ipchains -A input -j xyz
```

The first run creates a new chain called xyz. The second designates the xyz chain as an incoming one. You can then start adding specific filtering rules to that chain. For instance:

```
ipchains -A xyz -p TCP -j ACCEPT -I ppp0 -d $ALL ssh
```

You have now told your firewall to allow all TCP packets destined to the Secure Shell port at any IP address to come into your first PPP interface. You can further refine the xyz chain by running additional commands.

The /mnt/cdrom/firewall/ipfilter.rules.equiv script that comes on the IDG supplemental CD-ROM converts the ipfilter.rules script into several individual chains. Both scripts are functionally equivalent but the ipfilter.rules.equiv demonstrates the elegance of ipchains.

UNDERSTANDING IP MASQUERADING

Using IP masquerading is an elegant method for attaching your network to the Internet. IP masquerading (also call Network Address Translation, or NAT) converts an IP source address into another address. In this example, the source addresses of packets originating from within the Private Network get converted into the source address of the PPP connection on the Linux gateway/firewall. Once on the Internet they all appear to be coming from a single machine. No matter what computer on the Private Network you are using, all packets appear to come from a single computer.

If you use IP masquerading, then you do not need any official registration to allow your network to access the Internet. Without masquerading you would have to register with the InterNIC (the organization that distributes IP addresses) to obtain IP addresses for your network. It also conserves the quickly diminishing pool of IP addresses.

IP masquerading also provides the advantage of hiding your network behind a single address. Anyone trying to probe or attack your Private Network has to go through your single (and typically dynamic) address. Since IP masquerading is in effect a one-way street, most (if not all) attacks on your networked computers will die on the vine. That is because packets originating from the outside will not get translated into the address of a private network machine and, thus, never find their way to any computer. (Note that the only route that is configured on the Internet gateway atlas is the default route to the PPP connection. Returning masqueraded packets get shunted back into the private network via ipchains. There is no route to the Private Network for incoming, non-masqueraded, packets.)

The only way for a probe or attack to get a foothold is to hijack an existing connection. However, even if that's possible, the packets will have to be part of an existing connection originating from the Private Network. The packets will be treated as return packets and should never be able to start a new connection. IP masquerading has the effect of making your firewall safer than without it.

The last line in the ipfilter.rules script, in the section "Building a Working Filter," describes the masquerading rule for the paunchy.net network. IP masquerading converts one IP address into another IP address. That translation permits one or more computers to masquerade as single IP address. If that IP address is your dynamic, dial-up IP address, then your entire network can access the Internet.

What the rule says is that any local IP address 192.168.1.0 (the /24 specifies a subnet mask of 255.255.255.0) that shows up at the Linux gateway that is destined for the default route 0.0.0.0 is masqueraded. The default route is pegged to the PPP connection – ppp0 – which has a dynamic IP address given by your ISP. The source address of the packets destined for the Internet is changed to the dynamic IP address. For instance, if your PPP connection has the address 192.168.32.15 and the packets from the Windows box toluca have a source address of 192.168.1.1, then the packets that get sent to the Internet get the source address of 192.168.32.15. The computer toluca appears to the rest of the world as 192.168.32.15.

A little more happens during masquerading than just the source address translation. The source port also gets converted to another port. Recall that the TCP/IP protocols make use of both IP addresses and ports. Ports are used to separate network communication between different applications. For instance, the standard Hypertext Transport Protocol (HTTP) uses port 80 by default. If you look at the /etc/services file, then you see all of the standard applications and protocols along with their ports; the ports below 1024 are referred to as Well Known ports. During masquerading, the port gets changed to a number above 1024. This process allows the ipchains software to de-masquerade the returning, masqueraded packets back to their original locations.

When there's a response to a masqueraded packet, the reverse translation is performed. The returning packets have their destination IP address converted back to the originating IP address. The destination port is also converted back to the original port number.

CONFIGURE LINUX NETWORKING FOR MASQUERADING
The following instructions describe how to configure masquerading on your Internet gateway atlas.

1. Login to atlas as root.

2. The /etc/sysconfig/network script on atlas looks like the following. Modify the the FORWARD_IPV4 line from no to yes. (Also add the line DE-FRAG_IPV4 = yes so that atlas will defragment all IP packets. Setting that parameter protects ipchains from certain buffer overflow attacks.) IP masquerading requires forwarding to work.

```
NETWORKING=yes
FORWARD_IPV4=no
HOSTNAME=atlas.paunchy.net
DOMAINNAME=paunchy.net
GATEWAY=
GATEWAYDEV=
```

TIP You can verify that your kernel is set up for forwarding and defragmenting by looking at the contents of certain files in the /proc/sys/net/ipv4 directory. Recall that the /proc file system is a virtual file system that provides a view into the kernel state. Look at the values contained in the ip_forwarding and ip_always_defrag file as follows.

```
cat ip_forwading
cat ip_always_defrag
```

You should see the numeral 1 in both files. The 1 means true or yes which means that forwarding and defragmentation are turned on. Alternatively a zero means false or no.)

3. Your new network file should look as follows

```
NETWORKING=yes
FORWARD_IPV4=yes
DEFRAG_IPV4=yes
HOSTNAME=atlas.paunchy.net
DOMAINNAME=paunchy.com
GATEWAY=
GATEWAYDEV=
```

4. Uncomment the masquerading rule (the last line) in your `ipfilter.rules` script.

```
ipchains -A forward -j MASQ -s 192.168.1.0/24 -d 0.0.0.0/0
```

5. Any IP packet that shows up on `atlas`'s Ethernet NIC and is destined for an external location (any non `192.168.1.x` address) gets masqueraded as the dynamic PPP interface address; any packets originating within atlas do not get masqueraded because they inherit the PPP address.

6. Restart your network to put the change into effect.

```
/etc/rc.d/init.d/network restart
```

Give it a try from any computer on your Private Network. If, for instance, you open a Web browser on a Windows machine and click on `www.swcp.com/~pgsery/rhltoolkit`, your Linux gateway should dial up and connect to your ISP and then — after a few tens of seconds — you should see the web page.

AUTOMATICALLY FIRING UP YOUR FIREWALL

Whenever you connect to the Internet you should start your firewall as well. One simple and effective way of doing that is to have `diald` run the ipfilter.rules once the PPP connection has been established. You can do this by adding the following commands to the end of the `/etc/diald.conf` file.

```
ip-up /usr/local/etc/ipfilter.rules
ip-down /usr/local/etc/ipfilter.reset
```

The `ip-up` parameter forces `diald` to run the script that configures the `ipchains` rules. The `ip-down` runs the script that flushes all the `ipchains` rules and sets the default policies to accept.

CONFIGURING YOUR NETWORK FOR EXTERNAL ACCESS

The firewall described in this chapter works best when configured for one-way connections to the Internet. IP filtering presents a formidable wall with this configuration. However, when you start allowing connections from the outside, then your internal services can become exposed to attack.

You can replace your services with proxies (for instance, the TIS firewall or `www.tis.com`) to protect yourself, but that makes designing your firewall a more complex and difficult process. For small networks, my advice is to pay an ISP to provide general services, such as Web pages, and take the risks.

If you do want two-way communication, a good compromise is to use Secure Shell for incoming connections on your Linux gateway/firewall. Secure Shell can be configured to provide both host and user authentication, and can determine whether an incoming connection is from a trusted computer. It can also authenticate the incoming user (separate from the normal Linux user login process). Secure Shell is essentially an application-based firewall.

By modifying the IP filtering firewall to allow only incoming Secure Shell (port 22) you maintain the most of the firewall's integrity. There's only one possible port of entry and, if Secure Shell is configured correctly, there is very little that a cracker can attack. Using Secure Shell is discussed in Chapter 12.

Separating your firewall from your private network

The firewall system described in this chapter is a good compromise between maximum security and reasonable construction and maintenance costs. To take the next step up in security you will want to put your firewall on a separate network from your private network.

This system requires a second network called the DMZ. The Internet gateway at-las will sit entirely on the DMZ while chivas will be connected to both the private and DMZ networks and act as both a router and firewall. Figure 11-2 shows the topology of the networks.

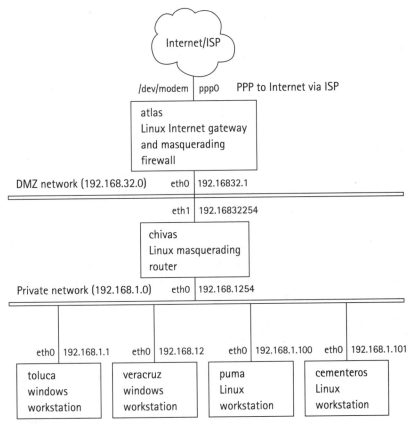

Figure 11-2: The DMZ and Private Networks

CONVERTING CHIVAS INTO A MASQUERADING ROUTER

1. Login to `chivas` as `root` and shut it down by running the command.

   `halt`

2. Turn off the power, wait for a minute to allow the power supply capacitors to bleed off (discharge) and remove the power cord. (You can never be sure that the capacitors have completely discharged so don't ever open the power supply.) Removing the power cord when you are working on a computer is essential for safety!!!

 There can still be dangerous electrical charge left in the power supply capacitors even after you remove the power cord. Don't EVER open up the sealed power supply and if you have one without proper shielding don't touch it! You should dispose of the power supply by replacing the computer case and take it back to the place of purchase or a qualified electrician.

3. Install a second Ethernet NIC. This NIC will be `eth1`. The existing NIC will remain as `eth0`.

4. Edit the `/etc/sysconfig/network` script as follows. (Note, add the line DEFRAG_IPV4 = true to force the kernel to defragment all IP packets. This makes the ipchains filter more robust.)

   ```
   NETWORKING=yes
   FORWARD_IPV4=true
   DEFRAG_IPV4=true
   HOSTNAME=chivas.paunchy.net
   DOMAINNAME=paunchy.net
   GATEWAY=192.168.32.254
   GATEWAYDEV=eth1
   ```

   The gateway points to the second Ethernet NIC eth1, which will have the address of 192.168.32.254. All packets destined for the Internet will now go through that interface.

5. Modify the `/etc/sysconfig/network-scripts/ifcfg-eth0` file to work with the new network configuration. Change the `IPADDR` parameter from 192.168.1.250 to 192.168.1.254.

   ```
   DEVICE=eth0
   IPADDR=192.168.1.254
   NETMASK=255.255.255.0
   NETWORK=192.168.32.0
   ```

```
BROADCAST=192.168.32.255
ONBOOT=yes
```

(If you have the `NISDOMAIN` parameter set don't change it.)

6. Create a new `ifcfg-eth1` file in `/etc/sysconfig/network-scripts` directory by copying the ifcfg-eth0.

```
cd /etc/sysconfig/network_scripts
cp ifcfg-eth0 ifcfg-eth1
```

7. The `ifcfg-eth1` file should contain the following information. It will sit on the DMZ network and will have an IP address of `192.168.32.254`.

```
DEVICE=eth1
IPADDR=192.168.32.254
NETMASK=255.255.255.0
NETWORK=192.168.32.0
BROADCAST=192.168.32.255
ONBOOT=yes
```

The 192.168.32.0 subnet will be referred to as the DMZ network.

8. Create the `/usr/local/etc/ipmasq.rules` script containing the following line.

```
ipchains -A forward -j MASQ -s 192.168.1.0/24
```

This rule converts (masquerades) all packets coming from the Private network. The masqueraded packets will inherit the network address of the second Ethernet interface — `192.168.32.254` — since that's where the default route points to.

CONVERTING ATLAS TO WORK ON THE DMZ

1. Log in to the Internet gateway `atlas` and shut it down.

```
Halt
```

2. Connect the Ethernet NIC to the DMZ network. Turn on the power switch.

3. Change the `/etc/sysconfig/network` script as follows.

```
NETWORKING=yes
FORWARD_IPV4=true
HOSTNAME=chivas.paunchy.net
DOMAINNAME=paunchy.net
GATEWAY=
GATEWAYDEV=
```

The `GATEWAY` and `GATEWAYDEV` entries are left blank because `diald` and `pppd` will dynamically create a default route (gateway) to the Internet.

4. Modify the `/etc/sysconfig/network-scripts/ifcfg-eth0` script as follows.

```
DEVICE=eth0
IPADDR=192.168.32.1
NETMASK=255.255.255.0
NETWORK=192.168.32.0
BROADCAST=192.168.32.255
ONBOOT=yes
```

5. Check the network connectivity of both machines on the appropriate networks as described in Chapters 1 and 2 and (hopefully it will be unnecessarily to refer to Chapter 3).

6. Check that `atlas` will dial up and connect to your ISP. You want to verify that `atlas` can communicate with the Internet before you worry about your private network.

7. Try sending a packet from `chivas` to the Internet. If you are lucky, it'll find its way out to the DMZ and then `atlas`. `atlas`, via `diald`, will fire up the modem, connect to your ISP and route the packet to the Internet.

8. If that test works, try browsing the network from any machine – Windows or Linux – on your private network.

This new firewall configuration is effective in several ways.

- It separates the firewall from the private network. Any intruder will first have to break into the firewall on the DMZ before attacking your private network.

- The Linux server `chivas` also gets into the firewall act. It effectively becomes a firewall via the masquerade mechanism. This masquerading system works in only one direction. Packets show up on `chivas`'s first Ethernet NIC and get converted to the IP of the second. When their return packets arrive at the second Ethernet NIC, they get converted back to their original IP address. However, any packets that show up at the second NIC, which don't match an existing connection, get dropped. This prevents any unauthorized connections.

- The DMZ provides a platform to place high-risk servers on. You can add an anonymous FTP server, for instance, to your menu and hang it on the DMZ. People will be able to access the server from the Internet, but you do not allow them any access to your private network.

FOLLOWING A PACKET TO THE INTERNET

If you want to understand how this new system works you should follow a packet from the Private network to the Internet.

1. Let's say that you are sitting at a `cementeros` on the Private network. You are using Netscape and click on your bookmark to my web page`http//www.swcp.com/~pgsery/rhltoolkit`.

2. Netscape sends a `gethostbyname` request to the Linux TCP/IP stack. The stack sends a request to the local DNS server `192.168.1.254`. If the DNS server cannot resolve the name locally and then sends the DNS request to the default route.

3. `diald` sees a packet show up on the default proxy interface `127.0.0.2` and fires up the modem, connects to the ISP and establishes a PPP connection.

4. The local name server finds the numeric IP address from the ISP's name server and returns it to the Linux workstation cementeros.

5. Netscape sends the first HTTP packet to the TCP/IP stack on cementeros. `cementeros` sends the packet to its default route. The default route is configured to send all packets to `192.168.1.254`. Thus, the packet goes onto the private network wire.

6. `chivas` picks up the packet. `chivas` sees the packet as destined for an external network and sends it to its own default route.

7. The `ipchains` system has a masquerading rule configured that converts every packet from the private network to the address of the default route NIC — `192.168.32.254`.

8. The packet inherits the source address of `192.168.32.254`. It goes onto the `DMZ` wire.

9. atlas picks up the packet. atlas sees the packet is destined for the Internet and and sends it to its own default address. The `ipchains` system has a masquerading rule configured that converts every packet from the DMZ network to the address of the default route NIC – ppp0.

10. The packet is routed through the ISP and finally finds its way to my web server. The web server processes it and sends it back to its source address. The source address is the masqueraded address of your ppp0 interface, which is most likely a dynamic address assigned by your ISP.

11. The `ipchains` program on `atlas` sees that the packet belongs to a masqueraded connection. It restores – de-masquerades – the packet. The destination address is converted from one belonging to the ppp0 interface to 192.168.32.1.

12. The return packet is routed back to `chivas` where it is de-masqueraded a second time. Its original source address and port number are given to the packet's destination address and port number. That packet is then send back to the original sender, which is cementeros in this case, and is displayed via Netscape.

13. The initial and all subsequent packets go out in the same way as described in steps 1 through 12.

Managing your Firewall

Maintaining a firewall is a lot of work, and there is no way around that fact. The following maintenance and observation tips are oriented towards pointing you in the right direction and should not be considered to be definitive. Firewall management, like every other aspect of computer security, is a moving target.

- ◆ The people and organizations who attempt to gain unauthorized access to your firewall and private computers are diverse in both scope and ability. There is no way to predict who will try to compromise your firewall or how. It is best to educate yourself about the bad guys. Please see the URLs in the section "Educate Yourself" in Chapter 12 for more information.

- ◆ Your log files (`/var/log`) provide a good mechanism to observe what is happening to your firewall. Keep a careful eye on them.

- ◆ You can effectively test your firewall with the nmap program. Please see the section "Using nmap" in Chapter 12 for more information.

- ◆ The `tripwire` program can tell you which files and directories have changed or been modified. Please see the section "Using tripwire" in Chapter 12 for more information.

- ◆ You can check your user passwords regularly with the crack system. Please see the section "Using crack" in Chapter 12 for more information.

Know your enemies

There is a great deal of media hype about computer and network break-ins. The problem that you face, now that you are immediately concerned with such issues, is making intelligent decisions about who and what the threats are.

Probably the best place to start is in a neutral position. Don't view the threat as either overwhelming or trivial. Many of the crackers out there do not have an intimate understanding of computers and the Internet protocols. They are referred to as kiddiescripters or scriptkiddies because they make use of readily available scripts and cracking tools.

On the other hand, there are enough smart crackers out there to worry about. There are both individuals and organized groups that make their living that way. The professionals have varying degrees of ability, of course, but they all should be treated as significant threats.

Whatever direction you are being attacked from, you can do a lot to protect yourself. The firewall described in this chapter is the essential cornerstone. Once it's in place, you need to actively monitor and manage it to assure that you present your best defense.

Know their tools and methods

There are numerous tools available to the unscrupulous cracker. One of them — nmap — is described in the section "Using nmap" in Chapter 12. You can investigate other tools by searching the Net.

There are also numerous methods for attacking systems. For instance, if you can gather information about a system or network, then you can go search the manufacturer's bug and vulnerability lists. By comparing the two lists you might be able to walk through an open door or slither through a crack. Another way is the well-publicized Denial of Service attack (DOS). By sending incorrect and incomplete packets into a computer, it is often possible to overload the internal network buffers of that computer and shut the service or entire computer down. No break-in occurs but the computer or network breaks down and all users are denied their use.

Again, this book is not intended to be an reference for security matters. It deliberately avoids detail on subjects such as this in order to concentrate on specific solutions. Please refer to the URLs listed in the section "Education is Your Firewall Too" to study this issue further.

Monitoring your log files

Your log files are often your best way of knowing what is happening, and has happened, to your system. They record system information about users and system processes. You can keep track of user logins and failures, modem/PPP connections to the Internet and many other functions.

There are many flags that you should keep an eye out for. Some of the most important are failed logins, logins at odd hours (that don't fit your users' general profiles), logins from unrecognized machines, etc. Also keep a close look at Super User (root) log ins. Limit the distribution of the root account password to yourself and one or two other people. Do not write down the password. In that way, it is possible to know when an unauthorized root login has occurred. The last command lists user logins. The last log shows the time of the last login for each of the users.

Keep an eye out for unusual /var/log/messages system information. The system logs much of its information to that file.

Other logs of interest are secure, xfer.log and the samba logs. The secure log records incoming connections to the Linux services (Telnet, imap, etc.). The xfer.log keeps track of data transfers from the Linux computer. The samba logs keep track of external Samba connections.

Troubleshooting

The two most difficult systems to install and maintain are the `ipchains` filtering firewall and the DNS server. Some basic troubleshooting hints and techniques are described in this section. The other systems discussed in this chapter deal with the monitoring and maintenance of the above services and are not difficult to set up or use.

IP chains

Setting up IP chains can be a confusing task at first. It's difficult to understand which packets are going where and through which interface. It is also hard to keep track of how the source and destination addresses — and port numbers — interact with the filtering rules.

When designing new rules or modifying existing ones, it is best to write out the rules on a piece of paper in order to get a better understanding of them. Make separate diagrams and lists for each direction: outgoing packets, incoming, and forwarding. (If you continue to use a simple network with a single Linux gateway, then the only forwarding rule that you're ever likely to need is the masquerading one.)

Once you have put into place the new rules, or are trying to better understand existing ones, then you can use the `dctrl` and `tcpdump` utilities.

The `dctrl diald` connection GUI provides a display of open TCP and UDP network connections. The source, destination and port information is shown. You can see new connections open up and old ones end. It is quite useful for seeing what is going on at your PPP connection.

The `tcpdump` is a packet sniffer. It comes as part of the Red Hat distribution and you can install it by logging in as root and entering the command `rpm -ivh /mnt/cdrom/RedHat/RPMS/tcpdump*`. This is a powerful tool because you can see every network packet that goes through your PPP connection. (You can also see every packet that goes by any network connection on your machine. This is one of the commonly used tools for sniffing information off a network. With enough experience and patience, you can discover passwords and other vital information. Beware.) If you are having problems getting a filter to work, then you can watch what packets are showing up at your PPP interface. With some work it is possible to then relate those packets back to your rule set and hopefully find the errant filtering rule.

Finally, you can try backing off on your filtering rules. Define a rule set that sets up default deny policies — as done in this book's `ipchains` scripts — but then set up input and output rules in each direction that allow all packets. For instance, try the following rules.

```
ipchains -F
ipchains -P output DENY
ipchains -P input DENY
ipchains -P forward DENY
ipchains -A output -j ACCEPT -s 0.0.0.0/0 -d 0.0.0.0/0
ipchains -A input -j ACCEPT -s 0.0.0.0/0 -d 0.0.0.0/0
```

These rules flush out any existing rules (it is essential to start from scratch when debugging filtering rules) and then set up a uniform denial policy. At that point your firewall is shut down tight. The final two rules open up the firewall to tcp, udp and icmp packets, coming from any location and going to any location from any port. Your firewall is now completely open.

Test your system and whatever Internet access you are after should work. The next step is to discover what IP protocol is getting stuck. Change the rules to include separate ones for both the TCP and UDP protocols as follows:

```
ipchains -F
ipchains -P output DENY
ipchains -P input DENY
ipchains -P forward DENY
ipchains -A output -p tcp -j ACCEPT -s 0.0.0.0/0 -d 0.0.0.0/0
ipchains -A input  -p tcp -j ACCEPT -s 0.0.0.0/0 -d 0.0.0.0/0
ipchains -A output -p udp -j ACCEPT -s 0.0.0.0/0 -d 0.0.0.0/0
ipchains -A input  -p udp -j ACCEPT -s 0.0.0.0/0 -d 0.0.0.0/0
```

You have now separated out the TCP and UDP protocols; the ICMP protocol is ignored in this example for simplicity and because it isn't a factor in nearly as many transactions as the other two. Try modifying the source and destination addresses to their correct values (for instance, for outgoing UDP packets set the source address to your PPP IP address.) You should consult the ipfilter.rules script for the details of the process.

Test your system again. Once you have narrowed the problem down to a protocol, then you need to find out the port.

Next, try setting up rules for the individual interfaces. You should pay particular attention to your internal interfaces such as eth0 and lo. It is very easy to set up rules for those interfaces that interfere with or deny communication on your Private Network. Once again, please refer to the ipfilter.rules script for more details.

Without going into more detail, you get the idea. As with all other troubleshooting, you want to successively narrow down the problem until you arrive at the solution.

Masquerading

If you are having problems getting masquerading to work, then first check that you have enabled IP forwarding in your Linux gateway. Check the file /etc/sysconfig/network and make sure that the IPFORWARD_IPV4 line is set to yes.

```
IPFORWARD_IPV4=yes
```

You need to restart your Linux networking to make the new rule take effect.

```
/etc/rc.d/init.d/network restart
```

Next, check that the masquerading rule has actually been set up with the `ipchains -L` command. You should see the following.

```
Chain forward (policy DENY):
target     prot opt    source          destination         ports
MASQ       all  ------  192.168.1.0/24  anywhere            n/a
```

If you still can not find the problem, then refer to Chapter 7 to make sure that your network connections are working correctly. Next, check the HOWTO documents and man pages.

Summary

This chapter describes how to set up a firewall to protect your Private Network from the worst of the Internet. The `ipchains` system is used as the heart of the firewall. It provides IP filtering that provides excellent protection for your private network. When combined with monitoring and testing tools, the firewall can be maintained to provide maximum protection at a reasonable cost.

Topics covered in this chapter include:

- An introduction to firewalls. Three basic types are described. The advantages of each are briefly discussed and the reasoning for the use of a hybrid firewall in this book is given.

- An introduction to the `ipchains` system. Its basic functions are explained. A simple example is given.

- Configuring a simple filtering firewall. A basic set of `ipchains` rules are described so that you can interactively experiment with them. By getting a feel for how the system works you can better install and manage the full rule set.

- A description of a full filtering rule set. It is displayed in the text but also stored on the companion CD-ROM. The rule set provides a template that allows the major protocols (such as www and FTP) to work through your firewall. You can modify the script to allow other protocols through your firewall as desired.

- The process of checking your log files. Log files provide you with the history of your system. By studying them, you can discover problems and possible break-ins before they progress too far.

Chapter 12

Securing your Server

IN THIS CHAPTER

♦ Adding active security measures to your network

♦ Detecting security problems before they occur with SATAN, crack, and tripwire

♦ Adding passive security measures to your network

♦ Increasing security and reducing the load on your Internet connection

♦ Removing all unnecessary daemons and applications from your firewall server

YOU CAN NEVER "FINISH" UP your security. As you grow as a systems administrator/ security monitor, you can add to the picture as you see fit. This chapter guides you through the process of layering security. You add both active and passive security measures to your network. Placing security-oriented software – active systems – on your critical servers, `atlas` and `chivas`, starts the process. You then refine the configuration – passive measures – of your servers in order to further enhance your security.

Layering your Security Measures

The concept of layered security was introduced in Chapter 9. The idea is to put as many layers between you and the bad guys as you can.

Determining exactly how to layer your security is a difficult process. Install too few layers and you'll end up compromised. Put in too many, and you'll end up reducing safety and the usability when your system becomes too complex to manage effectively. The complexity and size of your network and the type of users you support will determine what you need.

This chapter introduces some straightforward measures that will enhance your security without overwhelming you.

Adding Active Security to your Network

The `tripwire` and `nmap` systems, introduced in Chapter 9, are two useful programs to start building security into your network. Recall that tripwire uses the MD5 (message digest algorithm) to calculate a checksum on important system files (any file you wish to check, actually). These checksums can periodically be compared to the current files to see if any files have been changed to possibly hide a Trojan horse. `nmap` scans the hosts on your network to discover what operating systems they are running and what services they are providing.

In addition to presenting tripwire and `nmap`, this chapter introduces the crack system. It checks your existing passwords against words that can be found in dictionaries. By using crack, you can proactively protect your system from trivial or easily guessed passwords.

Using tripwire

`tripwire` is available as an RPM package on this book's CD-ROM. It is generally not considered good security practice to install a binary (especially of a code that is used for security itself) rather than to compile source code. The worry is that the binary can more readily hide viruses and back doors (fixed passwords or other entrances known only to the designer of the executable code) than source code can. However, I consider Red Hat to be a reliable source and trust them to have taken every reasonable precaution. Therefore, I have installed it on my system but leave it up to you to decide for yourself whether you accept my reasoning. If you wish to obtain the source code, it is available from a SunSITE.

I use tripwire on my File Server/Router. In my network, this is the most important computer, so I want to keep it as secure as possible. `tripwire` can also be configured to check other computers on the network (for example, the Firewall Server), so as long as it has access to the firewall network, it can be placed anywhere. The following instructions detail the installation of tripwire:

1. Log in to `atlas` as `root`.

2. Mount your IDG supplemental CD-ROM:

   ```
   mount /mnt/cdrom
   ```

3. Install `tripwire` by entering the following command:

   ```
   rpm -ivh /mnt/cdrom/security/tripwire-*.rpm
   ```

   `tripwire` is installed into the directories.

   ```
   /etc/cron.daily/tripwire.verify
   /etc/tw.config
   /usr/doc/tripwire-1.2-1
   ```

```
/usr/doc/tripwire-1.2-1/Changelog
/usr/doc/tripwire-1.2-1/FAQ
/usr/doc/tripwire-1.2-1/INTERNALS
/usr/doc/tripwire-1.2-1/README
/usr/doc/tripwire-1.2-1/README.FIRST
/usr/doc/tripwire-1.2-1/Readme
/usr/doc/tripwire-1.2-1/TODO
/usr/doc/tripwire-1.2-1/WHATSNEW
/usr/doc/tripwire-1.2-1/docs
/usr/doc/tripwire-1.2-1/docs/README
/usr/doc/tripwire-1.2-1/docs/appdev.txt
/usr/doc/tripwire-1.2-1/docs/designdoc.ps
/usr/doc/tripwire-1.2-1/docs/sans.txt
/usr/man/man5/tw.config.5
/usr/man/man8/siggen.8
/usr/man/man8/tripwire.8
/usr/sbin/siggen
/usr/sbin/tripwire
/var/spool/tripwire
```

4. Look at the `tripwire` configuration file, `/etc/tw.config`, which is partially shown below.

```
# $Id: tw.config,v 1.4 1993/11/22 06:38:06 genek Exp $
#
#     tw.config
#
{...}
@@define LOGFILEM E+pugn

# Config file
@@define CONFM E+pinugc

# Binary
@@define BINM E+pnugsci12

# Directory
@@define DIRM E+pnug

# Data file (same as BIN_M currently)
@@define DATAM E+pnugsci12

# Device files
@@define DEVM E+pnugsci

#
```

```
#
#     Ex: The following entry will scan all the files in
#         /etc, and report
#    Templates:        (default)  R :  [R]ead-only
{...}
# exclude all of /proc
=/proc E

#=/dev @@DIRM
/dev @@DEVM

#=/etc @@DIRM
/etc @@CONFM

# Binary directories
#=/usr/sbin @@DIRM
/usr/sbin @@BINM

#=/usr/bin @@DIRM
/usr/bin @@BINM

#=/sbin @@DIRM
/sbin @@BINM

#=/bin @@DIRM
/bin @@BINM

#=/lib @@DIRM
/lib @@BINM

#=/usr/lib @@DIRM
/usr/lib @@BINM

=/usr/src E

=/tmp @@DIRM
```

The configuration file tells tripwire to check each of the standard system directories/dev, /etc, /usr/sbin, /sbin, /bin, /lib, and /usr/lib. Each of these directories has a macro associate with it that tells tripwire what parameters to check . For instance, the macro for /usr/lib is @@BINM, which is specified at the top of the file. Its attributes are E+pnugsci12, which means that tripwire checks every possible change (please see the list of attributes in the beginning of the file).

The tripwire operations modes

tripwire has four operational modes:

◆ **Database generation.** tripwire needs a database of initial file integrity checksums to check current files against. It uses the configuration file /etc/tw.config to determine which files to generate checksums. This mode creates such a database.

◆ **Database update.** This mode updates the database to account for files that have legitimately been changed.

◆ **Interactive update.** This mode performs the same task as the previous one but prompts the user for which files to check.

◆ **Integrity checking.** This mode has tripwire check current files against their known, good values stored in the database.

You can tell tripwire to check on the directories of other machines on the network by defining the IFHOST macro.

A template also exists for a shell script that can be run daily by cron to check your system's integrity. The next several files are all documents describing tripwire. I recommend you read the FAQ and the README files; README.FIRST deals more with compilation issues so you can skip it. There are three man-page files. The siggen file is a program that lets you generate tripwire signatures without running tripwire itself.

For now, leave tripwire as is. I leave it to you to experiment with it as you gain experience with your system.

5. Next, you need to have tripwire initialize its database. tripwire can take a long time to run depending on the complexity of your system and its speed, so give yourself some time to run it.

Enter the following command (as root) to initialize the database:

```
tripwire -init
```

tripwire chugs away. If it finishes without problems, it looks like this.

```
###     Warning:    creating ./databases directory!
###
###     Phase 1:    Reading configuration file
###     Phase 2:    Generating file list
###     Phase 3:    Creating file information database
```

```
###
###     Warning:   Database file placed in
###     ./databases/tw.db_bart.tulane.com.
###
###         Make sure to move this file and the configuration
###             to secure media!
###
###             (tripwire expects to find it in
###             '/var/spool/tripwire'.)
```

6. Next, test your new system by making a trivial change to a system file. I recommend that you change a file that is changed often so that you don't have to recompile the `tripwire` database again. The `/etc/passwd` file is changed whenever you add or delete a user, so it is a good choice. (Otherwise, if you change a file like `/bin/login`, you could confuse yourself later on if you ever check it against the original distribution.) The `touch` program will modify the file timestamp without doing anything else (note that `tripwire` will not show that a file has been changed if you change the modification date and do not specify the modification timestamp — `m` — in the tw.config file). Enter the following command:

   `touch /etc/passwd`

7. Now run the `tripwire` integrity check by entering the following command:

   `tripwire -interactive`

8. `tripwire` shows that `/etc/passwd` has been modified.

   ```
   changed: crw-------  root   0   Oct 22 02:09:34 1999 /dev/ttyp2
   changed: drwxr-xr-x  root   333 Oct 22 02:10:22 1999 /etc
   changed: -rw-r--r--  root   589 Oct 22 02:09:53 1999/etc/passwd
   ```

   `tripwire` prompts you to update its database with the changed file. You have the option to enter **y** or **n** to update the database for that file or not. You also have the option to update all the files in which changes have been detected by entering **y**, but unless you are sure that you are the only person to have changed anything, I advise against doing so. Checking each file may be a lot of work, but it is an important process so you should just resign yourself to it.

9. Because your goal is to reliably check your current files for compromise, you must keep your database safe and pristine. You should not leave it on the machine that `tripwire` is to protect. The best way to store it is to copy it to a CD-ROM. But that isn't practical for most people, so a reasonable alternative is to copy it to a floppy, and flip the disk's write-protect tab. Doing so enables you to automatically run `tripwire` from `cron`. (If you require a more secure installation you could store the disk in a safe place. That prevents you from automatically running `tripwire` from `cron` but removes the possibility of the disk being physically modified.)

A compromise is to keep the `tripwire` database on the File Server/Router and create a separate checksum on it alone. You can take the simple precaution of marking it as readable by root alone to prevent anyone without root access from modifying it. Of course, if someone has modified a system file such as the `login` command to allow secret access as root, they can still modify the database. To minimize that possibility, you can then use your databases stored on floppy to check both the system database and the database checksum on a weekly or semiweekly basis. That way, if someone does compromise your system database you'll at least know it eventually and at the same time you can automate the daily checks.

TIP

If you have another Linux computer on your network, you can use it as your read-only file system. Store the `tripwire` database on the Linux computer and use NFS to export the file system read-only. Then, you can create a `cron` job on any Linux computer on the network to mount the file system and run `tripwire`. As long as the `tripwire` server is a well secured system, you will be able to run `tripwire` securely.

10. The Red Hat RPM `tripwire` package places the file `tripwire.verify` in the `/etc/cron.daily` directory. It is run automatically by `cron` every night in the early morning. The results are e-mailed to root. If nothing has been changed, the results appear as shown as below. This is another good function that comes ready to run out of the box. Log in as root and check your `tripwire` mail daily. Periodically compare the stored database to the one you saved on floppy disk.

```
Received: (from root@localhost)
          by chivas.paunchy.com (8.8.5/8.8.5) id BAA01746
          for root; Wed, 30 Jul 1997 01:14:07 -0600
Date: Wed, 30 Jul 1997 01:14:07 -0600
From: root <root@chivas.paunchy.net>
Message-Id: <199707300714.BAA01746@chivas.paunchy.net>
To: root@chivas.paunchy.net
Subject: File integrity report
Status: R
```

This is an automated report of possible file integrity changes, generated by the `tripwire` integrity checker. To tell `tripwire` that a file or entire directory tree is valid, as root run:

```
/usr/sbin/tripwire -update [pathname|entry]
```

11. Repeat steps 1 through 10 on `chivas` and any other Linux servers and workstations that you want to protect in this fashion.

Using crack

Your passwords are your first — and often last — line of defense. Linux makes it difficult to choose trivial or easily guessed passwords, but it is still important to check them. The cracker library makes the checking process a simple task to do.

The cracker program checks a file — either your `/etc/passwd` or `/etc/shadow` file — against dictionaries of common words and phrases. It looks at each word in the dictionary and encrypts it using the same algorithm that the Linux `passwd` program uses to generate the encrypted word that it generates after you enter your plain-text password. If the encrypted word matches one found in a passwd file, then it has found a match.

1. Log in to `chivas` as `root`.

2. Mount the IDG supplemental CD-ROM

   ```
   mount /mnt/cdrom
   ```

3. Install `crack` by entering the following command

   ```
   rpm -ivh /mnt/cdrom/security/crack*.rpm
   ```

   It installs itself into the `/root/crack-4.1f` directory because root should be the only user with access to it.

4. To run a check on the `/etc/passwd` file (`/etc/shadow` if you have installed shadow passwords), enter the following command:

   ```
   /root/crack-4.1f/Crack /etc/passwd
   ```

5. crack shows some information on the screen and then announces that it is running as a background task. After it is finished, it writes the results of its search to a file with the process ID as its suffix, such as `out.1978`. For demonstration purposes, I removed the password completely for `chivas` and ran a test on it.

   ```
   join: Dec 19 21:05:18 User xfs (in /etc/passwd) has a locked
   password:- !!
   join: Dec 19 21:05:18 User uucp (in /etc/passwd) has a locked
   password:- *
   join: Dec 19 21:05:18 User operator (in /etc/passwd) has a
   locked password:- *
   join: Dec 19 21:05:18 User bin (in /etc/passwd) has a locked
   password:- *
   join: Dec 19 21:05:18 User games (in /etc/passwd) has a
   locked password:- *
   join: Dec 19 21:05:18 User gopher (in /etc/passwd) has a
   locked password:- *
   join: Dec 19 21:05:18 User ftp (in /etc/passwd) has a locked
   password:- *
   ```

```
join: Dec 19 21:05:18 User daemon (in /etc/passwd) has a
locked password:- *
join: Dec 19 21:05:18 User adm (in /etc/passwd) has a locked
password:- *
join: Dec 19 21:05:18 User gdm (in /etc/passwd) has a locked
password:- !!
join: Dec 19 21:05:18 User lp (in /etc/passwd) has a locked
password:- *
join: Dec 19 21:05:18 Warning! rodbush (/home/rodbush in
/etc/passwd) has a NULL password!
join: Dec 19 21:05:18 User sync (in /etc/passwd) has a locked
password:- *
join: Dec 19 21:05:18 User shutdown (in /etc/passwd) has a
locked password:- *
join: Dec 19 21:05:18 User halt (in /etc/passwd) has a locked
password:- *
join: Dec 19 21:05:18 User mail (in /etc/passwd) has a locked
password:- *
join: Dec 19 21:05:18 User news (in /etc/passwd) has a locked
password:- *
join: Dec 19 21:05:18 User nobody (in /etc/passwd) has a
locked password:- *
```

As you can see, it found that the user rodbush has no password. (The standard Linux users have locked passwords, which means they can never be used as regular users.) That is unacceptable and I will add a password to it immediately. The /etc/passwd file used in this example is shown below.

```
root:asfdha;sdlfk:0:0:root:/root:/bin/bash
bin:*:1:1:bin:/bin:
daemon:*:2:2:daemon:/sbin:
adm:*:3:4:adm:/var/adm:
lp:*:4:7:lp:/var/spool/lpd:
sync:*:5:0:sync:/sbin:/bin/sync
shutdown:*:6:0:shutdown:/sbin:/sbin/shutdown
halt:*:7:0:halt:/sbin:/sbin/halt
mail:*:8:12:mail:/var/spool/mail:
news:*:9:13:news:/var/spool/news:
uucp:*:10:14:uucp:/var/spool/uucp:
operator:*:11:0:operator:/root:
games:*:12:100:games:/usr/games:
gopher:*:13:30:gopher:/usr/lib/gopher-data:
ftp:*:14:50:FTP User:/home/ftp:
nobody:*:99:99:Nobody:/:
xfs:!!:100:101:X Font Server:/etc/X11/fs:/bin/false
```

```
gdm:!!:42:42::/home/gdm:/bin/bash
paul:$1$dL7q5FEh$grmibnKLKASA4oF05Dg.S.:500:500::/home/paul:/
bin/bash
```

6. I want to add a not-too-difficult password to the user rodbush before I put my original, rather difficult one back in place. I run the passwd program and enter the string mybook as the new password. The passwd program objects to that choice by telling me that mybook is based on a dictionary word. Obviously, my and book are two real words that are simply joined together. I want to test crack, however, so I go ahead and confirm mybook and run crack again. It does not find the password even though passwd objected — but did not reject it. Combining two words was enough to foil this attempt at breaking into my own system.

7. Finally, copy the /etc/passwd (or /etc/shadow) file from the Linux computers on your network (atlas, cementeros, puma, etc.) and run crack on them. Change any passwords that are discovered.

8. Remove each password file once you run crack on it.

 Do not install crack on atlas. The last thing that you want to do is leave an intruder such a great tool to use against you.

Using nmap

The nmap program is a powerful security tool. It can be used for good purposes or not. It can be used against you, so, since it can be obtained off the Internet, you should use it to protect your network.

 You should not, under any circumstances, use nmap to scan machines that you do not control, or have permission to scan. Using nmap in an unauthorized manner is similar to walking up to a house and rattling the door. It is okay to test your own door, but not someone else's.

nmap does three things: simple and flexible pings, port scans, and computer fingerprinting. The functions are as follows:

♦ **Pings.** You can use nmap to see what machines are up on a network. The ping program sends out simple ICMP packets and displays their response. It is a workhorse for system administrators who want to see if a network device is alive.

◆ **Port scan.** This is the process where `nmap` sends TCP, UDP and ICMP packets with various settings to a host or entire network and the response is monitored. `nmap` can determine what ports are available (listening) depending on what the response is.

◆ **Fingerprinting.** A variation of the port scan sends out packets of varying type and setting. The responses can be correlated to determine what operating system is running on the target.

When you put all three (especially the latter two) functions together, you can gather a great deal of information about individual machines and the entire network. The more you know about a network, the more possibilities there are for attack. You should know at least as much about your network as an intruder, and `nmap` can help you do that.

`nmap` is a difficult system to master, because it takes a good understanding of the underlying TCP/IP protocols to make complete sense of the information that it can give you. The following examples are meant to give you a sense of what `nmap` can do and how to use the results (the `ping` function is useful but is skipped over in this discussion for the sake of brevity).

 Most of the interesting scans must be performed as root.

PORT SCAN YOUR LINUX SERVER

Log in as root on your Linux Internet gateway – `atlas` – and install the `nmap` package.

```
rpm -ivh /mnt/cdrom/security/nmap*
```

Run the following `nmap` scan against yourself.

```
nmap -sS 192.168.1.254
```

This is SYN scan. It sends the first part of a TCP handshake used for opening a TCP connection such as a Telnet session. When a response is sent, `nmap` sends another packet that immediately clears the connection. The result is that you can get a response from all active ports and the target system probably doesn't log any of the partial connections. That means you get the information but probably don't leave any trace.

The results from the default Red Hat installation without any firewall are as follows.

```
Starting nmap V. 2.07 by Fyodor (fyodor@dhp.com,
```

```
www.insecure.org/nmap/)
Interesting ports on atlas.paunchy.net (192.168.1.250):
Port     State        Protocol     Service
21       open         tcp          ftp
23       open         tcp          telnet
25       open         tcp          smtp
37       open         tcp          time
53       open         tcp          domain
70       open         tcp          gopher
79       open         tcp          finger
98       open         tcp          tacnews
109      open         tcp          pop-2
110      open         tcp          pop-3
111      open         tcp          sunrpc
113      open         tcp          auth
139      open         tcp          netbios-ssn
143      open         tcp          imap2
513      open         tcp          login
514      open         tcp          shell
515      open         tcp          printer
963      open         tcp          unknown
984      open         tcp          unknown
989      open         tcp          unknown
994      open         tcp          unknown
1024     open         tcp          unknown
1080     open         tcp          socks
6000     open         tcp          xterm
7100     open         tcp          font-service

Nmap run completed -- 1 IP address (1 host up) scanned in 1 second
```

That list corresponds to the /etc/services file. Those are the ports that are potential targets for all sorts of mischief. One way to tighten up your system is to eliminate all the services that you don't use. Services such as finger and gopher can be removed or commented out of your /etc/services file.

PORT SCAN ANOTHER LINUX BOX

Run a Stealth FIN port scan against another Linux box on your network. Enter the command.

```
nmap -sF 192.168.1.100
```

This scan is an attempt to use a combination of TCP packet flags to hide from detection programs. The results from an unprotected Linux computer are similar to the previous listing, and are not shown here for brevity's sake. But the end result is the same – you get more information about a system without necessarily revealing yourself.

PORT SCAN A WINDOWS COMPUTER

Run a port scan against a Windows machine.

```
nmap -sS 192.168.1.1
```

Returns the following:

```
Starting nmap V. 2.07 by Fyodor (fyodor@dhp.com, www.insecure.org/nmap/)
Interesting ports on toluca.paunchy.net (192.168.1.1):
Port    State        Protocol  Service
139     open         tcp       netbios-ssn
617     open         tcp       unknown
Nmap run completed -- 1 IP address (1 host up) scanned in 1 second
```

There is an unknown and a NetBIOS port. You could potentially use this information to attack the Windows box. For instance, a denial of service attack might be mounted against the NetBIOS.

FINGERPRINTING YOUR NETWORK

Now try detecting the operating systems that are running on your network. Enter the command.

```
nmap -sS -O 192.168.1.0/24
```

You should see all the unprotected network devices as follows:

```
Starting nmap V. 2.07 by Fyodor (fyodor@dhp.com, www.insecure.org/nmap/)
Interesting ports on toluca.paunchy.net (192.168.1.100):
Port    State        Protocol  Service
139     open         tcp       netbios-ssn

TCP Sequence Prediction: Class=trivial time dependency
                        Difficulty=0 (Trivial joke)
Remote operating system guess: Windows NT4 / Win95 / Win98

TCP Sequence Prediction: Class=truly random
{... the Linux ports edited out to reduce the length of this listing...}
                        Difficulty=9999999 (Good luck!)
Remote operating system guess: Linux 2.0.35-36
Nmap run completed -- 256 IP addresses (2 host up) scanned in 56 seconds
```

This shows that the paunchy.net network has two machines running without firewalls (and where Fyodor's preferences are!). Both operating systems are accurately detected; in fact almost the exact Linux version is found.

PREVENTING SCANS WITH A FIREWALL

This example uses the Linux box `atlas`. Login to it and install the `ipchains` package, if necessary. The simple filter shown below turns off all network connections, so you need to be at the console to enter the rules. (You can make your own filter script that allows, say, a Telnet connection, if you want.) Enter the rules.

```
ipchains -P output DENY
ipchains -P input DENY
ipchains -P forward DENY
```

Run any of the scans from the previous examples; or try new ones. Enter the following:

```
nmap -sX atlas
```

After about a minute `nmap` returns the following:

```
Starting nmap V. 2.07 by Fyodor (fyodor@dhp.com, www.insecure.org/nmap/)
Nmap run completed -- 0 IP addresses (0 hosts up) scanned in 80 seconds
```

`nmap` was not able to detect any open ports because the filter either prevented the packets from ever getting to the Linux box's network layer or else the filter prevented any return packets from getting back to the `nmap` server.

Read the Web page maintained by the `nmap` creator at `www.insecure.org` for a much more in-depth – and interesting – discussion of `nmap`.

 Do not install `nmap` on `atlas`. The last thing that you want to do is leave an intruder such a great tool to use against you.

Adding Passive Security to Your Network

Now that you have installed and configured your active security measures – the IP filtering rules, the dial-up connection, `tripwire`, SATAN, `crack` and so on – it is important to address the passive side of security. It is necessary to close all the possible entrances that you can think of. To that end, I want you to eliminate all the

Linux daemons, application programs, and programming libraries that the firewall absolutely does not need. The idea is that the fewer pieces of software exist, the fewer the possible security holes you have. I have you remove stuff in the following sections, not because I know of any particular security hole, but because one may be lurking out there (or could be in the future). The idea is to start configuring your firewall on a "clean" machine.

Using Secure Shell

The private network that is used in this book is potentially vulnerable to attack because all of the information traveling on it is in plain text. Anyone connected to the network can potentially look at the packets flying by. It is also possible for someone outside your private network to look at your information that travels out onto the Internet. This is called *packet sniffing*, and the `tcpdump` RPM that comes with Red Hat Linux can be used to display and log such packets. Those packets contain interesting information such as passwords and any information that is being passed on the network.

The firewall introduced in Chapter 11 is designed to allow network traffic originating from within the private network to go out to the Internet and allow return packets back in. No traffic originating from outside the private network – the Internet – is allowed back in. This creates an effective firewall but limits its use when you are not physically present at your network.

One solution to both problems is to use Secure Shell. The newest version of Secure Shell (`ssh2`) encrypts the information contained in the network packets, which provides a high degree of privacy and safety for your valuable information. If you modify your firewall to allow Secure Shell packets into your network, you sacrifice a small amount of safety for the convenience of accessing your private network.

UNDERSTANDING SECURE SHELL

Secure Shell is software that allows you to communicate between two computers via an encrypted connection. Secure Shell also permits you to validate that the machine you are connecting to is the correct one.

Secure Shell makes it very difficult for anyone to sniff your communication. Secure Shell does not send your password or general communication in plain text. Communication programs like Telnet send everything in readable form; it is possible to intercept the packets and reconstruct them to reveal passwords and other information. Secure Shell solves that problem.

The first time you connect to a Secure Shell server, you do not have its public key unless you have already placed it there. You get the message "Accepting host chivas key without checking." This means that your client machine is receiving the public key of the server without being able to verify that the server is the correct server. The new key is stored in a file in the `.ssh/hostkeys` directory.

Encryption methods and keys

Secure Shell uses several encryption methods: IDEA, three-key triple-DES, DES or Blowfish. Discussion of these methods is beyond the scope of this book and you should look to the following URLs for more information:

```
http://www.employees.org/~satch/ssh/faq/ssh-faq-2.html#ss2.5.2
http://www.sunworld.com/sunworldonline/swol-02-1998/swol-02-security.html
```

Public and private keys

Secure Shell uses the concept of public and private keys to perform authentication. A *public key* is a sequence of randomly generated numbers that is available to everyone. A *private key* is a another random number that you do not share with anyone else. Information that is encrypted with a public key can only be decrypted by the private key and vice versa. The public and private keys are totally independent of each other and one can not be derived from the other. This method is called *RSA authentication*.

Host authentication

Secure Shell makes use of the public and private keys to verify that all parties are who they claim to be. When you attempt to connect to a remote computer both the client and server generate random strings. The strings are exchanged in such a way that the combination of public and private keys proves that both the client and server are valid. The details of the process is interesting but beyond the scope of this book. Please refer to the other documents and URLs mentioned in this chapter, and `http://www.spotch.com/~robjen/sa/ssh/ sshtalk-1/sld032.htm`, especially slides 32 through 37.

It is essential that both the client and server verify that they are both who they say they are. Without verification, it is possible that a third party can pretend to be either the client or server, a process called *spoofing*. For instance: You are computer A and want to connect to computer B. However, if computer C pretends to be B by using the same IP address as B, then you might connect to C and send your valuable information to C. This is called a *man-in-the-middle* attack.

However, if you encrypt a random string, and send it to C, but do not get the same string back, then you know that the computer you are talking to either has changed keys or is a fake. RSA authentication prevents DNS, IP, and routing spoofing.

Secure Shell is based on a client-server model. You run a client program — ssh2 — to connect to a server daemon — ssh2d — on a remote computer. Once connected, you can interact with the remote computer as if you were sitting at its console.

User authentication

When you are creating your user keys with `ssh-keygen2` (discussed later in this chapter) you are asked to enter a *pass phrase*. The phrase can be up to 20 characters long and can include spaces. During the authentication process you are prompted for your pass phrase. Once it is correctly entered, you are logged onto the remote system. If the host authentication process fails, or you enter the wrong pass phrase, then Secure Shell reverts to the normal login process and you need to enter your regular login account password (You can turn off the normal login process in order to allow only pass phrase authentication. Please see the section "Configuring General Parameters" for more information).

Please see the URLs listed in the section "Encryption Methods" for more information on this subject.

 The article at the second URL discusses the operation of the first version of Secure Shell. Please keep in mind that Secure Shell 2 — used in this book — configures the keys differently from the version discussed in the article, but that overall the concept is the same.

DOWNLOADING SECURE SHELL

The Linux/UNIX version of Secure Shell is available via the Internet (`http://www.ssh.fi/sshprotocols2`) for non-commercial users only. Secure Shell must be purchased if it is to be used for commercial purposes. Please read the license agreement to determine whether you can legally use the publicly available version. The SSH Communication Security's home page at `http://www.ssh.fi` contains more product information.

 Data Fellows Ltd. at `http://www.datafellows.com` is a licensed reseller of Secure Shell products. In addition to the commercial version of Secure Shell, they also provide a free commercial trial version of Secure Shell.

To download the RPM version of `ssh2`, proceed as follows:

1. Log in to `atlas` as `root`.

2. Move to the /usr/local/src directory.

   ```
   cd /usr/local/src
   ```

3. Connect to `http//rufus.w3.org/linux/RPM/replay/crypto/linux/redhat/i386`.

4. Download the `ssh2`, `ssh2-client`, `ssh2-server`, and `ssh2-extras` RPMs.

INSTALLING AND CONFIGURING SECURE SHELL

Secure Shell requires that the machine to be connected to – the server – runs the `sshd2` daemon. You can connect to that machine from any other machine – the client – by using the `ssh2` client program once that you have configured both the client and server. The following sections describe how to configure both sides.

 TIP Your Secure Shell server and client can be placed on the same machine. Simply translate the following instructions for installing and configuring your client machine to your server. This is a good method to test Secure Shell if you do not have multiple Linux computers to work on.

INSTALLING SECURE SHELL ON THE SERVER COMPUTER   In this example, the Linux Internet gateway and firewall server `atlas` will function as the Secure Shell server. Any Linux computer on your network can provide this function. By placing one on the gateway, however, you can gain access to your private network from the Internet. (There is no limit on how many Secure Shell servers you can have. If you want to make your internal network more secure, then every Linux computer that you interactively communicate with should be a Secure Shell server.)

1. Log in to `atlas` as `root`.

2. Install the Secure Shell packages.

   ```
   rpm -ivh /usr/local/src/ssh2*
   ```

3. This command installs the `ssh2`, `ssh2-clients`, `ssh2-extras`, and `ssh2-server` RPM packages. When the `ssh2` RPM (the base package) is installed, it generates the public key (`hostkey.pub`) and private key (`hostkey`) as shown:

   ```
   Generating 1024 bit host key. This may take a while, go and
   have a coffee ;)
   Generating 1024-bit dsa key pair
   1 oOo.oOo.oOOo
   ```

   The process can take several minutes depending on the speed of your computer. The keys that it generates are stored in the `/etc/ssh2` directory.

4. When the `ssh2-server` RPM is installed it starts the `sshd2` daemon (and also installs the start up script `sshd2` in the `/etc/rc.d/init.d` directory).

At that point your Secure Shell server is ready to accept connections from clients. However, you still need to configure your client.

INSTALLING SECURE SHELL ON THE CLIENT COMPUTER   Only the Secure Shell base (ssh2) and client package (ssh2-clients) need to be installed on a client computer. In this example, chivas, the Linux file and print server, is used as the client.

1. Log in to chivas as root.

2. Install the Secure Shell base and client RPMs as follows.

   ```
   rpm -ivh /usr/local/src/ssh2-2*
   rpm -ivh /usr/local/src/ssh2-clients*
   ```

3. While the ssh2 base package is installing it will generate the client's keys. However, you will need to generate your own user keys. In this example the user frankcastle is used. Create that user with the useradd frankcastle command and create a password. Change to that user with the su - frankcastle command and run the following command.

   ```
   ssh-keygen2
   ```

4. The computer will spend more time generating the user's public and private keys. It will prompt you to enter a pass phrase, which is the Secure Shell equivalent of a password. The phrase can be up to 20 characters long, and can include space characters. Use your good judgment in creating a good password.

5. Once you enter the pass phrase, ssh-keygen2 places the public and private keys in the .ssh2 directory (which it creates). That directory is placed in the user's home directory which, in this case, is /home/frankcastle. The public file is called id_dsa_1024_a.pub and the private one is id_dsa_1024_a. Once again, the public file can be transported across the network, while the private one should be kept secret.

6. Next, you need to create an identification file on the client. That file tells the ssh2 client where to go to find its private key – id_dsa_1024_a in this case. From the user's home directory, change to the .ssh2 directory.

   ```
   cd ~/.ssh2
   ```

7. Enter the following command to create the identification file.

   ```
   echo "IdKey  id_dsa_1024_a" > identification
   ```

   The contents of /home/frankcastle/.ssh2/identification file will be as follows.

   ```
   IdKey id_dsa_1024_a
   ```

Secure Shell looks to the identification file to find out the name of the user's private key. This arrangement means that you can have multiple private keys assigned to each user. However, this example does not make use of that capability.

CONFIGURING THE SERVER COMPUTER   Now that you have created your personal public and private keys, you need to copy the public key to the server that you want access to.

1. Log in to the atlas as a regular user – in this case frankcastle (create the user with the useradd frankcastle command if necessary).

2. From the user's home directory, /home/frankcastle, create the .ssh2 directory.

   ```
   mkdir .ssh2
   ```

3. Go into the .ssh2 directory (cd ~/.ssh2) and copy the user frankcastle's public key – id_dsa_1024_a.pub – from the client computer. Use any method you want – smbclient, FTP or even sftp – to make the transfer, but be aware that anyone who intercepts the key before you install it on the server will conceivably be able to perform a man-in-the-middle attack. This is probably a remote possibility for most people, but beware. Therefore, it is considered good practice to use a floppy or some other media to hand carry the public key from machine to machine in order not to transport the key over a possibly porous network. Whether you want to take such precautions is up to you and depends on the degree of security that you want to maintain.

4. Once you have copied the id_dsa_1024_a.pub file to the server, rename it. The /usr/doc/ssh2*/SSH-QUICKSTART document uses the convention of calling it Local.pub. However, I personally find it easier to name the key after the user who will use it to connect.

   ```
   mv id_dsa_1024_a.pub key_of_frankcastle.pub
   ```

5. Create the authorization file in the .ssh2 directory on the server as follows.

   ```
   echo "Key    key_of_frankcastle.pub" > authorization
   ```

   The Secure Shell server daemon will look in the user's authorization file in the .ssh2 directory for the file containing user's public key on the server.

6. Both the server and client need to know the other's public keys for Secure Shell to work. The final configuration step requires you to copy the server's public key to your client. From atlas, copy the /etc/ssh2/ hostkey.pub file to key_22_atlas.pub in the /home/frankcastle/

.ssh2 directory. The new name contains the sshd2 port number – 22 – and the name of the server – atlas.

CHECKING THE CLIENT AND SERVER'S CONFIGURATION FILES The user frankcastle should have the following configuration and key files on the client and server. Note that the file random_seed is not discussed here because it is used by the Secure Shell programs and is not directly configured, or used, by the user, and is not included in Table 12-1.

TABLE 12-1 SECURE SHELL 2 USER FILES

Computer	Directory	File	Purpose
chivas	/home/frankcastle/.ssh2/	id_dsa_1024_a	Client private key
chivas	/home/frankcastle/.ssh2	id_dsa_1024_a.pub	Client public key
chivas	/home/frankcastle/.ssh2	Identification	Public key file name
chivas	/home/frankcastle/.ssh2/hostkeys	key_22_atlas.pub	Server public key
atlas	/home/frankcastle/.ssh2	key_from_chivas.pub	Public_key
atlas	/home/frankcastle/.ssh2	Authorization	Pointer to public key
atlas	/etc/ssh2	Hostkey	Private key of root
atlas	/etc/ssh	hostkey.pub	Public key for root
atlas	/etc/ssh	ssh2_config	Client configuration
atlas	/etc/ssh	ssh2d_config	Server configuration

CONNECTING TO YOUR SECURE SHELL SERVER

Try connecting to your Secure Shell server using the pass phrase.

1. Log in to the client computer chivas as the regular user frankcastle.

2. Try connecting to your server computer – atlas – via Secure Shell.

   ```
   ssh2 atlas
   ```

3. If you have configured both the client and server correctly, then you are prompted for the pass phrase that you entered while creating your client keys with ssh-keygen2.

```
Passphrase for key "/home/frankcastle/.ssh2/id_dsa_1024_a"
with comment "1024-bit dsa, created by
frankcastle@chivas.paunchy.net Sat May 29 19:27:40 1999":
```

4. Enter the correct pass phrase and you should be connected to the Secure Shell server via a secure, encrypted channel.

If your client machine does not have the server's public key the first time that you connect to it, then the /etc/ssh2/hostkey.pub file will be copied to the .ssh2/hostkeys directory in your home directory. Every subsequent time you connect to atlas you will not see the "Accepting host chivas key without checking" line in the login prompt. This is potentially a dangerous situation because full host authentication is not possible until each side has the other's public key.

If you have not configured the keys and other files correctly, then you can still connect to the remote Secure Shell server. You will be prompted for your regular password just as if you were connecting via Telnet.

```
frankcastle@atlas's password:
```

Enter your password and you will be connected. You are still connected over an encrypted channel, but Secure Shell is not able to correctly pass your public key back to your client machine. That means that you can not verify that the server you are connecting to is the correct one. You are potentially vulnerable to a man-in-the-middle attack where someone spoofs the computer that you are trying to connect to. In that case you would be using a perfectly encrypted connection to a fake machine.

Once again, you should use your judgment to determine whether the danger of potentially connecting to a false server is significant. If you are using Secure Shell to connect within your private network, then you should be able to judge the potential danger and act appropriately. If you are connecting from the Internet, then the potential danger might be much greater.

In this example, however, you are connecting to your own Secure Shell server from the server itself and thus have good reason to believe that there is no fake server involved. Continue with your connection and Secure Shell will create a known_host file in your home directory — /home/encryptme/.ssh/known_hosts:

```
Host 'atlas' added to the list of known hosts.
```

```
Creating random seed file ~/.ssh/random_seed.  This may take a while.
myuser's password:
```

If you look in the newly created `known_hosts` in the `.ssh` directory in your home directory — `/home/frankcastle` in this case — then you see that Secure Shell has created a key for your hosts.

CONNECTING TO DIFFERENT COMPUTERS

The previous example provides instructions for connecting from `chivas` to `atlas` only. If you want to go in the other direction, or want to connect to multiple computers, a little more configuration is necessary.

 You do not want to copy your private keys from other machines. This would violate the secrecy of the private key concept.

You need to create new private keys on each new client machine. Follow the previous instructions on each client computer for creating public and private keys. On the client computer you will need to have the `id_dsa_1024_a`, `id_dsa_1024_a.pub`, and `identification` files in your `.ssh2` directory; the public key such as `key_22_server.pub` should be put in the `.ssh2/hostkeys` directory. You also need to transfer the user's client public key to the user's `.ssh2` directory on the server machine and create the `authorization` file that points to it.

 If you have user accounts with different names on other computers, you can use the same keys to connect to them. The `ssh2 -l` option allows you to specify what account name to connect with. For instance, if your user account name is `gabe` on `veracruz` but you want to connect to `chivas` where your name is `frankcastle`, then you should use the command `ssh2 -l frankcastle chivas`. Otherwise, `ssh2` will use your name `gabe` which will not match up with `frankcastle` on `chivas`.

MODIFYING YOUR FIREWALL FOR SECURE SHELL

The firewall design from Chapter 11 is an effective and strong one. It gains much of its strength from the philosophy of not permitting any communication originating from the Internet into the private network; it allows only one-way communication. This model is quite useful but if you want to gain access to your network from outside — for instance, from your home — then it presents some problems.

A firewall based solely on IP filtering works very well in one direction. As soon as you allow IP packets from the Internet, however, you start opening potential holes in your firewall. For instance, I have used the network scanner nmap against this book's firewall defined by the ipfilter.rules script found in the /mnt/ cdrom/firewall directory on the Red Hat supplemental CD-ROM. The firewall tests very well, as every nmap configuration that I can conjure fails to return any information about my network sitting behind the firewall. However, when I add a rule to allow Telnet sessions in from the Internet, nmap then is able to see that service. An attacker then knows that there is a computer and/or networks at that IP address and can attempt to find a way in.

Allowing external access to network services like Telnet is not a direct danger in itself. However, it is a potential vulnerability for several reasons. First, if someone places a Trojan horse on your network, then access to the network is possible. (Otherwise, with a one-way firewall, even if a Trojan horse exists no one can gain access and use it.) Second, if there is a bug or backdoor in a daemon like telnetd, then an intruder can take advantage of it if external access is available. Finally, if someone is sniffing your incoming network traffic, then it's quite possible that your passwords will be discovered and access to your internal network gained via a service like Telnet.

The solution is to run a Secure Shell server on your Internet gateway/firewall and provide external access only to the Secure Shell server. In this case, atlas is the Secure Shell server and an ipchains rule is added to allow external clients access to it. This arrangement is safer than others for several reasons:

◆ First, all communication is encrypted, which makes all the information, such as passwords, very difficult to intercept, if not impossible.

◆ Second, if the authentication keys have been properly configured on both the client and the server, then you are assured that you are communicating with the correct machine. You cannot be spoofed by some third party on the Internet.

◆ Third, Secure Shell is in itself a type of firewall. It can be configured to require its own authentication before it will allow any access to itself (by turning off password-only authentication). Network packets coming in from the Internet and seeking access to the private network will be serviced by the Secure Shell daemon only. It essentially prevents unauthorized access to your private network just as an application-based firewall does.

◆ Finally, my nmap tests of my firewall with external access granted to Secure Shell do not show any response. That is, I scan the firewall and nmap does not see the Secure Shell port which is listening for incoming connection. nmap does not see the network just as before. This is not an exhaustive test but a very good indicator that the firewall is not going to break easily. (nmap is one of the most widely used and respected scanners available. It is highly adaptive to new conditions and continually being improved.)

The following rule is used to provide external access to your private network from the Internet.

```
# allow secure shell connections originating from the outside
ipchains -A output -p TCP -j ACCEPT -i ppp0 -s $ALL ssh -t 0x01 0x10
ipchains -A output -p UDP -j ACCEPT -i ppp0 -s $ALL ssh -t 0x01 0x10
```

These rules can be found in the /mnt/cdrom/firewall/ipfilter.rules file on the Red Hat supplemental CD-ROM. Remove the comments in order to activate them.

USING SECURE FTP

Secure Shell comes with a secure version of FTP called sftp. sftp can be used in place of FTP to transfer encrypted information. The sftp system is easy to use: you just enter the following command to connect to a computer — chivas in this case — running Secure Shell.

```
sftp chivas
```

The Secure Shell daemon handles the entire process. Unlike FTP, there is only one communication channel for both commands and data.

CONFIGURING GENERAL PARAMETERS

By default, the sshd2 configuration allows root logins. The better practice is to not allow direct root logins and force everyone to log in as a regular user. Those who have root privilege can use the su command to access root. That leaves an audit trail and also forces everyone to use two passwords instead of one to gain root access.

Edit the /etc/ssh/sshd2_config file and set the PermitRootLogin parameter from yes to no:

```
PermitRootLogin    no
```

Another useful change is to disallow password logins. The Secure Shell default operation is to revert to using the general Linux login password to authenticate the connection if the pass phrase fails. This could present an intruder with the opportunity to gain access if, for instance, the password file has been cracked or intercepted. Changing this option is not a panacea but does potentially provide extra protection. Change the parameter in the /etc/ssh/sshd2_config file to the following:

```
PasswordAuthentication    no
```

There are numerous other parameters that can be changed. Please consult the sshd2 man page for more information.

Eliminating all unnecessary system daemons

This section deals with eliminating unnecessary processes, daemons, and applications in order to increase the security of your firewall. With fewer processes (daemons) and software on the firewall, you simply have fewer potential – undiscovered – security holes available to be exploited.

I assume that you are starting with the base Red Hat Linux installed and running. To find the unnecessary processes, look at the process table by entering the following command:

```
ps x
```

You should see a list of processes.

```
PID TTY       STAT    TIME COMMAND
   1 ?         S       0:04 init [5]
   2 ?         SW      0:00 [kflushd]
   3 ?         SW      0:00 [kpiod]
   4 ?         SW      0:00 [kswapd]
   5 ?         SW<     0:00 [mdrecoveryd]
 260 ?         S       0:00 ypserv
 275 ?         SW      0:00 [ypbind]
 280 ?         S       0:00 ypbind (slave)
 306 ?         S       0:00 syslogd -m 0
 317 ?         S       0:00 klogd
 345 ?         S       0:00 crond
 359 ?         S       0:00 inetd
 366 ?         SW      0:00 [sshd2]
 380 ?         S       0:00 named
 394 ?         S       0:00 lpd
 412 ?         S       0:00 rpc.statd
 423 ?         SW      0:00 [rpc.rquotad]
 434 ?         SW      0:00 [rpc.mountd]
 449 ?         SW      0:00 [nfsd]
 450 ?         SW      0:00 [nfsd]
 451 ?         SW      0:00 [nfsd]
 453 ?         SW      0:00 [nfsd]
 454 ?         SW      0:00 [nfsd]
 455 ?         SW      0:00 [nfsd]
 456 ?         SW      0:00 [nfsd]
 457 ?         SW      0:00 [lockd]
 458 ?         SW      0:00 [rpciod]
 493 ?         S       0:00 sendmail: accepting connections on port 25
 524 ?         S       0:00 diald
 564 tty1      SW      0:00 [mingetty]
```

```
  565 tty2    SW    0:00 [mingetty]
  566 tty3    SW    0:00 [mingetty]
  567 tty4    SW    0:00 [mingetty]
  568 tty5    SW    0:00 [mingetty]
  569 tty6    SW    0:00 [mingetty]
  570 ?       S     0:00 /etc/X11/prefdm -nodaemon
  572 ?       S     0:00 update (bdflush)
 1197 ?       S     0:00 smbd -D
 1208 ?       S     0:00 nmbd -D
 1216 ?       S     0:01 smbd -D
 1710 ?       S     0:00 in.telnetd
 1711 pts/3   S     0:00 login - paul
 1725 pts/3   S     0:00 su -
 1729 pts/3   S     0:00 -bash
 1752 ?       S     0:28 /usr/bin/X11/X -auth /var/gdm/:0.xauth :0
 1761 ?       S     0:00 /etc/X11/prefdm -nodaemon
18466 ?       S     0:00 bash -login /etc/X11/gdm/Sessions/Default
18481 ?       S     0:00 /usr/bin/gnome-session
18503 ?       S     0:00 gnome-smproxy --sm-client-id default0
18509 ?       S     0:01 enlightenment -clientId default2
18522 ?       S     0:00 panel --sm-client-id default8
18524 ?       S     0:00 xscreensaver -no-splash -timeout 20 -nice
18526 ?       S     0:01 gmc --sm-client-id default10
18530 ?       S     0:00 gnome-name-service
18538 ?       S     0:00 gnomepager_applet --activate-goad-server
18540 ?       S     0:00 gen_util_applet --activate-goad-server
18547 ?       S     0:00 gnome-terminal
18548 ?       S     0:00 gnome-pty-helper
18549 pts/2   S     0:00 bash
18577 pts/3   R     0:00 ps x
18578 pts/3   S     0:00 more
```

There are several ways to eliminate the various daemons from running. You can delete the programs themselves, delete the links in the /etc/rc.d run-level directories, or modify the startup scripts. I prefer to modify the scripts that start up the various daemons because I can document what I have done – and why – by adding comments to the scripts. This leaves the computer in a near-original state, which helps you or whoever is working on the system in the future. (If you simply eliminate the links, for instance, it is far more difficult to document what you've done and why.)

The following steps serve to eliminate each of the unnecessary daemons. Start from the top and work your way down. The first few processes – listed within square brackets [ ] – are all part of the Linux kernel (see Chapter 4). The kerneld daemon is the first process we deal with in the next section. The klogd is part of the Linux logging process and we want to keep it. crond executes periodic processes and we want to keep it as well. The inetd, named (if you installed the optional Red Hat service in Chapter 1), lpd, sendmail, smbd, and nmbd daemons are all unnecessary for a firewall server, in my opinion. The remaining processes all relate to my own logins except for the update process, which is part of the kernel. The mingetty processes all process logins from the console and should not present any security problems. The login process and the bash shell (288 and 296) are logged in as root from the console and running the bash shell. You can also ignore the last several processes (308, 323, 324, and 336) because they are the processes that I used to log in remotely via Telnet (in.telnetd), and then changed to root (su), the shell for root (bash), and the command to show all the processes (ps x). I will, however, eliminate the capability to log in via Telnet in the section "Stopping inetd" later in this chapter, but for now it is okay because I am still configuring the Firewall Server.

The following sections describe how I configure my minimalist Firewall Server.

Stopping inetd

The idea is to eliminate as many possible security breaches as possible. One way to do this is to run as few daemons as possible. Many processes are started by the inetd daemon. inetd is called the super daemon because it is responsible for starting all sorts of processes on demand. Leaving one daemon in charge of starting many others means that you need only run one instead of many. You can either not run it at all or else edit its configuration file. In my opinion, it is best not to run inetd at all because there will be no doubt about what is and what is not running.

1. Log in to atlas as root.

2. There are numerous ways to not run inetd. First, you could remove the execution privilege by logging on as root and entering the following command:

   ```
   chmod -x /etc/rc.d/init.d/inet
   ```

3. You could also simply eliminate the link in the run-level startup directories. For instance, you could remove the /etc/rc.d/rc3.d/S50inet file, which is a link to the /etc/rc.d/init.d/inet script. Without the link, the inetd script will never be executed when you boot your computer.

   ```
   rm /etc/rc.d/rc3.d/S50inet
   rm /etc/rc.d/rc4.d/S50inet
   rm /etc/rc.d/rc5.d/S50inet
   ```

   (You could also simply rename the links and they won't be executed but you'll know their names should be if you ever decide to reinstate them.)

   ```
   mv /etc/rc.d/rc3.d/S50inet /etc/rc.d/rc3.d/_S50inet
   mv /etc/rc.d/rc5.d/S50inet /etc/rc.d/rc5.d/_S50inet
   ```

4. You can also delete the actual inet script.

```
rm /etc/rc.d/init.d/inet
```

(Or rename it.)

```
mv /etc/rc.d/init.d/inet /etc/rc.d/init.d/_inet
```

5. Repeat steps 1 through 4 on `chivas` and any other Linux servers and workstations that you want to protect in this fashion.

6. Reboot your computer and make sure that the change took effect and that your system runs as desired.

The end result is that your Linux computer will not be running any services started by `inetd`. The only daemons that will run on your system will be the ones that you see when you look at the process table.

Modifying inetd.conf

You may want to retain the convenience that the `inetd` daemon provides. In that case, you should edit the `inetd` configuration file `/etc/inetd.conf` in order to reduce the number of daemons that it will spawn to the absolute minimum. This will achieve nearly the same result as eliminating it altogether.

1. Log in to `atlas` as `root`.

2. Edit the `/etc/inetd.conf` file.

3. Remove all the unnecessary functions by deleting each line. I recommend removing all but the handful of services shown below.

```
#
# inetd.conf     This file describes the services that will be
available
#                through the INETD TCP/IP super server.  To
re-configure
#                the running INETD process, edit this file,
then send the
#                INETD process a SIGHUP signal.
#
# Version:       @(#)/etc/inetd.conf    3.10    05/27/93
#
# Authors:       Original taken from BSD UNIX 4.3/TAHOE.
#                Fred N. van Kempen,
<waltje@uwalt.nl.mugnet.org>
#
# Modified for Debian Linux by Ian A. Murdock
<imurdock@shell.portal.com>
#
# Modified for RHS Linux by Marc Ewing <marc@redhat.com>
```

```
#
# <service_name> <sock_type> <proto> <flags> <user>
<server_path> <args>
#
# Echo, discard, daytime, and chargen are used primarily for
testing.
#
# To re-read this file after changes, just do a 'killall -HUP
inetd'
#
# These are standard services.
#
ftp      stream  tcp     nowait  root    /usr/sbin/tcpd
in.ftpd -l -a
telnet   stream  tcp     nowait  root    /usr/sbin/tcpd
in.telnetd
#
linuxconf stream tcp wait root /bin/linuxconf linuxconf --
http
swat        stream  tcp     nowait.400       root /usr/sbin/swat
swat
# End of inetd.conf
```

The telnet and ftp services are not needed if you are running Secure Shell.
Secure Shell runs as its own daemon and provides both encrypted interactive terminal sessions and file transfer capabilities. You should consider removing Telnet and ftp from `inetd.conf` if you run Secure Shell.

The r* services: `rlogin`, `rsh`, `rdate`, etc. potentially provide remote users access to parts of or to your entire computer.

`finger` provides information about the users on your system.

`tftp` can provide unauthenticated access to your computer.

4. Save the changes and restart the `inetd` process by entering the following command:

   `killall -1 inetd`

5. Repeat steps 1 through 4 on `chivas` and any other Linux servers and workstations that you want to protect in this fashion.

6. Reboot your computer and make sure that the change took effect and that your system runs as desired.

Shutting down sendmail

Sendmail has traditionally been a source of many network security problems. It is a complex piece of software and that complexity has lent itself to unforeseen problems. Those problems have been greatly reduced in recent years and it is a reasonable system now. However, it should be run only when necessary.

Recall from Chapter 8 that two different e-mail systems were described. One method, the ISP-based e-mail model, sends and retrieves e-mail directly from your ISP. The other method, the locally-based e-mail server model, uses `sendmail` and `fetchmail` to create a local e-mail server for your private network. In the former case you should not run `sendmail` on any machine. In the later, `sendmail` should be run only on the e-mail server.

The following instructions describe how to turn off `sendmail` on a Linux computer. If you are using the ISP-based e-mail model, then run these instructions on every Linux computer on your network. If you use the locally-based e-mail server model, then run this script on every Linux computer except `chivas`.

1. Log in to your Linux computer as root.

2. Remove the `sendmail` RPM package.

   ```
   rpm -e sendmail
   ```

3. Stop any running `sendmail` daemons.

   ```
   killall -9 sendmail
   ```

4. Repeat steps 1 through 3 on any other Linux servers and workstations that you want to protect in this fashion.

Stopping the Samba startup script

A firewall should definitely not run any file- or printer-sharing utilities. If you do not set up your IP filter rules properly, your Samba shares can potentially be shared with the Internet!

1. Log on to your `atlas` as `root`.

2. Remove the Samba RPM packages.

   ```
   rpm -e samba-client
   rpm -e samba-common
   rpm -e samba
   ```

3. Stop any running Samba daemons.

   ```
   /etc/rc.d/init.d/smb stop
   ```

4. Repeat steps 1 through 3 on `chivas` and any other Linux servers and workstations that you want to protect in this fashion.

5. Reboot your computer and make sure that the change took effect and that your system runs as desired.

Removing unnecessary software

Continuing with our minimalist theme, eliminate the `routed`, `rusersd`, and `rwhod` packages if you have them installed.

1. Log in to `atlas` as `root`.

2. Remove the RPM packages.

   `rpm -e rsh`

3. Repeat step 2 for any packages that you don't need. Determining what is needed is quite difficult. I am working on a script for automatically removing packages. It is only experimental so be careful if you use it. You can find it in the `/mnt/cdrom/security` directory on the supplemental CD-ROM.

 A better way to create a minimal firewall computer is to install Red Hat Linux using the `kickstart` system. By using that method you only install the packages that you need in the first place. I am also working on a `kickstart` script and will include it in the `/mnt/cdrom/security` directory on the supplemental CD-ROM.

Removing all unnecessary compilers

Finally, remove any, and all, of the compilers from your firewall computer. Without a compiler, an intruder will have far fewer tools with which to work. On a Red Hat Linux firewall, use the RPM to find out which compilers you have installed.

1. Log in to your Linux file server/router as `root`.

2. Enter the following command to find installed compilers:

   `rpm -q -a | more`

3. Look for `egcc`, `glibc`, `libg`, `python`, `perl`, and so on. Remove those packages by entering the RPM `erase` command — like that shown for the GNU C-compiler:

   `rpm -e egcs`

4. Repeat step 3 for each compiler.

5. Repeat steps 1 through 4 on chivas and any other Linux servers and workstations that you want to protect in this fashion.

Adding a serial connection to your Firewall Server

You need to interactively communicate with your firewall to effectively manage it. The best compromise, in my opinion, is to use Secure Shell. However, an alternative is to add a serial line connection from chivas to atlas. Adding a serial connection enables you to work on your Firewall Server from anywhere on your private network.

You can then Telnet or use Secure Shell to connect to chivas. From there you use an interactive serial communication like dip to connect to atlas. You increase security by preventing direct communication with atlas except from chivas. chivas should be a more secure machine since it is a server that you control and manage.

The simplest method is to buy a preconfigured cable with the transmit (#2) and receive (#3) wires crossed over. This is called a Null Modem. Your remote computer sends outgoing data on line 2 and that data needs to be received on line 3 and vice versa.

You also may need to add a third serial interface if you use external modems and choose to have a separate phone line for incoming communication. You can purchase inexpensive serial interfaces to add another couple of interfaces.

You need to modify both computers to recognize the serial connection. This process is similar to configuring the dial-up connection described in Chapter 7. Complete the following steps:

1. Purchase or make a null modem cable. This is a serial cable with the send and receive lines crossed. Pin 2 on one connector becomes pin 3 on the other side.

2. Connect the two computers with a serial cable. PC serial ports are electrically buffered so you do not have to turn off the power to the computers to insert the cables, but be careful not to move them too much or you may damage the hard disks.

 If you are already using two external modems, you must install another serial port.

3. You need to modify the inittab file on the Firewall Server to enable logins via a serial port.

4. Log in to atlas as root.

5. If you have not already installed the RPM package `getty_ps`, which contains the `uugetty` that I use, then do so now:

```
rpm -ivh /mnt/cdrom/RedHat/RPMS/getty_ps-*.rpm
```

6. Make a backup copy of `/etc/inittab`:

```
cp /etc/inittab /etc/inittab.orig
```

You can skip this step if you have already made a backup copy of `inittab`, described in Chapter 10, in the section "Configuring Your Firewall Server for Dial-In." You may, however, want to make a copy of your dial-in modified inittab.

7. Edit the `/etc/inittab` file and modify the entry for the serial port that you want to enable. The entry for `uugetty` to monitor a serial device (`/dev/ttyS0`) for logins after the standard `mingettys` that monitor the console is as follows:

```
# Run gettys in standard runlevels
1:12345:respawn:/sbin/mingetty tty1
2:2345:respawn:/sbin/mingetty tty2
3:2345:respawn:/sbin/mingetty tty3
4:2345:respawn:/sbin/mingetty tty4
5:2345:respawn:/sbin/mingetty tty5
6:2345:respawn:/sbin/mingetty tty6

s0:3456:respawn:/sbin/uugetty ttyS0 38400 vt100
```

8. To force `init` to recognize all these changes, you must tell it to reread its configuration file. Enter the following command as root:

```
telinit q
```

If you look at the end of the message log `/var/log/messages` (`tail /var/log/messages`), you should see an indication that `init` did the job. It will also list any errors that occurred.

9. Test the new connection from `chivas` to `atlas` by using a serial-line communication program such as `dip` (you must be logged on as `root`):

```
dip -t
```

10. Set the port to the appropriate serial device and the speed to match the Firewall Server. I connect to `/dev/modem`:

```
dip> port modem
```

11. Change to terminal mode:

```
dip> term
```

12. You should get a login prompt from atlas. You can log onto it now. (If you get garbled text, you most likely have a speed mismatch.)

If you installed a dial-in modem connection (discussed in Chapter 10, in the section "Configuring Your Firewall Server for Dial-In") and have removed the network clients such as Telnet from the Firewall Server, you will want to configure the File Server/Router for direct serial connect as well. Without Telnet or rlogin, you will not be able to communicate with the private network without a serial connection capability. To communicate with the private network, you must be able to log on to the File Server/Router in the same way as you can log on to the Firewall Server.

To install uugetty on the File Server/Router, repeat Steps 4 through 8. You can then dial up and log on to the Firewall Server. At that point, you can use dip or another program to log on to the File Server/Router. From there, you can make use of the network application programs to access other machines on the private network.

Creating host-based firewalls

You can use the ipchains system to create a firewall for each of your Linux computers. The scaled down ipchains script is used to create each host-based firewalls.

1. Login to a Linux computer as root.

2. Mount the IDG supplemental CD-ROM.

```
mount   /mnt/cdrom
```

3. Copy the ipfilter.host script from the IDG supplemental CD-ROM to the /usr/local/etc directory.

```
cp /mnt/cdrom/security/ipfilter.host /usr/local/etc
```

The important rules are listed below.

```
# Flush out all existing chains
ipchains -F
# Flush out any empty chains (just to be sure)
ipchains -X

# Set built-in filters to deny everything on every network
interface
ipchains -P input   DENY
ipchains -P output  DENY
ipchains -P forward DENY
```

```
# Allow all internal network traffic
ipchains -A input  -i lo -j ACCEPT
ipchains -A output -i lo -j ACCEPT

# --- Going out to the private network

# TCP

ipchains -A output -p TCP -j ACCEPT -i eth0 -d $ALL -s $ALL

# UDP
ipchains -A output -p UDP -j ACCEPT -i eth0 -d $ALL -s $ALL


# --- Coming in from the Internet

# TCP

# Only allow TCP SYN packets back in
# (this creates a semi-stateful filtering system)
ipchains -A input -p TCP -j ACCEPT -i eth0 ! -y -s $ALL

# optionally allow secure shell connections originating from
the private net
#ipchains -A input -p TCP -j ACCEPT -i eth0 -d $ALL ssh
```

4. Start the script.

   ```
   /usr/local/etc/ipfilter.host
   ```

5. You now can go out onto your private network and the Internet via the gateway, but no one should be able to get into your system. No one should be able to scan your computer either.

6. Once you are satisfied that your computer behaves as desired, you can automate the startup and shutdown of the `ipfilter.host` script. Create soft links to the `ipfilter.host` script as follows:

   ```
   ln -s /usr/local/etc/ipfilter.host
      /etc/rc.d/rc3.d/S95firewall
   ln -s /usr/local/etc/ipfilter.host
      /etc/rc.d/rc4.d/S95firewall
   ln -s /usr/local/etc/ipfilter.host
      /etc/rc.d/rc5.d/S95firewall
   ```

You can shut down the local firewall by using the existing `/usr/local/etc/ipfilter.reset` script.

Providing web services

If you want to provide a Web Server to the world, then I advise that you pay someone else to do so. The reasons are as follows:

◆ You do not want to sacrifice your scarce Internet connection bandwidth to this purpose. If you have a puny PPP/modem connection, you'll immediately clog it up if you allow HTTP packets down your pipe. Even with higher speed connections, why sacrifice your own speed?

◆ You have extra security concerns when you allow HTTP packets into your network. Security measures are built into the protocol. CGI-bin is designed to isolate interactive services from passive ones (that is, straight browsing versus interactive browsing). But you still have to add IP filtering rules and configure your own HTTP system. Therefore, in my opinion, it is easier in most cases if you have your ISP run your Web server.

◆ Web serving is a huge and rapidly developing field. It will be time-consuming at best and better left to the professional to develop and manage.

The solution is to have your ISP act as your Web server. Most ISPs are set up to do just that and would love to do it. You never clog your Internet connection with that traffic and don't have to worry about configuring extra security.

Reviewing your Server

There you have it. You've got yourself a minimalist Firewall Server. It has just enough resources to perform its function. As a result, it has fewer temptations for burglars, too.

 I chose not to run X Window on the Firewall Server. If you have installed it on your Firewall Server, remove it with the RPM package. It takes away resources such as memory and disk space and is not needed. Remember that this is a simple machine and I like to run everything on it from a command line. You also save a valuable serial port by not having a mouse — that becomes important if you use a separate phone line for incoming communications and need the second serial port for that modem. Use the RPM query command to see how many X-related packages are installed and then remove them with the RPM `delete` command.

Listing the functions of the File Server/Router and Firewall

Table 12-2 lists the functions that the two servers (Firewall and File Server/Router) should perform.

TABLE 12-2 FUNCTIONS OF THE SERVERS

Function	Computer
File Server	chivas
Print Server	chivas
Router	chivas (if you use a bastion host)
nmap	chivas
tripwire	chivas, atlas
crack	chivas
IP masquerading	atlas, (chivas in the case of a DMZ based firewall)
PPP/diald	alas
IP Filtering	atlas, Linux workstations, (chivas in the case of a DMZ based firewall)
Secure Shell	chivas, atlas, Linux workstations
Dial-Up	atlas (optional)

Educating Yourself

The systems and methods described in this chapter provide a good starting point for securing your network. Security is a complex and ever-changing subject and you cannot remain static. Ultimately, your best defense is your own skill as a systems administrator.

The following URLs provide information that will be useful to educating yourself.

The Computer Emergency Response Team (CERT) web page at www.cert.org

◆ http://www.cis.ohio-state.edu/text/faq/usenet/computer-security/top.html

◆ http://olympus.cs.ucdavis.edu/

◆ http://www.cs.pdx.edu/~mchugh/cs510sc.html

◆ http://www.cs.umsl.edu/~sanjiv/security.html

◆ http://www2.pitt.edu/HOME/Security.old/

◆ http://www.insecure.org (one of my favorites and also one of the best!)

Check out the following newsgroups:

◆ comp.linux.security

◆ comp.firewalls

If you can find a college course on Internet or computer security, then that is certainly worthwhile. There are conferences that are very good at disseminating a great deal of information in a short time. Look up the schedules at www.sans.org and www.usenix.org to find very good tutorials on the subject.

Where to Go Next

That's it! You are now on your way to being a full-fledged systems administrator ready to design, build, and run client-server networks. Linux, Samba, ipchains, PPP and many other software systems are the reasons for your newfound profession. They provide the fundamental tools for building and managing commercial-quality client-server networks. Just as important, these tools are available to everybody.

UNIX in the form of Linux is no longer available only to a select few. The open nature of Linux has created a huge base of developers who aspire to create high-quality, functional software. The flux of ideas and tools has created an immensely creative environment. Thus, Linux – and its associated applications and utilities – is as high a quality and useful a product as anything else out there. No other operating system available is as easily obtained and used and yet so powerful. The fact that it is essentially free makes it that much better.

Everyone and every organization can now afford to have modern and productive networks. That means there is, and will be, that much more need for people with the skills and knowledge to manage these systems. Systems administrators need more systematic education.

With time, I hope and expect that more college level Systems and Network Administration/Engineering courses will appear. There will be a point where the discipline is recognized as an important and distinct field of study and degreed programs will be offered. This is necessary because the demand for systems people is expanding fast and this discipline needs to be taught in a systematic manner.

The time for ad hoc education is ending. My own education is as an electrical engineer. I share with my colleagues a common background. That educational background gave me a solid foundation with which to start my career. When I graduated, I knew the basics of my profession and more important how to learn the tasks presented to me. I also recognized what I didn't know and could better judge how to avoid potential hazards and thus grow professionally.

We all will benefit when our profession is acknowledged and treated like any other engineering or technical specialty.

 TIP Red Hat has recently proposed a certification program for training consultants and organizations in Linux, the Internet, and PC hardware. You can find out more about it at `http://www.interweft.com.au/redhat/`.

Summary

In this chapter, I describe how to add both active and passive security measures for the "real-world" Linux client-server network that I first introduced in Chapter 10. I cover the following topics in this chapter:

- ◆ Adding security monitoring systems to the Linux file and print server.

- ◆ It is best not to look for a silver-bullet security system. Any given system will have weaknesses and limitations. It is best to create layers of defenses.

- ◆ When you are creating a layered defense, it is best to use both active and passive systems.

- ◆ `tripwire` is a system that enables you to detect changes to important systems files that might mean an attempt to compromise your security.

- ◆ `crack` is a system that checks passwords for vulnerabilities.

- ◆ `nmap` is a TCP/UDP port scanning tool. It will tell you what services are available on the computers on your network. It will also tell you what operating systems are being used. You can also use it to test your firewall. It is a very powerful program and should be used with care.

- ◆ The `ipchains` system allows you to create excellent firewalls. You can use the scripts provided in this book and the IDG supplemental CD-ROM to create both Internet and host-based firewalls.

- ◆ Adding a serial cable between your File Server/Router and Firewall Server provides a safe, reasonably easy way to remotely communicate with your Firewall Server from your private network. Your Firewall Server does not run Telnet or `rlogin` for security reasons, so without the serial connection, you would have to work from the console.

Appendix A

Introducing vi

THE MOST UNIVERSAL SCREEN editor in Linux and UNIX is the Visual Editor, or vi. This appendix outlines the basic vi commands that let you perform simple edits on any text file.

I've been using vi for nearly 20 years now. I use it every day but I probably only know and use 20% to 30% of its capabilities. I'm not just lazy (well, I am lazy, but that's another matter) because I only need to use about 20% of its capabilities to get my job done.

I mention my limited knowledge of vi to illustrate its power. You only need to know the basics in order to get real work done. Looking at the vi man page can be daunting. vi is packed with features. Since it is command driven—there is no graphical interface—the wealth of features is difficult to learn. However, you can get by using a small subset of those features and I outline the ones that I find useful in this appendix.

Starting vi

You can start vi simply by entering the following at the shell prompt.

```
vi
```

You'll see a simple informational screen describing the basics of vi. If you enter the name of a text file as shown in the following example, vi will open that file automatically and show you the first page of text.

```
vi /etc/hosts
```

Introducing vi Modes

You can operate vi in either command or insert mode. The command mode is used to modify existing text and also to save changes to a file, insert text from files and to exit from vi. The insert mode is used to add text to a file.

Using the Command Mode

When you start vi it automatically defaults into command mode. The following table shows some common vi editing commands:

TABLE A-1 SIMPLE EDITING COMMANDS

Command	Description
x	Delete the character at the current cursor position
3x	Delete the next three characters, starting at the current cursor position
dd	Delete the current line
3dd	Delete three lines from the current one
dw	Delete the word that the cursor is sitting on
3dw	Delete the next three words from where the cursor is sitting
Ctrl+f	Page down one full screen
Ctrl+b	Page up one full screen
Up-arrow key	Move up one line
Down-arrow key	Move down one line
Right-arrow key	Move right one character
Left-arrow key	Move left one character

You can enter insert mode by pressing any of the following characters while you are in command mode.

TABLE A-2 CHANGE TO INSERT MODES CHARACTERS

Command	Description
a	Append characters from the current cursor position
A	Append characters to the end of the current line
i	Insert characters from the current cursor position

Command	Description
I	Insert characters at the beginning of the current line
o	Open a line below the cursor for test insertion
O	Open a line above the current line for text insertion

To return to the command mode press the `Esc` key.

Searching and Replacing Text

You can search forward for a text string by first pressing the slash (/) key. Any text that you then enter will be searched for. If the text is found, `vi` will place the cursor at the text. You can search backwards by using the question mark (?) in place of the slash.

You can search and replace text by using the following sequence.

```
:g/old/s//new
```

For instance, if you want to find the string `thatolddevilgravity` and replace it with `isbringingmedown` you enter the following sequence.

```
:g/thatolddevilgravity/s//isbringingmedown
```

`vi` will search and replace the first instance of the old string with the new string. You can direct `vi` to replace every occurrence of the old string you can use the following sequence.

```
:g/thatolddevilgravity/s//isbringingmedown/g
```

Saving and Quitting

To save your edits to a file, you must be in command mode. (Note that to change to command mode, you should press the `Esc` key.) The following sequence will save any changes that you have made to the file.

```
:w
```

To save and then exit `vi`, enter the following character sequence.

```
:wq
```

You can exit vi if you have already saved any changes by entering the following sequence:

:q

Alternately, you can exit vi and discard any changes that you've made by using the following sequence:

:q!

 TIP You can save and exit simply by entering the key sequence ZZ while you are in command mode. All changes that you've entered are saved and you return to the shell prompt.

With these few commands, you can get a lot of work done with vi.

Appendix B

Dynamically Assigning IP Addresses

THE EXAMPLE NETWORKS used in this book use static IP addresses. This is reasonable for small to medium sized networks – class C networks – where your workstations are stationary. However, if you use laptops, or if you tend to move your computers around, then you might want to use dynamic IP addresses.

You can use the Dynamic Host Configuration Protocol (dhcp) to assign IP addresses to any or all of the computers on your network. This appendix describes a simple dhcp example where mobile Windows and Linux computers use a portion of the 192.168.1.0 subnet.

Installing dhcpd

It is necessary to install the dhcp on a server. In our example network, the server chivas is used for this function.

1. Log in to chivas as root.

2. Mount the Red Hat CD-ROM.

3. Install the dhcp server.

   ```
   rpm -ivh /mnt/cdrom/RedHat/RPMS/dhcpd*
   ```

4. Create the /etc/dhcpd.conf file and enter the following information.

   ```
   option routers 192.168.1.254;
   shared-network PAUNCHY.NET {
           subnet 192.168.1.0 netmask 255.255.255.0 {
              range 192.168.1.40 192.168.1.50;
           }
        }
   ```

   The first section describes the range of IP addresses, within the class C subnet 192.168.1.0, that will be used by the dhcp clients.

5. Create the /etc/dhcpd.leases file

   ```
   touch /etc/dhcpd.leases
   ```

You don't need to put anything into this file. The dhcpd daemon dynamically puts information about the computers getting their IP addresses from dhcp. Those addresses are called – not surprisingly – leases.

6. Start the dhcpd server

```
/etc/rc.d/init.d/dhcpd start
```

Your dhcpd server chivas is now ready for Windows and Linux computers to get their IP addresses and routing information.

Configuring Linux as a dhcp Client

You only need to modify the /etc/sysconfig/network-scripts/ifcfg-eth0 file to make a Linux box look to the dhcp server for its network configuration. The file should look as follows:

```
DEVICE=eth0
BOOTPROTO=dhcp
ONBOOT=yes
```

 You can also use LinuxConf to modify your Ethernet NIC. Open up the network host configuration window and click on the dhcp radio button.

The next time you boot your Linux computer, or restart the /etc/rc.d/init.d/ network script, you will obtain the IP address, netmask, broadcast address and routing information from the dhcp server.

 If you manually modify the ifcfg-eth0 file you do not need to remove the static IP information. If you modify the PROTOCOL parameter to use dhcp your system will ignore the static information and pick up its parameters dynamically. However, your computer will revert to using the static parameters if the dhcp service is unavailable.

Configuring Windows as a dhcp Client

Setting up a Windows computer to use dhcp is very simple.

1. Log in to your Windows computer. (NT systems require you to log in as the administrator).

2. Open the Network Configuration dialog box.

   Start → Control Panel → Network

3. Open the TCP/IP properties dialog box.

4. Click the IP Address tab.

5. Click on the "Obtain an IP address dynamically" radio button.

6. Click OK.

7. Click the OK button in the Network dialog box.

8. When you are asked if you want to restart you computer click OK.

9. When your Windows computer restarts again it will be assigned an IP address between 192.168.1.40 and 192.168.1.50; the address will be 192.168.1.40 the first time that you use this system. You can prove this to yourself by looking at the /etc/dhcpd.aliases file and/or pinging the 192.168.1.40 address.

Your Windows computer will now obtain its address from the dhcp server on your network. For instance, you can now use your laptop on your both your home and work network (if they both use dhcp) without reconfiguring it each time.

Summary

This appendix introduces dhcp by giving very simple examples. Please refer to the dhcpd and dhcpcd man pages and the documentation in /usr/doc/dhcpd and /usr/doc/dhcpcd for more information.

Appendix C

What's on the CD-ROMs

This book comes with two CD-ROMs. CD-ROM 1 contains the Red Hat Linux Publisher's Edition distribution. CD-ROM 2 contains my own scripts plus supplemental software that is referenced in this book.

CD-ROM 1

The official Red Hat Linux Publisher's Edition is contained on CD-ROM 1. The major directories are:

◆ images: The files used to create boot images used during the Red Hat Linux installation.

◆ RedHat/RPMS: The RPM packages that contain the Linux and supporting system.

◆ dosutils: Utilities used to assist in the installation of Red Hat Linux. These include MS-DOS programs for making room for Linux on existing file systems.

CD-ROM 2

The second CD-ROM contains scripts and software that are used in the book and/or that I find useful.

◆ Applixware: A demo of the powerful office software suite for Linux.

◆ Arkeia: The Knox Software Arkeia backup system. This system provides a network-based, automated backup system.

◆ diald: The dial-on-demand `diald` system monitors your network for outgoing network communications. When it detects outgoing traffic, it automatically dials up your ISP and opens a PPP connection.

◆ dns: This directory contains several domain name service (DNS) scripts. The scripts match the instructions used in the book and will create a DNS server right out of the box.

◆ email: This directory contains several sendmail scripts. The scripts match the instructions used in the book and will create an e-mail server right out of the box.

◆ extras: Several software packages are contained in this directory. These are packages that I find to be useful but are not discribed in the book.

◆ firewall: This directory contains several `ipchains`-based scripts that are used to create firewalls.

◆ misc: Two simple scripts are located here. One is a `crontab` script that is oriented towards preventing the `diald` system from accidentally holding a phone connection open overnight. There is also an script containing aliases that I find useful.

◆ security: This directory contains software that is used to increase your computer security.

◆ chapters: This directory contains two virtual chapters for the book. History covers the origins of Linux and Samba; Resources tells you how to access additional Linux resources.

Index

Symbols and Numerics

Continued

Continued

Continued

IDG Books Worldwide, Inc.
End–User License Agreement

4. <u>Restrictions on Use of Individual Programs</u>. You must follow the individual requirements and restrictions detailed for each individual program in Appendix D of this Book. These limitations are also contained in the individual license agreements recorded on the Software Media. These limitations may include a requirement that after using the program for a specified period of time, the user must pay a registration fee or discontinue use. By opening the Software packet(s), you will be agreeing to abide by the licenses and restrictions for these individual programs that are detailed in Appendix D and on the Software Media. None of the material on this Software Media or listed in this Book may ever be redistributed, in original or modified form, for commercial purposes.

5. <u>Limited Warranty</u>.

    (a) IDGB warrants that the Software and Software Media are free from defects in materials and workmanship under normal use for a period of sixty (60) days from the date of purchase of this Book. If IDGB receives notification within the warranty period of defects in materials or workmanship, IDGB will replace the defective Software Media.

    (b) IDGB AND THE AUTHOR OF THE BOOK DISCLAIM ALL OTHER WARRANTIES, EXPRESS OR IMPLIED, INCLUDING WITHOUT LIMITATION IMPLIED WARRANTIES OF MERCHANTABILITY AND FITNESS FOR A PARTICULAR PURPOSE, WITH RESPECT TO THE SOFTWARE, THE PROGRAMS, THE SOURCE CODE CONTAINED THEREIN, AND/OR THE TECHNIQUES DESCRIBED IN THIS BOOK. IDGB DOES NOT WARRANT THAT THE FUNCTIONS CONTAINED IN THE SOFTWARE WILL MEET YOUR REQUIREMENTS OR THAT THE OPERATION OF THE SOFTWARE WILL BE ERROR FREE.

    (c) This limited warranty gives you specific legal rights, and you may have other rights that vary from jurisdiction to jurisdiction.

6. <u>Remedies</u>.

    (a) IDGB's entire liability and your exclusive remedy for defects in materials and workmanship shall be limited to replacement of the Software Media, which may be returned to IDGB with a copy of your receipt at the following address: Software Media Fulfillment Department, Attn.: *Red Hat Linux Network Toolkit, 2E,* IDG Books Worldwide, Inc., 10475 Crosspoint Blvd., Indianapolis, IN 46256, or call 1-800-762-2974. Please allow three to four weeks for delivery. This Limited Warranty is void if failure of the Software Media has resulted from accident, abuse, or misapplication. Any replacement Software Media will be warranted for the remainder of the original warranty period or thirty (30) days, whichever is longer.

(b) In no event shall IDGB or the author be liable for any damages whatsoever (including without limitation damages for loss of business profits, business interruption, loss of business information, or any other pecuniary loss) arising from the use of or inability to use the Book or the Software, even if IDGB has been advised of the possibility of such damages.

(c) Because some jurisdictions do not allow the exclusion or limitation of liability for consequential or incidental damages, the above limitation or exclusion may not apply to you.

7. **U.S. Government Restricted Rights**. Use, duplication, or disclosure of the Software by the U.S. Government is subject to restrictions stated in paragraph (c)(1)(ii) of the Rights in Technical Data and Computer Software clause of DFARS 252.227-7013, and in subparagraphs (a) through (d) of the Commercial Computer — Restricted Rights clause at FAR 52.227-19, and in similar clauses in the NASA FAR supplement, when applicable.

8. **General**. This Agreement constitutes the entire understanding of the parties and revokes and supersedes all prior agreements, oral or written, between them and may not be modified or amended except in a writing signed by both parties hereto that specifically refers to this Agreement. This Agreement shall take precedence over any other documents that may be in conflict herewith. If any one or more provisions contained in this Agreement are held by any court or tribunal to be invalid, illegal, or otherwise unenforceable, each and every other provision shall remain in full force and effect.

GNU GENERAL PUBLIC LICENSE

Version 2, June 1991
Copyright (C) 1989, 1991 Free Software Foundation, Inc.
59 Temple Place – Suite 330, Boston, MA 02111-1307, USA

Preamble

The licenses for most software are designed to take away your freedom to share and change it. By contrast, the GNU General Public License is intended to guarantee your freedom to share and change free software--to make sure the software is free for all its users. This General Public License applies to most of the Free Software Foundation's software and to any other program whose authors commit to using it. (Some other Free Software Foundation software is covered by the GNU Library General Public License instead.) You can apply it to your programs, too.

When we speak of free software, we are referring to freedom, not price. Our General Public Licenses are designed to make sure that you have the freedom to distribute copies of free software (and charge for this service if you wish), that you receive source code or can get it if you want it, that you can change the software or use pieces of it in new free programs; and that you know you can do these things.

To protect your rights, we need to make restrictions that forbid anyone to deny you these rights or to ask you to surrender the rights. These restrictions translate to certain responsibilities for you if you distribute copies of the software, or if you modify it.

For example, if you distribute copies of such a program, whether gratis or for a fee, you must give the recipients all the rights that you have. You must make sure that they, too, receive or can get the source code. And you must show them these terms so they know their rights.

We protect your rights with two steps: (1) copyright the software, and (2) offer you this license which gives you legal permission to copy, distribute and/or modify the software.

Also, for each author's protection and ours, we want to make certain that everyone understands that there is no warranty for this free software. If the software is modified by someone else and passed on, we want its recipients to know that what they have is not the original, so that any problems introduced by others will not reflect on the original authors' reputations.

Finally, any free program is threatened constantly by software patents. We wish to avoid the danger that redistributors of a free program will individually obtain patent licenses, in effect making the program proprietary. To prevent this, we have made it clear that any patent must be licensed for everyone's free use or not licensed at all.

The precise terms and conditions for copying, distribution and modification follow.

TERMS AND CONDITIONS FOR COPYING, DISTRIBUTION AND MODIFICATION

0. This License applies to any program or other work which contains a notice placed by the copyright holder saying it may be distributed under the terms of this General Public License. The "Program", below, refers to any such program or work, and a "work based on the Program" means either the Program or any derivative work under copyright law: that is to say, a work containing the Program or a portion of it, either verbatim or with modifications and/or translated into another language. (Hereinafter, translation is included without limitation in the term "modification".) Each licensee is addressed as "you".

   Activities other than copying, distribution and modification are not covered by this License; they are outside its scope. The act of running the Program is not restricted, and the output from the Program is covered only if its contents constitute a work based on the Program (independent of having been made by running the Program). Whether that is true depends on what the Program does.

1. You may copy and distribute verbatim copies of the Program's source code as you receive it, in any medium, provided that you conspicuously and appropriately publish on each copy an appropriate copyright notice and disclaimer of warranty; keep intact all the notices that refer to this License and to the absence of any warranty; and give any other recipients of the Program a copy of this License along with the Program.

   You may charge a fee for the physical act of transferring a copy, and you may at your option offer warranty protection in exchange for a fee.

2. You may modify your copy or copies of the Program or any portion of it, thus forming a work based on the Program, and copy and distribute such modifications or work under the terms of Section 1 above, provided that you also meet all of these conditions:

   a) You must cause the modified files to carry prominent notices stating that you changed the files and the date of any change.

   b) You must cause any work that you distribute or publish, that in whole or in part contains or is derived from the Program or any part thereof, to be licensed as a whole at no charge to all third parties under the terms of this License.

   c) If the modified program normally reads commands interactively when run, you must cause it, when started running for such interactive use in the most ordinary way, to print or display an announcement including an appropriate copyright notice and a notice that there is no warranty (or else, saying that you provide a warranty) and that users may redistribute the program under these conditions, and telling the user how to view a copy of this License. (Exception: if the Program itself is interactive but does not normally print such an announcement, your work based on the Program is not required to print an announcement.)

These requirements apply to the modified work as a whole. If identifiable sections of that work are not derived from the Program, and can be reasonably considered independent and separate works in themselves, then this License, and its terms, do not apply to those sections when you distribute them as separate works. But when you distribute the same sections as part of a whole which is a work based on the Program, the distribution of the whole must be on the terms of this License, whose permissions for other licensees extend to the entire whole, and thus to each and every part regardless of who wrote it.

Thus, it is not the intent of this section to claim rights or contest your rights to work written entirely by you; rather, the intent is to exercise the right to control the distribution of derivative or collective works based on the Program.

In addition, mere aggregation of another work not based on the Program with the Program (or with a work based on the Program) on a volume of a storage or distribution medium does not bring the other work under the scope of this License.

3. You may copy and distribute the Program (or a work based on it, under Section 2) in object code or executable form under the terms of Sections 1 and 2 above provided that you also do one of the following:

   a) Accompany it with the complete corresponding machine-readable source code, which must be distributed under the terms of Sections 1 and 2 above on a medium customarily used for software interchange; or,

   b) Accompany it with a written offer, valid for at least three years, to give any third party, for a charge no more than your cost of physically performing source distribution, a complete machine-readable copy of the corresponding source code, to be distributed under the terms of Sections 1 and 2 above on a medium customarily used for software interchange; or,

   c) Accompany it with the information you received as to the offer to distribute corresponding source code. (This alternative is allowed only for noncommercial distribution and only if you received the program in object code or executable form with such an offer, in accord with Subsection b above.)

The source code for a work means the preferred form of the work for making modifications to it. For an executable work, complete source code means all the source code for all modules it contains, plus any associated interface definition files, plus the scripts used to control compilation and installation of the executable. However, as a special exception, the source code distributed need not include anything that is normally distributed (in either source or binary form) with the major components (compiler, kernel, and so on) of the operating system on which the executable runs, unless that component itself accompanies the executable.

If distribution of executable or object code is made by offering access to copy from a designated place, then offering equivalent access to copy the source code from the same place counts as distribution of the source code, even though third parties are not compelled to copy the source along with the object code.

4. You may not copy, modify, sublicense, or distribute the Program except as expressly provided under this License. Any attempt otherwise to copy, modify, sublicense or distribute the Program is void, and will automatically terminate your rights under this License. However, parties who have received copies, or rights, from you under this License will not have their licenses terminated so long as such parties remain in full compliance.

5. You are not required to accept this License, since you have not signed it. However, nothing else grants you permission to modify or distribute the Program or its derivative works. These actions are prohibited by law if you do not accept this License. Therefore, by modifying or distributing the Program (or any work based on the Program), you indicate your acceptance of this License to do so, and all its terms and conditions for copying, distributing or modifying the Program or works based on it.

6. Each time you redistribute the Program (or any work based on the Program), the recipient automatically receives a license from the original licensor to copy, distribute or modify the Program subject to these terms and conditions. You may not impose any further restrictions on the recipients' exercise of the rights granted herein. You are not responsible for enforcing compliance by third parties to this License.

7. If, as a consequence of a court judgment or allegation of patent infringement or for any other reason (not limited to patent issues), conditions are imposed on you (whether by court order, agreement or otherwise) that contradict the conditions of this License, they do not excuse you from the conditions of this License. If you cannot distribute so as to satisfy simultaneously your obligations under this License and any other pertinent obligations, then as a consequence you may not distribute the Program at all. For example, if a patent license would not permit royalty-free redistribution of the Program by all those who receive copies directly or indi-

rectly through you, then the only way you could satisfy both it and this License would be to refrain entirely from distribution of the Program.

If any portion of this section is held invalid or unenforceable under any particular circumstance, the balance of the section is intended to apply and the section as a whole is intended to apply in other circumstances.

It is not the purpose of this section to induce you to infringe any patents or other property right claims or to contest validity of any such claims; this section has the sole purpose of protecting the integrity of the free software distribution system, which is implemented by public license practices. Many people have made generous contributions to the wide range of software distributed through that system in reliance on consistent application of that system; it is up to the author/donor to decide if he or she is willing to distribute software through any other system and a licensee cannot impose that choice.

This section is intended to make thoroughly clear what is believed to be a consequence of the rest of this License.

8. If the distribution and/or use of the Program is restricted in certain countries either by patents or by copyrighted interfaces, the original copyright holder who places the Program under this License may add an explicit geographical distribution limitation excluding those countries, so that distribution is permitted only in or among countries not thus excluded. In such case, this License incorporates the limitation as if written in the body of this License.

9. The Free Software Foundation may publish revised and/or new versions of the General Public License from time to time. Such new versions will be similar in spirit to the present version, but may differ in detail to address new problems or concerns.

   Each version is given a distinguishing version number. If the Program specifies a version number of this License which applies to it and "any later version", you have the option of following the terms and conditions either of that version or of any later version published by the Free Software Foundation. If the Program does not specify a version number of this License, you may choose any version ever published by the Free Software Foundation.

10. If you wish to incorporate parts of the Program into other free programs whose distribution conditions are different, write to the author to ask for permission. For software which is copyrighted by the Free Software Foundation, write to the Free Software Foundation; we sometimes make exceptions for this. Our decision will be guided by the two goals of preserving the free status of all derivatives of our free software and of promoting the sharing and reuse of software generally.

NO WARRANTY

11. BECAUSE THE PROGRAM IS LICENSED FREE OF CHARGE, THERE IS NO WARRANTY FOR THE PROGRAM, TO THE EXTENT PERMITTED BY APPLICABLE LAW. EXCEPT WHEN OTHERWISE STATED IN WRITING THE COPYRIGHT HOLDERS AND/OR OTHER PARTIES PROVIDE THE PROGRAM "AS IS" WITHOUT WARRANTY OF ANY KIND, EITHER EXPRESSED OR IMPLIED, INCLUDING, BUT NOT LIMITED TO, THE IMPLIED WARRANTIES OF MERCHANTABILITY AND FITNESS FOR A PARTICULAR PURPOSE. THE ENTIRE RISK AS TO THE QUALITY AND PERFORMANCE OF THE PROGRAM IS WITH YOU. SHOULD THE PROGRAM PROVE DEFECTIVE, YOU ASSUME THE COST OF ALL NECESSARY SERVICING, REPAIR OR CORRECTION.

12. IN NO EVENT UNLESS REQUIRED BY APPLICABLE LAW OR AGREED TO IN WRITING WILL ANY COPYRIGHT HOLDER, OR ANY OTHER PARTY WHO MAY MODIFY AND/OR REDISTRIBUTE THE PROGRAM AS PERMITTED ABOVE, BE LIABLE TO YOU FOR DAMAGES, INCLUDING ANY GENERAL, SPECIAL, INCIDENTAL OR CONSEQUENTIAL DAMAGES ARISING OUT OF THE USE OR INABILITY TO USE THE PROGRAM (INCLUDING BUT NOT LIMITED TO LOSS OF DATA OR DATA BEING RENDERED INACCURATE OR LOSSES SUSTAINED BY YOU OR THIRD PARTIES OR A FAILURE OF THE PROGRAM TO OPERATE WITH ANY OTHER PROGRAMS), EVEN IF SUCH HOLDER OR OTHER PARTY HAS BEEN ADVISED OF THE POSSIBILITY OF SUCH DAMAGES.

*****END OF TERMS AND CONDITIONS*****

How to Apply These Terms to Your New Programs

If you develop a new program, and you want it to be of the greatest possible use to the public, the best way to achieve this is to make it free software which everyone can redistribute and change under these terms.

To do so, attach the following notices to the program. It is safest to attach them to the start of each source file to most effectively convey the exclusion of warranty; and each file should have at least the "copyright" line and a pointer to where the full notice is found.

```
one line to give the program's name and an idea of what it does.
Copyright (C) yyyy  name of author

This program is free software; you can redistribute it and/or
modify it under the terms of the GNU General Public License
```

as published by the Free Software Foundation; either version 2
of the License, or (at your option) any later version.

This program is distributed in the hope that it will be useful,
but WITHOUT ANY WARRANTY; without even the implied warranty of
MERCHANTABILITY or FITNESS FOR A PARTICULAR PURPOSE. See the
GNU General Public License for more details.

You should have received a copy of the GNU General Public License
along with this program; if not, write to the Free Software
Foundation, Inc., 59 Temple Place - Suite 330, Boston, MA
02111-1307, USA.

Also add information on how to contact you by electronic and paper mail.

If the program is interactive, make it output a short notice like this when it starts
in an interactive mode:

Gnomovision version 69, Copyright (C) *yyyy name of author*
Gnomovision comes with ABSOLUTELY NO WARRANTY; for details
type 'show w'. This is free software, and you are welcome
to redistribute it under certain conditions; type 'show c'
for details.

The hypothetical commands 'show w' and 'show c' should show the appropriate parts of the General Public License. Of course, the commands you use may be
called something other than 'show w' and 'show c'; they could even be mouse-
clicks or menu items--whatever suits your program.

You should also get your employer (if you work as a programmer) or your
school, if any, to sign a "copyright disclaimer" for the program, if necessary. Here is
a sample; alter the names:

Yoyodyne, Inc., hereby disclaims all copyright
interest in the program `Gnomovision'
(which makes passes at compilers) written
by James Hacker.

signature of Ty Coon, 1 April 1989
Ty Coon, President of Vice

This General Public License does not permit incorporating your program into
proprietary programs. If your program is a subroutine library, you may consider it
more useful to permit linking proprietary applications with the library. If this is
what you want to do, use the GNU Library General Public License instead of this
License.

The BSD License

my2cents.idgbooks.com

Register This Book — And Win!

Visit **http://my2cents.idgbooks.com** to register this book and we'll automatically enter you in our fantastic monthly prize giveaway. It's also your opportunity to give us feedback: let us know what you thought of this book and how you would like to see other topics covered.

Discover IDG Books Online!

The IDG Books Online Web site is your online resource for tackling technology — at home and at the office. Frequently updated, the IDG Books Online Web site features exclusive software, insider information, online books, and live events!

10 Productive & Career-Enhancing Things You Can Do at www.idgbooks.com

- Nab source code for your own programming projects.

- Download software.

- Read Web exclusives: special articles and book excerpts by IDG Books Worldwide authors.

- Take advantage of resources to help you advance your career as a Novell or Microsoft professional.

- Buy IDG Books Worldwide titles or find a convenient bookstore that carries them.

- Register your book and win a prize.

- Chat live online with authors.

- Sign up for regular e-mail updates about our latest books.

- Suggest a book you'd like to read or write.

- Give us your 2¢ about our books and about our Web site.

You say you're not on the Web yet? It's easy to get started with IDG Books' *Discover the Internet,* available at local retailers everywhere.

CD-ROM Installation Instructions

Red Hat® Linux® Network Toolkit, Second Edition, is accompanied by two CD-ROMs: on the first is a special one-disk distribution of Red Hat Linux, version 6.1; on the second is an assortment of software, scripts, and bonus chapters that provide you with more information and resources.

For instructions on how to install Red Hat Linux from Disk 1, see Chapter 1, which covers the process in detail. For information on how to install each package on Disk 2, see the readme files included with each package. For more information on the contents of these two disks, see Appendix C.

Notice from Red Hat Software, Inc.:

This book includes a copy of the Publisher's Edition of Red Hat Linux from Red Hat Software, Inc., which you may use in accordance with the GNU General Public License. The Official Red Hat Linux, which you may purchase from Red Hat Software, includes the complete Official Red Hat Linux distribution, Red Hat Software's documentation, and 90 days of free e-mail technical support regarding installation of Official Red Hat Linux. You also may purchase technical support from Red Hat Software on issues other than installation. You may purchase Official Red Hat Linux and technical support from Red Hat Software through the company's web site (www.redhat.com) or its toll-free number 1.888.REDHAT1.